Freedpeople in the Tobacco South

Freedpeople

in the Tobacco South

Virginia, 1860–1900

JEFFREY R. KERR-RITCHIE

The
University
of North
Carolina
Press
Chapel Hill
and London

© 1999 The University of North Carolina Press

All rights reserved

Designed by April Leidig-Higgins

Set in Monotype Bulmer by Keystone Typesetting, Inc.

Manufactured in the United States of America

The paper in this book meets the guidelines for
permanence and durability of the Committee on
Production Guidelines for Book Longevity of the
Council on Library Resources.

Library of Congress Cataloging-in-Publication Data

Kerr-Ritchie, Jeffrey R.

Freedpeople in the tobacco South : Virginia, 1860–
1900 / by Jeffrey R. Kerr-Ritchie.

p. cm. Includes bibliographical references and index.

ISBN 0-8078-2460-7 (cloth: alk. paper).

ISBN 0-8078-4763-1 (pbk.: alk. paper)

1. Freedmen—Virginia—History—19th century.
2. Afro-American farmers—Virginia—Economic
conditions. 3. Tobacco farms—Virginia—History
—19th century. 4. Virginia—Economic conditions.
I. Title. II. Title: Freed people in the tobacco South.

F235.N4K47   1999   98-22751

975.5′00496073—dc21   CIP

03 02 01 00 99   5 4 3 2 1

To the freedpeople,
their historians,
and emancipation

CONTENTS

MAPS AND FIGURES

Maps

Figures

TABLES

ACKNOWLEDGMENTS

Few of us can honestly claim our intellectual paths are simply the product of our own individual exertions. Even fewer of us could echo Gibbon's famous dictum that although conversation enriches understanding, solitude is the school of genius. I would first like to thank Sally Warwick-Haller, my undergraduate adviser at Kingston Polytechnic (now University) for believing in me all those years ago, and for encouraging an early interest in the American past, especially the Revolutionary period. Thanks to Lee Cassanelli, then History Department chair, for supporting a foreign student's application to graduate school. Special thanks are also extended to Robert F. Engs, who mentored, tolerated, and supported me during the rigors of graduate school at the University of Pennsylvania. He also stimulated an abiding passion in that other defining moment of the American past.

Many thanks also to my Penn Pals: Thomas Heinrich, for all those debates over the meaning of republicanism to two "aliens"; to David Kerans, for putting me right on all those complex details concerning rural farming methods; to Joel Kaye, for discussing the "big" questions; to Lawrence Mbogoni, for his timely conceptual critiques of bourgeois political economy; and to Komozi Woodard, for all those kitchen discussions on black history and politics, past and present.

I would further like to thank Dolores Janiewski, Bruce Laurie, and Kathleen Housley for their initial encouragement of this project. I would especially like to thank Joseph P. Reidy for his constant support and encouragement over the years. His comments have always been useful and interesting. (I promise we will have that drink or two sometime.) I would also like to thank Harold Forsythe for sharing his insights and knowledge about postwar Virginia. His work on Afro-Virginian Southside politics promises a great deal. I have also benefited over the years from the kind words and encouragement of Eric Foner and Barbara J. Fields. My debt to the stimulating work of Steven

Hahn, Leslie Rowland, Harold Woodman, and Eugene Genovese should become evident; so should the lessons learned from an older generation of British Marxists, including Rodney Hilton, Christopher Hill, Eric Hobsbawn, Edward Thompson, and Raymond Williams. My ultimate acknowledgment of an intellectual group must be to those earlier scholar-activists of black history and struggle, including W. E. B. Du Bois, C. L. R. James, Walter Rodney, Carter G. Woodson, Althreus A. Taylor, and Luther P. Jackson, whose work has informed so many of us.

Primary historical research without professional assistance is usually impossible, or at best, exceptionally difficult. It would also make an often tedious task even more mundane. I would like to thank the following archivists for their support over the years: Michael Plunkett at the Alderman Library, University of Virginia; Kent Olson at the Law Library, University of Virginia; Fritz Malval at the Hampton University Archives; and Lucious Edwards at the Virginia State University Library. Heartfelt thanks are also extended to the numerous archivists and workers who serve diligently but often anonymously at the following repositories: the National Archives, the Virginia Historical Society, the Virginia Library (formerly the Virginia State Library and Archives), the Virginia State Law Library, and the Law Library at Yale University. Many thanks also go out to the patient staff at the interlibrary loan office at Wesleyan, especially the late Steve Lebergott, Kathy Stefanowicz, and Deborah O'Brion.

This book would not have been completed without the financial support provided by Wesleyan over the years, including three Meigs grants from the history department in 1993, 1996, and 1997. These facilitated research trips. They also allowed me to listen to the quiet rural rhythms and occasional noisy clashes of distant postwar Virginia life from the solitude of Middletown. Thanks also to the Center for the Humanities at Wesleyan for a semester fellowship enabling me to concentrate on this book. Cheers for the constant intellectual and collegial support provided by Ron Schatz, Richard Buel, Ashraf Rushdy, Kate Rushin, and Erness Brady. A special thanks to Richard Vann for some last-minute proofreading. I would also like to thank Donna Martin for her administrative assistance over the terms.

Many thanks to the people at UNC Press, especially copyeditor Stephanie Wenzel, managing editor Ron Maner, and executive editor

Lewis Bateman. A final word about personal support. Three families have been particularly supportive over the years: the Engs family, including Jean, Robbie, Barbara, Robert, Leia, Joi, and Mrs. Engs; the Gardiners, including Bud, Rita, Clarke, and Jason; and the Jacksons, including Barbara, Michael, and Mrs. Georgia Collins. None are professional historians, but they all understand the importance of the past to the present. They have helped someone else listen to African American voices. The result is neither singularly authentic nor definitive, but it is hopefully insightful.

A final thanks for the patient support of Leah C. Gardiner, the most important person in my life.

Middletown, Conn.
March 1998

Freedpeople in the Tobacco South

On the eve of the First World War, English traveler Arthur G. Bradley recalled a bygone era:

> People generally, I think, led happy lives there, not yet greatly harassed by the shifting of the negroes townwards, which in the eighties began to create the labour difficulty, indoors and out, that now, more than ever, is the curse of American rural life. . . . Virginia is now, however, an utterly different country. Black labour, for which there was no substitute, has practically disappeared from the country districts, and flocked into big cities, to mines, and to public works. With the dying out of the old planter class, born and reared under the old conditions, everything that made Virginia humanly and socially interesting to a stranger vanished. Their successors are quite different. The very young people, even in my day, were generally a great falling off from their parents. The chaos of war and succeeding poverty had indeed suspended all advantages for that particular generation which, to be candid, was often conceited as well as ignorant, with rarely any of the charm of their elders. But they have long forsaken country life, and with their children been distributed through many successful channels north, south, and west, of American industrial life. They are merely a new type of modern American, with the physical and superficial attributes of the South upon them, and concern neither the reader nor myself. For the old Southern life is long dead.[1]

Bradley's recollections captured some essential features of life in postemancipation Virginia. The Civil War was undoubtedly a turning point in the fortunes of the Old Dominion and the nation at large. The abolition of slavery had unshackled labor from the land. The plantocracy was slowly withering away alongside the dissolution of the former slave system. Many Virginians had freed themselves from the familiar countryside. An old established region was succumbing to the throes of national modernity; its peculiarities were engulfed by sweeping national forces emanating from northern military victory, Republican political and legal domination, and capitalist transformation.

Bradley's nostalgic account was also flawed and incomplete. Most obviously, his "negroes" were still "servants." They were depicted in terms of what they did and no longer do for the plantocracy. Furthermore, despite emancipation and emigration, many former slaves, former masters, and their descendants continued to work the land. Far from simply disappearing, these Virginians struggled over the nature and fruits of productive labor in the tobacco and cereal fields. The postemancipation decades were earmarked by social struggles among those remaining behind trying to eke out a living and make sense of this hard new world. If the nationalization of Virginia life became inevitable, this was also resisted, especially through ideological convictions grounded in older ways of living. The following work seeks to explain these contradictory aspects of both dissolution and stasis resulting from emancipation, prolonged agricultural depression, and a transformed tobacco economy.

How does a working-class Londoner, with roots in midland England and Egypt, become interested in agrarian life in postwar tobacco Virginia? Part of the answer is attributable to the usual causes: a combination of inspirational ideas along with a glaring lacuna in the existing scholarship. In my particular case it was exposure to the fascinating world of nineteenth-century southern and African American history, while much of the historiography continued to be ruled by King Cotton at the expense of other regional economies (rice, sugar, indigo, hemp, cereal, and tobacco). But there were also deeper structures of feeling at play. I have often wondered why so many non-American scholars are drawn to study either the Revolutionary or the Civil War periods. Perhaps it is because those conflictual historical moments are comfortably familiar to those from older worlds. More specifically, I kept hearing familiar echoes of benignity and exceptionalism reverberating through the historical literature on Virginia. It was once fashionable to argue that English history was one long happy saga of progressive nation-building overseen by a beneficent establishment and supported by a forelock-tugging quiescent rural folk. The last few decades have witnessed some radical scholarly challenges to this traditional picture.[2]

Similarly, commentators and historians used to trumpet the Old Dominion's benign and exceptional past. Some familiar benchmarks included the state's seminal contribution to the American Revolution and early nation-building, the state's unique executive service of providing four of the first five presidents to the fledgling republic, the most benign form of antebellum slavery (compared with that in the Deep South), and reluctant secessionism (compared with that of radical fire-eaters). Postwar benchmarks included more genteel forms of rural and racial protest, uniquely benevolent paternal leadership, and moderate race relations during the so-called 1890s nadir of lynching, segregation, and disfranchisement elsewhere.[3]

This classic portrait has since been touched up with many new shades and tints scraped from the palette of social history. Building upon the pioneering insights of an earlier generation of African American heterodox scholars, we now have far more sober and critical accounts of the origins of racial slavery, its colonial and antebellum practices, and the advent of emancipation during the Civil War and its aftermath.[4]

Much of this recent work, however, only faintly brushes over the older canvas. We can still see vestiges of benignity and exceptionalism. Even those black scholars, whose intellectual ancestors pioneered the earliest challenges to Old Virginia historiography, have produced scholarship that still seems to echo traditional notions.[5] Thus, while some have argued that the ephemeral success of postwar Hampton's black community demonstrates what freedom might have looked like if only it had been allowed to work, others maintain that African Virginians played an exceptional role during the Civil War, both as African Confederates as well as African Yankees.[6] Even the venerable Virginia Historical Society has recently prepared its palette, rinsed its paintbrushes, and begun to dab the old canvas.[7]

An alternative approach to this restored exceptionalism is the focus on the Upper South's regional difference, especially Virginia's close proximity to the North and West. Some historians have seen this relationship in fairly straightforward terms as Virginia being on the geographical, economic, and cultural edge of the American South.[8] The most refined conceptual statement has been issued by those who see the Upper South states as meandering "crab-like" toward industrial capitalism, especially through the triumph of free labor over slave labor. Here Maryland and its fellow border states are seen as the regional harbingers of a broader historical process that eventually embroiled the American South within an unfolding dynamic of industrial capitalism. The Chesapeake region in particular is seen to have emerged out of precapitalist slavery into a new capitalist world due to internal and external contradictions.[9]

This peripheral approach, while broadening our understanding of the regional complexity of the American South as well as its relationship to broader historical change, is also limited in a number of ways. The geographical focus is primarily on the Chesapeake, and the timeframe is geared toward the Civil War era. This work focuses on postwar internal Virginia and extends the analysis through the late nineteenth century.[10] Furthermore, limited attention has been given to the Upper South's central cash crop, presumably because traditional tobacco fits awkwardly with arguments stressing change. In contrast, I focus on the central role played by a transformed tobacco economy in affecting postwar social relations.[11] Finally, the definition of free labor has remained tied primarily to the classic tenets of the wage labor relationship, rural dispossession, and out-migration. This work focuses on freedpeople as a means for understanding broader features of the postemancipation landscape.

The Virginia tobacco belt, I argue, was intimately caught up in the throes of nineteenth-century global capitalism. It was unexceptional in its subservience to postwar northern capitalist domination. It was exceptional because the region articulated new as well as older forms of social relations of agricultural production. Agrarian capitalism both dissolved as well as maintained existing conditions. Planters and ex-masters were replaced by shadows of their former selves. Former slaves, yeomen, and nonslaveholders played a crucial role in dissolving this old world, but they did not do it simply by themselves. They were part of a confusing postemancipation world that they also struggled to comprehend. Their understanding was drawn from reservoirs of thought tanked up during the struggles of antebellum slavery.

The book's argument is simple enough: slave emancipation combined with transformed market conditions gradually eroded traditional

4

forms of social discipline. Each section and chapter explores subarguments. The opening four chapters chart the important beginnings of emancipation between the early 1860s and the early 1870s. Chapter 1 opens with the social organization of slavery in the Virginia tobacco belt, its interaction with the national and international marketplace, and the subtle shift in social relations during the fulcrum of the Civil War. Its central purpose is to delineate the contours of an older way of life whose ideas were to gain even greater saliency just as that old world was slowly dissipating. The second chapter explores the struggle over free labor among former slaves, former masters and new employers, and the Bureau of Refugees, Freedmen, and Abandoned Lands (BRFAL). The central task is to explore the ways in which the presence of the BRFAL, along with its free labor ideology, effected a transformation in social relations that continued to haunt the tobacco fields long after the federal government's withdrawal. The political conflict engendered by this transformation is pursued in Chapter 3. Chapter 4 traces the erosion of traditional relations through the pages of the premier regional farming journal, the *Southern Planter and Farmer*, and Hampton Institute's self-help monthly, the *Southern Workman*. The objective here is the excavation of old ideas from the new quarry of emancipation. In sum, this opening section situates emancipatory struggles within the shifting context of an older slave world.[12]

The following three chapters explore the nature of prolonged agricultural depression and transformations in the tobacco economy from national, regional, state, and local perspectives between the early 1870s and the early 1890s. Chapter 5 traces the undermining of the Virginia tobacco economy by superior western leaf competition. It also follows the subsequent political struggles between tobacco farmers and merchants both in and out of the Virginia general assembly during the mid-1870s. The tobacco merchants eventually won with the abolition of old state inspection tobacco laws. This represented the free market erosion of the paternal state. This setback in political power, however, was balanced by new laws that effectively guaranteed the protection of property in free labor relations by the early 1880s. The struggle over the law of free labor in the context of emancipation and depression is the subject of Chapter 6. Here I argue that state law was invoked as a means of constructing an agricultural proletariat. The major legal case was *Parrish v. The Commonwealth*, and its impact was especially felt in the tobacco belt. Chapter 7 traces the structural transformation of the tobacco economy, especially with the takeoff of the cigarette industry and monopoly capitalism through the formation of the American Tobacco Company (ATC). This highest stage of combination is also traced through the unusual emergence of local producer alliances in tobacco Virginia.

The final chapter examines the socioeconomic breakdown of the Virginia tobacco belt. This breakdown, or shifting terrain, represented the climax of the erosion of social discipline especially through the twin peaks of freedpeople's landholding and freedpeople's emigration. It also reflected the erosion of the more recent social discipline of the black family and freedom's older generation.

This work is fueled by two central concerns: first, to illuminate the shifting frontiers of a world caught in the transition between a postemancipation society no longer defined by slavery and emergent capitalist forces that were not yet fully matured; second, to chart the different understandings of this bewildering process by contemporaries as well as historians. One of our major concerns is to capture the contradictions and confusions engendered by postemancipation transformations such as the mixture of wage and tenant labor, landownership and emigration, and dark chewing/bright smoking tobacco economies.

The spatial and temporal dimensions are clear enough: The Virginia tobacco region encompassed the central and lower piedmont between the fall line and the Blue Ridge Mountains. Its central division in the postbellum period was between the dark tobacco belt, or the traditional shipping producing counties located in the central piedmont, and the tobacco southside, or the newer bright-producing counties adjoining the North Carolina border. The chronological period encompasses roughly forty years, beginning with the Civil War era and concluding early in the new century. The actual years themselves are less important than their location within crucial transformatory historical moments.

Throughout the book, I use particular terms that require introductory explanation. By *freedpeople* I mean a more inclusive category than usually suggested by either *freedmen* or *former slaves*. I also mean a social relationship to former masters with transitory, contractual, and ideological components. I further mean a generational shift that includes freedom's first and second generations.

By *class* I mean social groups defined in relationship to one another primarily according to their access to the means of agricultural production. Thus, former slaves were once owned but ended up owning themselves. They continued to be the major productive class in the tobacco region. Former masters are characterized by their transformation from laborlords to landlords.[13] Of course, the social relations between such groups were conflictual as well as exploitative; most obviously, former masters continued to try and exploit former slaves, a relationship that was subtly changed through the advent of emancipation and depression. The focus on this relationship does not preclude occasional lengthy analysis of other classes and even intraclass cooperation. However, one of the major conceptual premises is the centrality of the former relationship, whose change had rippling effects.

By *exploitation* I mean the continued deprivation of freedom from the freedpeople as well as denial of the just fruits of their labor. It was in both production and exchange in the marketplace that the surplus profit from freedpeople's work was enjoyed by the landlords despite their own experiences with defeat, low prices, and hard times. The notion that emancipation either reduced or ended exploitation remains the wishful thinking of neoclassical economists. We do not pursue progressive exploitative statistics whereby the former slaves' 13.5 percent rate of appropriation improved from the 55 percent rate for slaves.[14] What this view does is simply mystify exploitation under various guises of compensation for work. Postslave relations, as the ancestors of a stolen people knew (and know), continued to be exploitative even if they were different and less naked. The freedpeople's struggle to realize their self-emancipatory aspirations can only be adequately understood within the context of the knowledge of past and present appropriation. Exploitation was part of a historical continuum rooted in slavery that remains unresolved to this day.[15]

By *culture* I mean lived struggle. This book does not follow an older school of monocrop determinists who simplistically defined a people's culture in terms of the crops they grew.[16] Nor does it subscribe to a popular anthropological definition that posits lived experience as "known meanings and directions, which its members are trained to; the new observations and meanings, which are offered and tested."[17] Rather, culture is "located within a particular equilibrium of social relations, a working environment of exploitation and resistance to exploitation, of relations of power which are masked by the rituals of paternalism and deference."[18]

For *household economy* I follow the classic definition of a rural family household engaged primarily in subsistence economy but also in some market activity with any surplus agricultural production.[19] The freedpeople, however, attempted to reconstruct their familial units away from a previous preoccupation with work even while having to work in order to survive. The objective here is to challenge the claim that former slaves were simply acquisitive accumulationists because they were either *homo economicus* or familiar with market relations during antebellum slavery.[20] While exploring the extended nature of this household economy in terms of the activities of freedwomen and freedchildren, I do not believe such an extension fundamentally changes the basic definition.[21]

By *ideology* I mean contradictory attempts by social groups to make some sense of their complex world through various actions and expressions. These often amounted to "nightmares on the brain of the living."[22] Thus many former masters viewed emancipation as disastrous because their proslave ideology prepared them to think no other way. The BRFAL officials were often imbued with the tenets of northern free labor ideology despite the obvious barrenness of southern soils. The freedpeople welcomed freedom, but an older generation became haunted by older notions of landholding that were being increasingly undermined by more recent agricultural and regional changes.

The book's theoretical premises are a qualified historical materialism. Its major emphasis is on the struggle between social classes as the motor of historical transformation away from older forms of unfreedom. This social process, however, was evolutionary rather than revolutionary.

Several additional points require brief comment. Work and the struggle around it take center stage. This was the central historical experience of freedpeople.[23] Second, the book concentrates on the relationship between race and class. As other southern historians have pointed out, the interaction between the two concepts is infinitely more interesting than some simplistic duality.[24] Third, freedwomen are focused on as vital historical subjects. In response to a male-centered historiography, more work is appearing that focuses on freed-

8

women. This book follows, although less is made of, gender differences precisely because of the very different historical reality of postemancipation conditions that often forced freedpeople's cooperation rather than conflict.[25] Finally, I use the term *postemancipation* in contrast to the more traditional term, *postbellum*, because it captures more accurately the centrality of transformed social relations of freedom.

The book's method is different from its theoretical premises. It is comparative in the hope that such an approach will raise new questions as well as challenge old exceptionalisms. It is both large and small, microcosmic and macrocosmic. Thus we swing from struggles over the freedpeople's household economy in the tobacco fields to political infighting in the state general assembly, from the ups and downs of international leaf markets to legal adjudications in the state supreme court, and back to the shifting human terrain in the tobacco belt. This relational aspect was a crucial part of the historical process according to the contemporaries themselves. They experienced it, tried to fathom it, and acted accordingly. It is incumbent upon subsequent commentators to record this awareness (or nonawareness) even if our contemporary era of academic professional specialization encourages otherwise.[26]

A word about my language. This study attempts to use historically accurate language even while recognizing its limitations. Thus we encounter slaves, freedmen, Negroes, Yankees, bureau officials, planters, farmers, former masters, merchants, middlemen, and monopolists. These terms reflect the linguistic understandings of the day; they do not preclude critical analysis. Freedmen, for instance, were a class of former slaves designated as such by the federal government in the immediate years following the Civil War. The term, however, does not prevent us from talking collectively about freedmen, freedwomen, and freedchildren. (I also switch to freedpeople after the BRFAL's withdrawal.) Furthermore, I have tried not to sanitize either the spoken or the written word. What is most important is listening to the struggles of historical agents, not engaging in pleasant-sounding jargon to make their brutal past appear less brutal. I have occasionally used the term *black* instead of *African American* or *African Virginian*, both of which seem presentist and oddly out of place. Besides, the term *black* does have an older usage by progressives. It is preferred by many black people as a collective national expression; it is equatable with the term *white*; and it avoids the insidious notion that black Americans are simply another ethnic group of American hyphenates in this ever progressive, pluralistic, incorporative, and multicultural society.

A word about sources. This book has unearthed a few new sources. These are duly noted, especially the BRFAL monthly reports and letters, state and county legal records, and the U.S. Bureau of the Census tobacco schedules. The book mainly, however, suggests new ways of looking at older sources. The BRFAL reports, agricultural journals, and land tax records have all been exposed to careful scrutiny for their silences as well as their more obvious facts. To paraphrase another historian, any historical methodology that has former slaves as its subject must also consider the "discursive formation" behind the emergence of such a subject.[27]

This work is also an exercise in challenging a rich historiographical tradition. Some postmodernists claim there is no history except historians. I would argue that such simplemindedness, apart from its vacuous politics, ignores the fascinating dialectical relationship between actual history and doing history in postemancipation Virginia. I am clearly critical of an older school of Virginia thought as well as many of its critics. And this is not simply an argument for the equality of different perspectives.

One of the central objectives of this study is to assert the freedpeople's historical agency. If you visit some of the tobacco farms in southern Virginia today, you will not encounter many of the freedpeople's descendants. Instead, much of the work is being done by Mexican migrant laborers whose presence is authorized by Richmond. This is the newest free labor in the Virginia tobacco belt. (The rationalizations for exploiting these workers—that they are volunteers, that they receive higher wages than they would in Mexico, that they are naturally docile—are eerily reminiscent of older ideas on the cusp between slavery and emancipation.) Still, the fields and structures were once worked and inhabited by freedom's generations. It is their voices this work seeks to recover. Indeed, I am writing against the view of a hegemonized slave people. The struggles of the freedpeople in the postemancipation Virginia tobacco belt suggest the essential failure of former masters in imposing their moral, political, and legal *dirige* (direction) on ex-slaves. The freedpeople materially contradicted the ideological residues of proslavery thought and actions. (Indeed, at the risk of oversimplification, I argue that the freedpeople managed freedom better than their former masters did.) The complex nature of such a social process has fueled, and continues to fuel, the intellectual curiosity of an array of foreign travelers, albeit from radically different perspectives.

CHAPTER ONE

Slavery, Tobacco, and Old Dominion

> You can make a nigger work, he said, *but you cannot*
> *make him think.*
> —Slaveowner W to Frederick Law Olmsted
>
> Used to wuk in family groups, we did. . . . In dat way one
> could help de other when dey got behind.
> —Ex-slave Frank Bell
>
> Of course, when the master was away, they didn't make
> much.—Ex-mistress Sarah Payne

Unfree labor and tobacco production were spawned by European colonialization and transatlantic mercantilism in the New World, along with popular luxury consumption in the Old World.[1] The 250 years spanning the early seventeenth to the mid-nineteenth centuries saw the making of Virginia, its westward expansion, its cash crop production, and its social organization of slavery. By the eve of the Civil War the Old Dominion had established a long and venerable past. This history drew upon old English roots. These sprang up variously: Virginia led the ideological and military challenge to the British monarchy, provided disproportionate leadership in both the executive and the legislative branches of the new government, and nourished Jeffersonian republicanism as crucial to the political culture of the young nation. This proud state was also a society in which African slaves worked under the supervision of Anglo-American masters. This Old Dominion became increasingly exposed to a series of both internal and external pressures. The exigencies of war provided a quick shock to this traditional and relatively stable polity. The postwar decades were all about an Old Dominion struggling to come to terms with emancipation.

Cash crop production reigned supreme in the Old Dominion on the eve of the Civil War. During the 1859 agricultural season, slaves produced nearly 122 million pounds of tobacco leaf. This crop fetched an estimated $7 million in market sales and amounted to record high production levels. This poundage represented 28 percent of the total tobacco production in the United States, making the region the most valuable tobacco real estate in the nation (and probably globally). Cereal grains, especially wheat, were also an important component of Virginia's export economy. During the same season, slaves helped produce nearly 11 million bushels of wheat worth over $15 million. Former slaves in Virginia recalled their arduous labors. Archie Booker never forgot "dem days dey raise co'n, wheat an' terbaccy," when they would "wuk fum sun to sun." Eighty-six-year-old Henrietta Perry remembered her harsh work regimen and tobacco's role in it. She recalled distastefully, "Use to get sick of seein' de weed. Use to wuk fum sun to sun in dat old terbaccy field. Wuk till my back felt lak it ready to pop in two. Marse ain' raise nothin' but terbaccy, ceptin' a little wheat an' corn for eatin', an' us black people had to look arter dat 'baccy lak it was gold."[2]

There was some local consumption of these crops, but most were raised for export purposes. Tobacco was marketed to local urban areas such as Richmond, Petersburg, Danville, Lynchburg, and Clarksville. Once there, it was processed by factory workers into snuff for sniffing, plug for chewing, and shredded leaf for pipe smoking. The Old Dominion's tobacco industry was estimated to be worth over $12 million in 1859. Its outlet was primarily domestic exportation for consumption southward in the cotton states. Planters and farmers consumed these tobacco products, as did slaves and free blacks. Cereal produce was also marketed to urban areas where it was milled into flour and grain and shipped to the cotton states as well as to northern states and Brazil. It should be added that profits from this slave agricultural production were also shipped northward; financial control of marketing and manufacturing radiated from New York City's financial district.[3]

Despite the prime position of Virginia tobacco as an established

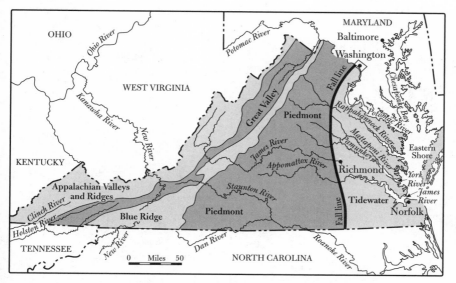

MAP 1.1. Virginia's principal geographic regions (adapted from Dabney, *Virginia*, 417, by permission of the University Press of Virginia)

staple crop that was part of a broader antebellum economy, specters of leaf competition loomed from bordering states. Kentucky's rural producers had harvested a small tobacco crop in 1839. Twenty years later slave and free labor produced over 108 million pounds, or around one-quarter of the nation's total poundage. The specter was also raised southward. North Carolina produced nearly 33 million pounds (7 percent of the national total) in 1859.[4] Especially noteworthy was the emergence of a lighter and more pliable leaf called bright tobacco, which eventually became the favorite of tobacco manufacturers.[5] Farther west the wheat fields were expanding. In 1849 farmers in the relatively new state of Illinois (1818) had produced nearly 10 million bushels of wheat compared to 11 million bushels from Virginia; a decade later these farmers produced nearly 24 million bushels compared to 13 million bushels. Indiana, Wisconsin, and Ohio all reported greater wheat production than the Old Dominion.[6] These specters that haunted the Old Dominion's cash crop economy were to sweep all before them in the postwar decades of emancipation and agricultural depression.

There was a temporary halt to tobacco's dominion when Virginia's rural producers switched crops to meet the exigencies of a Con-

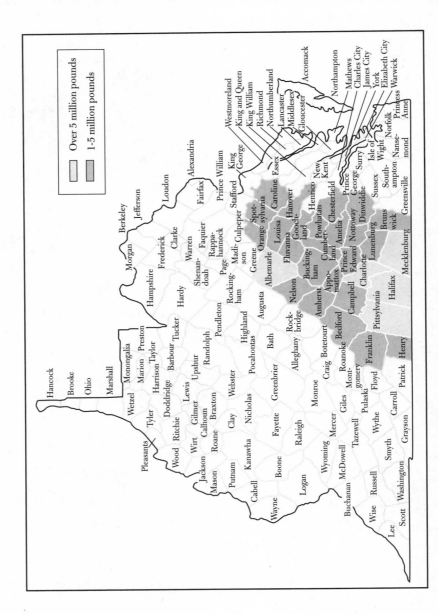

MAP 1.2. Tobacco production in Virginia, 1859 (USBC, *1860, Agriculture*, 155–63)

federacy at war. On March 3, 1862, the Confederate congress assembled in Richmond passed a joint resolution "recommending the planters of the Confederate States to refrain from the cultivation of cotton and tobacco and devote their energies to raising provisions."[7] Many planters appear to have heeded this advice. On June 13, 1862, J. B. Lundy, a slaveholder from Brunswick County in southside Virginia, wrote to the Confederate secretary of war requesting the return of impressed slaves from fortifying Richmond since "it is as necessary to till the land as to fight the battles." Lundy went on to inform the secretary, "We planted full Crops of Corn for all our hands our determination being to raise grain and meat. We have planted all our best lands in Corn, (no tobacco is planted with us)."[8] This substitution of subsistence for staple crops was widespread throughout internal Virginia during the war. According to Laurent Marcellin Joseph de Give, a Belgian consul reporting to his foreign minister on conditions in the Confederacy during the fall of 1862, tobacco production had all but ceased. "Tobacco raising in Virginia during 1862," de Give wrote, "was affected by the same circumstances: like cotton, the crop hardly existed. It is estimated at not over a fifteenth of an average crop. Indeed during the autumn when I went through the region formerly planted to tobacco, I looked in vain for those immense fields of green which one used to see everywhere: the long, yellow corn stalks had crowded out the broad green tobacco leaves."[9]

This regional shift from intensive to extensive agricultural production was undoubtedly the result of the exigencies of war; it was also probably inevitable given the special labor requirements of leaf production. It is likely that this reduction in the labor-intensive agricultural routine of slaves in the Virginia tobacco belt marked an embryonic stage in the gradual erosion of older forms of social control. This transformation would have to await the military reality of Appomattox. Not until the 1870s did the full impact of western tobacco and cereal competition begin to undermine seriously an older dominion. And only during the century's final two decades did the cigarette industry revolutionize an older tobacco world and its social relations.[10]

If cash crop production was one side of the Old Dominion, its other was unfree labor. African chattel slavery spread into the Virginia piedmont during the early eighteenth century. By 1750 the region's 40,000 slaves represented one-third of Virginia's total slave population. By the end of the eighteenth century the region had virtually trebled its slave populace. The piedmont held half of the state's total slaves, compared with the one-third held in the tidewater. Tobacco's lucrative profits drew slaveholders and forced slaves westward. In Pittsylvania County in southwestern Virginia, the slave population increased from 271 in 1767 to 4,200 by 1800, primarily through westward expansion. Just over a generation later, rural producers in this county were responsible for nearly 6.5 million pounds of tobacco; its population at this time had reached 24,400, of whom 11,558 (47 percent) were slaves.[11]

Creoles soon began to dominate the region's slave population. This became evident in their use of acculturation to facilitate resistance against slavery. The usage of English language skills, the relative stability of family life through reproduction, slave naming in opposition to master's naming, the rise of evangelical Christianity, and an increase in plantation units replacing smaller farms all encouraged the growth of slave communities in Virginia's eighteenth-century interior regions. This piedmont life developed quite quickly in contrast to the slower maturation of tidewater society. By the late antebellum period, however, there was a remarkable degree of convergence as the piedmont had become an established extension of the Old Dominion.[12]

By the final antebellum decade the Virginia piedmont constituted the heart of the state's slave economy. According to the region's most recent historian, "Economic and political changes in the tidewater steadily molded the plantation upcountry into a specialized hinterland that served as an occasional labor reserve for commercial and industrial interests, in addition to funneling raw materials to seaboard factories and ports." The modern forces of factories, mines, railroads, and urban areas, it is further argued, pulled slaves out of the undeveloped tobacco region into the developing mixed economy of the eastern seaboard. These slaves and free blacks apparently gained some familiarity with the market economy, especially the "rudiments" of wage labor, which they took back with them into the hinterland. These antebellum experiences purportedly prepared these African Virginians for emancipation in contrast to their slower cotton-belt cousins who were less exposed to urban, commercial, and industrial relations.[13]

SLAVERY, TOBACCO, AND OLD DOMINION

The social organization of slavery was sovereign in the Old Dominion. In 1860, Virginia led the fifteen southern slave states with 52,128 slaveholding households and 490,865 slaves. These masters and slaves were overwhelmingly concentrated in eastern Virginia, constituting 80 percent of all masters and 87 percent of all slaves in the state. Most of the sixty-nine counties east of the Shenandoah Valley had either majority or high minority populations subjected to the social discipline of slavery. Furthermore, of the 5,810 slaveholders with more than twenty slaves, 5,410 lived in eastern Virginia. The tobacco belt that embraced the central and southern piedmont was the most concentrated region of planters, slaveholders, and slaves. This entrenchment of unfree labor stood in marked contrast to the free labor farming practiced in trans-Allegheny Virginia, which had few large farms and almost no slaves. The political consequences of this regional division became manifest with the advent of the Civil War when slave Virginia sided with the secessionist slave South and free western Virginia stayed with the Union.[14]

Slave relations also characterized urban Virginia. The most recent student of urban slavery estimates that around 12,843 slaves, mostly males, worked in the tobacco factories of Richmond, Lynchburg, and Petersburg. Over half of these slave semiproletarians were hired out by their owners for the factory season encompassing the spring and fall months. Indeed, these tobacco slaves are seen as only part of a broader hiring process that encompassed free blacks as well as skilled white laborers. These semifree and free laborers were part of a versatile economy. During slack parts of the agricultural seasons, they worked in factories, furnaces, coal mines, railroads, and canals and engaged in domestic work in urban households.[15] It is difficult to determine the exact number of these hired laborers, their origins, and the precise nature of their work. But two points seem fairly clear. These slaves were more likely to emanate from the tidewater region because of its mixed economy rather than the piedmont with its year-round labor-intensive tobacco calendar. Furthermore, the number of these slave hirees was always very small whether we think of them either as a manifestation of the slave system's versatility or as a contradiction of the social organization of slavery.[16]

The Old Dominion knew aggressive geographical expansionism from the British Isles to the southern Atlantic Seaboard and beyond.

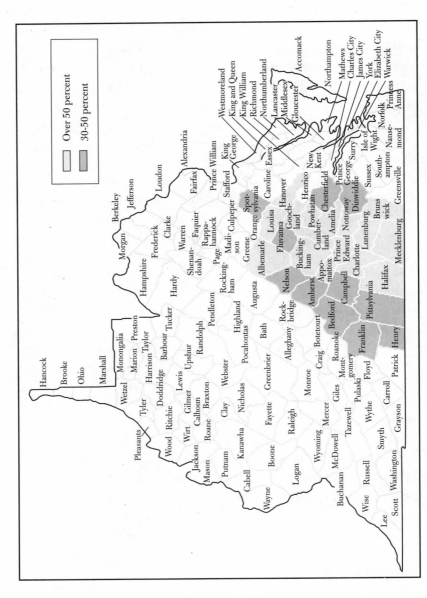

MAP 1.3. Slave population in the Virginia tobacco region, 1859 (USBC, *1860, Agriculture*, 243–45)

Unfree labor was central to this expansionist process. Slavery linked the various southern regions together as well as production on the land and manufacturing in the city. Southwestern expansion and the search for cotton and sugar profits redirected the unfree labor surplus of the Upper South to the newer colonized regions. The most recent student of the antebellum slave trade estimates that during the preceding half-century around 441,684 slaves were sold out of the state. By the 1850s this human exodus ranged from 67,000 to 83,000. This commonality was politically expressed through southern secession but also in the Old Dominion's insistence, contrary to that of South Carolina, that the foreign slave trade not be reopened because it would prove detrimental to the state's financial interests.[17]

The ideological expression of this dominant social organization was proslavery. Drawn from a combination of Christian precepts and phenotypical racial theory, proslave thought originated as a defense of slavery as an unfortunate but necessary political and economic evil; it evolved into a defense of slavery as a positive good for civilizing backward Africans, ordering society, and maintaining social discipline against destructive modern forces. Its key rationalizations were drawn from the Bible, history, paternalism, and reciprocal rights. Virginia slaveholder, scholar, and essayist Thomas Roderick Dew offered a biblical defense of slavery published in the aftermath of the 1821 Nat Turner insurrection: "With regard to the assertion, that slavery is against the spirit of Christianity, we are ready to admit the general assertion, but deny most positively that there is any thing in the Old or New Testament, which would go to show that slavery, when once introduced, ought at all events to be abrogated, or that the master commits any offence in holding slaves. The Children of Israel themselves were slave-holders, and were not condemned for it."[18] Furthermore, great civilizations had always been based on slavery. To those who "*contended that slavery is unfavourable to a republican spirit*," Dew replied, "but the whole history of the world proves that this is far from being the case." Indeed, "in the ancient republics of Greece and Rome, where the spirit of liberty glowed with most intensity, the slaves were more numerous than the freedmen. Aristotle, and the great men of antiquity, believed slavery necessary to keep alive the spirit of freedom."[19] Thirdly, paternalism was evoked as the Christian slaveholder's duty. South Carolina slaveholder and politician James Henry

Hammond put this eloquently enough in his influential 1845 "Letter to an English Abolitionist." "Though a slaveholder," Hammond wrote, "I freely acknowledge my obligations as a man; and that I am bound to treat humanely the fellow-creatures whom God has entrusted to my charge."[20] One final proslave principle was the natural reciprocity of master-slave relations. Virginia planter, lawyer, and journalist George Fitzhugh thundered against callous free labor relations in his "Southern Thought," published in 1857: "But the free laborer has nightly care superadded to incessant daily toil, whilst his employer is exempted as well from the labor of life, as from most of its cares. The former is a slave, without the rights of a slave; the latter, a master, without the obligations of a master. What equality of condition can there be in free society?"[21] The transformation of proslave ideology from a necessary evil into a positive good was increasingly sharpened upon the anvil of northern abolitionist and free labor attacks from the 1830s onward.[22]

In the slave agricultural South, proslavery manifested primarily in the debate over the most efficacious ways of attaining efficient slave management. How best to school backward, indolent, and inferior Africans? The consequence was a plethora of advice literature propagated through southern agricultural journals. An older historiographical tradition interpreted this literature primarily in terms of agricultural reform.[23] Alternatively, other historians have argued that these slave management difficulties often reflected varying degrees of both direct and indirect resistance to the coerced nature of their lives; these were vital ways for challenging an exploitative and dehumanizing process.[24] Unfortunately, the older focus is creeping back into some of the more recent historical literature.[25] Our focus is on the legacy of slave management debates that reflected the continuation of proslave thought in emancipatory conditions. When freedpeople acted against the best interests of former masters, the logical consequence was the "problem" of free labor.[26]

Slave management was deemed particularly important for tobacco production. This cash crop required constant and close supervision all year round. Quality tobacco production was especially demanding.[27] One Virginia slaveholder, "W," informed visiting northern journalist Frederick L. Olmsted that he "cultivated only the coarser and lower-priced sorts of tobacco because the finer sorts required more pains-taking and discretion than it was possible to make a large gang of negroes use." The same slaveowner believed that it was possible to make slaves work but not to make them think.[28] Perhaps the first sentiment was accurate, although the abundance of advice literature on slave management argues against its facility. The second idea, however, was clearly inaccurate. Slaves learned different lessons from the school of slavery, including farming knowledge, familial cooperation, and ideas about labor and its fruits. This was protoemancipation at work on the job. Slaves gained farming knowledge while in the fields despite their hard regimen. Their expertise grew with emancipation, but the seeds were sown during slavery.[29]

Former Virginia slave Gabe Hunt described his past agricultural regimen to Works Progress Administration interviewer William T. Lee. "You see," Hunt recalled, "de fust pickin' come roun' de fust of August," when workers would "git de wheat in, den come de tobacco." Hunt and the "boys" were then ordered to "git de smoke house in order," and they would "clean out de barn," "rake out all de leavin's and dirt an' clean de mud an' dirt out whar de fire box is." "Barns was built on hills," he explained, "so's you kin lay de sticks way fum top to bottom" and pack "de top fum de upper winder right level wid de groun' an' pack de bottom fum de do'." This full day's task was followed by picking the tobacco leaves. "Got to pick dem leaves what's jus' startin to brown." If you pick "too soon dey don't cure, an' you pick 'em too late dey bitters." Furthermore, you had "to break 'em off clean at de stem an' not twist 'em cause if dey bruised dey spile. Hands git so stuck up in dat old tobaccy gum it git so yo' fingers stick together. Dat ole gum was de worse mess you ever did see." After spreading "de leaves on a cyart an' drag it to de barn . . . de women would take each leaf up an' fix de stem 'tween two pieces of board, den tie de ends together." Afterward they "hand 'em all up in dat barn an' let it smoke two days an' two nights. Got to keep dat fire burnin' rain or shine, 'cause if it go out, it spile de tobaccy."[30]

Gabe Hunt's account eloquently captures the labor intensity, sexual division of labor, and downright grubbiness of slave work in the Virginia tobacco fields. Throughout the harvesting, barn cleaning and preparation, tobacco picking, carting from the fields, leaf stemming and tying, housing and curing, all the slaves were kept busy. Adult slave women were singled out for stemming and tying. All of these tasks were hot and dirty: harvesting under the July sun, raking out muck and dirt from the barn, picking gum-sticking leaves, and curing in a stiflingly hot wooden barn for forty-eight hours. Hunt's description further suggests that he understood, and understood very well, the nature of his work, in contrast to the view held by contemporary slaveowners. Barns had to be built a particular way in order to best accommodate the hanging of tobacco sticks. Leaves had to be picked carefully at the right time in order to maximize their curing potential and to avoid bruising. Once the tobacco was housed, it required careful attention, especially with its heating, in order to cure properly. In short, the intensive and specialized peculiarities of tobacco cultivation armed the slaves with a degree of farming knowledge that they carried directly into the postemancipation period.[31]

Former slave Frank Bell also recalled his work experience in the Virginia fields. His owner John Fallons "wasn't much on no special house servants." The master put

> everybody in de field, he did, even de women. Growed mostly wheat on de plantation, an' de men would scythe and cradle while de women folks would rake and bind. Den us little chillun, boys an' girls, would come along an' stack[.] Used to wuk in family groups, we did. Now we and my four brothers, never had no sisters, used to follow my mom an' dad. In dat way one could help de other when dey got behind. All of us would pitch in and help Momma who warn't very strong. 'Course in dat way de man what was doin' de cradlin' would always go no faster dan de woman, who was most times his wife, could keep up.

Although some overseers would not let families work together on other plantations, Bell continued, "Marse John Fallons had a black foreman, what was my mother's brother, my uncle. Moses Bell was his name, and he always looked out for his kinfolk, especially my mother."[32]

Much like those of Hunt and other Virginia slaves, Bell's experiences conveyed both hard work and a primitive division of labor. All slaves were required to work, while basic tasks were accorded by either sex or age. Bell's account also suggests the importance of cooperation among the slave family work unit. This collective support was expressed not just as physical assistance but also in terms of productivity and task time. These rural rhythms, while often circumscribed by the harsh realities of slavery, overseership, and slave trading, provided the crucial groundwork for emancipation. In short, despite primitive social organization and labor intensity, slaves in the Virginia tobacco belt learned tobacco cultivation skills, engaged in cooperative kinship relations, and thought about the nature of their work and its worth—all of which proved to be of vital preparation when freedom came. Along with the presence of free blacks, slave hiring, and slave-marketing activities, the nature of slave agricultural work contained the seeds of quasi-freedom.[33]

With the advent of the Civil War the social organization of slavery became vitally challenged. Secession was pursued to defend slavery, but slavery almost immediately became indefensible. The Confederate war machine required slave labor to build its fortifications, work its factories, quarry its mines, fix its railroads, defend its harbors, tend its urban areas, and serve its soldiers. These enslaved workers often hailed from the fields and farms of the Old Dominion. This reallocation of labor only deepened antebellum contradictions of unfree labor working in semifree conditions as slaves familiarized themselves with their new surroundings, escaped, and supported the Union war effort.[34]

According to some pioneering historical studies and much of the best recent literature, many slaves emancipated themselves during the Civil War by embracing Union armies whenever these appeared.[35] There was certainly evidence of this slave self-emancipation in the Virginia tobacco piedmont. On December 4, 1861, John B. Spiece, a slaveholder from Albemarle County, wrote to the Confederate attorney general decrying the actions of newly mobile slaves. "There is," he complained, "also a serious evil in impressing slaves for the service in North Western Virginia:—Whilst there they get to talking with Union Men in disguise, and by that means learn the original cause of the difficulty between the North and South: Then [they] return home and inform other negroes:—Not long since one of my Neighbors negro men went to his master, and desired to let him go again to the North western army—adding 'I wish you to let me go futher [sic] than I went before.'"[36] The following spring L. H. Minor, a major slaveholder from Hanover County, wrote to the Confederate secretary of war protesting Rebel complicity in "encouraging" slave runaways. "Many

FIG. 1.1. The slaves' tobacco regimen. Note the labor intensity, primitive division of labor, and slave solidarity throughout the production process. (Drawing by Chester Hunt after P. H. Mayo and Brother's Calendar [ca. 1870], Robert, *Tobacco Kingdom*, frontispiece)

farmers in Virginia," he complained, "are injured by a practice which has become habitual and extensive among the soldiers of our army. The soldiers employ runaway negroes to cook for the mess, clean their horses, and so forth. The consequence is that negroes are encouraged to run away, finding a safe harbour in the army. Two of my neighbors have each recovered runaway negroes within the last few weeks; who were actually found in the employment of the soldiers on the peninsula and these negroes had been runaway many months."[37] The Virginia interior, like many other pockets of the Civil War South, also appears to have had its moment of truth.[38]

The vast majority of slaves, however, did not steal themselves away. They stayed on their isolated plantations and farms and pursued the far less dramatic action of stealing their own labor from their absentee owners. Such a course was probably most practical during the unpredictability of war. Furthermore, the military enlistment of many central and southern piedmont slaveholders and nonslaveholders must have considerably eased the burdens of coercive agricultural production for the slaves. According to one recent study of the Forty-fourth Virginia Infantry, nine companies came from the heart of the central piedmont with recruits from Amelia, Appomattox, Buckingham, Charlotte, Goochland, Louisa, and Prince Edward Counties. A survey of the 534 members of the Forty-fourth Virginia Infantry whose antebellum occupation was known revealed 91 farmers, 67 overseers or farm managers, 4 tenant farmers, and 1 planter. A smaller survey of four companies from Amelia, Appomattox, and Fluvanna Counties revealed that 51 percent of the soldiers were either slaveholders or the sons of slaveholders. A further 10 percent of these men were either overseers or laborers on farms with slaves.[39] In other words, the fundamental basis for coercive slave-based agricultural production in the southern and central piedmont, namely supervision, had been removed to the battlefront. If the Forty-fourth Virginia Infantry was exemplary, then the clear majority of the region's slaveholders and overseers must have flocked to the Confederate standard with a corresponding loss in supervision.[40]

This withdrawal of vital slaveholding supervision was exploited in a variety of ways by slaves in the Virginia interior. Their striking actions drew on a past tradition of disobedience, recalcitrance, and troubling management. Some took advantage of the opportunity to enjoy a unique degree of control at the point of agricultural production. Former Virginia slave Levi Pollard pointed to the change in his work routine on Charles Bruce's plantation in Charlotte County during the Civil War. "My overseer," he recalled, "went ter war en I wus my own boss. I start plowin' dat fall en' I plow'd all dat year, den de next fall I gits me two horses ter plow with, en den af'er dat I keep ter plowin' with two horses en I ain'n never seed dat bucket no mo' dat I toted 'fore I start ter plow. I even plow part in de day Lee surender'd."[41] Most slaves in the region, however, appear to have engaged in an informal slowdown in the fields. According to the contemporary vernacular, they either "loafed" or performed "demoralized" labor. The nature of this wartime demoralization was captured by a former slaveholding mistress from Campbell County. Sarah Payne recalled in a letter to her cousin Mary M. Clendenin: "You know the men were taken in the army, first from eighteen to thirty five, then from eighteen to forty five, and towards the last, from sixteen to fifty. Of course, the greater number, nearly *all* of the labouring men were taken from the fields. A great many were not accustomed to work with their hands but had a large number of negroes under them. Of course, when the master was away, they didn't make much."[42]

This theme of slave recalcitrance during the Civil War was subsequently echoed by the southern-tinted views of some historians. Bell I. Wiley, for example, noted that although "instances of effective work done under the direction of women and slave drivers are numerous and often very striking, there can be no doubt that plantation labor suffered considerably from the absence of overseers during the war."[43] Clement Eaton not only thought that the "impact of the war on the agricultural economy of the South was felt in the serious weakening of control of the planters over the slaves," but "as the great majority of the able-bodied white men were drawn into the army[,] the lot of the slaves in general became easier."[44] This important aspect of slave self-emancipation on the domestic front complements the more dramatic illustrations of the destruction of slavery on the battlefront during the Civil War. This process also suggests that the unraveling of the social organization of slavery occurred as much in the region as outside it.[45]

On the morning of April 9, 1865, in a small private residence in the heart of Virginia's central piedmont, the fate of the Confederacy's military resistance and political secession was finally sealed. For over two and a half centuries the Old Dominion was slavery and tobacco. It took hold in the Virginia piedmont for much of the century prior to the Civil War. Slaveholders coerced their slaves into labor-intensive staple crop production; slaves, while forced, also became acquainted with the rural rhythms of the land, ways to work that land, and the value of their labor. In early 1865, of course, this knowledge meant little outside the shadow of slavery. Levi Pollard plowed while Lee surrendered. Isaac Petty was busy plowing his master's fields in nearby Pittsylvania County at the moment of the surrender; if he paused at all, it was probably only to wipe his brow under the hot spring sun.[46]

The shadow, however, was retreating as former slaves and former masters were about to grapple under the very different conditions of emancipation. This difference was reflected in social relations shaped by either proslave management or emancipatory aspirations that weighed heavily on the brains of the living. This difference was made even more evident with the presence of triumphant Union troops and, in particular, military representatives of the victorious federal government, the BRFAL. What ensued was the erosion of older forms of social discipline under the ideology of republican free labor.

CHAPTER TWO

Free Labor Struggles in the Field, 1865–1867

Freedmen on the place took up an acrimonious idea that
the land and every thing upon it belonged to them.
—Justice of the Peace A. W. Thompson

You have now every inducement to work, as you are to
receive the payment for your labor, and you have every
inducement to save your wages, as your rights in what
you possess will be protected.—Colonel Orlando Brown

Order and labour on the Plantation to be the same in
every respect as formerly.—Planter Grey Skipworth

On February 28, 1866, Captain J. W. Sharp, assistant superintendent
of the BRFAL in Dinwiddie County, Virginia, penned his monthly report to state commissioner Brigadier General Orlando Brown in Richmond. "To a casual observer," Sharp began, everything "would look
bright and promising. There are but ten freedmen who draw Government rations and these are all old and infirm; most of the young and
able-bodied are working for the whites at either remunerating wages in
money or for a share of the crop. There are no apprehensions of
insurrection and, in general, mutual good feeling exists between the
whites and the blacks." Although Sharp had arbitrated many "trivial"
cases, he knew of little abuse of the freedpeople by the whites. These
observations were, however, only "the superficial view," and for those
who sought "to understand the true state of affairs, things [did] not
look so promising."[1]

Captain Sharp devoted the majority of his report to these difficulties. Some of the freedpeople insisted on pursuing subsistence

farming, risking poverty and dependency while injudicious land-holders encouraged them to do so. Sharp wrote,

> Just freed from slavery and infactuated with the new and dazzling idea of liberty, many of the blacks have settled on miserably poor lands in the fallacious hope of making a crop. These lands have been rented or leased to them for the one fourth of their product by persons who realize that an ear of corn is better than nothing—for, without these settlers, the land is valueless. In most cases, the freed-men have to build a cabin to live in, fence the land, and clear so much land; and all this without a supply of provisions, without money, without wagons, ploughs or harrows—in some cases with and in others without an old and worthless horse, the former being much the better off, as they have no horse to feed.

Captain Sharp feared that emancipation in his region might develop in the same negative way as it had in other postemancipation societies: "Some of the inevitable results of this pernicious system, the full effects of which are seen in Jamaica, have already developed them-selves here, and others equally baleful remain to be developed in the future."

One immediate problem was interference with the smooth opera-tion of the free market system in wage labor. "Many honest and reliable farmers," Sharp complained, "offering from five to ten dollars a month and board, have not many laborers as they desire and others have none at all—and, of course, their lands will remain untilled or be so much the less productive." Since the "would-be planters" were unable to support themselves, these freedpeople "must resort to theft to eke out a subsistence." Sharp received daily complaints "although I by no means believe that in all cases the freedmen are guilty." Along with "ill will and bad feeling" between the whites and the blacks, Sharp thought the "prospective evil most to be dreaded is that they will not raise enough of corn and meat to support them and will become dependents on the charity of the Government" or "perish of want and the deseases thereby engendered."

Not all the freedpeople "who have located on lands" were in such a bad way. Sharp reported a "few of them have good lands, have provi-sions, teams and money enough to make a crop, and are thriving so handsomely that it makes me feels proud and glad when I visit them."

He proposed to "break up the worst of them—those most destitute and most egregiously misled by their improvidence and folly," and have them hire out to "farmers who will treat and pay them well." Sharp's superior, the BRFAL district superintendent, however, had previously informed him that this "cannot be done, and I would respectfully ask [Colonel Brown] what can be done, or must the evil go on getting worse and worse every day?"

Captain Sharp noted a "few cases of injustice towards the blacks," but these originated from select "classes." These included "disreputable men who never had any character in the county," "old men whose ideas have become crystalised and who cannot accommodate themselves to changed circumstances," and "idle women whose tongues are busier than their hands."

Especially onerous for the local BRFAL official was implementation and enforcement of the free labor contract system. "One of the difficulties" encountered by Sharp was "a propensity the freedmen have to break their contracts. In some cases they wander about the country either idly or seeking employment but very often they go directly to a neighbor . . . I am very frequently inclined to believe, has persuaded them to come to live by promising them higher wages, though the person who promises unusually high wages I have found are the worst to pay—a fact which few of the Freedmen can yet appreciate." This was the context for Sharp's ominous conclusion: "I must state that as far as my experience has gone, the oft quoted remark that 'the nigger won't work' is false, and that under proper regulations I believe he will become an honest, good, and useful member of society—but that locating at his pleasure and that of unprincipled whites, on poor lands—subject to no control but the indolence and gross appetites engendered by slavery—will make him a thief, a pauper, and a curse to the country."

This remarkable BRFAL monthly report contours free labor struggles in the field during the opening postemancipation seasons. The freedpeople squatted, subsisted, contracted, and moved away from older forms of social control in search of autonomy. Some proved successful; the desperate determination of others was suggested by their toleration of near-starvation and their resorting to theft. Many resisted the local official's improvement plan. Former masters and landlords controlled land but no longer the labor that had made such land so valuable.

Indeed, in their desperation for laborers at the beginning of the agricultural season, some of these employers enticed laborers away from their existing contracts. Traditional class collaboration was further hampered by those who could not adjust to emancipation. As for Captain Sharp, his free labor agenda of wage labor, self-support, and equitable relations was constantly undermined by the actions of former slaves and former masters. Despite his duteousness, supervision, and best efforts, he feared the failure of emancipation reminiscent of other postslave societies. Sharp's monthly report unwittingly captured the weakening of older forms of social control. These became the hallmark of social relations in the Virginia tobacco region.[2]

The role of the federal government in facilitating the transition from slavery to freedom in the American South was made clear very early, even before the official cessation of hostilities. While General Grant was chasing the ragged remnants of General Lee's shoeless army across Virginia's central piedmont in early March 1865, Congress passed an act establishing the BRFAL for the duration of the war and one year thereafter. The BRFAL was the culmination of various convergent forces, including the American Freedmen's Inquiry Commission, the Treasury's *Rules and Regulations*, and dealing with wartime runaway "contrabands." Its stated objectives were to provide clothing, rations, and fuel to needy former slaves as well as to distribute abandoned and confiscated lands to loyal refugees and freedpeople.[3]

The BRFAL soon established itself as a major military and political presence in the defeated South. On May 12, 1865, President Andrew Johnson appointed General Oliver O. Howard as commissioner of the BRFAL. Before the month was out, Howard had appointed nine assistant commissioners for the South, including Colonel Orlando Brown for Virginia, headquartering at Richmond. In early July this Yale-educated physician and former freedmen's director in the southeastern peninsula divided the state into eight districts. Three districts covered the Virginia tobacco region: District 2, covering the southern piedmont under the authority of superintendent Captain Stuart Barnes; District 4, partially covering the central piedmont under superintendent Captain Thomas F. P. Crandon; and District 7, containing nine counties in the southwestern piedmont superintended by Captain Robert S. La-

FREE LABOR STRUGGLES IN THE FIELD

cey. The headquarters for these districts were Petersburg, Charlottesville, and Lynchburg, respectively. Over the next few months Colonel Brown appointed military officers as provost judges and supervised the establishment of local freedmen's courts in the counties. On January 29, 1866, Brown issued Circular Order 6, which required district superintendents to provide regular monthly reports "of the condition of Bureau affairs, the state of feeling between the Whites and the Freedmen, and other facts connected with the welfare of the Freedmen." These monthly reports became the arteries of northern political power and Republican free labor ideology.[4]

Of course, describing the establishment of the BRFAL begs the question of its nature and operation. What function did this federal organization serve in the immediate aftermath of Appomattox? Did it smooth the transition from slavery to freedom? Was it biased toward the interests of former slaves or former masters? What impact did it have on the outcome of emancipation? These issues have been debated extensively over the years. Some have argued that the BRFAL was a benevolent organization created to help the freedpeople in their transition from slavery to freedom and was largely successful. Lieutenant Marcus S. Hopkins ended his tenure as the local BRFAL official in Orange County with fulsome praise for "the much abused Bureau [as] one of those great successful national works for the amelioration of the condition of mankind which marks epochs in history and constitute the visible steps by which we are enabled to trace human progress."[5] Hopkins's superior, General Howard, offered a more sober assessment in his subsequent autobiography. The BRFAL "became a school in which he [the freedman] learned the first practical business of life."[6] These flattering contemporary views have been mirrored by numerous historians who have argued that the BRFAL, in the words of one recent student of postbellum Virginia, "struggled mightily to ease the freedmen's transition from slavery to freedom."[7] Others have been more harsh in their appraisal of the BRFAL's activities. For many former Confederates, the bureau represented the worst evidence of federal intrusion, while some northern opponents resented any extension of federal governmental power. Revisionist historians have condemned the hostile racist attitudes of BRFAL officials toward former slaves, charging the organization with overall failure in its mission.[8]

More recently, some historians have depicted the BRFAL as an organ

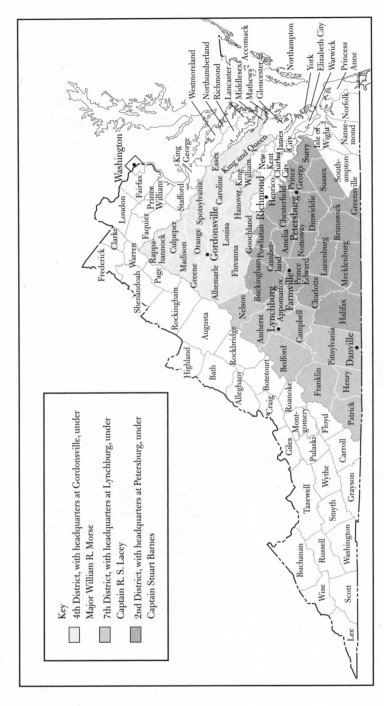

MAP 2.1. BRFAL districts in the Virginia tobacco region (Alderson, *Freedmen's Bureau*, 8–10)

of federal/state power imbued with the principles of Republican free labor ideology. The personal attitudes and racial identity of BRFAL officials are not so much ignored as subsumed under the mantle of a powerful federal military and political structure primarily concerned with the implementation of free labor relations.[9] The following argument supports this interpretation. Its major contribution, apart from providing further regional emphasis, is the systematic pursuit of Republican free labor ideology in relation to the rural rhythms and clashes of agricultural seasons. This relationship is often evoked but rarely analyzed. We should insist on the seasonal context of these early emancipatory struggles in the field(s).

Republican free labor ideology had helped begin, sustain, and win a Civil War. Its principles of worker dignity, fair relations between employee and employer, contract labor, self-sufficiency, upward mobility, and property ownership had been enshrined a decade earlier in the fledgling Republican Party.[10] If federal troops introduced emancipation on the point of a bayonet during the war, their BRFAL cousins were charged with imposing free labor negotiation under the nib of a pen. In May 1865 BRFAL commissioner General Howard ordered the implementation of new social relations in the former secessionist states. Assistant commissioners were instructed "to introduce a practical system of compensated labor." They must further "remove prejudices from late masters who are unwilling to employ their former servants." The freedmen were to be corrected in their occasional "false impression" that they could live without labor. Only the helpless among the refugees were to be provided for, while "the able-bodied [were] to labor for their own support." The freedmen must work without government support. "The negro," Howard directed, "should understand that he is really free but on no account, if able to work, should he harbor the thought that the Government will support him in idleness." Howard described the essence of these instructions: "to rehabilitate labor, to establish the actual freedom of the late slave, to secure his testimony in the local courts, [and] to bring the freedmen justice in settling past contracts and in making new ones." This work also aimed to support northern philanthropic "school work" and to operate a self-supporting agency.[11] The collective meaning of such ideas is buried by historians' discourse of either sympathy or antipathy; rather, these ideas entailed the rigorous implementation of a new, more judicious, free labor system along the lines of work, capital-labor equality, independence, and improvement.

In Virginia the assistant commissioner was quick to explain the BRFAL's new policy. The day preceding his official installation as chief in Richmond, Colonel Brown issued Circular Order 5, which commanded the discontinuance of relief as soon as possible, the assistance of the freedpeople in self-support, protection of loyal refugees and free laborers, and agency aid for land distribution. A few weeks later Brown issued another order, which emphasized the bureau's free labor policies regarding assistance, protection, education, the mutuality of capital and labor, antivagrancy, and self-support.[12]

The most salient expression of Colonel Brown's free labor tenets was a published address, "To the Freedmen of Virginia," issued on July 1, 1865.[13] He began on a duteous note: "It becomes my duty to look after all matters that pertain to your welfare" and to "teach you how to use that freedom you have so earnestly desired, and to prevent the abuse of it by yourselves and others." Brown noted the changed condition of the freedpeople. Formerly they were "directed," the "proceeds" of their labor "taken by your masters." Now "you are to direct and receive the proceeds of your own labor and care for yourselves." The key to success was to "help yourselves" through being "industrious and frugal." Their incentive would be to "receive the payment for your labor." Through saving "your wages" and thrift, the freedpeople provide for "sickness and old age."

Although Brown believed that most of the freedpeople would "feel the responsibilities of your new condition," some would "act from the mistaken notion that Freedom means liberty to be idle." Vagrancy, he warned, would not be tolerated. Free labor, he continued, did not mean "your former masters have become your enemies." Rather, "honest, industrious and frugal" labor would beget employers of "kindness and consideration." If not, "you will find the Government, through the agents of this Bureau, as ready to secure to you, as to them, Liberty and Justice." Schools were also to be established, since "in your condition as *freedmen*, education is of the highest importance." Individual responsibility must be forthcoming especially since governmental "protection and assistance" would soon be withdrawn. Most importantly, freedpeople should stay put "in a location where work is to be obtained at fair wages," because "it is much better for you to remain than to be looking for something better." If they followed these directions, were "quiet, peaceable, law-abiding citizens" and "industrious" and "frugal," then "the glory of passing successfully from Slavery to Freedom, will, by the blessing of God, be yours."[14]

This address deserves special attention because it became the official free labor constitution of postemancipation Virginia during the tenure of the BRFAL. Its tenets of compensation, self-help, independence, industry, frugality, thrift, schooling, citizenry, and progress represented a veritable Republican manifesto. Forged in the furnace of previous antislavery political struggles, Republican free labor attempted to fasten its steel-like rivets on the postemancipation South. Its complex meaning was perhaps most succinctly conveyed in Indiana Republican politician George W. Julian's reference to "that principle of eternal justice, a fair day's wages for a fair day's work."[15] It might be added that such ideas of free labor represented the global triumph of capitalist ideology that was promulgated throughout numerous postemancipation societies.[16]

Of course, we have no way of knowing what the freedpeople's response was to Colonel Brown's proclamation. We can fairly assume that more freedpeople heard about it than read it because of high rates of slave illiteracy. Some points do seem clear. Brown was a federal authority who was obviously at odds with the former slaveholders, but his address also smacked of another form of management. He emphasized freedom, but mainly the freedom to work in exchange for compensation. Brown's address offered minimal welfare support by the BRFAL, but only in cases of dire necessity. The freedpeople's mobility was not outlawed, but it was restricted. Most importantly, older slave ideas of the unfair appropriation of labor by masters who had previously directed slave labor and taken its proceeds were officially confirmed by this federal authority.[17]

It is also difficult to gauge the response of either former masters or new employers to Brown's address. Its emphasis on work and industry would have surely met with their approval. So would the federal government's opposition to vagrancy and the limitations imposed on the freedpeople's mobility. But the address also contained some disturbing elements. Most obviously, it betokened unwanted federal power in the Old Dominion. It promised external management. It also equalized employee-employer relations in a very different way. The emphasis on education offered a new type of schooling altogether. And it described a labor theory of value very much at odds with that of proslavery. The resulting clash between the former masters' proslavery controls, the former slaves' emancipatory aspirations, and the bureau's free labor ideas reverberated throughout the postemancipation seasons.

The precise function of the BRFAL was soon revealed in the aftermath of Appomattox. Part of its raison d'être was almost immediately canceled by President Johnson's Amnesty Proclamation, issued on May 29, 1865. Under its terms many former Confederates were pardoned through simply swearing an oath of allegiance to the Union. Their pardon was followed by the return of those lands that they had "abandoned." The BRFAL oversaw a rapidly dwindling supply of either land belonging to those outside the proclamation or "confiscated" territory that had once belonged to the Confederate government. In Virginia this process amounted to the rapid restoration of former landownership. By the end of 1865 the BRFAL controlled a mere 75,653 acres of Virginia real estate, of which 2,625 acres were arable, 49,110 acres were uncultivated, and 23,918 acres were unclassified. Most of this abandoned and confiscated land was in the tidewater region. A mere 3,366 acres of land in the Virginia piedmont was held by the federal government. In other words, former slaveowner Robert Hubard's 6,000 acres in Buckingham County made him a greater regional landowner than the federal government. A year later BRFAL holdings in the state fell to around 50,000 acres; by the summer of 1868 these had dwindled to under 10,000 acres, all of which had been returned by the year's end.[18]

If the BRFAL was not to concern itself with abandoned lands, this was also true of its provisioning for refugees. As we have seen already, senior officials such as General Howard and Colonel Brown made it clear that one of the crucial aims of Republican free labor was the creation of independent freedpeople and freedmasters. Captain Sharp's report suggests the extent to which self-sufficiency trickled down to the fields. Free labor was to replace slave labor as a means of creating such independence. The sort of welfare provisions associated with wartime refugeeing ran contrary to this objective. Such federal welfarism was thought of as only a last resort. That it was still needed, especially by those freedpeople who slipped between the basic support of a slave

FREE LABOR STRUGGLES IN THE FIELD

regime and an emergent free labor society, was noted by the likes of Captain Sharp. Lieutenant Colonel John W. Jordan, the local bureau official for Prince Edward and Cumberland Counties, was even more adamant. He informed his district superintendent that rations were provided to "a number of freedmen who by means of infancy, old age or infirmity are incapable of providing for their own wants," but not to those "who are *able* to work." Jordan deemed this bureau welfarism crucial since the freedmen "cannot look to their old masters for assistance or support," while "no definite action has been taken by the proper County authorities toward providing for them."[19]

By streamlining welfarism and facilitating reclamation of ex-Confederate land, the BRFAL was effectively transformed from an agency that had the potential to redistribute land into an agency that primarily supervised free labor relations.[20] Its major means were through the system of labor contracts between former slaves and former masters— preferably written and preferably stamped with the approval of the local bureau official. In early May 1865 General Howard issued his eleventh circular order, requiring all planters and farmers to engage in labor contracts with the freedpeople, either under the auspices of officials in the field or independently.[21] Such orders were almost immediately followed in the Virginia interior. On May 12 employer Edward B. Goode contracted with "Lucious, Horace, John, Tom, Amelia, Lucy, Ann and Harvie" whereby the "laborers" agreed to "serve" their employer "faithfully and diligently on his farm" in Mecklenburg County until the first of January 1866. As "compensation for their service," the freedpeople were to receive food rations as well as "one fourth of the corn, fodder, peas and sorghum." Those freedmen who worked on "reaping and securing the crop of wheat" were to be paid one dollar daily; other "hands," fifty cents; and "women and boys," twenty-five cents.[22] On June 7, 1865, former master William R. Baskerville contracted with his former slaves Gilbert, Plummer, London, Douglas, William, Ned, Glouster, John, Ben, Gilbert, Daniel, and Pitt. These freedmen were to "work diligently on his plantation" in Mecklenburg County until December 24, 1865, for which they were to "secure as remuneration one fourth (¼) part of the proceeds of the crops of corn, wheat, fodder, potatoes and peas." Over the next two days employer Baskerville signed another eight contracts with former slaves Grayson, Gilbert, Meckles, Taswell, Nammo, Hardy and Louisa, Essex, and Billy to work in either the fields or the household in exchange for either a share of the crop or board and provisions.[23]

Labor contracting supervised by the BRFAL occurred elsewhere in the region. Between June 12 and August 5, 1865, employer Lewis E. Harvie separately contracted with freedpeople Archer Binton, Madison Crump, Dick Hardaway, Cornelius Scott, Sally Clairborne, Dick Craddock, John Thompson, D. Isham, and Jim Smith. In exchange for their services as "farm laborer[s]" on his Dykeland plantation in Amelia County for the remainder of the season until December 31, 1865, Harvie agreed to provide "good and sufficient food" along with monthly wages ranging from $3.50 for Sally to between $5.00 and $7.00 for the others.[24]

Labor contracting was particularly active in Louisa County. On May 11, 1865, seven freedmen engaged in separate contracts with William E. Langan at wage rates between $1.00 and $2.50 daily plus board. One week later fifteen freedmen signed a collective contract with M. Pendleton for board and clothing, as did six ex-slaves with William Waddy. Throughout the rest of the summer, former slaves and former masters continued to contract in the area. By mid-September around thirty-two contracts had been signed between 23 employers and 183 freedmen in Louisa County. As was the case with Baskerville, many former masters contracted with their former slaves. At least 117 "former servants" signed with at least 12 "old masters." This flurry of labor contracts in the first flush of emancipation points to the role that the BRFAL played in negotiating the transition from unfree to free labor in tobacco Virginia.[25]

These written contracts suggest the degree to which BRFAL influence penetrated the Virginia tobacco region. They also highlight the ways in which former masters and new employers sought to utilize the new contract system to gain maximum control over their former charges. Employer Goode's contract with eight freedpeople stipulated that should the laborers "become disorderly, or disobedient to reasonable commands," he reserved the right to "dismiss him or her from his service at his discretion" along with fines.[26] The contract between ex-master Baskerville and eleven freedpeople stipulated that "the said negroes, formerly slaves, are to conduct themselves in an orderly respectable and respectful manner." If they did not, they were to forfeit their shares in the crops. Furthermore, the freedpeople had to work from sunrise until sunset and were responsible for overseeing the work tasks of their families: "Those of the negroes, formerly slaves, who have wives or children who do not labor in the field are to return, out of their portion of the crop when gathered," all that corn consumed by them between the contract date and settlement.[27] Planter Harvie's three-page contract with Dick Craddock was quite eloquent in its expression of the freedman's free labor duties. Should Craddock "fail to work faithfully and industriously or be guilty of any insubordination or other misconduct," the employer reserved the right to discharge the laborer. The freedman would also forfeit "all that may be due him for work done," while his employer "may apply to any public officer or authority which was empowered to compel a faithful compliance with this contract." Craddock's welfare was now his responsibility, with sickness costs and doctor bills payable through "deductions." Dick's wife Meloina(?) was also required to labor "for the same time for her rations for herself and infant child subject herein to the same conditions as herein before expressed."[28]

Similar employer stratagems to remake free labor in the image of older discipline were pursued in other parts of the region. The contract between William Waddy and his six former slaves insisted the latter "bind ourselves to work as we have done heretofore." Eight other contracts from Louisa County made the same stipulation. While employers William MacGhee and Charles G. Trevilian signed equal liability clauses with the freedpeople, several employers included forfeiture clauses in the contracts that applied exclusively to the laborers. In his contract with seven of "his servants" and their families, N. H. Crawford reserved the right to expel the laborers if they misbehaved and to collect their pay of "thirds" if they left voluntarily.[29] These ex-masters and new employers also combined to support the efforts of one another in their attempts to reassert domination through labor contracting. Not only were the stipulations, format, and language of these contracts similar, but a number of the contracts were endorsed by fellow employers. Charles C. Goodwin claimed to be a "disinterested party and disinterested witness" in a contract between William B. Cocke and five freedmen, yet he had a contract with fifteen freedmen witnessed by a fellow local employer. Employer combination was stark in the case of the settlement clause inserted into the contract between David R. Shelton and eight freedmen, in which "part of the crops made on the farm of the said Shelton the present year (1865)" was to be determined by "any 2 white gentlemen of the neighborhood [who] shall say [what] is just and right."[30] We may fairly assume these gentlemen's agreements favored gentlemen only. Such employer endorsements were made for the edification of the local BRFAL official; they also reflected class-conscious employers and provided an important collective means for exerting pressure on the freedpeople. Free labor here was construed to mean the freedom to labor only under the direction and supervision of former masters. The supervisory nature of these written labor contracts clearly exposed the entrails of proslavery.

It would be misleading, however, to extrapolate the complete story of free labor negotiations only from labor contracts. Otherwise the freedpeople would appear mute. They often signed an "X" by their names, suggesting an inability either to read, verify, or dispute what they had put their mark on.[31] Rather, the struggle over work itself in the fields and on the farms and plantations casts a more accurate light on the nature of new social relations. Freedman Anderson's actions were a good example of some of the dimensions of this new relationship. On June 1, 1865, Anderson contracted to work for himself, wife Milly, and their six children on the plantation of William Overton for the duration of the year in exchange for food, clothing, and "being taken care of." The contract further stipulated that the freedpeople work "as they have heretofore." On July 22 Overton wrote to his local BRFAL official complaining of Anderson's disobedience. Apparently, manager John S. Sargent "ordered Anderson to take a load of wheat from the threshing yard to the barn in the ox-cart which he (Anderson) was driving." The freedman "refused to do so, alleging that he had a headache." The manager then "told him to let another person take his cart and carry it, which he insolently refused to do himself, or suffer to be done by another." Overton was vexed since he felt that Anderson was abusing his good treatment. The "support of Anderson and his family is much more than their labour is worth," he argued, and "I retained them more for their benefit than my own, having from the first come to the conclusion to send none of them off who would behave themselves." If they did not behave, he added, "it will be impossible for me to retain them." Overton might well have given special treatment to freedman Anderson and his family; he may also have been engaging in tendentiousness calculated to appeal to the free labor

FREE LABOR STRUGGLES IN THE FIELD

equity of the BRFAL. (His postcript drips with the threat of dependent freedpeople in ways reminiscent of Captain Sharp's report.) Most importantly, Anderson was exerting a degree of control over his own labor time that formerly would have been quickly circumscribed by the punishment of the slave regimen. The point is not that disobedience was new; rather, the action, its reportage, and adjudication indicate new expressions of negotiation in the field.[32]

There were other tensions implicit in free labor negotiations. On May 27, 1865, J. W. Pendleton signed a share contract with at least eight freedmen in which it was stipulated that the employer would manage the farm. Apparently differences arose as to what such management actually entailed; freedman John Robinson was summarily discharged without any further explanation. On September 18, 1865, employer Goodwin contracted with twenty freedpeople, including Dabney. Three weeks later Captain John Smith endorsed a contract termination between Goodwin and Dabney that was "mutually agreed." It is possible that Dabney was not fulfilling the terms of the contract to the letter, since her employer was awarded her share of the crop when harvested; alternatively, Captain Smith might have simply sided with the employer. Planter Leighton Nuchalls was not even prepared to tolerate the new labor system beyond the requirements of the current agricultural season. His share contract signed with fourteen freedmen on August 23, 1865, stipulated that "the said Negroes are after putting in all the above crops specified no longer in my employment and must leave my farm."[33]

Settlement time harvested these free labor tensions. The central dispute was over the precise dispensation of the crop. The freedpeople brought the consciousness of their right to the fruits of their labor. (These were those "acrimonious ideas" referred to by Judge Thompson in the opening quotation.) They also fueled the "pernicious system" described by Captain Sharp. The BRFAL's legal emphasis on the wage as property became a very useful tool in the hands of the freedpeople, who could use such Republican free labor ideology to argue their claims. After all, Colonel Brown had officially directed that the freedpeople were to receive the proceeds of their own labor. Such "rights" clashed with the views of former masters and new employers who were unable to accept that workers' wages were their property that had been won during the season in the fields. At settlement time, labor contracts were transformed from frozen legal articles into moving targets of contested compensation.[34]

Sometime during the 1865 agricultural season, freedman Sam, Ella, and their family had contracted to work the remainder of the season for part of the crop on Mrs. Henderson's place in Cumberland County. With the busiest part of the season over, however, the employer had decided to discharge her laborers prematurely without compensation. The freedpeople immediately protested to their local BRFAL official. On July 24, 1865, Henderson received a curt letter from Captain John L. Liny. "Madam," it read, "the negroes herein named have been at work for you through the business of this season and now you turn them off with[out] the proportion of pay which would have been due them if they had remained on your place till the close of the year." This was "unjust and the parties turned away must receive the following compensation for their services." Liny then ordered Henderson to pay Sam "in addition to what he has had (5) five bushels corn or wheat" and "Ella and family in addition to what they have had (3) bushels of corn and wheat." Henderson was also instructed to "allow them the garden stuff of their own to be gathered as soon as practicable." "You have," Liny explained, "made no complaint to me of your labor not doing their duty and living up to their contract."[35]

This settlement dispute highlights some of the features of the free labor system. For Henderson, compensation was less a contractual obligation than was her own arbitrary dispensation. (Her actions were similar to those of the unreconstructed "old men" described by Captain Sharp.) For Sam, Ella, and their family the prime concern was with compensation for their seasonal labor, and they were prepared to use the local authorities to seek redress. For Captain Liny productive work was to be judiciously rewarded as befitted employer-employee relations. Since Liny had no reason to assume otherwise, the new system of contract labor was to be strictly enforced.[36]

Sometimes the freedpeople went to extraordinary lengths to defend their free labor rights. For the 1865 season, freedman Ned and others contracted to work the "Banister place" owned and managed by the Miller brothers in Pittsylvania County. Apparently a dispute arose over the division of the corn at settlement time. The freedmen complained to the BRFAL. Local official Captain J. F. Wilcox, assistant superintendent at Danville, instructed the Millers to compensate the freedmen with "the 10th part of the corn crop." The Millers subsequently protested to A. W. Thompson, the military justice of the peace of the second district, claiming they "had agreed to pay them [freedmen] the tenth," but their proposition "was treated with insolent contempt." It was a rather irate Justice Thompson who informed Captain Wilcox, the "freedmen on the place took up an acrimonious idea that the land and every thing upon it belonged to them." The freedmen "went so far as to bar the entrance of the place against a manager who was employed by him [Miller] and resisted one of the neighbours authorized by him [Miller] to gather parts, saying that Mr. Miller had no right to sell or dispose of it in any way." Justice Thompson also described "a large and expansive family many children and old women" who "have been idle and insolent throughout the year, going off and returning to the plantation at will." Even though Miller was described as being a "kind lenient and humane master" who fed, clothed, and treated his laborers well, the freedmen "have forced him to sell out and rent the land in self-defence." All of "these facts," Justice Thompson concluded, "will be testified to by any of his neighbors of high respectability." While the local justice's report was probably somewhat tendentious, it clearly suggests that Ned and his fellow freedmen were prepared to defend their compensatory rights by all means. They were even prepared to defend these rights against their landlords, local respectable neighbors, and a hostile military justice of the peace.[37] Captain Sharp was not alone in being unable to budge determined freedpeople.

The control over free labor time was a crucial component of these struggles in the fields. While BRFAL officials construed work time as a neat contractual obligation, former masters maintained that work time lasted all day and all calendar year, and freedpeople saw their labor time as amounting to daily and seasonal crop obligations. These competing notions clashed once the crops had been harvested. John G. Gilliam, Tandy Holman, and Moses A. Spencer, employers in Buckingham County, became embroiled in a contract dispute with the freedpeople over the length of the agricultural work season. On October 16, 1865, these employers wrote their local BRFAL official that they had made a contract with the "hands on our farms" for "one third" of the corn and pork along with provisions. The laborers "obligate[d] themselves to work faithful on our farms the present year under our control." But now, they protested, "we beg leave to report to your honor that our hands refused to sow our crops of wheat and to do any work connected with the crop for the present year, and we wish to have your advice as to the steps proper to be taken in the premises."[38]

On Harvie's plantation in Amelia County the freedpeople construed their contracts to mean they were to labor in the crop only during the day. The employer informed the local BRFAL official that they refused to obey orders especially regarding working after sunset. Both these cases suggest conflictual understandings of the work seasons. For the employers it meant the long day and year in ways reminiscent of slavery. For the freedpeople, work obligations ceased at either the end of the day or the end of the season, in contrast to former patterns. For the BRFAL the freedpeople were to work according to the provisions of the contract. The ambiguities of such contracts were hammered out on the anvil of free labor, sometimes in favor of the freedpeople, other times in favor of their employers.[39]

The end of the first agricultural season after Appomattox saw the institutional and ideological establishment of the BRFAL. Its major function had become the implementation of a new system of labor relations through contracts. This system drew upon a Republican ideology of free labor aimed at forging judicious employers from tyrannical masters and independent laborers from dependent slaves. This is what appeared to be happening. Years later General Howard recalled "the first results of free labor efforts" were encouraging during the first season in Virginia, where the "vast majority of freedmen were already at work."[40] Underlying strains and tensions, however, revealed a different social reality. Former masters and former slaves struggled to control the evolving emancipation process. The labor contract was contested, especially during settlement time. The significance of these written agreements defies easy statistical generalizations. Even the most exhaustive search of the national and state archives reveals a mixture of differing compensations, including supplies, rations, shares, and cash. The central point is that these contracts allow us to trace the early stirrings of free labor contestation. If employers often used the BRFAL to bolster their claims, the freedpeople used the same federal military and political agency to adjudicate their compensatory rights. The ripples of these struggles over contracting, settlement, and work time became a river the following season. On January 15, 1866, the Virginia general assembly passed a vagrancy act. It stipulated that the able-bodied idle were to be hired out for three months. Should vagrants abscond, they were required to work an extra month without wages. This legislation was reminiscent of numerous previous efforts by BRFAL officials and military commanders to force the able-bodied idle, especially in and around urban areas, into fruitful employment. The legislation was soon canceled, however, by General Alfred H. Terry, military commander in Virginia, who considered it too draconian. The general assembly also passed a labor contract law requiring written agreements between freedpeople and employers to be witnessed by a public official. Unlike the short-lived vagrancy law, this contract law lasted much longer since it complemented the BRFAL free labor agenda.[41]

While some freedpeople refused to contract either because of continuing hopes for land redistribution or because of the failure of employers to compensate them for their previous season's work, many others began to contract under the supervision of the BRFAL. These freedpeople needed to work in order to live, while employers needed their labor to begin sowing potentially bumper cash crops whose cultivation had been interrupted for the last several years. Captain John W. Barnes reported supervising sixty contracts costing $30 in fees charged between February and May 1866 in his district.[42] Captain J. F. Wilcox notarized around eighty agreements in Pittsylvania County.[43] Numerous other bureau officials reported labor contracting activities in their jurisdictions.[44] Labor negotiations between employer Lewis E. Harvie and twenty freedpeople at the Dykeland plantation were closely supervised by W. J. Cheatham, the local assistant superintendent in Amelia County. The latter contracts also contained a termination clause which stipulated that such contracts were only to be "canceled by the mutual consent of the parties in it, in the presence of some agent connected with the Freedmen's Bureau authorized to act in such matters in this county."[45] This clause was a telling comment on the reach of BRFAL's free labor agenda into the shadow of the Blue Ridge.

The contemporary contestation over labor contracting in the tobacco South has been mirrored by recent historical debate. Some have argued for the emergence of labor contracting within the context of local planter-client relations.[46] Others have argued for the immediate incidence of share payments resulting from the declining efficiency of worker organization units.[47] The most recent historian of postwar

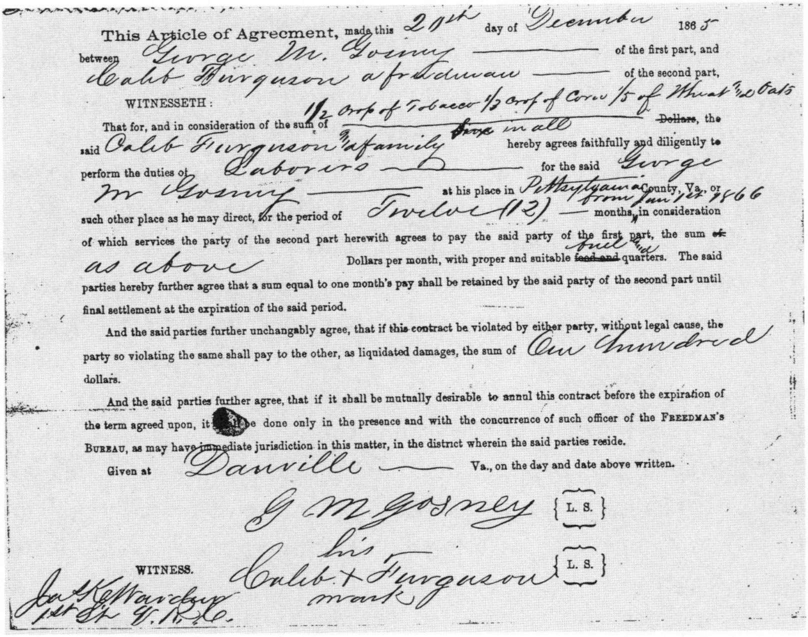

This Article of Agreement, made this 20th day of December 1865
between George M. Gosney —— of the first part, and
Caleb Furguson a freedman —— of the second part,

WITNESSETH:

That for, and in consideration of the sum of 1/2 crop of Tobacco 1/3 crop of Corn 1/5 of Wheat 1/2 Oats ~~Dollars~~, the said Caleb Furguson & family in all hereby agrees faithfully and diligently to perform the duties of Laborers for the said George M Gosney at his place in Pittsylvania County, Va., or such other place as he may direct, for the period of Twelve (12) from Jan 1st 1866 months, in consideration of which services the party of the second part herewith agrees to pay the said party of the first part, the sum ~~of~~ as above Dollars per month, with proper and suitable ~~food and~~ Fuel & quarters. The said parties hereby further agree that a sum equal to one month's pay shall be retained by the said party of the second part until final settlement at the expiration of the said period.

And the said parties further unchangably agree, that if this contract be violated by either party, without legal cause, the party so violating the same shall pay to the other, as liquidated damages, the sum of One hundred dollars.

And the said parties further agree, that if it shall be mutually desirable to annul this contract before the expiration of the term agreed upon, it [shall] be done only in the presence and with the concurrence of such officer of the Freedman's Bureau, as may have immediate jurisdiction in this matter, in the district wherein the said parties reside.

Given at Danville Va., on the day and date above written.

G M Gosney {L. S.}

WITNESS. Calib his + mark Furguson {L. S.}

Jas K Warden
1st Lt V. R. C.

FIG. 2.1. BRFAL labor contract between freedman Caleb Furguson and employer George M. Gosney, 1865 (BRFAL Labor Contracts, 3950, Pittsylvania County, RG 105)

Virginia concludes that by the beginning of the second crop season, "working on shares on annual contract was the predominant form of agreement for freed families across the tobacco belt."[48] All seem plausible depending on one's research and accompanying agenda, but the search for easy statistical generalizations also seems largely irrelevant. Many labor contracts were oral, and we shall never know exactly how many there were. The most thorough search of national, state, and university archives reveals only a fraction of these surviving remnants of the past. A more useful approach is to view these contracts as targets of conflictual compensation grounded in free labor struggles.

Rummaging around the archives over the last several years, I have unearthed over 600 contracts from fifteen counties in the Virginia tobacco region. I closely scrutinized 41. These reveal some bare statistical bones. Most were struck at the season's beginning between December 1865 and February 1866. They involved 28 employers and 162 freedmen and their families in eleven counties. They reflected a mixture of compensatory negotiations: 21 for cash, 15 for shares, 3 for

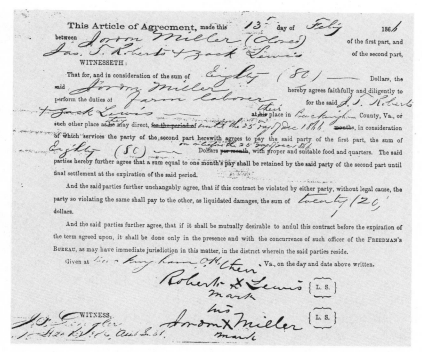

FIG. 2.2. BRFAL labor contract between freedman Jordon Miller and employers J. T. Roberts and Zack Lewis, 1866 (BRFAL Labor Contracts, 3905, Buckingham County, RG 105)

rations/lodging, and 1 for rent. Full settlement was invariably projected for the end of the calendar year. The work year primarily involved farm labor with some accompanying domestic labor.[49]

Employer A. L. Brent engaged in five separate labor contracts with freedpeople M. A. Miller, P. Miller, M. Smith, N. Smith, Lizzy Willis, and their families at Recess plantation in Fluvanna County. The freedpeople were to provide their "services" for the year and "to discharge cheerfully and promptly all duties" in exchange for food, lodging, and monthly wages ranging from $3 to $8 payable "when the crops of 1866 are secured."[50] Employer Samuel Allen contracted with freedmen Ben Miller, Willis Chambers, George Sharp, Archer Chambers, Jessie Lewis, Henry Holman, Adam Holman, Walker Cabell, and Jack Miller "to work his farm on James River Buckingham County Va for the year 1866." Allen would furnish the work animals, fodder, and rations for the freedmen along with "one half of the corn, wheat, oats and tobacco made on the farm" providing the freedmen "hereby bind themselves to attend to the business and to work constantly and diligently."[51] These contracts alone suggest a wide array of differing labor organization, nature of work, and compensatory arrangements.

If these contracts "stubbornly refuse to be reduced to statistical form,"[52] they do point to some general processes characterizing free labor relations in the opening post-Appomattox seasons. Much like the contracts of the previous year, they highlight the local power of the BRFAL. They also point to an older form of class collaboration. Some contracts stipulate neighborhood rates that reflect a particular agreement signed among employers themselves, while others were witnessed by family members or fellow employers. Edwin James Harvie oversaw several of L. E. Harvie's contracts in Amelia County, while Dr. I. Spraggins witnessed contract agreements in Charlotte County.[53] More specifically, these contracts replicated employers' attempts to wrest maximum control over the freedpeople, their lives, and their labor. Planter Grey Skipworth demanded from the thirty-one freed-people with whom he contracted that the "order and labour on the Plantation to be the same in every respect as formerly." Freedman Edmund Burke agreed to "furnish Four (4) good able bodied work hands (two men & two women)" and to assume personal responsibility for their supervision and behavior. The "management and direction," however, "of all the operations on the place, shall be under the control of the said C. B. Lowry, or such agent as he may employ." Here were the echoes of proslavery management.[54]

Accompanying old echoes were new sounds. One was the freeing of labor from its minimal protective moorings. Free labor contracting entailed work only; it had nothing to do with any provisions outside the work calendar. Freedmen Frederick Woodson, Aleck Woodson, Lewis Booker, and Charles Alexander, who contracted with Eliza B. Haskins for half-share wages, were required "to board themselves and pay their own take, and medical bills" along with "the sum of thirty dollars for house rent and fire wood for their families." We can fairly assume that the BRFAL approved of this agreement based strictly on work between capital and labor. It severed all other relations of dependency and indicated independent support and self-sufficiency on the part of both classes.[55]

One of the central tenets of Republican free labor ideology was this balance between the classes. Employers needed labor and employees needed work; their mutual interests would be arbitrated through the marketplace and legally guaranteed by a contract, written or otherwise. The proliferation of contract negotiations for the impending agricultural season did not preclude the realization of conflicting free labor agendas. This was particularly evident through employer "enticement" during the early winter months of 1866. Although BRFAL officials reported that many of the freedpeople were working either "well" or "hard," others were being enticed into severing their contracts through offers of more lucrative wages elsewhere. The custodians of Republican free labor chafed at this annoying trait of the new system. From Lunenburg County, Lieutenant J. Arnold Yeckley informed his superior "that many white men are enticing freedmen to break fair contracts by the offer of higher wages." Even though Yeckley "compelled the freedmen to live up to his [sic] contract," he bemoaned the fact that there was "no law to punish the white man."[56] Lieutenant Connelly, assistant superintendent at Farmville, reported from his district of Prince Edward and Cumberland Counties that "numbers of the freedmen through a want of a thorough understanding of their contract but mainly owing to the inducements held out to them by designing Whites are leaving the plantations of their present employers and hiring themselves out again to any party who may offer more wages than they have received at their old place." Connelly ordered the freedmen to return to their original places of employment immediately.[57]

Of course, Connelly's frustration and Yeckley's concern at this blatant disregard for the contract system missed the point. The freedpeople could have been ignorant of their contracts; they might also have been responding to past contract iniquities that the BRFAL might or might not have resolved. The freedpeople could have been the dupes of better-paying employers; they might also have sought to fulfill their emancipatory aspirations, especially through their recently found mobility.[58] BRFAL descriptions of "designing Whites" are equally debatable. Apart from silencing the freedpeople by blaming the employers, they also skirt the realities of burgeoning market competition for free labor. Gone were former controls; now there were BRFAL contracts freezing some labor and mobility freeing other labor, all during a promising new tobacco season. These enticements also breached planter solidarity, pushing employers beyond class solidarity. In short, these BRFAL ideas were an awkward fit for the new social relations, although they did capture the decline of older forms of social control.

By the spring of 1866 much of this early seasonal chaos had dissipated because of agricultural duties, BRFAL clampdowns, and antienticement laws. Free labor struggles, however, continued unabated, often in far less noisy terms than those expressed at either settlement time or the season's beginning. These conflicts took place on plantations and farms as minute daily struggles over the extent, nature, and control of free labor. The details of these seasonal struggles in the Virginia tobacco fields are perhaps best exemplified through events in Charlotte County, in the heart of the tobacco southside. The local BRFAL official conducted a series of surveys that were completed by several planters. These interrogatories provide fine detail on the local activities of the BRFAL, especially its adherence to the tenets of free labor relations. They also throw light on the planters, the nature of their farming systems, and their difficult adjustments to emancipation in the immediate aftermath of the Civil War. This collection further provides fascinating glimpses into the meaning of freedom for local freedpeople.

On April 6, 1866, Lieutenant Edwin Lyon assumed leadership of the assistant subdistrict of Charlotte County. The novelty of the position, the lack of records kept by his predecessor, and a sense of duteousness prompted Lyon to devise a "plan for supplying the necessary information" describing his new jurisdiction. He put together a survey consisting of twenty-nine questions that was distributed to "the leading planters of the county with request to reply, *giving their own views*, on the subject of free labor, the condition of the freedmen, and the feeling between the two classes." Seven planters replied. Despite being "interested parties," Lyon felt that their status as "men of standing," together with "their honest views," would make their returns useful for his superior, Colonel Brown, ensconced in his Richmond headquarters.[59]

The starting point of these surveys was their indication of the BRFAL's local power. Lyon set up his headquarters at Charlotte Court House, which was within easy range of the surrounding countryside. Most of the planters who fell under Lyon's jurisdiction lived within a twenty-five-mile radius of the courthouse, less than a morning's horse ride. In contrast to Lieutenant Louis Ahrens, his more casual predecessor, Lyon issued his federal interrogatories and demanded immediate compliance. The BRFAL's new free labor agenda offered a marked contrast to both the more relaxed practice of Lyon's predecessor and an older dominion.[60]

The power of these local planters undoubtedly derived from their former ownership of slaves, together with their large landholdings and presence in the community. William Spaulding, while "evidently uneducated," owned a 1,000-acre plantation near Wylesburg, about twenty-five miles from the courthouse. John A. Spencer, "a young man with the reputation of being a good manager," also owned a 1,000-acre plantation. Dr. Dennis, "a man of standing and education," lived near Colt's Ferry on the Stanton River, about fifteen miles from the courthouse, where he managed his father's 900-acre plantation. Dr. I. D. Spraggins, also a "man of standing," operated a 635-acre plantation ten miles from the courthouse. William A. Smith, clerk of the county court, a "very intelligent, active man," operated a 900-acre plantation about twelve miles from the courthouse. Lawyer J. R. Watkins, who moved to Charlotte County as executor of his deceased father's estate, held 2,020 acres. William L. Scott, owner of a 960-acre plantation, was district representative in the general assembly as well as "the leading politician of the County." Together these landlords owned around 7,415 acres of local real estate.[61]

If landholding planters persisted, so did their local farming systems. Between one-third and one-half of the landholdings were arable. Spaulding had 250 of his 1,000 acres in production, while Smith cultivated 350 of 900 acres. This approximated older regional patterns. All the planters grew cash staples supplemented with corn and oats. Tobacco was the major cash crop although its careful cultivation entailed a small acreage. Only 240 acres, or around one-tenth of all seven planters' arable land, was devoted to tobacco cultivation. Spaulding put 200,000 plants in 50 acres, while Dennis seeded 100,000 plants on 25 acres. The Tharp brothers, tenants on Watkins's plantation, devoted 8 acres to tobacco. The planters' 855 acres devoted to corn made up between one-third and one-half of all the arable acreage. Spencer put 90 of his 210 arable acres in corn, while Spraggins put in 70 of his 350 arable acres. Scott and Watkins also pursued a little truck farming. Lawyer Watkins's tenants provided the most detailed breakdown of their arable acreage. The Tharps devoted 40 acres to corn, while

Watkins's siblings put 50 acres in tobacco, 70 in wheat, 175 in corn, 120 in oats, and 20 in rye. There was little report of crop rotation practices, although Scott pursued the familiar three-field system on shifts of about equal quality and fertility, with one field lying idle or left for pasturage every year.[62]

To the "casual observer"[63] such as Lieutenant Ahrens, Colonel Brown, or even some historians, a quiet perusal of these planter surveys suggests little had changed in the sleepy tobacco southside. A similar impression is made regarding the labor system. The surveys reported that of the 135 employed freedpeople, nearly half were former slaves who had remained with their former masters. It was further reported that some of the freedpeople worked "as well" as when they were slaves, and most were "respectful towards their employers." Four of the planters even noted that the freedpeople had "strong local attachment" to the area, while virtually all of them reported no "disposition on the part of the freedmen to emigrate."[64] These descriptions of regular work habits, settled labor, and relative calm among the newly freed classes boded well for the transition from slave to free labor.

Such a view, by both contemporaries and historians, would miss deeper "structures of feeling" that underlie the surveys.[65] Postwar planters, for all their seeming nonchalance, remained former masters grappling with the reality of defeat and emancipation, which challenged their old dominion. Meanwhile, the freedpeople struggled to realize their emancipatory aspirations, which promised a new dominion. These reports of free labor's workings in the fields of Charlotte County during the first spring of freedom help challenge existing generalizations of either planter paternalism, neoslavery, *homo economicus*, or simply immutability. Emancipation entailed a dialectical process that cannot be unraveled outside the conflictual relationship between former slaves, former masters, the federal government, and all their divergent pasts.

The compensation arrangements reported from Charlotte County were straightforward. Unlike many other areas of mixed payments, most planters paid the freedpeople cash wages. Some freedpeople were employed for monthly wages: the twenty-one freedpeople on Spaulding's plantation received $6 to $8 monthly. Others were paid in provisions as well as cash: the six freedpeople on Smith's place were paid $8 monthly plus rations. Still other freedpeople were paid monthly wages according to the season's business plus rations: employer Watkins paid $5 for January and February, $6 for March and April, $10–$11 for the next six months, and $5 in November and December.[66] This simple compensatory system, however, was marked by tension. Employer Scott explained that he had "never tried them [freedmen] by the crop but I prefer to employ them by the month for many reasons one of the chief of which would be that I could direct and manage the crop according to my judgment, and a bargain of this kind is much more easily understood by the Freedman."[67] Scott's explanation captures the clash between older notions of labor management and emerging ideas of free labor. This free labor struggle became stark concerning the freedpeople's household economy.

During slavery, slaveowners exerted virtually complete control over both the productivity and the social reproduction of their human property. The masters' economy predominated in staple crop regions. This control extended over the labor of the entire slave household. The promise of this domination was the major motivation behind the adoption of legal slavery especially for labor-intensive tobacco production in colonial Virginia.[68] With the advent of emancipation, however, the freedpeople began to shift their households away from an exclusive preoccupation with staple crop production. In particular, the freedpeople moved away from the sort of labor controls imposed by the former regime. They turned toward autonomous institution building, especially the family, church, and school, as important components of their freedom.[69] This often entailed the selective withdrawal of freedwomen and freedchildren from agricultural labor. Such freedpeople could never completely withdraw from work, as has been implied by some recent scholarship, but they struggled to balance their subsistence needs with their emancipatory aspirations.[70]

All seven planters from Charlotte County reported the withdrawal of women from field labor. Planter Dennis, for example, noted that none of the "women work in the field."[71] Withdrawal from agricultural labor was largely selective. Lawyer Watkins, for instance, observed that "women are very reluctant to work in the field and very few of them do so." Reluctance and limited numbers did not spell total withdrawal, however.[72] Two freedwomen worked planter Spaulding's fields, while three of twelve freedwomen worked in Spencer's fields.[73] Some of the freedwomen pursued field work only during the busy seasons. On Smith's plantation the "wives and daughters work in the field when called on in the busy season of planting," while the freedwomen who worked for Spraggins only "agreed to work on the tobacco crop."[74] This selective withdrawal of the freedwomen from agricultural labor was an important index of the freedpeople's control of their own work in the fields. It was, however, always seasonal and contested.[75]

Planter William Scott provided a lucid expression of this upheaval in the household economy after the slaves were freed. These women, he reported, "do not work well either in or out of doors and I think there is a growing disposition among them to do little or nothing anywhere." They are only "employed in the lighter labors of the farm, but I find they are becoming rather disinclined to work for an employer either in the house or in the field." Furthermore, their husbands "have but little control over them" and encouraged them in their idleness by constantly "buying from [their] employer all the provisions required for their support." Planter Scott could not "conceive of a more injudicious plan and disagreeable situation than to have 9 or 10 idle women upon my plantation over whom there can be no control exercised either for their own good or the good of their families." These women "may do a little spinning and that is all the raw material of which they have to buy and which does not amount to employment more than one day in the week." Scott concluded "that all must labor white and colored, male and female, old and young," before there could be an improvement in social conditions.[76]

Scott's invective provides insight into some eloquent expressions of feeling. The freedwomen were working—as farmworkers, family providers, and clothes makers—but not in ways that were derived from the slave economy. Freedmen supported this selective withdrawal of freedwomen's agricultural labor because of the importance of familial reconstruction away from an exclusive preoccupation with cash crop production for planter profits. This issue of the freedmen's families became particularly contentious.

All these Charlotte County planters deplored the "loose government" of the freedmen's families. Spaulding complained that "the negroes have not good control over their families."[77] Smith concurred: "As a general rule the government is very loose."[78] A more accurate note was struck by Dr. Dennis, who believed the "freedmen have control over their families but do not exercise it."[79] These families were less controlled than they had been during slavery. Presumably the reestablishment of greater control over the freedmen's families would lead to greater agricultural productivity.

Charlotte County planter and representative William Scott was particularly eloquent on this familial change. He believed the freedpeople's "government is very loose and uncertain," while "the parents take but little authority over the children and consequently the children do not know the importance of obedience and training for the promotion of their future welfare." Scott thought the explanation lay in poor parental training since emancipation. "I might further add," he continued, "that I think the present generation of Colored people who have lately emerged from a state of Slavery must be very imperfectly qualified for training the young in habits of industry, and teaching them the art of living and making provision for their future comfort, happiness, and prosperity."[80] Poor parenting, in other words, meant failure to discipline the freedchildren for work. It entailed the shift of familial control away from the master's economy and its preoccupation with agricultural production. Scott's view vindicated the managerial principles of proslavery; it also reflected the distance traveled by freed families toward emancipation.

Lawyer Watkins provided the bluntest comment. It was lamentable "that among the freedmen, parents seem totally blind to the importance of a proper government and discipline of their families." Such freedmen "will neither govern their families properly nor suffer their employers or former masters to do so." Watkins thought that young "people (I mean children) white and black are not naturally disposed, I think, to be industrious," and there "must be compulsion, from some source, to make them so."[81] This compulsion was formerly provided by the slave family and legitimated by the principles of proslavery. The advent of emancipation and the struggle of freedpeople to regain total control of their families challenged this former dominance. Emancipation had prematurely closed the harsh school of slavery, much to the delight of the freedpeople and much to the regret of former slaveholders.[82]

Freedpeople also appear to have earned poor grades at the free labor school run by the BRFAL. Their primer stressed constant work for the able-bodied. Lieutenant Lyon seemed only slightly less exasperated than the planters at the freedmen's withdrawal of the labor of their families. "One of the strangest developments of negro character under the free system," he remarked, "is their indisposition to work their wives and children." He was amazed that "even the most industrious freedmen encourage their wives and daughters in idleness, so that field labor is materially affected thereby." "Very few women," he concluded, "work in the field, and very few have any work to do indoors, so that in cases where there are large families, there is a degree of poverty where there should be plenty."[83] This admonishment of the freedpeople's actions only superficially resembled the planters' objections. They had been trained in expectations of familial work, household control, and slave dependency. The BRFAL criticism of labor withdrawal was fueled by a Republican free labor agenda of work and independence. These descriptions of freedmen's household economies during the spring months of 1866 were an important register of the oscillating needle on the barometer of emancipation.[84]

Some of the tensions implicit in these reports of social relations from Charlotte County emerged full-blown during the first full harvest after the Civil War. By July and August 1866 much of the agricultural labor for the season had been accomplished with the harvesting of the crops. The returns were impressive. From several counties, record tobacco crops were reported. In Halifax County, although only one-third of the average wheat yield was anticipated, oats, "corn and tobacco promise a large yield."[85] The eventual harvest in the entire state reaped over 114 million pounds of tobacco grown from 160,000 acres and fetching over $15.5 million.[86] This bounteous harvest was hardly unexpected; it was the first full agricultural season since the interruptions wrought by war and emancipation.

Contested compensation during settlement time was expected. After the 1865 harvest many employers and freedpeople had clashed over whether work time encompassed the calender year or merely a single season. During the 1866 harvest many employers challenged the freedpeople's understanding of their contracts. Claiming the freedpeople had failed to follow their contracts, these employers began to discharge them once most of the season's labor had been completed, the crops gathered, and settlement was imminent. Throughout the region BRFAL officials reported employers terminating labor contracts either during or after the harvest. From Bedford County, Assistant Superintendent

B. F. Shaun informed his superior that although the freedpeople were complying with their contracts, many employers were forcing violations so as to avoid settlement because "the most necessary and hard labor, on the farms is done, and persons can do with less, or can now employ hands for less than the contract calls for."[87] In Louisa County, with the "most important labor on farms being performed, many of the farmers [were] trying to discharge their hands regardless to contracts made for the term of a year" and "giving some mischief done by the employee as a reason in the most cases."[88]

This premature dismissal of freedpeople without compensation was reported elsewhere in the Virginia tobacco region. From bounteous Halifax County, Lieutenant George Buffum wrote that there "is displayed on the part of a certain class of citizens, a desire, now that the crops are in a condition to require less labour, to break their contracts with the freedmen and defraud them in part or in the whole of the products of their labour particularly those who are working for a share in the crop, and pursue such a course, in many instances towards the freedmen as to irritate them and cause them so to conduct themselves as to furnish an excuse for discharging them."[89] The major BRFAL official in Nottoway and Lunenburg Counties informed state commissioner Colonel Brown that he had "known of as many as twenty cases, in which the employer would pick a quarrel with his laborers, for the purpose of dismissing them when the crop would be harvested without any compensation for their past services and upon the trumped up charge of insolence."[90] Many of the freedmen in Amelia County were reportedly "discharged for frivolous reasons, or a difficulty goten up to get rid of them now that they are not needed in the crop." "Their place," Lieutenant F. W. White added, "has been made uncomfortable and they do not desire to return." Consequently the freedpeople "take what they can get and seek employment elsewhere at less wages."[91] From Franklin County, Lieutenant William F. D. Knight reported that any "insolence whatsoever on the part of the freedmen, shall furnish sufficient cause for his white employer, at his discretion, to at once dismiss him, with the loss of the entire fruits of his labor up to the time, and regardless of the sacrifice of his prospects for the future; at perhaps the worst season of the year."[92]

This employer subterfuge and contract breaking worsened during the season's twilight. From Albemarle County, Captain William L.

Tidball reported that the "disposition on the part of some citizens to take advantage of the freedmen" was "manifesting itself in more numerous instances as the Autumn approaches." "Some laborers," he continued, "are discharged by their employers, without pay for the labor already performed, under the pretext that the laborer has violated his contract." In some cases, he added, they are owed "a sum considerably above fifty dollars."[93] By the end of September, employer subterfuge had gone from bad to worse in Lunenburg County. Captain A. Jerome Connelly reported that "large numbers of freedmen have been drove off the plantations, by their employers during the last month, and none of them have received any compensation for their services."[94] In short, BRFAL monthly reports from the field suggest that many planters continued to appropriate the freedmen's proceeds.

BRFAL officials were clearly frustrated at these employer contract violations as well as the denial to the freedpeople of the just fruits of their labor. Settlement time unsettled the making of free laborers and free employers out of former slaves and former masters. Unfulfilled compensation also raised the specter of freedpeople's dependency. Local officials were often powerless to prevent this contract breaking by employers, especially in the face of hostile local laws and class collaboration. From Louisa County came a report that the civil authorities sanctioned contract breaking by employers. The aggrieved freedpeople had their employer "referred to the magistrates," who were "of course in favor of the White men" and approved "the discharge, which only benefited the employer."[95] Local law here reflected employer class consciousness. Indeed, the social function of law protecting property became naked enough for some BRFAL officials to recommend the passage of a countervailing lien law, which would be passed by military ordinance, to protect freedpeople's rights in the crop. From Albemarle county, Tidball wrote to Brown to "respectively recommend that the legislature be requested to give the laborer a lien on the crops he cultivates, as mechanics have a lien on the structures they build."[96]

But these triumphs by former masters and new employers did not prevent freedpeople from fighting for their just rights. Freedpeople rather than eagle-eyed BRFAL officials frequently lodged complaints about the breakdown of the free labor system. Along with the freedmen plaintiffs in Louisa County, twenty freedpeople brought their cases to Captain A. J. Connelly for adjudication in Nottoway and

Lunenburg Counties.[97] Most importantly, it was the *potential* of BRFAL fair adjudication that explained the freedpeople's continual and repeated complaints. A lucid expression of this process came from the subdistrict of Prince Edward, Cumberland, Buckingham, and Charlotte Counties. Lieutenant Colonel John W. Jordan reported that "scarcely a day passes in which complaints are not made by the Freedmen that the white man is defrauding them in various ways in making their divisions." He noted one case where the employer, "although he had two barns unoccupied positively refused to let his freedmen use either of them for preparing their share of the tobacco for market—and this too in the face of the fact that these men had not only worked faithfully but had succeeded in making for him a good, if not better crop than he ever had before—they providing for themselves and families the whole time." In such cases, argued Jordan, "if the protection of the Bureau was *withdrawn* from the freedmen they would soon be reduced to a condition compared with which their former slavery system would be a blessing." He also added that "a small force of U.S. troops" helped "protect the freedmen" in receiving "their just and equitable rights," probably much to the delight of the freedpeople and the chagrin of their employers.[98]

Other freedpeople responded to their employers' contract reneging by simply withdrawing from agricultural production altogether and emigrating townward. Both Lynchburg in Campbell County and Farmville in Prince Edward County attracted dispossessed freedpeople from their surrounding hinterlands. Lieutenant Louis W. Stevenson reported that "the col'd. people crowd to this city [Lynchburg] from the adjoining counties, and once here it is almost an impossibility to induce them to leave." These migrations often incurred the ire of BRFAL officials. Stevenson complained to Brown that Lynchburg's "streets are literally blocked up with idlers every few days." His solution was the passage of "some judicious plan compelling a portion to leave the city." Indigenous town residents apparently were no less irate. Stevenson reported, "Old residents (col'd.) complain bitterly about the country people flocking to the town, cutting down prices and doing nothing." "They say," he added, "there ought to be a law passed preventing it."[99]

Other BRFAL officials opposed the freedpeople's urban trekking. Lieutenant Colonel J. W. Jordan criticized tobacco factory workers in

Farmville because seasonal unemployment contradicted full-time active labor. Whereas the tobacco season in the fields lasted all year, in the factories it was much shorter, usually running from April through September. During the winter the tobacco manufacturers were closed. This suspension of the tobacco industry "has thrown all those out of employment who pursue this kind of labor for a living." Consequently there were a "number of freedmen who are in this immediate locality out of employment at this time." It is probable that the specter of dependent freedpeople haunted Jordan's imagination. In the meantime, the freedpeople had acted as free laborers. They worked during the season, were denied settlement, and thus withdrew their labor for more secure prospects elsewhere.[100]

This rudimentary free market expressed itself in other ways. Lieutenant L. W. Stevenson reported from Lynchburg that "several northern enterprises which have been started, in my district, are paying wages which the community look upon as ruinous especially as they settle weekly."[101] Some freedpeople were drawn to the laying of rail tracks. Railroad companies in Kentucky and Tennessee attracted freedmen because of higher wages that were regularly paid.[102] Other freedpeople from the region ventured farther afield. Around 150 freedpeople emigrated from Mecklenburg County southward to North Carolina and the Southwest because of their dissatisfaction with the existing labor system. Many of these freedpeople had reportedly finished the agricultural season, whether working for cash or shares, in debt by $30 to $40.[103] From Lunenburg and Nottoway Counties came reports that "quite a number of the most industrious and intelligent freedmen of these counties" had emigrated to Kentucky, Tennessee, and Mississippi under contract for $12 to $15 monthly and rations. These freedmen had emigrated eagerly since they "start with a fair prospect of having some money, and a belief that they will receive their wages when due, which the conduct of their last employers, has convinced them that they will not receive here."[104] This search for alternative work through emigration represented an important feature of the new system of free labor.

It might be added that these last two monthly reports encapsulate many BRFAL free labor assumptions. Both Captain A. Jerome Connelly and Lieutenant G. F. Cook thought that the migration of freedpeople in the face of employer abuse would serve as a good lesson to the planters, who would consequently adopt fairer treatment toward their employees in the future. Faced with an ever decreasing supply of available labor, they believed, former masters would soon learn to compensate the freedpeople. The free market would teach the planters a harsh but necessary lesson. Yet a recurrent theme in these monthly reports was the planters' refusal to accede to the normal dictates of rational economic behavior. Employers would entice laborers into breaking legal contracts; they would dismiss their laborers without compensation; and they would attempt to rehire at will. Similarly the freedpeople would break their contracts, challenge their subordination, and not work in the ways expected. One of the most vital tensions in these monthly reports was precisely this clash between economically irrational behavior on the part of former masters and slaves and the free market assumptions of BRFAL agents.[105]

Although some freedmen left the fields, many remained to renegotiate for the following agricultural season. Explanatory models of *homo economicus* are not that useful. Faced with failed compensation, the freedmen should have followed the laws of supply and demand and sought adequate remuneration elsewhere. Some did, but most did not. We may quickly dismiss freedmen incompetence since much of the previous evidence suggests, despite its circumscription, an agency of struggle. Perhaps the freedpeople were loyal to both community and rural custom. Planter Spencer from Charlotte County thought the freedpeople had "strong local attachment." This comment might have said more about the planter than the freedman, and it was contradicted by employers such as Dr. Dennis, who did not "think that they have strong local attachment."[106] Its more general refutation can be seen in agency ranging from wartime self-emancipation to postwar emigration—freedmen were either "idle wanderers" or familial reconstructionists.[107] More compelling explanations have to do with the nature of the actual struggle in the field.

Many freedpeople had to remain in the fields despite the potential liberation of free labor. Emancipation freed them from the bare support provided from slave ownership—whether motivated by benevolence, paternalism, or simple self-interest on the part of the master. The BRFAL determined that a central feature of postemancipation society was work for independence. This would prevent dependency except in the most dire circumstances. Freedpeople could rely only on their labor power. In order to live and survive, they had to submit, however unwillingly, to certain postwar realities. These often included working somewhere with someone under conditions that were far removed from the successful realization of their emancipatory aspirations. The difficulties were reported from the field. Captain A. Jerome Connelly informed Richmond that Nottoway County employers "furnished" the freedpeople with "food and necessaries, at such extortionate prices that after paying their debts, they will hardly have anything left to commence the year with." This observation raised the specter of freedmen dependency emanating out of employer duplicity. It also pointed to the stirrings of debt peonage as employers attempted forms of provision peonage to control their laborers for the following year.[108]

Much as they did for the previous season, contract negotiations for the 1867 agricultural calendar defy easy statistical generalization. A random search has unearthed around sixty contracts from eight counties in the Virginia tobacco region for this period. This paltry figure amounted to only 10 percent of an already small percentage made for the 1866 season. Ten of these fragments from the past have been carefully examined. They were all made at the end of the calendar year between eight employers and twenty freedmen and their families. The compensatory arrangements were mixed, with six for cash, three for shares, and one for rations and lodging. Settlement was to be at the end of 1867. Work was primarily agricultural, with some freedwomen also agreeing to engage in domestic work.[109]

Employer George C. Hannah signed one collective contract with freedmen Phil Walker, Tom Harrah, Horace Lacy, Cornelius Green, Lazarus Clay, Henry Clay, Harley Johnson, George Branch, Paul Johnson, Stokes Clark, and Wyatt Gardiner on January 1, 1867. In exchange for the "faithful performance" of their "labor" at Gravel Hill plantation in Charlotte County for 1867, the freedmen were to receive annual cash wages ranging from $44 to $100, with food rations. The freedmen also agreed to pay their employer for any provisions used by their families "at neighborhood prices," as well as forfeiture of half their wages for any contract "violation." The contract was witnessed by William Marshall.[110] One week earlier, freedman James Gregory had agreed to work as a "farm hand" on E. B. Goode's place in Mecklenburg County at $6 monthly "for Jan'y, Feby, March, April, November + December" and $8 per month for "May, June, July,

66

August, Sept, and Oct." The difference was due to the season's business. The contract was witnessed by W. E. Bevil.[111] Freedman Fountain H. Fontaine engaged in a more unusual rental agreement with his landlord Elizabeth Hunter. Both agreed to "operate as farmers in partnership for the year 1867." Hunter would provide the land, lodging, and firewood for Perkins. She also agreed to share all other costs accruing from the team, "laboring hands," "new tools," blacksmiths, new farm buildings, and newborn stock. Perkins was to meet the remaining requirements, manage the farm, and receive "as his share one half of all the crops, or crop, he may make during the said year." The contract was witnessed by A. L. Perkins.[112] These free labor negotiations all point to differences in labor organization, the nature of work, and compensation arrangements for the 1867 season.

Despite their variations these labor contracts also suggest some general processes characterizing free labor relations in the opening seasons after Appomattox. Local contracting was supervised by the BRFAL, while fellow employers collaborated as contract witnesses. But this 1867 contracting was also informed by previous encounters in the fields. For some freedmen an earlier desire for socioeconomic autonomy, especially through land settlement, was reinforced by employer subterfuge during settlement time. Some freedmen managed to make rental arrangements the following season. From Brunswick and Greensville Counties in the southside came reports that the freedmen declined to contract after the harvest in the belief "that they can do better upon rented land" next season.[113] Lieutenant Robert Cullen informed Colonel Brown that many of the freedmen in Mecklenburg County would "rent land (to cultivate) during the ensuing year and with a little economy on their part can live independently until the next crop matures."[114] In Goochland County, freedman Charles Scott rented the farm of V. A. Powell for "one half of the crop made."[115]

Such rental agreements, however, remained the exception rather than the rule. This was primarily due to the employers' control of land and tools and their desire to supervise the freedmen's labor in old ways. After all, a generation of slave management ideology was not exactly the best preparation for accepting the freedpeople's autonomy. It is unlikely, for instance, that those Charlotte County planters who filled out Lieutenant Lyon's surveys subsequently rented out land to the freedmen. According to Captain A. Jerome Connelly, the planters "will not rent, lease or sell land to freedmen" in Lunenburg County.[116] This planter antipathy toward the freedmen's tenancy was probably typical for the region as a whole. Lieutenant L. W. Stevenson reported that freedmen's tenant farming in Nelson and Amherst Counties resulted in the "almost universal complaint on the part of the citizens that the negroes have done nothing."[117] Even BRFAL officials opposed freedmen's tenancy, especially when it raised the specter of want and dependency. Many freedmen tenants were deemed worse off than they had been the previous year. "This is attributable," explained Stevenson, "to lack of judgment on their part, which induced them to locate on poor land without any means of cultivating the soil other than a hoe, and that borrowed."[118] This flirting with subsistence living and seemingly irrational economic behavior might alternatively be explained by the freedmen's seeking freedom from previous forms of control in ways similar to the actions of freedmen in Dinwiddie County reported by Captain Sharp. It might also be explained as a response to the sort of employer subterfuge of the previous season, when Stevenson himself reported that "insubordination is generally met by a 'knock down argument,'" and freedmen were expelled without their share of the crop.[119]

As a result of the previous season's failures of share waging together with opposition to tenant farming, many freedpeople contracted for cash wages for either the year, the season, or the month. This option was facilitated somewhat by the increased availability from the sale of cash crops after the first full season of agricultural production in tobacco Virginia. Despite the severe credit scarcity resulting from abolition and the decline of the antebellum factorage system, there was not a scarcity of hard currency after the sale of the 1866 staple crops. As noted already, the tobacco crop fetched over $15 million, while the wheat and corn crops sold for over $12 million and $17 million, respectively.[120] Lieutenant G. Buffum repeatedly reported record cash crops in fine shape raised in Halifax County. From the perspective of the freedpeople, cash wages promised to be a more open and less risky form of remuneration than shares because these could be paid daily, weekly, or monthly as well as annually. Short-term hiring also offered greater opportunities for free labor mobility. Fixed figures promised at least some compensation when settlement time came around. Wage compensation also promised to ease provision peonage.

These conditions suggest the reasons why many of the contracts that were made for the 1867 season were cash arrangements. Of the total number of labor contracts examined, forty-two were for wages. This propensity for cash contracting was also reported from the field. According to BRFAL officials the freedpeople were disposed to hire monthly, while their employers preferred annual cash hiring in Albemarle and Franklin Counties.[121] In Amelia and Powhatan Counties the going system was to pay monthly cash wages ranging from $7 to $10 for adult freedmen, along with food, lodging, and fuel.[122] A clear statement of the freedmen's preference for cash wage compensation for the ensuing season appears in a BRFAL report issued from the bounteous fields of Halifax County. "Many are making their bargains for the next year," noted Lieutenant G. Buffum; the "greater portion will be for wages, the system of working for part of the crop not proving satisfactory in many cases." "Very few," he added, "who have been cropping on shares will according to present indications consent to do so again."[123] These observations suggest that postwar devastation and credit scarcity did not automatically translate into preponderant share wage agreements.

At the same time, it is important to recall that these cash "bargains" did not preclude an array of other strategies and labor arrangements by the freedpeople.[124] Some simply left for alternative work elsewhere. Other freedpeople refused to rehire with former employers. Planter Goode does not appear to have recontracted with his former laborers; his three contracts for 1867 were with other freedpeople.[125] Employer Hannah contracted with ten freedmen in 1866; this had increased to eleven employees in 1867. However, three of the original freedmen did not recontract and disappeared.[126] Other freedmen rented, shared, or simply survived as best they could. Captain Sharp and others testified to their varying fortunes. The point is that these contracts were moving targets of competing definitions of the freedom to labor. They helped set the framework for seasonal struggles but were by no means solely determinative. The advent of freedmen's politicking during the spring of 1867 betokened a whole new level of struggle in the field.

CHAPTER THREE

Black Republicanism in the Field, 1867–1870

105,832 freedmen registered to vote for the 1867 Virginia election. . . . 93,145 freedmen (88 percent) voted in the 1867 Virginia election.
—Lowe, *Republicans and Reconstruction*, 122, 126

Of all [the] ridiculous and mischievous legislating, that of giving an ignorant, uninformed class of people the right to vote and the chance of being set over the whites of the land, takes the lead.—Former mistress Sarah P. Miller

I would rather pay a high tax upon land and work it myself than to work for other people for nothing.
—Representative Frank Moss

For the first two agricultural seasons, the struggle over emancipation was largely confined to the socioeconomic terrain. The BRFAL attempted to oversee and implement a new system of contract labor based on the precepts of Republican free labor. Former masters and new employers attempted to exert older forms of management and control. In contrast the freedpeople struggled to fulfill their aspirations for emancipation, through limited access to land, increased control over the work season, fair compensation, and reconstructed family life. The 1866 agricultural harvest had also yielded a struggle over the fruits of free labor. By the postseason, bumper crops were accompanied by deep social tensions. The seeds of class conflict between anti-emancipation employers and dispossessed freedmen were scattered far and wide. The following spring these seeds prematurely burst forth into political bud.

Between the founding of Jamestown and the victory at Yorktown, Virginia was an English colony. The two generations following independence saw the flowering of a political culture imbued with Jeffersonian republicanism that played an influential role in national politics. The Civil War changed all this. During the conflict itself, the Old Dominion was torn between a secessionist west, which became independent in 1863, a Unionist north around the government of Francis N. Pierpont in Alexandria, and the centralizing tendencies of the Confederate States of America situated in Richmond. With the Confederacy's defeat at Appomattox, the traditional polity was further challenged through the presence of federal power. Although Virginia never actually experienced "radical reconstruction," its politics were far from independent for the remainder of the decade. Its executive leadership, whether antithetical to Reconstruction, like Francis H. Pierpont (1865–68) and Gilbert C. Walker (1869), or sympathetic, such as Henry H. Wells (1868–69), was always powerfully influenced by federal authorities. President Johnson, for instance, recognized the Whig Unionist government of Pierpont, while Virginia's military commander Major General John M. Schofield temporarily replaced Pierpont with the Michigan lawyer and unionist soldier Wells.[1]

The postwar general assembly was likewise influenced by the federal authorities. Although conservative domination remained intact throughout the period, the state legislature was forced to deal with federal power, especially the military. In January 1866 the general assembly passed a vagrancy act that was almost immediately terminated by the state military commander, General Alfred H. Terry. The legislature also passed new contract laws between employers and former slaves that were subsequently appropriated as BRFAL policy governing new labor relations. During 1867–68 the new Virginia legislature, popularly known as the Underwood Convention, was convened under the order of the new military commander, General Schofield, while many former officials and supporters of the former Confederacy were temporarily disfranchised.[2]

The state judiciary was perhaps the least influenced by federal

Reconstruction. Virginia's judicial code continued to operate throughout the period. (Many employers and freedpeople probably vouchsafed this continuance albeit from opposing perspectives.) The federal authorities, however, also influenced state laws. BRFAL state commissioner Colonel Brown had established freedmen's courts for each county consisting of the assistant superintendent, elected freedmen, and white representatives. This local judicial apparatus continued until May 1866, when it was terminated, having been superseded by the Civil Rights Act of March 1866, which legalized freedmen's testimony in court.[3] With the advent of military districting the following year, the nature of the legal hierarchy was left in no doubt. As General Schofield reminded his military commissioners in an order emanating from his Richmond headquarters on August 8, 1867, they were to be "governed in the discharge of their duties by the laws of Virginia, so far as the same are not in conflict with the laws of the United States, or orders issued from these headquarters, and they are not to supersede the civil authorities, except in cases of necessity."[4] Most importantly, the actual adjudication of the law often occurred at the local level under the auspices of representatives of the federal government, namely victorious military officers of the Union army or northern BRFAL officials.

In response to the limitations of presidential reconstruction, Congress passed two Reconstruction Acts in March 1867. This legislation provided the following: military districting of the former Confederacy; disfranchisement of the Confederacy's major officials; ratification of the Fourteenth Amendment, guaranteeing federal protection of civil liberties to all citizens through the rule of law; and the drafting of new state constitutions through representative conventions. The political objectives of this legislation were clear, ranging from a radical Republican desire to establish regional political control to a more moderate Republican objective of facilitating regional independence through federal withdrawal.[5]

The freedmen responded with political rallies, mass voter registration, and popular embrace of suffrage. These activities took on a crucial communal component and formed the basis for a burgeoning class consciousness for the realization of emancipatory aspirations. These activities also elicited strong opposition from former masters and new employers for whom the freedmen's politicking promised the further weakening of old forms of social control. The politicization of emancipation promised a collective struggle that transcended the narrower confines of either individual contracting, occasional emigration, or difficult recontracting. A freedmen citizenry had liberating (or subversive) potential. The freedmen's political activities were often supported by BRFAL officials as a means of consolidating the new system; these also often clashed with the dictates of Republican free labor ideology, threatening greater social instability.[6]

General Schofield was made responsible for the implementation of the new Reconstruction laws in Virginia. He was required to set up voting districts, register new voters, supervise the election, and put the new constitution to a popular referendum. Voter registration boards were set up throughout the state. The registrars included BRFAL officials, army officers, Union veterans, and local loyalists. The employment of BRFAL officials as registrars received the stamp of approval from BRFAL commissioner General Howard. He instructed local officials to register all eligible voters in their respective districts. This duty was no doubt facilitated by the Republican political sympathies of many BRFAL officials.[7]

During the busiest months of the 1867 agricultural season the freedmen engaged in political activities en masse. BRFAL officials reported freedmen attendance at political meetings and rallies throughout southside Virginia, including Pittsylvania and Halifax Counties.[8] From the central piedmont Colonel J. W. Jordan, provost marshal in Farmville, Prince Edward County, reported freedmen joining the Union League. Other Union League activities involving the freedmen were conducted in Albemarle, Fluvanna, and Louisa Counties.[9] These local Republican clubs often stood as beacons of political education. Eric Foner has captured some of the flavor of these local political education groups that "convened in black churches, schools, and homes, and also, when necessary, in woods and fields." There was usually a Bible, a copy of the Declaration of Independence, and a farming implement. The meeting was opened with a prayer by the attendant minister, oaths by new members sworn, "and pledges followed to uphold the Republican party and the principles of equal rights."[10] The popularity of such meetings was evident from additional reports of freedmen voter "registration" in Nottoway, Lunenburg, Franklin, and Brunswick Counties.[11] Other freedmen were reported to be drilling, organizing, and marching in Caroline County.[12]

BLACK REPUBLICANISM IN THE FIELD

It is important to stress the communal nature of these political activities. The freedmen's Republicanism in the field assumed a communal mantle that challenged the gendered straitjacket of male suffrage. Many of these meetings took place in churches, schools, homes, and fields, spaces also vitally shaped by the contributions of freedwomen. Their advocacy had already been reported by some BRFAL officials. It was a rather piqued Provost Marshal Jordan who observed that some freedpeople, "especially among the females," "do not comprehend the new relation they sustain to the white man." These "females" were "influenced by impractical and exaggerated ideas of freedom" that "cause all classes serious annoyances." They "go about poisoning the minds of the colored people against the whites—by gross misrepresentations—circulating dangerous rumors—interfering with contracts—and generally disturbing the relations between the races."[13] It is likely that these freedwomen were equally vociferous in "generally disturbing" political relations. Indeed, they might well have annoyed some of their more quiescent husbands, brothers, sons, and grandsons. It is more definite that these freedwomen engaged in communal solidarity over the collective rights of emancipation. As postwar Virginia's leading political historian succinctly concludes, the freedwomen "joined secret societies affiliated with the Union Leagues, conducted fund-raising activities to support black organizations, encouraged their men to vote, and used their influence to pressure wavering black men to stay solid for black rights."[14] This represented a new challenge to the traditional polity.

The freedwomen's "going about" and "circulating," as Jordan put it, pointed to another important dimension of the communal politics of freedpeople. These were primarily local, but they were also part of a broader pattern of emancipatory politics. This wider circumference was provided by itinerant lecturers, political leaders, and circuit riders whose political ripples transcended local communities to link them to broader platforms. Throughout the American South, itinerant lecturers and local leaders descended on local communities and spread the gospel of political Republicanism. Political circuit riders such as the Reverend John V. Given from South Carolina visited Lunenburg County in southside Virginia after he learned a freedman had been killed. "I shall go there, and speak where they have cowed the black man so that they dare not even register . . . and by the help of God, give them a dose of my radical Republican pills and neutralize the corrosive ascidity [*sic*] of their negro hate."[15] Dr. Henry Jerome Brown, characterized later as a "Mulatto Charlaton," engaged in political organizing in Virginia and North Carolina before moving on to the village of Darlington, South Carolina.[16] Prior to the Republican state convention held in Richmond in April 1867, James W. Hunnicutt, editor of the *New Nation* and advocate of freedmen rights, crisscrossed eastern and southside Virginia addressing numerous gatherings of freedmen.[17] Similarly, local activists and future leaders of the region circulated political messages. These included freeborn James D. Barrett, prominent Union League activist in Fluvanna County; freedman Joseph R. Holmes in Charlotte and Halifax Counties; and freedman John Robinson. The latter was described by General Schofield, military commander of Virginia, as one who "commands the entire confidence of the negroes" in Cumberland County.[18]

The efficacy of this political activity became clear with the coming of the 1867 fall election to decide whether to have a constitutional convention and who the representatives to it would be. By election day, 105,832 freedmen had registered to vote statewide, with 40 percent of these registrants hailing from the Virginia piedmont. In many of these counties freedmen registrants were in either the majority or the high minority, except in the southwest counties of Franklin and Patrick. Their extensive political activities were widely reported by BRFAL officials throughout the region.[19] With the coming of election day on October 22, 1867, many freedmen exercised their historic political rights and chose the "radical" or "republican" ticket. Altogether, 93,145 freedmen, or 88 percent of those registered to vote, eventually went to the polls in the 1867 Virginia election. If we allow for parity with registration statistics, it is probable that around 40 percent of these voters hailed from the piedmont, as did 40 percent of those 92,507 freedmen who approved a new constitutional convention.[20] Statistical exactitude, however, is far less important than seeing the 1867 election as the culmination of the freedpeople's communal activities and their class consciousness.

The result of this political activism in the field was the election of representatives to the Underwood Convention. Named after a nonnative white Republican justice, the convention began its deliberations in Richmond on December 3, 1867. There was a total of 105 convention members, of which 68 had been elected by the freedmen. There were 36 conservatives, 23 "carpetbaggers," 21 "scalawags," and 24 freedmen representatives.[21] Around 32 delegates hailed from the Virginia tobacco region. According to General Schofield's appraisal of the delegates, about two-thirds were "radicals."[22] Some were northerners, or carpetbaggers, such as the New York preacher and distiller Sanford M. Dodge of Mecklenburg County and Union army veteran and lawyer Edgar "Yankee" Allen of Prince Edward and Appomattox Counties. Others were southern Unionists, or scalawags, such as tobacconist C. L. Thompson of Albemarle County and teacher H. A. Wicker of Pittsylvania County.[23] It is important to stress, however, that these representatives were elected by the freedmen. Representative Dodge was, according to General Schofield, "elected on Watson's popularity." John Watson was a freedman activist for schools and churches as well as convention representative for Mecklenburg County.[24] Representative Wicker taught at freedmen's schools. These convention delegates were spatial and temporal conduits of the freedmen's emancipatory aspirations.

Of the 24 freedmen representatives at the Underwood Convention, eleven hailed from the Virginia tobacco region. They were James D. Barrett (Fluvanna County), James W. B. Bland (Prince Edward County), David Canada (Halifax County), James B. Carter (Chesterfield and Powhatan Counties), Samuel Kelso (Campbell County), William Moseley (Goochland County), Francis Moss (Buckingham County), Edward Nelson (Charlotte County), John Robinson (Cumberland County), James T. S. Taylor (Albemarle County), and John Watson (Mecklenburg County). All were native-born except James B. Carter from Tennessee. Barrett, Bland, Moss, and Taylor were freeborn; the other eight were slave-born. Their occupations were often multiple and included 5 farmers, 4 shoemakers, 3 ministers, 2 teachers, 1 carpenter, 1 mason, 1 boatman, 1 laborer, 1 lawyer, and 1 storekeeper. Six were reported literate. Most appeared propertyless; others, such as William Moseley, who purchased a 500-acre plantation belonging to his former slaveowner, became large landholders. Many did not continue long in public life, but others, such as Moseley and Moss, went on to serve in the Senate (1869–71), as did John Robinson (1869–73). Moss served in the House of Delegates (1874–75), while Bland became a federal official. As other historians have noted, these were Reconstruction's lawmakers responsible for carving out the emancipatory aspirations of the freedpeople.[25]

What were the politics of these freedmen at the Underwood Convention? Most appeared to have played a fairly quiet role in the proceedings. Others were vocal in their call for equal citizenship. Representative James W. B. Bland of Prince Edward and Appomattox district proposed a military order to allow convention delegates first-class accommodations on public transport. He also proposed the right of "every person to enter any college, seminary, or other public institution of learning, as students, upon equal terms with any other, regardless of race, color, or previous condition."[26] Others called for the disfranchisement of former Confederates. James T. S. Taylor of Albemarle County called for Rebel disfranchisement, as did Lewis Lindsay of Richmond. Bland, interestingly enough, opposed this measure, as did Joseph Cox of Richmond.[27] It was the land question, however, that posed the greatest radical political challenge.

Minister and dentist Thomas Bayne was elected from Norfolk to become the most powerful freedmen leader at the Underwood Convention. Much like Representative Bland, he called for equal citizenship rights. But his most powerful statements concerned taxing the land of planters and former slaveholders. "The poor people have to bear all the burdens of taxation in this State," Bayne pointed out. "I am in favor of all taxes except that tax that carries me back to that old slaveholding hell of touching the lands lightly. The lands of Virginia have never been taxed properly."[28] This call for land redistribution had not come out of a vacuum. Many of the freedmen laboring in the fields had based decisions on it. Joseph T. Wilson from Norfolk had attended numerous Republican meetings during 1867 calling for land confiscation.[29] Lewis Lindsay led the call for land confiscation and Rebel disfranchisement at the convention.[30]

This call for land redistribution was central to the freedpeople's challenge to the old dominion. One of its most eloquent spokesmen was Frank Moss. Freeborn in Buckingham County around 1825–26, he had earned his living in farming and picked up some literacy skills. He was sent as the sole representative of Buckingham County to the Underwood Convention by a large majority of 2,871 registered voters, of whom over 62 percent were freedmen. When he reached the capitol building, his seat was contested by a group of conservatives. He demanded his right of representation. The military governor agreed and sent a letter to the credentials committee, which ruled in his favor. Land taxation became a stormy issue. Representative Moss argued, "If we do not tax the land we might just as well not have come here to make a Constitution." He added, "I'd rather pay a high tax upon land and work it myself than to work for other people for nothing." Moss also opposed freedmen working for shares because it denied them their independence. The freedmen needed land, they had worked hard for it, and they deserved that part in which they had invested their past lives and labors. This was the freedmen's labor theory of value. Moss also insisted that emancipatory rights entailed education and suffrage.[31]

Clearly, Moss made an impact. "Illiterate but energetic and enterprising. Radical," was how General Schofield rated Moss at the Underwood Convention. The Richmond press caricatured him as "Francis Forty-Acres-of-Land-and-a-Mule Moss" because of his obsession with land redistribution. These descriptions raise an important issue. Moss drew criticism because of his radicalism. He was a representative who struck a chord with his freedmen constituents. On one occasion outside the courthouse in Buckingham County, he gave a speech encouraging freedmen to vote against the two local candidates. A riot was narrowly averted by Union troops when local whites and freedmen began to draw guns from their coats.[32] Moss went on to serve his freedmen constituents in the state senate for 1869–71 and the House of Delegates in 1874–75. In both houses he continued to argue for land redistribution and against sharecropping.[33] In sum, Moss was a particularly prominent example of the local grassroots leader who clarified the political dimensions of seasonal struggles for both the freedmen and the former masters.[34] These ripples of class consciousness waved through Readjusterism, populism, and beyond.

Frank Moss embodied the dangerous potential of class consciousness among the freedmen. This view ranged from conservative opposition to press derision to General Schofield's description of Moss as radical. It materialized in former masters' and new employers' condemnation of the freedmen's politicking. Such activities, they claimed, detracted from the freedmen's "natural" agricultural proclivities. This antipathy was further fueled by the belief that republicanism was a political tradition exclusive to either antebellum Black Republicans or newly enfranchised slaves. Former masters were especially galled at their own disfranchisement. Most importantly, they opposed the class conscious potential of this political identity. They no longer faced this wage worker, that tenant, this dependent, but freedmen united in their emancipatory aspirations that were clearly ranged against the interests of former masters and current employers.[35]

For many former masters and new employers, the freedmen's political activities detracted from their agricultural duties.[36] These former slaves had no business exercising such a degree of control over their own labor time. Opposition was expressed in several different ways. One was intimidation. Captain A. Jerome Connelly, assistant subassistant commissioner in Lunenburg and Nottoway Counties, reported that whites in his area attempted to prevent black laborers from registering to vote. Another method was the threat of bribery through booze. In Franklin County, Lieutenant William F. D. Knight was informed "by one colored man" that the whites "intend to get the negroes all drunk when the election comes off, so as to make them vote for whoever they, the whites, may select."[37]

The most popular expressions of this opposition to freedmen politicking were employer threats to discharge their laborers. These threats were especially prominent during preelection days. From Pittsylvania County, Colonel G. B. Carse, assistant superintendent, reported white opposition to the freedmen's voting as well as voter intimidation in remote sections of the county. He added, "Some men I am informed say they will discharge any of ther employees who may go to hear any political speech." Similar threats were reported from Prince Edward, Cumberland, Buckingham, Charlotte, and Albemarle Counties in July 1867. This employer opposition continued after polling day in late October. From the seventh subdistrict, Lieutenant Louis W. Stevenson reported employer threats to discharge freedmen because they had voted the "radical ticket." From Bedford County it was reported that since the election "many more are threatened with discharge." There could be no more powerful comment on the significance of freedmen politicking.[38]

Many employers followed through on their threats. During the previous harvest, employers had discharged the freedmen without compensation for supposedly not fulfilling the terms of their labor agreements. This practice of employers breaking contracts at settlement time was repeated the following season, only this time the freedmen's political activities served as the rationale for their dismissal. Lieutenant J. M. Kimball, assistant superintendent for Brunswick County, reported that "thirty complaints have been made at this office, during the month of July by freedmen who were driven away from their employment many of them having an interest in a proportionate part of the crops." "Much of this persecution of the freedmen," he explained, "has grown out of the exercise of their political rights in registering; and is calculated to defraud them out of a great part of their years labor, it being invested in the growing crops."[39] From the second subdistrict, Colonel Jordan reported that employers discharged their laborers because of their attendance at political meetings.[40] Firing freedmen was especially pronounced in the aftermath of the October election. In Dinwiddie County some freedmen were dismissed for voting Republican, while from both Goochland and Pittsylvania Counties it was reported that other freedmen were discharged for general political activities.[41]

A succinct statement of this conflict over the political dimensions of free labor between the freedmen and their employers was reported from Bedford County in the shadow of the central Blue Ridge mountains. Employers threatened to discharge the freedmen for voting the Republican ticket on October 22, 1867. But the freedmen went ahead anyway. "Since the election," Lieutenant B. F. Shaun reported, "many have been discharged, and many more are threatened with discharge, for this cause." Many freedmen also risked their homes as well as their work. Shaun observed that a "general disposition is evinced on the part of the white employers, to punish the freedmen for this act, by discharge, turning out of houses rented by them." Politically active freedmen were not the only ones to suffer the wrath of indignant employers. The "same treatment, in some instances, has been meted out to poor laboring white men by their more wealthy employers, for the same causes." Events in Bedford County were no better the following month. Not only had the freedmen's condition deteriorated since the election, but daily and monthly hirees were refused work, and employers hired "neither white or colored" who voted the radical ticket. While ostensibly outside the purview of strict contracting, such activities had everything to do with the broader evolution of free labor relations.[42]

Despite the widespread nature of these employer threats and dismissals, however, many of them simply failed to materialize. Some were precluded by the swift actions of local BRFAL officials. Captain A. Jerome Connelly informed Richmond that some employers in his subdistrict "have tried to commence their yearly amusement and tricks of beating and driving off their laborers after the crop is almost made." Unlike the previous year, however, their actions had been "quickly remedied."[43] Other checks to repeated employer duplicity arose from the emergence of a burgeoning and chaotic free market. Emancipation loosened bonds that challenged former methods of control and stability. This was especially significant in the Virginia tobacco region, where the agricultural economy was labor-intensive. From Brunswick County, Lieutenant J. M. Kimball reported few problems since "one race is equally as dependent as the other."[44] From his subdistrict, Lieutenant L. W. Stevenson reported that despite numerous threats to discharge the freedmen for radical voting, these had rarely been carried out.[45] Even in Bedford County, scene of some of the worst employer contract-breaking because of the freedmen's political activities, a quasi-free market operated. Lieutenant B. F. Shaun's final report of the year sounded a very different note from those of a month or so earlier. "The parties," he reported, "who were in favor of discharging every colored man, who voted contrary to their desire, have utterly failed." "They are compelled," he explained, "to have their labor, and can get no others to replace, in their stead, except of the same class."[46] A similar theme was heard in Albemarle County, where Lieutenant A. F. Higgs reported that threats to discharge the freedmen ended up "all moonshine, as labor is too scarce to be trifled with."[47]

Perhaps the clearest expression of how a burgeoning free market could check the freedmen's premature dismissal was provided by Lieutenant Newton Whitten from Franklin County. He reported he had "yet to learn the first instance of discharge of freedmen from employment on account of voting their chosen ticket." "This latter subject," he continued, "I have made one of especial inquiry and investigation and although no such discharges have taken place, it must not be understood or indicative of any liberality or concession on the part of the whites toward the freedmen, relative to the right of suffrage of the latter for such is not the fact." Rather, it was because of the operation of the free market system: "Capital and labor are so evenly balanced in this section that the former could not dispense with the latter without serious injury."[48] These checks were especially salient during contract negotiations for the following agricultural season. Such observations by BRFAL officials highlighted an important feature of the new system of free labor: former masters and new employers now had to weigh their economic interests in relation to their political interests. In the interstices between the two, the freedmen struggled to carve out some emancipatory niches.

The freedmen also had to carve out niches of freedom from the clash between free labor principles and Republican politics overseen by the BRFAL. Some local officials believed that the principles of the free labor system would educate members of a former slave regime out of their old habits. Thus labor requirements would check the freedmen's premature dismissal, the freedmen's emigration would teach landlords to be fairer toward their labor in the future, and freedmen would consume less because excessive provisioning resulted in a form of debt peonage. However, some of the BRFAL officials' responses to the freedmen's politicking revealed a less nuanced understanding of the new system. Although Congress had countenanced the freedmen's politics and BRFAL officials oversaw registration, voting, and local Republicanism, some of the stewards of free labor in the fields were concerned that political activities detracted from the primacy of the freedmen's agricultural obligations. From Halifax county, Lieutenant G. Buffum complained that the freedmen's political activities detracted from their farming activities during the busy season.[49] Colonel Jordan was particularly incensed at the freedmen's activities in his subdistrict. In the spring Jordan complained that freedmen were "neglecting" agricultural affairs for political meetings. They continued to do so throughout the summer months. In August freedmen attended Union League meetings and club rallies rather than attending to their crops. Jordan was still complaining in his fall reports.[50] These "distractions" were believed to be especially onerous by BRFAL officials since the political season coincided with the busiest months of the agricultural calendar from spring planting through early fall harvesting. There was no more eloquent comment on struggles in the field than this clash over contrasting understandings of free labor as only the freedom to labor as opposed to labor's freedom.

With the end of the 1867 agricultural season many of these political struggles elided into disputes between the freedmen and their employers at crop settlement time. Many of the previous season's latent tensions sprang up. Employers sought to deny the freedmen their contractual compensation, while many freedmen complained to the BRFAL of employer subterfuge. From Brunswick County, Lieutenant J. M. Kimball reported freedmen complaints about unfair crop divisions and some employer discharging.[51] Similar reports were received from Franklin County.[52] The freedmen in Lunenburg County complained to Agent W. H. H. Stowell about being owed back wages,[53] while the freedmen in Pittsylvania County barraged officials with complaints that they had not been paid for their previous season's work.[54]

Few of these complaints were based on simple misunderstandings. From his subdistrict Agent E. C. Morse noted some "honorable exceptions" but bewailed the fact that "there are too many as yet, who seem unable to see and realize that those whose labor had heretofore belonged to them are entitled to enjoy its fruits."[55] Agent Stowell, however, made a more penetrating observation. In Lunenburg County he had received daily complaints from freedmen for "wages due them for last year's work." Although, he continued, "the people are poor in consequence of the small crops raised last year, yet I cannot but think, from all I see and hear, that the *failure* to pay results as much from the disposition *not* to pay as from the poverty of the debtors."[56] Indeed, the production of around 90 million pounds of tobacco fetching over $11 million for the 1867 season supports Stowell's view.[57] Despite the destruction of the former credit system, the tobacco crop was generating cash for wages. It seems probable that employers were using back wages as a means of retaining the freedmen's labor and controlling their mobility—always risking the unrecompensed flight of their free labor, the ultimate free market possibility.

A new legal weapon in the employers' armory was the passage during the summer of 1867 of the Bankruptcy Act, which basically provided financial protection against indebtedness. Many employers

BLACK REPUBLICANISM IN THE FIELD

took advantage of the new legislation to avoid compensating the freed-men for their previous season's labor. From Nottoway and Lunenburg Counties came reports that many employers were taking advantage of the new legislation to avoid paying the freedmen and "swindling" them out of their earnings.[58] Some employers used the new law to deny all compensatory claims since the inauguration of the new system of free labor. From Mecklenburg County, Agent Alex D. Bakie ex-pressed his consternation at "numerous persons who owe the freemen being about to take advantage of the bankrupt law." Consequently, the freedmen "will lose considerable money coming to them in settlements yet due for 1866 and in some cases 1865."[59]

These contractual tensions had an important impact on negotia-tions for the following 1868 agricultural season. Recontracting con-tinued to represent a moving target of contestation over free labor that cannot simply be reduced to statistical generalization or behavioral *homo economicus*. The seasonal struggle was omnipresent; its nuances, localized. From Franklin County, Lieutenant A. R. Egbert reported the freedmen "are not anxious to work—as they *fear their employers will be unable to pay—when the money falls due.*"[60] From Nottoway and Lunenburg Counties it was reported that "fair farmers" were attracting "good hands" and the freedmen were contracting for the next year "at about the same terms." There was also "an increasing desire among them [freedmen] to rent land and cultivate the same on their own account and many have made arrangements to do so the present year."[61] Lieutenant J. R. Clinton reported that freedmen in Amelia County were contracting for both cash and shares, while some were renting.[62] From Brunswick County came a report that a "good many of the farmers" rented out land to the freedmen, while freedmen in Prince Edward County "rent[ed] small pieces of land by giving the owner part of the crop and in that way barely make enough to support their families."[63] A clear expression of the contested nature of recon-tracting was provided by Major William R. Morse, who reported that "most of the freedmen I think have contracted for the present year—some for wages, and others for a share of the crops" although "many prefer to take their chances for a crop rather than the loss of wages by bankrupt employers."[64]

The actual labor contracts for 1868, much like their predecessors, defy narrow categorization. There do appear, however, to have been noticeably fewer written negotiations. Several of those that were analyzed were for mixed compensation. Freedman Henry Puryear contracted with employer Edward B. Goode to hire out his son James for 1868 to "serve in any capacity he [Goode] may direct." The compensation agreed on was food and clothing for the freedboy and $30 to the freedman, payable at the year's end.[65] Seven freedmen contracted to work for Sam Allen for the year on the latter's farm in Buckingham County in exchange for a third of the crops, payable after the harvest. These freedmen on Allen's plantation provide an interesting insight into free labor struggles. The seven freedmen were down from nine contractees for the 1866 season, of which only two, Henry and Adam Holman, were still with their original employer.[66] One rental agreement between Richard Malone and Mary Vaughn for was for halves of corn, tobacco, and oats in Buckingham County. This rental agreement did not work out because it was officially canceled under the auspices of the local BRFAL office on June 9, 1868.[67]

That summer saw further clashes over the political dimensions of free labor. The Underwood Convention had been scheduled for a popular referendum on June 2, 1868. It was postponed, however, by General Schofield because of the lack of state funds for an election. Both the state Republican Party and conservative opponents organized nominating conventions in anticipation of an early election, although Congress eventually deferred the referendum until December.[68] Meanwhile the freedmen continued to meet and discuss the upcoming referendum in preparation for endorsing the new state constitution. Numerous employers issued threats of dismissal if the freedmen voted the Republican ticket or agreed to the passage of a new constitution. Agent Thomas Leahey reported from Charlotte County that "the employers . . . are acting very unjust with the colored people on account of their political principles." "They threaten," he continued, "to turn them away and let them starve before they will give them anything to do if they (the col. men) vote against the instructions and wishes of the whites." He added ominously, "And in some instances they have already put their threats into execution."[69] From adjoining Halifax County Agent Stowell reported that "much trouble also arises between the White and Colored from the prejudices caused by the different political views of the two parties."[70] Indeed, these tensions were so great in some areas that amidst threats to discharge freedmen who would not vote the way whites wanted, a mini-riot broke out at Lunenburg Court House on the last court day.[71]

These tensions, however, were most stark in Pittsylvania County in the Virginia tobacco southside. White hostility against the former slaves had occasionally been reported from this area ever since the end of the Civil War. In June 1865 it was reported that "the people throughout the county are feeling bitterly towards the colored people and are determined to make their freedom more intolerable than slavery."[72] In July 1866 Lieutenant Colonel G. B. Carse, assistant superintendent for the seventh district, reported that while freedmen Thomas Dillard, Miles Taylor, and Orange Womack and their families were busy at work in the crop, their employers William G. "Lynn and Bro. with others came with firearms and by force drove Dillard and the men employed by him from the fields," without compensation.[73] The summer of 1868 saw a ratcheting up of this white hostility. In mid-July Agent William Leahy reported from Pittsylvania Court House that employers threatened to discharge freedmen if they voted for the new constitution. Freedmen continued to complain to the BRFAL of their employers' failure to compensate them for their seasonal labors. On July 20 there occurred a "breach of the peace" in which several people were reportedly injured. Furthermore, the freedmen complained to the BRFAL that they were being driven off plantations and farms for violating contracts, for refusing to vote against the new state constitution, and for claiming back wages for labor during previous seasons.[74]

The following month things went from bad to worse. Lieutenant William Leahy reported a "great many complaints have come to this office within the past month of assaults committed on the Freedpeople by the whites." Some were "beaten with Sticks," and several "have been cut and stabbed with knives." This maltreatment was especially common "in the remote part of the county," where the freedmen "are taken out of their houses at night by men armed and disguised who beat them with sticks." The freedmen's lives were threatened and their attackers "take their Guns, Knives and any weapon they may find," and "in several cases they have demanded money." The family of freedman Wesley Edwards was singled out for special punishment. The attackers "threatened the life of his wife who was sick in bed and then ravished his daughter." If the freedmen "report these outrages to this office" their lives "are threatened." Indeed, Lieutenant Leahey reported that several "colored men have been compelled to leave their cabins and sleep in the woods," while at "least 100 guns and Pistols have been stolen from the freedpeople by these mid-night marauders."[75]

The ownership of such firearms suggests that some of the freedmen were not exactly defenseless. On the morning of August 24, 1868, freedman Morton Wicker shot and killed Alexander Dodson, a white man. According to the official report, they "had quarrelled several times and Dodson went to Wicker's house that morning to renew the quarrel." After an angry exchange, the freedman shot his visitor, who "lived about 24 hours." Leahey reported that "Wicker immediately came to my office and gave himself up." The BRFAL, however, turned him over to the civil authorities, who presumably tried him for murder.[76]

These reports of increased violence and near-anarchy did not completely subvert the rule of law supervised by the local BRFAL in Pittsylvania County. From June through October 1868 twenty-nine cases were reported that were primarily concerned with contractual disputes and white violence. Sometimes the decision went against the freedmen. Freedman David Williams reported that J. W. Tinsley and wife "refuse to give him his part of the wheat crop." Both parties were ordered to appear before the BRFAL. In Danville on July 14 the case was settled in favor of the defendant, with "Tinsley to have all the wheat[,] Williams failing to comply with contract." Freedman Silas Cunningham complained that his employer Mr. Lumkin "drove him away from work." The plaintiff was ordered to return to "Lumkin's employment and fulfill his contract." At other times the decision went against the employer. In July freedman Rupert Motley reported that his employer drove him from the plantation "in violation of contract." At the settlement hearing in Danville on July 16 the employer "settled by paying Rupert Motley $40" and was ordered to let the freedman "have his garden vegetables."[77]

There are several likely explanations for these increased tensions during the summer of 1868. Settlement time usually highlighted contestation. Political differences over the new state constitution undoubtedly focused much tension between Republican freedmen and disfranchised, conservative Democratic whites. This friction cannot have been helped by the extended drought in southern Virginia that continued unabated for several weeks during July and August. Further-

BLACK REPUBLICANISM IN THE FIELD

more, on July 25 Congress decided that by January 1, 1869, the BRFAL was to be "withdrawn from the several states within which it has acted." The exception was the "educational department and the collection and payment of money due to soldiers, sailors and marines, or their heirs," which "shall be continued as now provided by law until otherwise ordered by Act of Congress." The federal government intended to complete its military, financial, and educational objectives in classic Republican fashion. Meanwhile, its impending withdrawal pointed to the specter of a post-Reconstruction state. For the freedpeople this meant using the BRFAL as much as possible. For former masters this federal withdrawal promised a return to an older dominion.[78]

Indeed, it is difficult to read the final monthly reports of BRFAL officials and overlook the implications of federal withdrawal. Of course, we should guard against the twin dangers of self-congratulation and impending closure that might tend to exaggerate the BRFAL's importance and influence. It is also conceivable that some of the dire forecasts in these final reports were tendentious in the hope of continuing the BRFAL. However, these reports ring true and feel accurate. Their structures of feeling remain solid during imminent bureaucratic dissolution. On Wednesday, September 23, 1868, Major Marcus S. Hopkins confided to his diary that several "cases of outrages were reported to me by freedmen most of which I am powerless to redress."[79] From Brunswick County, Lieutenant J. M. Kimball thought that "a further continuance of the Bureau" was "of little importance unless it can be armed with more authority, sufficient to accomplish its purpose and maintain its dignity."[80] From his subdistrict in the southern piedmont the new local BRFAL official made his presence quickly felt by halting three illegal transactions between employers and freedmen. However, he added, "I am informed that as soon as I leave here they will go on with the sales."[81]

The implications of the BRFAL's impending withdrawal were particularly salient during the traditionally tense settlement time. The 1868 crops had been harvested. The tobacco crop exceeded 93 million pounds although its relatively poor leaf quality resulted in a reduced market price of just under $8 million. The corn and wheat harvests compared favorably to those of the previous two seasons.[82] Many BRFAL officials penned their forebodings in their concluding reports. From

Pittsylvania County, Agent William Leahy reported employer duplicity whereby the "freedpeople are losing large amounts of money."[83] From Brunswick County, Lieutenant J. M. Kimball reported receiving numerous complaints from the freedmen. These complaints he referred to the local authorities although he thought this would be "poor consolation to them [freedmen] however in most cases."[84] It was a rather somber final report from Agent E. C. Morse, who informed Richmond that "many accounts still remain unsettled the parties not having disposed of the tobacco crops." He added, "I fear that much wrong and injustice will result to the freedmen."[85]

The most succinct statement of the implications of the BRFAL's withdrawal was penned by Agent Stowell in his final missives from Halifax County. "Bureau business," he wrote, "has been very lively the past month, and both civil and criminal complaints have been made in unusual numbers over 200 having been lodged at this office during the month, of which 21 were for assault and battery." Stowell attributed the increase "to disputes which arise at the close of the year in the division of crops between employers and their hands, these disputes in many cases ending in blows." He concluded that "the withdrawal of the Bureau will take place at the worst time of the year possible, as it is the time of settlement between the farmers and the freedmen, and in the interval which will elapse between the withdrawal of the Bureau, and the adoption and practical inauguration of a new state government, I can foresee nothing but anarchy and injustice to the freedmen." Stowell's predictions proved accurate. His final report noted even greater difficulties with settlement disputes due particularly "to the general belief which has existed during the month that the Bureau would be continued only till the 1st of January 1869." It is important not to forget that both the freedmen and their employers were acting with foresight.[86]

The following year witnessed the decline of federal Reconstruction. The BRFAL withdrew from the state, excepting its educational activities. The conservatives regrouped in the face of the Radical Republican threat, while the Republicans split over opposing gubernatorial candidates. On July 6, 1869, an amended Underwood Constitution was approved, moderate Republican Gilbert C. Walker was elected governor, and conservatives won clear majorities in the Senate (30 to 43) and the House (96 to 138).[87] The *Norfolk Journal* declared that Virginia was "redeemed, regenerated and disenthralled."[88] For some historians this "redemption" depressed the hopes of many freedmen in Virginia.[89]

Post-Reconstruction was more complex. Former masters had retained their land, resumed tobacco production, and waved a bitter adieu to Howard's bureau. This federal representative had struggled mightily for "the amelioration of the condition of mankind which marks epochs in history."[90] If the BRFAL was not quite as successful as was claimed, however, neither was it unimportant to the early years of emancipation. It clearly failed to implement and consolidate Republican free labor relations in the field. But it was a local military, legal, and political power with which the freedpeople and their former masters had to struggle. Its withdrawal promised the reimposition of an older dominion. But the conditions for redemption had changed; emancipation had made a vital impact. Former masters still owned their land and the tools of production, but they also faced the logical consequence of proslave management outside the social system of slavery. Although the freedpeople failed to win land redistribution and were forced to work to subsist, neither were they simple converts to the free market. They would insist on reconstructing emancipation in their own image. They had tasted the fruits of freedom in the fields. It was often bitter, but unforgettable. The long-term legacy of these free labor struggles in the field was to be the dissolution of the old dominion of social control. Its short-term legacy was ideological confusion reflected in agricultural literature.

CHAPTER FOUR

The Impact of Emancipation, 1865–1872

The negro had been emancipated and a new system of
culture had been introduced.—Dr. Benjamin W. Arnold Jr.

Devoted to the Industrial Classes of the South.
—Motto, *Southern Workman*

Agricultural production in the Virginia tobacco region experienced significant disorganization immediately following the Civil War. Numerous explanations have been given for this postwar crisis: war devastation, freak climatic conditions, excessive taxation, and faulty census enumeration. The central explanation, however, must be sought in the transformation of older social relations wrought by emancipation. Many former slaveholders attempted to master this transformation through the resurrection of older ideas of strict labor control and management. Other rural employers attempted to embrace the changes for the better. Advocates for the freedpeople's education, such as the sponsors of Hampton Institute, attempted the reorganization of agricultural production along the lines of the free labor system contoured by the departed BRFAL. These conflictual interpretations were debated through the pages of the agricultural press and monthly journals. Their differing understandings of the impact of emancipation were invariably based on past ideas in relation to present conditions. Behind all the debates, however, was the central recognition that emancipation had made a profound difference, and that it was the actions of the freedpeople themselves which were directly responsible. Let us begin with the changed landscape itself.

The Civil War reduced the size, nature, and value of Virginia lands. In 1860 the Old Dominion ruled over 31 million acres. The successful secession of the western counties in 1863 reduced the state's size to just over 18 million acres. The tobacco region increased its proportion from less than one-fifth to more than one-third of the state's total size. There was also a decline in the state's arable land, or improved acreage. In 1860 over 11 million acres of the Old Dominion were devoted to agricultural production; a decade later the amount was down to just over 8 million acres. Arable land in the tobacco belt declined from 3.3 to 2.9 million acres over the decade. This decline was uneven. Arable land in Halifax County declined from 277,913 acres to 183,771 acres. Arable acreage in Pittsylvania County fell marginally from 247,156 to 239,018, and some of the smaller counties registered slight increases in their arable land.[1]

Along with size and nature, the value of Virginia real estate was significantly reduced by the Civil War. According to one contemporary estimate, land prices throughout the state fell by over one-fourth during the 1860s.[2] The federal census reported more modest declines—from around $14 to just under $12 an acre over the decade.[3] These estimations provide a rough guide to the fall in land values for the state as a whole but gloss over important regional differences. In the tobacco region, real estate prices fell from around $12.70 to $7.95 per acre over the decade. This decline was especially marked in the tobacco southside. Land prices in Halifax County plunged from $14.59 to $7.42 per acre, or by half over the decade. Land prices in other parts of Virginia experienced a far less precipitous decline. In the tidewater region, prices fell from $13.65 to $11.27 per acre, while in Loudoun County, situated in the northern piedmont, they actually increased from $35.82 to $39.36 per acre over the decade.[4]

This regional as well as statewide decline in land values challenges proponents of postwar planter persistence in landholdings.[5] It is undisputable that old landownership remained essentially intact in postbellum Virginia.[6] As we saw earlier, the BRFAL only ever controlled a small amount of land for a small amount of time. Much of this old land, however, plummeted in value because of emancipation. In the words of Chester, an anonymous contributor to the *Southern Planter and Farmer*, "Unfortunately, nearly all the money capital of the South was invested in negro labor, and with the freeing of the slaves the capital

THE IMPACT OF EMANCIPATION

was lost. The land was left, and without corresponding working capital has in many instances become a burden to the owner."[7] This transformation of laborlords into landlords highlights the importance of the abolition of chattel slavery, or human capital, as the central determinant of land values.[8]

Agricultural production from the land was also disorganized by the Civil War. This was especially marked in the tobacco region during the decade. The Old Dominion's record high of over 123 million pounds in 1859 plummeted to a record low of just over 37 million pounds a decade later. The six leading tobacco counties of Brunswick, Charlotte, Halifax, Lunenburg, Mecklenburg, and Pittsylvania reported a major decline from around 37 million pounds to about 14 million pounds during the decade. Halifax County, the leading area in 1860, reported its production halved from 8.5 million pounds to 3.8 million pounds. Other tobacco counties reported far greater devastation, especially in the central piedmont. Tobacco cultivation in Albemarle County, for instance, fell from 5.4 million pounds to 1.7 million pounds. In Orange County, leaf production virtually disappeared, falling from 1.7 million pounds to 46,000 pounds.[9]

This decline in Virginia tobacco production was accompanied by the consolidation of the domination of the national tobacco economy by the western states. During the waning antebellum years the fresher soils of Kentucky, Tennessee, and Missouri produced newer, more pliable products, which increasingly challenged the Old Dominion. With the passing of the Civil War, this challenge was finally confirmed. In 1869 Kentucky reported tobacco production exceeding 105 million pounds, or 40 percent of the national product. In contrast Virginia accounted for a record low national share of 14 percent.[10]

Virginia's cereal grain production was also affected. In 1860 the Old Dominion reported the production of over 61 million bushels of corn, wheat, and oats. A decade later cereal grain production fell to just under 32 million bushels. The six leading tobacco counties in the tobacco southside had their second most valuable cash crop (wheat) halved from 973,538 bushels to 488,457 bushels. In contrast, oat production, which was primarily for consumption rather than marketing, experienced the smallest decline. While some counties reported small declines, others increased their oat production. Rural producers in Halifax County increased their oat production from 129,790 bushels to 168,970 bushels. Other counties registered similar increases, including Nelson, Campbell, Orange, and Greene.[11] It is not unlikely that the freedpeople engaged in this subsistence production as part of their search for independent farming.

Along with cereal grains and tobacco the region's other major agricultural activity, animal husbandry, was adversely affected by the Civil War. In 1860 the Old Dominion reported livestock worth nearly $48 million. By 1870 this had fallen to just over $28 million (or 40 percent). The value of livestock in the Virginia tobacco region fell at a similar rate (35 percent), as did the value of the region's slaughtered animals.[12]

There have been numerous explanations for postbellum Virginia's agricultural decline. It is clear that Civil War devastation played some part. Most obviously, the Old Dominion was a major theater of military operations from the first battle of Bull Run through Appomattox. In Albemarle County federal troop incursions during the latter stages of the war were responsible for the destruction and loss of animals. By 1870 the number of horses in the county had reportedly declined to 3,418 from 5,195 a decade earlier.[13] The most recent historian of postwar Louisa County has estimated that one-third of the county's livestock was lost as a result of the Civil War. According to the federal census returns, livestock values in the county went down even more drastically, from $556,856 to $272,220.[14] One local historian has observed that although Goochland and Nelson Counties were "outside major combat areas," the former county "suffered several raids that were accompanied by the destruction of property," and these "raids may account for Goochland's greater decrease in agricultural production."[15]

Civil War devastation alone, however, provides an insufficient explanation for postbellum agricultural decline. The Virginia interior, especially the tobacco region, was not a major theater of operations for the Civil War. Unlike the tidewater region, it was spared much of the military havoc. Indeed, as was argued earlier, the Virginia interior experienced less dramatic forms of slavery's self-destruction and a longer war in contrast to many other parts of the state and the South seized early by Union armies. The Virginia tobacco region was the area to which slaves were evacuated from more active battlefronts and Union armies, while the southern piedmont around Danville, in

THE IMPACT OF EMANCIPATION

Pittsylvania County, served famously as the last bastion of the Confederacy.

Unusual climatic conditions were more important in accounting for the decline in Virginia's agricultural production during the late 1860s. The climate is usually fairly mild, with an average mean annual temperature of 56.6 degrees Fahrenheit and an average mean annual precipitation of 42.20 inches. Between 1868 and 1870, however, the Virginia interior experienced unusually hot summers and a series of severe droughts. In June and July 1868 average summer temperatures soared to 85 degrees Fahrenheit, while the following summer was only slightly less hot at close to 80 degrees Fahrenheit. This intense heat did not let up; from July 5 through September 18, 1870, the whole of the state experienced severe drought conditions.[16]

These severe climatic conditions had a devastating impact on crop production. According to one contemporary the corn was burned up in "nearly all the fields I have seen."[17] Commenting on the same 1869 agricultural season, an editorial in the *Southern Planter and Farmer* observed that from the Virginia seaboard to the upper end of the Shenandoah Valley, a "fair" crop of corn was impossible and that "one third of the tobacco" had been destroyed. The same editorial reported the desperation of the circumstances. "We have heard," it noted, "of instances in which commercial manures were used, where the entire crop of corn or tobacco will not satisfy the claims of the commission merchant." The editor mentioned seeing "many fields in South-side Virginia where the average yield of corn was not more than a barrel, and of tobacco not more than 400 lbs to the acre."[18]

If the hot summer months of 1868 compounded free labor difficulties in the Virginia tobacco region, this was no less true the following year when drought conditions impinged on the freedpeople's schooling efforts. According to the BRFAL's superintendent of schools for Virginia, northern philanthropic societies had reduced their financial aid for the education of freedpeople. This increased the local burden of supporting such educational activities. The severe weather made matters worse. According to BRFAL superintendent J. W. Alvord, "the difficulty of maintaining schools has been greatly enhanced by the drought and short crops of last summer." He explained that this "cause has not been properly understood by societies and people at a distance," since with "one half of the whole 'stay and stuff' of bread cut off, there is not enough left for food, and nothing to sell." The consequences were dire for the freedpeople. "For a people thus situated," Alvord observed, "to board their teachers and help build and repair their school-houses, is to bear a vastly heavier burden than any community in a similar condition of poverty, in any Northern State, is required to bear."[19]

The ensuing agricultural season brought little relief. According to one *Southern Planter and Farmer* editorial, the state was drought-stricken for nearly ten weeks during the harvest. As a result the corn crop was halved, the plowing for winter wheat was delayed, and corn land had to be seeded in wheat because there was insufficient time for fallowing.[20] While it is pointless to measure in precise terms, it seems clear that this unusual run of hot weather and drought conditions toward the end of the 1860s played a major role in the state's decline in agricultural production, especially in its major cash crop region.

Contrary to historian Ulrich B. Phillips's famous dictum, however, neither the weather nor its extremities can solely explain these postwar agricultural conditions.[21] Hot and dry conditions had intermittently ruined agricultural seasons in the Old Dominion for generations. As we saw, the 1865 through 1867 agricultural seasons appeared to be quite favorable (even if social relations of free labor were not). Furthermore, it is sometimes tricky to determine whether journal editors were merely responding to poor weather conditions or the limitations of free labor. As we shall see, such commentaries cannot be explained outside old ideas in new postemancipation conditions.

More recently, some historians have explained postwar decline through federal census inaccuracies. They argue that with the aftermath of the Civil War came confusion together with statistical undercounting. The implication here is that the agricultural production figures for the postbellum South are also suspect. The region assumed, it is argued, better shape more quickly than either contemporaries or statisticians have previously suggested.[22] Although such explanations are certainly plausible, they automatically assume a more accurate knowledge through hindsight than that of contemporaries. This might be more statistically accurate, but what does it tell us historically? Furthermore, it only addresses the rate of agricultural decline; the decline itself does not seem to be in question and still remains to be explained.

Although Civil War devastation and extreme weather conditions contributed to postwar agricultural decline in Virginia, the most significant explanatory factor concerned the new social relations of emancipation. Agricultural production in the Old Dominion had been based on the coercion of slave labor. While many slaves challenged this unfree regime through either indirect or direct resistance, others awaited the opportunities presented by the exigencies of war. For many slaves in the Virginia interior, however, these latter opportunities were limited and came late. Most of these regional slaves had to settle for a reduction in coercion at the point of production through the breathing space afforded by absentee masters. With the advent of emancipation came the freedpeople's outright rejection of the type of domination experienced during slavery. This rejection was expressed through a variety of autonomy-seeking strategies. The new degree of control enjoyed by the freedpeople in, for instance, the reconstitution of the household economy, entailed a subsequent loss to former masters and new employers. In short, the reduction in land values, the crisis of credit, and the decline in agricultural production in the region can primarily be explained through emancipation.[23]

This impact of emancipation was reported by numerous visitors to the region. M. P. Handy, a northern journalist, told his readers that with "no crop has the emancipation act interfered so much as with this, and the old tobacco planters will tell you with a sigh that tobacco no longer yields them the profits it once did: the manufacturers are the only people who make fortunes on it nowadays."[24] Fellow journalist Edward King echoed Handy's observations in his renowned travelogue *The Great South*. In the antebellum period, King wrote, Albemarle County "was a region of large plantations, principally devoted to tobacco, of which hundreds of slaves raised five millions of pounds annually." By the early 1870s, he continued, "the Production amounts to but little more than a million and a-half pounds yearly; but it will in due time regain the old number; for no section of Virginia is more rapidly recovering from the disorganization of labor, and the discouragements which followed upon the war, than Albemarle and her fertile sister counties at the foot of the Blue Ridge."[25] While both reports were not totally correct—tobacco manufacturers' fortunes were a later phenomenon, while King Tobacco never ruled postemancipation Albemarle County—they do suggest that emancipation made an impression on regional labor-intensive tobacco production.[26]

The most elaborate commentary on the impact of emancipation on the Virginia tobacco region was penned by one of its earliest scholars. Dr. Benjamin W. Arnold Jr., who taught at McCabe's University School in Richmond, argued in his 1897 survey that freedom was incompatible with efficient tobacco cultivation. "The negro," he argued, "was not as good a laborer in the new as in the old system." "Many of them," he continued,

> would work for "neither love nor money," and the labor of the few that could be persuaded to work was expensive, for overseers had to be employed to insure efficient service. The majority became so self-important in their new liberty that they refused to "hire out," but must needs rent farms on shares. They were in a position to force their claims, and the negro share-owner became a new factor in the production of the State. As he took many holidays, being a faithful attendant upon all camp-meetings, political gatherings and church festivals, he did not add much to the sum-total of the State's production.[27]

Arnold's criticism of the freedpeople's emancipatory behavior suggests a disparity with the close supervision and efficient management of a former regimen. These old beliefs were undoubtedly encouraged by W. E. Dibrell, editor of the *Southern Tobacconist and Manufacturers Record*, and J. F. Jackson, editor of the *Southern Planter and Farmer*, both of whom Arnold gratefully acknowledged for assisting him in his scholarly endeavors.[28]

Arnold's observations point to an inescapable conclusion concerning free labor. The freedpeople experienced a hitherto unique degree of control over their own labor. They had to work in order to survive; this was the material reality of the freedom to labor. However, the freedpeople also valued control over their own time, communal activities, and civic incorporation. The price of freedom was a decline in agricultural production that was particularly significant with labor-intensive tobacco production.[29]

This relationship between the withdrawal of free labor and reduced agricultural productivity might be termed the *freedom crop index*. It provides a crude measure of the distance traveled, simply in terms of labor and exploitation, from slave to free labor.[30] The freedpeople in the Virginia tobacco region struggled to free themselves from coercive agricultural production. Their struggles were similar to those of other freedpeople in the New World.[31] This partial withdrawal constituted a crucial aspect of their new freedom. To critics, however, whether bewailing inefficient tobacco cultivation in the Upper South, reduced cotton production in the Lower South, or declining rice and sugar production elsewhere, such drops pointed to the failure of the new system. These cash crop declines vindicated the ideology of proslavery management during emancipation. This became especially apparent in debates over free labor management conducted in the pages of the Virginia agricultural press.

Between November 20 and 22, 1866, a group of planters assembled in Richmond under the auspices of the Virginia State Agricultural Society (VAS). They assembled for numerous reasons, including discussing how best to pursue agriculture in harsh postwar conditions, comparing labor under the slave system with hired labor in the new system, and devising means of obtaining more labor and capital to work their lands. Several committees were appointed to address these issues. President Willoughby Newton inaugurated the proceedings; his opening address advised landholding retention and opposed "the wretched *metayer* system" because it "invariably makes poor landlords and wretched tenants." J. R. Jones, head of the Labor Committee, advised the engagement of labor for annual wages rather than shares in the crop. Jones's report also encouraged immigration to meet the current labor shortage. William Frazier noted the scarcity of capital in the state. This caused, he argued, an acute crisis, since "the change in the labor system of the South requires now the constant use of money in the affairs of agriculture." The committee on usury laws resolved to advise the state legislature to maintain 6 percent as the legal interest rate but to allow higher interest rates providing such contracts were in writing.[32]

The VAS passed other resolutions. One was to research the possibility of using labor-saving implements to counter the Negro's labor withdrawal. Another was the establishment of scientific agricultural schools and clubs throughout the state. William T. Sutherlin, influential tobacco planter and manufacturer from Pittsylvania County, concluded the meeting with a call for the paternal management of labor. He advised "the settlement of negro laborers upon a place, and creating in their minds feelings of local attachment and domiciliary influences." This approach "would render such a place much more valuable to a planter, and not only increase its value if put into market, but also render it more salable because desirable." "These laborers," he added, "would form a sort of peasantry, whose presence on a place would give [the] purchaser the best assurance of obtaining labor for its cultivation." Sutherlin closed his comments in an upbeat fashion. "The abolition of slavery," he remarked, "much as we may deplore it, has not only unlocked the labor of the country, and placed it within the reach of all who have energy, industry and intelligence, but it has also unlocked the broad acres of the country, and opened up their cultivation." The implication here was that since emancipation had freed labor from the land, and land from its capital dependency on labor, planters and farmers should make the best of the new conditions.[33]

This discussion of harsh postwar conditions and how best to deal with them proved to be efficacious. The VAS drafted a new usury bill calling for higher maximum interest rates and presented it to the general assembly. It failed, but a similar bill raising the legal maximum rate of interest from 6 to 12 percent was eventually passed in 1870. Similarly, the Labor Committee's resolution to encourage immigration was sent to the state legislature with a request for appropriations. This resolution eventually resulted in the founding of the Board of Immigration, along with a plentiful supply of literature selling the state to potential immigrants.[34]

The most salient feature of this VAS meeting, however, was its acknowledgment of the free labor problem. What were the best ways to cultivate particular crops? How were employers to derive the best benefits from free labor? What was the most efficacious means of free labor management? What was the best payment system? How was capital to be attracted to a credit scarce environment? How best to maintain, retain, or enhance land values? These questions dominated agricultural life in postemancipation Virginia. They were publicly aired, argued, and inflected through the pages of the *Southern Planter and Farmer*, the most influential agricultural magazine in Virginia. Most importantly, these issues provide a window, sometimes clear, at other times foggy, into the ideological interpretation of emancipation by former masters and new employers.

The *Southern Planter*, whose masthead proclaimed devotion to "Agriculture, Horticulture, and the Household Arts," was first produced in January 1841 under the editorship of Charles T. Botts. Its central objective was to propagate practical farming advice similar to that found in northern agricultural magazines. It often became the mainstay of advice literature on how to improve crop cultivation, how to better manage recalcitrant slaves, and how to maximize productivity efficiency. Publication was suspended during the Civil War, but a phoenix-like rising occurred in 1867 under the more inclusive title the *Southern Planter and Farmer*, edited by Charles B. Williams.[35] There was little ostensible change in the magazine's postwar objectives. Indeed, many of its articles resembled their antebellum cousins. This was, however, only a superficial resemblance. Improved supervisory management and efficient production had been promoted to deal with the silent sabotage of recalcitrant slaves; its postemancipation evocation was demanded by the free labor "problem." Emancipation also promoted greater ideological conflict between proponents of traditional ways and those advocating newer and modern methods of free labor management.

The pages of the *Southern Planter and Farmer* were replete with articles, letters, and comments from planters, farmers, and employers on what to do about the problem of free labor. The journal also published contributions from agricultural club members, snippets from other agricultural periodicals, and leading editorials. In only its second postemancipation issue, editor Williams bemoaned the unavoidability of the share payment system. He went on to report that although some tobacco and wheat producers of the previous year had been able to avoid the share arrangements because they "acquired means of paying the wages of labor in money," the rest had been forced to "submit to the evils of a bad system."[36] Anonymous contributor H expounded on these necessary evils in his "Hints on the Labor Question." After Appomattox, H wrote, planters faced a severe money scarcity and had to pay their labor with a share of the crop. This was an unfortunate necessity and should cease as soon as possible. Its worst drawback was a loss of control through the sharing of management, especially with ex-slaves. H deplored this loss of managerial control: "Why should a planter admit as partners in his business his daily laborers, any more than the merchant or mechanic?" He answered his own question: "The only excuse for it is a want of funds to pay wages, and the owner of the soil ought to be willing to economize and sacrifice, that he may pay regularly a money value for labor, and thus *control* the product of his soil, as well as all the operations conducted thereon." Indeed, H added, many large planters had "test[ed] the negro as manager for himself," providing farming tools and implements, but rarely had the experiment been successful.[37]

A month later H offered some further hints on how to control free labor. It was his view that the existing labor scarcity would be met in the long term by immigrant labor. In the short term there was a need for greater control of labor. The best means, H argued, was the reduction of cultivated acreage, close supervisory management, and the prompt monthly payment of wages. This latter suggestion, he admitted, entailed some risk, since short-term labor arrangements obviously facilitated labor mobility. The solution proposed by H was that once a good laborer had been obtained, it was imperative to "*make him comfortable.*" He elaborated further. The Negro should be given "a good cabin, a garden, and let him surround himself with such things as tend to make a home and then let him, and his wife and children understand that upon their industry and good conduct depends their continuance in a comfortable home." Since the "negro has strong local attachments," employers "must use the strong points in his queer nature, to control him." The plan, H enthused, "has been tried with great success by a gentleman in Albemarle County, Virginia, in the past two years, and I believe that a combination of the three recommendations herein given, will tend greatly toward the removal of the difficulty of keeping and controlling labor." H clearly shared William T. Sutherlin's earlier expressed belief that the best way to control the freedmen's labor was through a benevolent wage labor system based on the encouragement of "local attachments."[38]

This emphasis on the need to control emancipated labor through inducements rather than coercion offers striking testimony to the differences provided by free labor. H, much like many of his contemporaries, despised Negro tenancy and concluded with condemnation of

THE IMPACT OF EMANCIPATION

this worst evil of the free labor system. He drew on the experience of "Colonel W" in adjoining Caswell County, North Carolina. Apparently the colonel's ten supervised "hands" had produced 15,300 pounds of tobacco worth $4,891.03, 104 bushels of wheat, and 220 barrels of corn during the 1867 season. In contrast the colonel's Negro tenants working independently had produced only 4,758 pounds of tobacco worth $739.02, no wheat, and only 200 barrels of corn. Clearly, freedom did not work as well as traditional forms of management. Meanwhile, H opposed the partial autonomy of freedpeople's tenancy as much as those Charlotte County planters interviewed by BRFAL official Lieutenant Lyon eighteen months previously.[39]

The views of H on the wage labor system as being the most efficacious means of controlling free labor were shared by others in the region. At a meeting of the Goodwyn Agricultural Club, located in bordering Granville County, North Carolina, club president Nathaniel A. Gregory thought the "progressive, high-farming, wages system" was infinitely superior to the costly and "extravagant" share system. E. H. Hicks concurred with Gregory, having long since quit share arrangements in disgust. "What," he asked, "can we make of a partnership with an individual whose highest aim is a suit of 'sunday clothes'?" Not all club members agreed. Mr. Davis reported trying every system and found share payments were the least expensive, or at least the method by which there was "less to be lost." Davis also asked Gregory, "Under his idea, what was to become of all the labor?" Surely "it would be calculated to run it all out of the country?" Gregory conceded that shares were the only means to secure labor. Meanwhile, Mr. Horner preferred "independent" white labor to "dependent" black labor. "We must," he directed, "get labor that will work without all this persuasion and attention." Mr. Cooper appeared more sanguine with his view that black labor was employable "profitably, both on shares and wages."[40] What all these club members were clearly wrestling with was the most important manifestation of free labor: reduced control of the productive process through lack of coercive control along with the constant threat of the freedpeople's voluntary mobility.[41]

One solution to the free labor problem advocated through the *Southern Planter and Farmer* was simply the replacement of black labor with white labor. For some planters immigration offered the prospect of plantation preservation. Frank G. Ruffin, planter and perennial editor of the *Southern Planter and Farmer*, issued an urgent appeal for foreign immigration in his address to the Border Agricultural Society, an influential improvement club in the tobacco southside. Ruffin identified 51,342 farms averaging 340 acres each with 103,068 black male laborers in Virginia. This entailed a land-labor ratio of one worker for every 170 acres. This poor land-labor ratio, he added, was compounded by the withdrawal of the Negro family from the agricultural production. "As a general rule," he noted, "I know hardly an exception—women and children do no farm work." He concluded with a plea for new immigrants to take up the plentiful supply of land and urged the state government to take a lead in the campaign. For Ruffin and many of those who supported him, foreign immigration offered one tangible way to reduce the existing market "power" of free black labor.[42]

Ruffin drew on comparative emancipation to bolster his point concerning Virginia's disadvantageous land-labor ratio. He argued that emancipation had failed in other former slave societies, especially the British West Indies and Haiti. These former slaves were not prepared for freedom. Their lack of preparation was exacerbated by poor land-labor ratios that favored the breakdown of free labor control and resulted in the failure of emancipation. The exception was the British colony of Barbados, where the land-labor ratio of one "soul" per acre pushed real estate values as high as \$800–\$1,000 per acre.[43] The necessity for slave management had been a central tenet of proslave ideology; it was confirmed by the failure of emancipation in other postslave societies.[44] Free labor struggles in the field confirmed rather than refuted such a principle. These were important lessons from the past to recall and bear in mind for those currently embroiled in postemancipation struggles.[45]

For others immigration offered the prospect of plantation destruction and the emergence of an independent white yeomanry whose labor was demonstrably superior to Negro labor. This rationale worked nicely with the notion of an all-white state. In January 1868 *Southern Planter and Farmer* readers were treated to a short article titled "How to Secure White Labor," penned by "A Virginian." The anonymous writer expressed dissatisfaction with the "present disorganized and demoralized condition of negro labor" and issued a call for white immi-

THE IMPACT OF EMANCIPATION

grants who could do twice the work of "blacks." The writer further advised the break-up of the "black quarters" and the shooing off of the idle so that "Virginia will be a white man's state."[46] The sentiments of the Virginian were echoed by "An Augusta Farmer." This anonymous contributor recalled a farming experiment conducted in Charlotte County the previous year. Thirteen Negro farmers, furnished with mules and implements and provisions, raised 94 barrels of corn, 7 stacks of oats, and 5,000 pounds of tobacco. In contrast, two white farmers, likewise furnished with mules, implements, and provisions, raised 112 barrels of corn, 10 stacks of oats, and 8,000 pounds of tobacco. Furthermore, the mules returned by the white farmers were fat and sleek, while those returned by the Negro farmers were in a poor and emaciated condition.[47] It was the considered opinion of both authors that white labor was clearly superior to that of Negro labor and should predominate as quickly as possible if Virginia was ever to recover its older dominion.[48]

European colonization was one solution offered to the problem of free labor. William H. Richardson advised the encouragement of European immigrants to replace unreliable "negro labor" that "cannot now be relied upon" in order to "improve state agriculture." One difficulty with this proposal, however, was limited state support and the refusal of many planters and farmers to provide adequate funding for immigration.[49] In response J. D. Imboden, the newly appointed Virginia commissioner for immigration, proposed a colonization scheme designed to attract settlers en masse. Imboden advocated the provision of a compact colony of 10,000 acres at cheap prices to be mortgaged through a lien on the property. Potential settlers would be approached in Europe and brought straight to Virginia, presumably to avert the risk of their settling elsewhere. The state commissioner was convinced of the plan's feasibility especially if two or three "leading men" from the various counties supported it. The proposal gained a polite hearing at a convention on immigration held in Burkeville, Nottoway County, in August 1868.[50]

These rationales, appeals, and suggestions notwithstanding, it soon became clear that large-scale immigration to Virginia was unlikely. This was explainable by the contradictory motives of immigration propagandists. Some saw immigration as a means of breaking up the plantation system, while others saw immigration as the best way to preserve it. In addition, many immigrants probably viewed attempts to control freedpeople's labor as only one short step from controlling their own labor. As early as the end of 1867 the president of the VAS called for the adoption of labor-saving machinery because white immigration was not forthcoming. Responding to a call by H. Wise on the need for immigration, Newton reluctantly admitted that "immigration to Virginia will not, in this generation, be sufficient to justify the cultivation, exclusively, of small farms, and that we shall find it necessary to stick to the reaper and the drill."[51]

This argument of machines for men was echoed by numerous *Southern Planter and Farmer* contributors. Editor Williams adapted an old adage: "The scarcity of labor and the prices demanded for it are the principal incentives to invention."[52] He repeated his call several months later, noting that the overthrow of the southern labor system meant "we must adopt all labor-saving machinery."[53] An eloquent call for labor-saving machinery was issued at the Border Agricultural Fair in Danville, Pittsylvania County, during the fall of 1868. According to William T. Sutherlin, Thomas P. Atkinson, and George Williamson, prominent members of the Border Agricultural Society, agricultural machinery was the only effective solution to the labor question. "We must learn," they intoned, "the important truth that as iron muscles require neither food nor clothing, and demand lower wages, in as much as one man with them can do the work of five without them, we must introduce and use upon our farms all those labor-saving machines which the experience of others may recommend and our judgment shall approve." The efficacy of this approach, they concluded, would be the "dispensing with all unnecessary and extra labor."[54]

The burgeoning free market was not slow to capitalize on this seeming necessity for labor-saving machinery for agricultural production. The pages of the *Southern Planter and Farmer* soon filled with advertisements for labor-saving implements. George Watt and Company, for instance, located at 1450 Franklin Street, Richmond, advertised "The Watt Plough." This machine was headlined as "A Plough For The Times" and was introduced as warranted "to do far better work, and one fourth more work, with the same power." It was endorsed by planter W. C. Wickham, who favored the Watt plow to others especially "when the ground is at all foul." "It will do better," Wickham advised, "and more work, with less labor to the team and

THE IMPACT OF EMANCIPATION

teamster, than either of the others and . . . it is decidedly the best two-horse plough I have ever had."[55] H. M. Smith, located at 1532 Main Street, Richmond, advertised a whole series of "Agricultural Implements and Machinery," including threshers, horse-powers, wheat fans, corn shellers, straw cutters, well-fixtures, corn planters, gleaners, plows, harrows, rollers, cultivators, and cider mills. This company also sold larger machines for cereal production, including cultivators such as the Rockaway Wheel Horse Rake and harvesters such as McCormick's Reaper.[56]

Such advertisements were undoubtedly a reflection of technological progress and burgeoning manufacturing interests. They also provided revenue for the fledgling *Southern Planter and Farmer*. Most importantly, they were nourished by the rich soil of the free labor problem. Much like immigration proposals, however, they ran into trouble. Credit shortages circumscribed the buying potential of planters and farmers especially with regard to purchasing expensive farm machinery. An even more challenging obstacle was the peculiar nature of tobacco production. Unlike cereal crops, tobacco remained a labor-intensive cash crop that did not lend itself easily to technological methods. The nature of the plant stubbornly refused modernity. In this sense the tobacco plant along with former masters shared an older dominion.[57]

The campaign of machinery for men was similarly echoed in the promotion of manure and fertilizer for free labor in agricultural production. Despite a vigorous campaign for home manures and artificial fertilizers to combat soil exhaustion during the antebellum era, many planters and farmers failed to respond, especially in the Virginia tobacco region.[58] During the Civil War Samuel M. Janney had written an agricultural report for the U.S. Department of Agriculture (USDA) that argued for the productiveness of the Virginia piedmont. There "is no doubt," Janney wrote, "it might be made to yield far heavier crops by more thorough farming and use of fertilizers."[59] The campaign was reinvigorated after the Civil War but under very different emancipatory conditions. Formerly it was primarily to meet soil exhaustion; now the old problem was compounded by the shortcomings of free labor. If the problem of slavery was that it exhausted the soil, then the problem of free labor was that it did not work the land sufficiently.

G. C. Gilmer of Albemarle County provided a clear expression of the dilemma and its possible solution. It was difficult, he argued, to pursue agricultural cultivation with "demoralized labor." Gilmer advised heavy manuring and the reduction of cultivated acreage. He was especially impressed with "Baugh's superphosphate and Old Dominion fertilizer," which he had used for corn production. While his tenants had produced 100 barrels of corn and "nubbins" on fifty acres without the use of fertilizer, Gilmer had produced 250 barrels of corn and nubbins on half the acreage. "I am perfectly satisfied," he concluded, "that we must manure more and hire less labor—the manure pays better than the worthless labor now generally afloat in these parts." A few months later Gilmer repeated his call for a new farming system in which manure farming would alleviate a situation where "labor is so very unreliable" and agricultural production was constantly interrupted by "our wandering freedmen." He even went so far as to advocate a plan for cereal grain cultivation whereby manure costs would exceed labor costs. Thus, if the planter's total expenses amounted to $2,950, then $1,200 should be spent on fifteen tons of manure, while labor costs for two hands, food and board, and extra harvest help should amount to the smaller amount of $850. The remarkable proposal here was that judicious fertilization might compensate for the limitations of free labor.[60]

The efficacy of exchanging manuring/fertilizing for free labor was argued by other contributors to the *Southern Planter and Farmer*. The anonymous "Nansemond" argued for soil improvement through grass farming as a more viable means of capital investment than the less manageable, unstable, and unreliable system of free labor. "The question of labor in connection with the improvement of our soils," he explained, was very important, "and if a very large percentage of the cost of improvements can be saved by throwing the onus on the land, making it work in the production of green crops for manures, it is reasonable to conclude that this is the true economy, the best investment of capital that can be made, since experience proves that the system is safe, permanent, and most reliable." It was certainly deemed safer than the precariousness, temporality, and irregularity of emancipated labor.[61]

The sentiments of Nansemond were echoed by "Southsider," who issued a call for the improved usage of manure and fertilizer farming especially in tobacco production. According to this writer, it was important to "apply four, five, and even six hundred pounds per acre, so as to make the tobacco large and thus economize labor." Southsider went on to explain the necessity of replacing free labor with fertilizer and, in doing so, also offered revealing commentary on the agrarian habits of planters and farmers in tobacco Virginia. "It is thought by some," he noted, "that the cultivation of tobacco requires too much labor to be profitable, and many persons have discontinued its cultivation in consequence." However, he continued, tobacco production "can not be safely dispensed with here," since "it is our main money crop" and "no other crop can be substituted in its place." Consequently, "attention must be directed to the best mode of lessening the cost of production." "This is to be done," Southsider advised, "by increasing the productiveness of the soil, by heavy manuring, and thus make[ing] large tobacco." Indeed, he added, "it requires no more labor to make a large plant weighing half a pound than it does to make a small one weighing one eighth of a pound. The cost per pound may be greatly lessened in this way."[62] In the tobacco South it was popularly believed that rubbing fertilizer on a child's feet would make the youngster grow into a strong, healthy, and productive adult.[63] Perhaps systematic manuring and fertilizing would help meet the deficiencies of the new free labor system. More important was tobacco's old dominion in the minds, hearts, and pockets of former masters and new employers.

The promotion of fertilizer to deal with free labor's shortcomings was, much like labor-saving machines, quickly endorsed by the marketplace. Fertilizer sales only superficially resembled those of the antebellum period. The products found themselves in different soil, while manufacturers promoted their wares as the best means of shaking off the cobwebs of war. In the spring of 1867, fertilizer manufacturers and merchants began to advertise in the revitalized pages of the *Southern Planter and Farmer*. E. B. Bentley, agent for the James River Manufacturing Company in Richmond, advertised the company's readiness "to supply the Planters and Farmers of Virginia and North Carolina with its well-known FERTILIZER, which will be found equally beneficial to the crops of Tobacco and Oats, as it has proved to be to that of Wheat." The Southern Fertilizing Company (SFC), also of Richmond, advertised numerous artificial fertilizers, including "Fine Crushed Peruvian Guano," "Old Dominion," "Phospho Peruvian," and "Tobacco

Fertilizer." This latter product, planters and farmers were informed, was "prepared with special reference to the requirements of the Tobacco crop," which included quality production as well as careful supervision.[64]

As part of their advertising campaign, fertilizer agents began to use prominent planters to endorse their products. Tobacco planters W. A. Pace and J. C. Farrar of Mecklenburg County, along with Thomas R. Dew of Dinwiddie County, endorsed Excelsior fertilizer on behalf of Baltimore manufacturers J. J. Turner & Co.[65] Willoughby Newton, in his capacity as president of the state's leading agricultural society, recommended Ober's phospho peruvian as the most useful fertilizer for agricultural activities.[66] Gilmer, while advising the benefits of fertilizer farming in postwar conditions, also slipped in a recommendation for Baugh's superphosphate and Old Dominion fertilizer to the *Southern Planter and Farmer* readership. It is probable that he received either a special fertilizer dispensation or a small gratuity for his efforts.[67] Other prominent planters and farmers also endorsed fertilizer products. Twenty planters from the tidewater, piedmont, and valley regions emulated Newton in recommending Ober's fertilizer, while five others extolled the virtues of another brand called Chesapeake Guano.[68] Fertilizer advertisements provided an array of benefits, including revenue for the *Southern Planter and Farmer*, customers for fertilizer manufacturers, and forms of support for planters. The product also promised a quality crop despite the deficiencies of free labor.

It was not long before these fertilizer products began to promise a little too much. Some merchants attempted to profit from unsettled free labor conditions. This became easier in a climate where many writers were promoting organic farming to compensate for the shortcomings of free labor. As one *Southern Planter and Farmer* editorial succinctly put it, the combination of exhausted soils and the scarcity and high price of labor stimulated a search for the "best and cheapest auxiliaries for producing the most abundant crops." Consequently, there was an "energetic rivalry, and vigorous competition, among the manufacturers and sellers of these various fertilizers, struggling for the market and tempting the confidence of the unsuspecting farmer."[69] Desperate planters, farmers, and employers were often hoodwinked, as exemplified by the *Mason v. Chappell* legal dispute. Although Chappell's fertilizer had been strongly recommended, it proved to be

THE IMPACT OF EMANCIPATION

of limited worth. Farmer Mason, however, was unable to prove fraud on the part of the fertilizer agent. Consequently, the farmer never recovered his costs. In the future, the *Southern Planter and Farmer* editor warned, the buyer should demand an "express written guaranty." Such advice would have been more judicious if it had acknowledged its own role in the promotion of such substitutes for the deficits of free labor.[70]

Together with agricultural advice, discussions on free labor, immigration schemes, and advertisements for labor-saving machinery and fertilizer, the pages of the *Southern Planter and Farmer* fairly crackled with hints and suggestions for the most efficacious farming systems. The call for planters, farmers, and employers to switch to less labor-intensive crop cultivation was particularly pronounced. This too was not a new call, but emancipation and dire agricultural conditions made it particularly urgent. One writer argued that since there was "not sufficient labor in Virginia to grow the quantities of tobacco and wheat formerly raised," and because planters and farmers did not have "the capital to fertilize and cultivate the same extent of land," they should switch to less labor-intensive potato production.[71] Peanut farming was also occasionally promoted as providing a more profitable alternative to the region's traditional cash staples. The *Southern Planter and Farmer* reprinted an extract from another agricultural journal that drew attention to the extraordinary profitability of peanut production. Average peanut prices ranged from sixty to eighty cents per bushel with productivity returns of 75 to 100 bushels per acre. Indeed, some farmers reportedly raised as much as 500 to 1,000 bushels from six to ten acres. Examining Sussex, Surry, and Southampton Counties in the Virginia southside, the author went on to advise planters on the best means of cultivating the peanut and outlined the advantages of post-harvest pasturage that were available from peanut farming.[72]

The call for a switch in cash crops was echoed in various federal reports. In "Cultivation of the Peanut" the anonymous writer estimated that Virginia's peanut crop during the 1868 season amounted to 300,000 bushels. At $2.75 per bushel this totaled around $825,000. With improved peanut farming, the author postulated, by 1869 production could reach 1 million bushels worth $2.75 million. His central point, however, was the comparative profitability of peanut cultivation over other staple crops, especially cotton and tobacco. Cotton, he argued, was raised at 225 pounds per acre and, at twenty- five cents per pound, was worth $56.25; but it involved a tedious amount of labor. Tobacco leaf was raised at 600 pounds per acre and, at ten cents per pound, was worth slightly more than cotton at $60. However, it was also labor-intensive, and its cultivation was expensive. In contrast, peanuts could be raised at 50 bushels per acre and sold for $2.50 per bushel. This would bring in $125 for each acre of peanuts, and the labor involved was far less. Indeed, the author concluded, some farmers in Amelia, Nottoway, Halifax, and Brunswick Counties had already seen the advantages and were beginning to switch from tobacco to peanut cultivation.[73]

The notion of the comparative profitability of crop cultivation through reduced labor costs was the subject of a detailed investigation by the anonymous H. He compared the labor costs, acreage production, and labor productivity of tobacco, wheat, and corn. With labor costs at 60 cents a day, he calculated tobacco cultivation required 67 days of labor at $40.20, wheat cultivation needed 14 days costing $8.75, and corn, 15 days at $9. The net profit from each crop per acre would be $78.05 for tobacco, $33.39 for wheat, and $34.37 for corn. But, H pointed out, even though leaf was the most profitable crop per acre, one hand could only cultivate 2.5 acres compared with 10 acres of either wheat or corn. Thus, cereal grain production worked out to be the most profitable. H further advised the "necessity of curtailing tobacco culture" through crop rotation and diversity.[74] The efficacy of mixed farming for emancipated labor was echoed by a subscriber from Orange County who informed the *Southern Planter and Farmer* editor that due to "our labor system being essentially changed, it behooves us to make a corresponding change in our farming operations." He recommended that a "system of mixed husbandry must now be adopted, otherwise I think a failure will be inevitable." The anonymous writer went on to recommend grass farming, pasturage, and the specialized production of small crops of corn, tobacco, oats, and wheat as the best substitute for the failings of free labor.[75]

The clearest expression of this correlation between improved farming and emancipated labor was heard in calls for more specialized tobacco cultivation. Faint echoes during the late antebellum era became trumpet blasts in the immediate postemancipation years. Walter

W. Bowie's essay "Culture and Management of Tobacco" urged southern tobacco cultivators to engage in small-scale quality tobacco production. Because of emancipation, Bowie argued, employers were unable to pay high prices for the unstable labor of migratory freedmen. Furthermore, large-scale tobacco cultivation simply could not compete with small, well-managed crops. If leaf producers followed his advice, they could expect around 2,400 pounds of tobacco from each laborer, fetching between $480 and $720—and from only three acres. Bowie contrasted the profitability of such specialized tobacco production with that of slavery, the "old system," in which eight acres were worked by two or three hands for the much smaller return of $240.[76] Planter J. B. Ficklin echoed this call for specialized leaf production in a letter to the *Southern Planter and Farmer*. Tobacco growers, he advised, should pursue specialized cultivation especially through fertilization, manuring, small-scale quality production, and a reduction in arable acreage. If leaf growers followed his advice, Ficklin claimed they could expect a "good price for a good crop of tobacco" despite emancipation.[77]

The major feature of specialized tobacco production was the switch from dark leaf cultivation (quantity) to yellow leaf production (quality). Bright tobacco, or yellow leaf, had become increasingly popular during the final antebellum years. Its finer, richer texture was more suited to the growing demands of indigenous manufacturers and foreign buyers than the traditionally darker and coarser Virginia leaf. Although bright tobacco production was temporarily interrupted by the Civil War, planters and farmers soon resumed its cultivation once hostilities had ceased. With the advent of emancipation and the corresponding loss of human capital, however, the cultivation of this increasingly valuable commodity became even more urgent. At least editor Williams thought so. Bright leaf cultivation was important enough to warrant a reprint of planter Samuel C. Shelton's 1861 article on the management of yellow tobacco in the revived *Southern Planter and Farmer*. Shelton had advised the manuring of plant beds, the application of guano to old lands, "good wages to the hand," and the employment of young, active hands to cultivate "fifteen thousand hills each," which would amount to 2,000 pounds of quality leaf. Much like that of his fellow adviser Bowie from Maryland, Shelton's notion of specialized leaf production worked out to about three acres per hand. He added that previously slaves, or "old hands," had cultivated up to 20,000 hills each, but now this was too much for quality production.[78]

The *Southern Planter and Farmer* did not halt its campaign promoting bright tobacco cultivation. Toward the end of the 1868 season Thomas P. Atkinson, a prominent planter in the tobacco southside, articulated the reasons why tobacco growers should switch from dark to bright leaf production. Apart from the "fabulous prices" being fetched by the yellow leaf, he argued, few planters could "afford to make the ordinary shipping tobacco, whilst they shall be subject to the present high taxes and to all the evils consequent on free labor." Hence "the necessity of turning their attention to producing the only kind which will amply remunerate them for the outlay and the labor required to make it." Atkinson also described the bright tobacco calendar in order to assist planters and farmers in the cultivation of yellow leaf. Recalling an earlier, more famous tobacco salesman, he signed the article "Walter Raleigh."[79] An anonymous J.V.B. from Halifax County also promoted bright leaf cultivation in the context of emancipatory conditions. Since the region had been impoverished because of the loss of its slave capital, he argued, bright tobacco was the most profitable crop. Furthermore, because it was "a crop which requires a great deal of labor and handling," it "is absolutely necessary that the land in cultivation should be rich, that the tobacco may be large and heavy." Otherwise, "it is the most unprofitable crop the farmer can engage in." J.V.B. also provided tips on the yellow leaf calendar, advised the pursuit of "mixed husbandry," and called for a reduction in total arable acreage in order to maximize quality production.[80] In short, the call was for quality crops over quantity crops at a time when free labor was scarce, lacking in quality, and difficult to supervise.

The labor-intensive peculiarities of tobacco production during this period were succinctly captured by one tobacco planter in an article written for the agricultural journal in early 1868. C. W. Dabney, in describing the intense labor requirements demanded by leaf cultivation, also fleshed out the particular difficulties facing tobacco employers in the context of emancipation and the new free labor system. "Many of the vicissitudes attending the crop," he observed, "may be obviated by labor. For instance, if the beds don't flourish, they may be dressed and manured if there is anybody to do it. If plants are late, and seasons scarce, the crop might be pitched, if we had the people to do it. If the season is rainy, and grass constantly growing again, one must have hands to repeat the tillage. If worms come in a glut, as was again the case last year, you must redouble your labor, or lose your investment."[81] Of course, the whole point concerning agricultural production in postemancipation Virginia was that the transformation in social relations entailed reduced control over the freedpeople and the availability of their labor. There was an urgent need to curtail labor requirements through specialized crop production, especially through the cultivation of small-scale fine leaf. In this sense the promotion of yellow tobacco for black labor provided merely the sharpest edge to the free labor problem.[82]

Meanwhile, eighty-two miles southeast of the *Southern Planter and Farmer*'s Richmond address, a postemancipation advice literature aimed at a very different audience was beginning to take shape. At the recently founded Hampton Institute, free labor was viewed more as an opportunity than a problem. Of course, in order for its potential to be realized, the freedpeople had to pursue the tenets of thrift, industry, good character, property ownership, education, patience, and Christian fortitude. Much of this message had already been propagated by officials of the BRFAL. Although much of the BRFAL apparatus officially withdrew from the American South after January 1, 1869, its message gained a new lease on life, especially in postemancipation Virginia. The watchman was a former Union general and BRFAL superintendent, the beacon was Hampton Institute, and the guiding light was Hampton's illustrated monthly periodical, the *Southern Workman*.

The ideological nexus between the BRFAL's notion of free labor and emancipation's potential was exemplified in the personage of Samuel Chapman Armstrong and his Hampton idea. Born of missionary parents in Hawaii, Armstrong was schooled in the moral liberalism of Williams College in remote northwestern Massachusetts and was disciplined through enlistment and service in the Union army during the war. After a brief stint on the Rio Grande, he returned to Virginia to serve as the BRFAL superintendent for the Ninth District, headquartered at Fortress Monroe in the southeastern peninsula. Moral uplift of the so-called despised races, civilizationism as Christian duty, industriousness through discipline and regimentation, and rewards for effort were all influences in Armstrong's past that converged in his creation of Hampton Agricultural and Normal Institute, which opened in April 1868 for the business of transforming slaves into industrious freedpeople.[83]

Although Hampton Institute stressed manual labor and technical training, its major objective became teacher training in the school of free labor. Students were primarily exposed to moral training and only secondarily to intellectual instruction. As Booker T. Washington later recalled of his classmates in the early 1870s, the "great and prevailing idea that seemed to take possession of every one was to prepare himself to lift up the people at his home."[84] After graduation these young freedmen and freedwomen were expected to embrace local rural communities and propagate the educational gospel of hard work, moral advancement, and social uplift. Their spiritual guidance was Hampton's theme of education for life.

Hampton's message resonated early in some quarters. In his Franklinesque second autobiography Washington reported overhearing a conversation about Hampton in a darkened coal mine in Malden, West Virginia. "It seemed to me," he recalled, "that it must be the greatest place on earth, and not even Heaven presented more attractions for me at that time than did the Hampton Normal and Agricultural Institute in Virginia." Emboldened by this ethereal vision and spurred on by the communal encouragement of "the older colored people," Washington embarked on the 500-mile trek from Malden across tobacco Virginia to Hampton in the southeastern peninsula. After "a long, eventful journey," he was met by "the sight of the large, three-story, brick school building [that] seemed to me to be the largest and most beautiful building I had ever seen." After passing the famous broom-sweeping entrance exam, he entered the hallowed halls of his divine inspiration.[85]

The message also echoed through the more earthly corridors of the state general assembly. A decade earlier the U.S. Congress had passed the Morrill Act, which provided federal land-grant assistance for agricultural and technical colleges. Various state institutions of higher education, including Washington College, Virginia Military Institute, and the University of Virginia, attempted to gain access to these federal funds through proposals to initiate agricultural and technical pro-

THE IMPACT OF EMANCIPATION

grams. Instead, during the 1871–72 session the general assembly used two-thirds of the funds to establish a new agricultural and mechanical college at Blacksburg for white students; the remaining third went to Hampton for the training of freedpeople. This remarkable legislative support for freedpeople's schooling from a post-Reconstruction conservative legislature was partially the result of Armstrong's skillful machinations. It also owed its passage to the work of vocal freedmen legislators such as Senator James W. B. Bland, representing Prince Edward and Appomattox Counties, and Senator Daniel M. Norton of James City and York Counties. It was also, however, a practical political measure designed to capitalize on the reality of the freedpeople's schooling and the legislative fiat toward public schooling initiated by the Underwood Convention. It was an attempt to give direction and control to such educational activities and represented the grafting of current state policies onto past federal objectives.[86]

In 1872, one year after the institute's first graduating class and four years after the founding of Hampton Institute, Principal Armstrong initiated the *Southern Workman*, which he subsequently edited. This illustrated monthly served as Hampton Institute's major newspaper. It provided commentary on school activities, events, functions, and student affairs as well as broader contemporary issues. It also served as a major fund-raising tool, especially in its propagation of educating the freedpeople in their correct role and place in postbellum society. As Armstrong later informed his friend and Hampton trustee Robert C. Ogden, he hoped the *Southern Workman* would become a "power." In its subsequent appeasement of both northern philanthropists and southern moderates, the *Southern Workman* proved to be very successful.[87]

It is also important to recognize that the *Southern Workman* functioned as a missionary tool for the propagation of Hampton Institute's educational gospel of hard work, moral advancement, and social uplift. Both its title and pithy motto pointed to work as constituting the mainstay of the potential emancipation of the freedpeople. The subjects of the magazine's title were the freedpeople whose major purpose was to work in the South. The *Southern Workman*'s motto, "Devoted to the Industrial Classes of the South," was particularly salient. Devotion entailed Hampton Institute's commitment to the freedpeople; it also implied that the freedpeople were its paternal brethren. Industriousness, as we have already seen, meant hard and constant work in the litany of nineteenth-century Republican free labor ideology. The purpose of the *Southern Workman* was to keep Hampton alumni constantly informed of the correct lessons of emancipation. Armed with copies of the journal and fortified by its message, these graduates fanned out into the darker recesses of the Virginia interior to spread the missionary gospel of work, progress, and social uplift. They might have left Hampton, but through the school newspaper Armstrong ensured that Hampton never left them.[88]

In January 1872 the *Southern Workman* began its mission. Devoted to the freedpeople of the South, it consisted of four short pages. Purchasable for one dollar annually in advance, it featured numerous short articles, advertisements, prints, homilies, and snippets. These addressed an array of subjects including church and school activities, domestic life, agricultural living, student affairs, children's folktales, and home advice. It also had advertisements for insurance as well as farms for sale. Additional items in the first edition included a selection from a Lincoln speech, a sermon titled "Prayer and Potatoes," and a lecture on Temperance. Its central business was expressed in the lead editorial. Editor Armstrong trumpeted the essence of its Christian mission. "Together," he wrote, "we must fight intemperance, dishonesty, laziness—those vices which drag us down lower than the beasts; together, we must build up homes all over this southern land—homes whose foundations shall be laid in honesty, sobriety, industry, cleanliness, and intelligent Christian faith."[89] In a subsequent editorial Armstrong's message was even more forthright. "Be thrifty and industrious," he informed *Southern Workman* readers. "Command the respect of your neighbors by a good record and a good character. Own your own houses. Educate your children. Make the best of your difficulties. Live down prejudice. Cultivate peaceful relations with all. As a voter act as you think and not as you are told. Remember that you have seen marvelous changes in sixteen years. In view of that be patient—thank God and take courage."[90] This message echoed Colonel Orlando Brown's Republican free labor manifesto published several years previously. It can only be presumed it met with the glowing approval of Hampton trustee General Oliver O. Howard.[91]

The message of the *Southern Workman* ostensibly resembled that of the *Southern Planter and Farmer*. Emancipation had wrought fundamental changes in social relations between former slaves and former masters. The freedpeople had to be educated into hard, consistent, and diligent work. They also had to stay where they were instead of migrating, especially to the towns. However, such similarities cloak crucial distinctions. In the pages of the Hampton journal, emancipation promised opportunity for the freedpeople rather than crisis for former masters and new employers. All the freedpeople had to do was to adhere to the correct principles prescribed by their new teachers. Industriousness promised the freedpeople the fruits of their labor in property accumulation, no longer to be siphoned off by avaricious employers. Stability further ensured the freedpeople's accumulation of property rather than a stationary workforce for planters. Most importantly, the *Southern Workman*'s emancipatory objective was the moral training of the freedpeople for social uplift as opposed to the reimposition of controls reminiscent of slave conditions. The keyword here was neither stasis nor tradition but progress in the classic, nineteenth-century sense of the term.[92]

In the spirit of Hampton Institute's agricultural improvement program, the *Southern Workman* offered advice to the freedmen on farming systems. This was done primarily through graduates advising local farmers and was supported through the pages of the magazine.[93] Armstrong, for instance, noted the efficacy of leadership through teacher-farmer advice to the freedmen.[94] Graduates would often advise local farmers on the best way of farming. Writer C informed the editor that he had advised the "colored people" in his section of Henry County to diversify their crop production because of tobacco overproduction. The freedmen, he reported, "say if they don't raise tobacco, they can't make any money, this year they have made so much tobacco that they can't get any price for it." The writer's advice was "to raise more corn, wheat, oats, cattle, hogs and sheep." "Most of them," he added, "do raise enough corn and wheat to last them the year around, while others do not."[95]

The *Southern Workman* also functioned as an organ promoting communal stability. It expressed institutional support for the consolidation of the family household. For the purposes of familial reconstruction, for instance, the journal regularly published an "information wanted" column that listed freedpeople inquiring after lost family members. This resembled the policy of "quirin" letters first adopted in freedpeople's churches immediately after emancipation. The *Southern Workman* also promoted the education of the freedchildren as well as older freedpeople. In the late summer of 1872, Hampton alumnus William P. Brown reported the establishment of a freedpeople's school in Hanover County. It was the first school to be opened in the area since the war. The schoolhouse was erected on one-half acre of land. The local community converted the old church into a "neat school house" and raised $600 for the construction of a new church. The next school session was scheduled to begin on September 1, 1872, although this depended on the availability of the teacher. Brown was impressed with the local community's educational zeal and "truly believe[d] that the colored people desire[d] the education of their children more than anything else." So did the *Southern Workman* desire household stability, which was conducive to the progress of emancipatory aims.[96]

These educational strivings, however, were not without struggle. As some letters from alumni suggest, the lack of adequate finances and resources often curtailed the most eager schooling efforts of the freedpeople. This paucity must have been further exacerbated by prolonged agricultural depression that gripped much of the state, nation, and world after late 1873.[97] Many freedpeople were forced to reconcile the material needs of farmwork with their emancipatory ideals of schoolwork. William H. Wilkins, for instance, opened a new school at Otteville, Bedford County, in the fall of 1872, noting that "the parents of the children are very poor and at times they are compelled to keep their children at home to work and to help them about the farm."[98] Teacher Thomas Cayton reported that attendance at his Glendow school in Albemarle County was invariably affected by the demands of the agricultural calendar: "During the last two months my school has been greatly increased, mostly by young men and women who cannot come more than two months of the term."[99] "We would have begun [the term] sooner," explained one Hampton teacher, "but the farmers have been having such a very dry time with their crops that they could not afford to spare their children to go to school."[100]

The abolition of slavery transformed social relations in the Virginia tobacco region; this transformation was evident from the nature of

THE IMPACT OF EMANCIPATION

agricultural decline. The response of many former masters and new employers was to call for agricultural reform. Its central component was the effective management of labor. An older tradition was evoked, but the challenge of free labor management was very different from slave management. The extent of its challenge encouraged some to call for greater modernization. Meanwhile, others saw free labor in terms of improvement; this was a more recent hangover from the BRFAL. The freedpeople had to struggle against both approaches in the ensuing postemancipation decades. The business of agricultural reconstruction, unlike political reconstruction, was only just beginning. It almost immediately faced prolonged depression.

CHAPTER FIVE

The Contested Tobacco State,

1873–1877

When we consider the efforts being made in Kentucky,
Tennessee and Missouri, to produce an article equal to
that in Virginia and North Carolina, we cannot flag in our
resolution to bring ours "fully up to the standard."
—John Ott

CHAP. 316.—An ACT to revise the laws relating to the inspection of tobacco, and warehouse charges, and to insure the proper delivery of tobacco to the consignees,
and to repeal all acts on the subject which were in force
on the 1st January, 1877.—*Acts*, 1876–77

The old "hands," trained in the operations of priming,
topping, assorting, and the various details of cultivation
and management, are dying out, and the younger generation is decidedly inferior to the old as trained and
skilled laborers.—Joseph B. Killebrew

In May 1873 the financial journal *Bankers' Magazine* pointed out the
excessive centralization of capital in New York City. "Is it surprising,"
it read, "that capital concentrates here from the wilds of Maine, the
recesses of Connecticut, the prairies of the West, or the tobacco fields
of the South, to be used at one or two percent per month, instead of six
per cent at home?" "We caution," it urged, "our country bankers to
keep a healthy reserve at home, and not to trust too large a fund in Wall
Street on 'call.'" The journal's warning proved to be ominous. Four
months later, in early September 1873, the major American bank of Jay

Cooke and Company folded after engaging in exorbitant price speculation in Northern Pacific Railroad stock. A fragile house of financial cards quickly fell all across the United States as banks crashed, the stock market temporarily closed, and factories shut down. Financial panic ensued as credit became less and less available. This was the beginning of the first major crisis of mature industrial capitalism.[1]

What began as a financial panic became a prolonged period of industrial, commercial, and agricultural depression that dominated the waning decades of the nineteenth century. Between 1873 and 1896 there were three major bouts of depression encompassing 1873–78, the mid-1880s, and 1893–96. Despite temporary recoveries, this quarter-century represented the longest and severest depression until that point. Based on pig iron and coal production, cotton consumption, railroad revenues, merchandise imports, and bank clearances, there was an economic decline of 32 percent between 1873 and 1878. (This compares with the 55 percent decline of the Great Depression between 1929 and 1932.) A brief recovery in 1879–81 was followed by the return of depressed conditions during the mid-1880s. Again, recovery was followed by a sharp downward turn between 1893 and 1896. By the end of the century this unique prolongation of depressed conditions had earned the contemporary description of the Long Depression.[2]

The 1873 financial panic in New York City was felt around the world. After a record boom that earmarked mid-century Victorianism, Europe plunged into depression. German share values fell by around 60 percent between the peak of the boom and 1877, while almost 50 percent of blast furnaces in the main iron-producing nations stopped working. The river of immigration to the United States dried up to a stream during the 1870s. In 1889 a German business guide noted that "since the stock market collapse of 1873 . . . the word 'crisis' has constantly, with only brief interruptions, been in every one's mind." These thoughts were echoed the same year across the Atlantic by an American expert who described the world economy since 1873 as being marked by "unprecedented disturbance and depression of trade." Its uniqueness, he observed, was its "universality," embracing warring and peaceful nations, stable and unstable currencies, free trade and protectionist policies, old countries as well as new nations, Europe as well as its colonies, and centers as well as peripheries.[3]

These global financial reverberations were also felt in the tobacco

THE CONTESTED TOBACCO STATE

South. On Monday, September 29, 1873, George Hunt, a farmer in the Darlington Heights district of Prince Edward County, Virginia, confided to his diary, "Farmers very busy, labor scarce." He added that labor was "almost impossible to get for love or money." "*Most* of the *banks* have been closed," he continued, while "money [was] scarce."[4] Farther south, financial depression wreaked havoc on the cotton economy around Macon in central Georgia as well as the state as a whole.[5] Farther north, the advent of depression helped transform rural and urban life in Maryland, including emigration from the countryside, city unemployment, and the proliferation of itinerant tramps around railroad lines and urban centers.[6]

This global depression was particularly evident in agriculture. The two decades following the American Civil War witnessed a marked increase in U.S. agricultural production, especially its cereal economy (see table 5.1). In 1873 rural producers returned 322 million bushels of wheat grown on nearly 25 million acres. Seven years later national production had rocketed to 502 million bushels grown on over 38 million acres.[7] Subsequent developments in railroad and steam transportation whisked this increased produce from outlying fields to the towns, cities, ports, and markets of the world. Consequently, there was a rapid fall in prices. In 1873 rural producers earned $1.17 per bushel. Seven years later this had fallen to 95 cents per bushel. By 1894 global wheat prices had plummeted by nearly two-thirds from their 1867 market value.[8] In cereal-producing England the annual average price of wheat also fell by two-thirds, crashing from sixty-three shillings and nine pence per imperial quarter in 1868 to twenty-two shillings and ten pence by 1894.[9] As economic historian Eric Hobsbawn has summarized, the "decades of depression were not a good time in which to be a farmer in any country involved in the world market."[10]

American rural producers were no less immune to the prolonged ravages of the marketplace. This was particularly apparent in the constant price declines for major agricultural produce. Cereal prices across the nation fell dramatically. In 1873 corn, oats, and barley fetched 48 cents, 37 cents, and 96 cents per bushel, respectively. By 1880 prices had dropped to 39 cents, 35 cents, and 66 cents. Wheat, the most lucrative cash crop nationally, fell from $1.17 per bushel to 95 cents over the same period. The market price of the leading staple crop in the American South also dropped precipitously. In 1876 rural

TABLE 5.1. U.S. Wheat Production, Acreage, and Crop Value by Six Leading
States and Virginia, 1869–1899

Year	State	Bushels	Acreage	$ Value
1869	Illinois	29,200,000	2,607,142	22,192,000
	Wisconsin	24,000,000	1,568,627	16,320,000
	Iowa	23,500,000	1,807,692	12,220,000
	Indiana	20,600,000	1,430,555	19,158,000
	Ohio	20,400,000	1,316,129	21,012,000
	California	20,000,000	1,098,901	18,600,000
	Virginia	8,642,000	823,047	10,456,820
	Total U.S.	260,146,900	19,181,004	244,924,120
1879	Illinois	44,896,830	2,400,000	48,039,608
	Iowa	44,445,408	3,214,400	30,163,930
	Indiana	43,709,960	2,153,200	51,140,653
	Ohio	36,591,750	1,876,500	43,910,100
	California	35,000,000	2,500,000	43,050,000
	Minnesota	31,886,520	2,592,400	29,973,329
	Virginia	8,851,320	962,100	11,241,176
	Total U.S.	448,756,630	32,545,950	497,030,142
1889	Minnesota	45,456,000	3,113,406	30,455,338
	California	43,781,000	3,291,820	30,646,844
	Dakota Terr.	41,652,000	4,431,034	24,991,032
	Indiana	41,187,000	2,801,803	29,242,418
	Illinois	38,014,000	2,375,863	26,609,666
	Ohio	36,865,000	2,524,990	28,017,289
	Virginia	6,804,000	810,057	5,851,560
	Total U.S.	490,560,000	38,123,859	342,491,707
1899	Minnesota	68,223,581	5,091,312	37,522,969
	N. Dakota	51,758,630	4,043,643	26,396,901
	Ohio	39,998,006	2,816,761	25,598,724
	S. Dakota	37,728,339	3,526,013	18,864,170
	Kansas	36,468,044	3,721,229	18,963,383
	California	33,743,909	2,393,185	20,921,223
	Virginia	6,330,450	753,625	4,368,010
	Total U.S.	547,303,846	44,592,516	319,545,259

Sources: USDA, *Annual Report* (1869), 32; USDA, *Annual Report* (1879), 135;
USDA, *Annual Report* (1889), 210–11; USDA, *Yearbook* (1899), 766; Shannon,
Farmer's Last Frontier, 161–65; Ferleger, *Agriculture and National Development*,
table A.10, 354, lists higher U.S. totals for wheat production and acreage.

THE CONTESTED TOBACCO STATE

producers harvested nearly 4.5 million bales of cotton on over 11 million acres and fetched 9.71 cents per pound. Ten years later these original producers, with additional tenant farmers, produced over 6.5 million bales on over 18 million acres and brought in just over 8 cents per pound. There were brief price recoveries for all these commodities. For instance, cotton fetched 10.66 cents per pound in 1881, while cereal prices rose in 1881 and 1890. These price rises, however, were merely temporary crests in a sea of troughs. The trend in market prices for agricultural produce throughout the period was inescapably downward.[11]

Rural producers in the tobacco South were no less affected by the reduction in prices received for their principal crops during this period. In 1873 they cultivated 382 million pounds of tobacco on 513,000 acres and sold it for 8.6 cents per pound. By 1879 national production had increased to 472 million pounds on 633,000 acres, and the price had fallen to 6.1 cents per pound.[12] These depressed trends were even more pronounced at the state level. Tobacco prices plummeted in Virginia from 9.3 cents per pound in 1873 to 5 cents per pound through 1878–79.[13] Cereal prices for rural producers in Virginia also fell markedly. In 1873 the price of wheat was $1.46 per bushel. By 1879 it had fallen to $1.27 cents per bushel. The prices per bushel of corn, oats, and rye fell from 59 cents, 45 cents, and 79 cents to 49 cents, 38 cents, and 63 cents, respectively, over the same six-year period.[14] This drop in agricultural prices for the major staple crops of Virginia was a crucial part of the context in which emancipation was fought in the waning decades of the nineteenth century. If it was not a good time to be a planter/farmer in the global marketplace, neither was it easy for those living in staple crop regions who had recently been freed from slavery, denied the tools for independent production, and had only their labor power to sell to survive.

The increase in the production, distribution, and exportation activities of numerous nations posed a mounting challenge to the traditional tobacco leadership of the United States. The Chesapeake and the Old Dominion had dominated tobacco production from the seventeenth century through the final antebellum decade. During the Civil War era other nations had pursued staple crop production because of the suspension of southern exports. This global cultivation of staples continued after the conclusion of the war. In 1876 European production amounted to nearly 187 million pounds of tobacco, mostly grown in Hungary (44 percent), Baden (27 percent), and France (20 percent). By 1890 the statistician for the USDA reported a marked increase in European production. "The product of Europe," he noted, "is nearly equal in quantity to the average production of the United States." This constituted around 500 million pounds of tobacco annually with Austria-Hungary producing one-third; Russia and Germany, one-tenth; and France, about 35 million pounds[15] (see table 5.2).

It is important to remember that despite burgeoning global competition, U.S. tobacco production continued to dominate the world's marketplace. In 1876 total U.S. leaf production amounted to around 466 million pounds, or over twice the combined total of all European production.[16] However, the waning years of the nineteenth century saw several incursions into this U.S. domination. Most obviously, other nations pursued tobacco production and redistribution on an unprecedented scale. Furthermore, the rise in foreign production provided alternative crop sources for those nations that participated in the tobacco trade. Alex Bramwell Bremner, a tobacco operator in London, noted the rise of alternative supplies of tobacco in the aftermath of the poor tobacco season of 1874. High prices, he informed John Ott, secretary of the SFC, went against the "ultimate interest" of planters "because they tend to encourage the growth of other sorts, and at the same time improve them." Hungarian, East Indian, and French tobacco production had taken off as a result. Operator Bremner added that there were other disadvantages. "There is no substitute," he noted, "for fine Virginia Tobacco; but the inferior can be supplanted by other growths, if there is a heavy difference in the price; and, therefore, the present great rise in price may prove injurious when the Virginia crop is again so large as to require European markets for its consumption."[17]

U.S. tobacco domination was challenged in other ways. Global tobacco production provided an element of competition to the U.S. domestic market. Although this was small, it was unprecedented and growing. It can be traced through the gradual rise in foreign imports of tobacco. Between 1877 and 1886 the United States imported nearly 11 million pounds of tobacco annually worth $5.5 million; by 1900 net imports of foreign leaf had risen to over 26 million pounds. The

THE CONTESTED TOBACCO STATE

TABLE 5.2. The Global Tobacco Economy: Leading Producers, Exporters, and Leaf Types, ca. 1875

Nation	Year	Output (in thousands of pounds)	Acreage	Value (in thousands of dollars)	Exports (in millions of pounds)	Leaf Type
United States	1875	379,347	559,049	30,342	256.0	C, S
Virginia	1875	57,000	90,476	4,845		C
Germany	1871–72	78,701	80,330	8,274	16.3	C, S
Germany	1872–73	99,516				
Hungary	1875	45,000				C, S
Hungary	1876	82,698				
Turkey	1875	43,000				C, CT
Brazil	1873				34.4	C, S
Cuba	1872			20,000	18.2[a]	C, S
Philippines	1872	22,000			7.3[b]	C, S
Philippines	1875			6,167		
Japan	1872				6.6	C
Colombia	1868–69				12.5[c]	S
Java	1875	33,000				C, S
France	1854–68	45,843				C
France	1876	38,036				
Puerto Rico	1870	21,100				U
Santo Domingo	1873				14.8	U
Holland	1870				6.3	S, SN
Russia	1875			23,820		U
Switzerland	1875	2,200				U
Ecuador	1875				1.6	S

Sources: Ort, *Tobacco: Outlook in America*, 9–25; USDA, *Annual Report* (1875), 30; USDA, *Annual Report* (1876), 266.

Notes: Export leaf types: C = cutting; S = seed-leaf; CT = cigarette; SN = snuff; U = unclear. Leaf producers but limited or no data on production and exports: Venezuela, Mexico, Greece, British India, Australia, Argentina, Paraguay. Leaf producers but mainly home consumers: China, Guatemala, Russia, Africa. Leaf consumers/distributors only: Great Britain, Canada, Malta, Gibraltar, Spain, Egypt, Italy, Belgium, Sweden, Norway.

[a]Havana, Cuba, exported 18,210,800 pounds of leaf and 225,139,000 cigars in 1872.

[b]The Philippines exported 7,321,107 pounds of leaf and 110,850,000 cigars in 1872.

[c]For the rise and fall of the Colombian tobacco economy, see Harrison, "Evolution of the Colombian Tobacco Trade."

United States, however, still had an extremely favorable balance of trade regarding its tobacco economy.[18]

The most significant change in the tobacco economy, however, was the rise in leaf consumption by indigenous manufacturers and the decline of U.S. tobacco exports. There are no returns for manufacture consumption of tobacco prior to 1879 with which to compare tobacco exports. However, in 1873 the United States produced 382 million pounds of tobacco, of which nearly 214 million pounds (56 percent) was exported as leaf tobacco worth $22.6 million, and an undisclosed tobacco poundage worth $2.6 million was exported as manufactured tobacco. By 1879 the gap between exports and manufacturing had closed. Of a total U.S. tobacco production of 472 million pounds, nearly 226 million pounds were exported (48 percent, down from 56 percent), while over 216 million pounds were consumed by manufacturers (46 percent). In 1890, of 648 million pounds of U.S. leaf, 246 million (38 percent) were exported, compared with 349 million pounds (54 percent) used by manufacturers. Tobacco's Rubicon appears to have been crossed after 1886 when exports never again exceeded figures for manufacturing consumption.[19]

One statistician's report for the USDA in particular called attention to these alarming trends in the U.S. tobacco economy. European tobacco production, it claimed, was increasing. Although Europe would continue to import tobacco from the United States because it "is very cheap, and it is desirable for mixing and fortifying European leaf," U.S. exports were declining compared with usage for indigenous manufacturing. "Our exportation," the federal official noted, "is not increasing; the proportion of our crop exported is declining and will continue to fall as our population increases." He added, "Much the larger portion was formerly exported; now the larger part is annually manufactured." His concluding observation was that manufacturing in 1888 exceeded exports by 49 million pounds.[20] A subsequent investigation into the U.S. tobacco economy confirmed these fears. Of a total production of 852 million pounds of leaf, just over 308 million pounds were exported (36 percent), compared with over 386 million pounds (45 percent) consumed by manufacturers.[21]

This U.S. tobacco economy, of course, especially around the Chesapeake and the Old Dominion, was obviously no stranger to the global marketplace. Transatlantic tobacco exchange had characterized colo-

THE CONTESTED TOBACCO STATE

nial, early national, and antebellum life. This cash economy had always been marked by depressions, gluts, and price rises. However, the postemancipation period witnessed a global shakeup of the tobacco economy. The United States continued to be the major tobacco producer, but it was faced with growing global competition. It continued to be the major exporter of tobacco because its leaf was both cheap and desirable, but exports gradually declined in importance in the face of rising indigenous manufacturing demand.[22] The important point here is that Virginia's tobacco economy was severely affected by these changes during the 1870s. The Virginia tobacco economy had to compete with increased production and changing demands. The region's primary tobacco type was dark leaf, which was an export crop. Increasingly, this type became elbowed out of the market in place of lighter leafs grown elsewhere that were usable for growing manufacturing interests. These new competitors, while occasionally global, were much closer to home and primarily of western extraction.[23]

The U.S. tobacco economy was characterized by phenomenal productive growth during the last decades of the nineteenth century (see table 5.3). In 1869 the United States produced nearly 274 million pounds of tobacco leaf raised on over 481,000 acres. Virginia repeated its old dominion, leading the nation in tobacco production with 65 million pounds (one-fifth) grown on over 155,000 acres (one-third). The western states of Kentucky, Tennessee, Missouri, and Ohio together produced nearly 110 million pounds of leaf on around 166,000 acres.[24] Less than two decades later, U.S. tobacco production exploded. In 1889 national production reached nearly 566 million pounds grown on over 747,000 acres worth over $43 million. In twenty years tobacco production had doubled while its acreage had increased by one-half. The four western states now produced over 377 million pounds on nearly 444,000 acres worth more than $28 million. They had nearly quadrupled their production and tripled their acreage. Meanwhile, tobacco Virginia produced a more modest 64 million pounds from a reduced 127,052 acres worth $3.8 million.[25]

The major challenge to tobacco Virginia came from Kentucky. Its tobacco production began during the early decades of the nineteenth century primarily as a result of western migration by European settlers from the eastern seaboard's older tobacco regions, including tidewater Virginia. Slaveholders, planters, and farmers moved their slaves and

TABLE 5.3. U.S. Tobacco Production, Acreage, and Crop Value by Leading
States, 1869–1899

Year	State	Pounds	Acreage	$ Value
1869	Virginia	65,000,000	155,502	6,695,000
	Kentucky	40,000,000	59,970	3,640,000
	Tennessee	35,000,000	63,868	4,555,000
	North Carolina	33,500,000	65,944	4,589,500
	Missouri	18,500,000	18,649	1,961,000
	Ohio	16,000,000	22,857	992,000
	Total U.S.	273,775,000	481,101	32,206,325
1879	Kentucky	126,880,000	160,000	6,344,000
	Virginia	86,524,200	113,400	4,326,210
	Tennessee	44,160,000	55,200	2,208,000
	Pennsylvania	29,617,700	20,300	2,665,593
	Maryland	25,826,400	40,800	1,291,320
	Missouri	15,050,100	22,700	752,505
	Ohio	14,091,000	21,000	845,460
	Total U.S.	391,278,350	492,100	22,727,524
1889	Kentucky	283,306,000	323,409	21,247,971
	Virginia	64,034,000	127,052	3,842,052
	Tennessee	45,641,000	67,119	3,651,274
	Ohio	35,195,000	39,105	2,745,171
	North Carolina	25,755,000	57,107	1,931,644
	Pennsylvania	24,180,000	19,500	2,587,260
	Total U.S.	565,795,000	747,326	43,666,665
1899	Kentucky	314,288,050	384,805	18,541,982
	North Carolina	127,503,400	203,023	8,038,691
	Virginia	122,884,900	184,334	7,210,195
	Ohio	65,957,100	71,422	4,864,191
	Tennessee	49,157,550	71,849	2,748,495
	Wisconsin	45,500,480	33,830	2,898,091
	Pennsylvania	41,502,620	27,760	2,959,304
	Total U.S.	868,163,275	1,101,483	56,993,003

Sources: USDA, *Annual Report* (1869), 34; USDA, *Annual Report* (1879), 137;
USDA, *Annual Report* (1889), 229; USBC, *1900, Abstract*, 274; Ferleger, *Agriculture and National Development*, table A.10, 356, has slightly different U.S. totals
for tobacco production and acreage.

their tobacco seeds across the Alleghenies. In 1810, for instance, John Small and Edmund Curd emigrated from Virginia, while two years later Virginian Martin Hogan and North Carolinian Thomas Morrow commenced tobacco cultivation in Logan County, Kentucky. Between 1810 and 1820 William C. Browder and John P. Moore, also from Virginia, commenced tobacco production. By 1840, explained federal investigator Joseph Killebrew, the emergence of "better home markets" established by tobacco dealers "who stemmed tobacco and put it up for the English markets" had boosted this regional economy in the Upper South. On the eve of the Civil War the Kentucky tobacco economy ranked a close second behind that of the Old Dominion, poised to assume national tobacco leadership. It would take Civil War, prolonged depression, and the rise of the cigarette industry to both confirm and consolidate this cash crop leadership.[26]

The Civil War does not appear to have markedly affected tobacco production in Kentucky. In 1860 the state had produced over 108 million pounds; by 1870 this had only slightly decreased to just over 105 million pounds. This appears to have been the moment when Kentucky assumed a national tobacco leadership, edging out its venerable eastern competitor. This domination was confirmed throughout the following decades. In 1877 Kentucky returned its largest and best crop ever of over 182 million pounds. Two years later it produced over 170 million pounds on around 226,000 acres at a yield of over 750 pounds per acre. This crop reportedly fetched at least $5 million. In 1889 Kentucky produced over 283 million pounds on over 323,000 acres. This accounted for half the entire national production and over four-tenths of all U.S. tobacco acreage. This major share of U.S. production contrasts with the state's earlier shares of 14 percent of production and 12 percent of acreage only twenty years earlier. Meanwhile, Virginia's tobacco economy had slumped in the national rankings, falling from 50 percent to 11 percent of production and from one-third to under one-fifth of national acreage between 1869 and 1889. The Bluegrass State was part of tobacco's new dominion.[27]

According to Killebrew's exhaustive federal investigation, tobacco production was being pursued in several major regions of Kentucky. Its heart was known as the White Burley district. This encompassed about 3,000 square miles and consisted of Boone, Kenton, Campbell, Gallatin, Grant, Pendleton, Bracken, Carroll, Owen, Harrison, Robertson, Mason, Lewis, Fleming, Montgomery, Nicholas, Bourbon, Scott, Franklin, Henry, Trimble, Oldham, Shelby, and Woodford Counties. This region's tobacco growth was so dynamic that Killebrew predicted it "may soon embrace several other districts." In 1879 this district alone accounted for around one-fifth of the state's tobacco production and acreage. It also provided exceptionally high tobacco yields of over 876 pounds per acre compared with the state average of 750 pounds per acre.[28]

More specifically, this region's white burley leaf undermined the more traditional dark leaf produced in Virginia. The momentous effects were fully described by Killebrew. "It is believed," he reported, "that fully four-fifths of the plug tobacco used in the east, north, and west is made from this variety, and its introduction and culture has worked one of the most remarkable revolutions known to the agriculture of this country." He added, "Within the last ten years the whole of what is now called the White Burley district has abandoned every other variety." Although small amounts were exported to Europe, this leaf was mostly used by manufacturers of cutting tobacco, with "nine-tenths of the whole product [being] consumed in the United States." Indeed, white burley leaf had become so popular, it was replacing other leaf types on the market. Since the mid-1870s plug manufacturers from New York, Richmond, Petersburg, Lynchburg, Chicago, and elsewhere were demanding white burley. "The consequence," Killebrew explained, "is that, while all shipping styles of tobacco have been dull or depressed, the leaf tobacco of the White Burley district has commanded prices double, and sometimes quadruple, those paid for the best shipping leaf produced in other regions of the state." Neither, he added, was "the profit confined to the increased prices received for the White Burley tobacco." It was also secure in more ways than one: "The labor necessary for making this variety is much less than that demanded for the export tobacco, and the risk of curing, by not using fire, is reduced to the minimum."[29]

By the waning years of the nineteenth century the challenge of white burley for older tobacco types had become irreversible. The devastating impact of white burley on traditional leaf producers had become consolidated. "In recent years," one federal source noted, "the white Burley has been coming into great favor for the same purpose that the Maryland and Virginia tobaccos were formerly used for." The result

THE CONTESTED TOBACCO STATE

was that the "very much larger yield of the White Burley has lowered the price of the Maryland and Virginia tobaccos almost below the point of profitable production." The free market was burying the Old Dominion.[30]

The other major challenge to Virginia's tobacco economy came from northwestern Tennessee. Its tobacco economy, much like that of Kentucky, originated with European American settlers who moved from the eastern seaboard to the Cumberland Valley and brought tobacco seeds and African slaves from the old tobacco kingdoms of Virginia and North Carolina. In 1840 this leaf culture had become regionally important, with Henry County alone producing over 9 million pounds of tobacco. The antebellum period also saw the establishment of Clarksville as a major leaf market and locale for tobacco manufactories. By 1860, for instance, there were sixteen stemming factories processing 2 million pounds of leaf in Clarksville alone. That same year Tennessee produced over 43 million pounds of leaf, ranking third in national production behind Kentucky and the Old Dominion.[31]

Unlike in Kentucky, but much as in Virginia, the Civil War had a major impact on Tennessee's tobacco economy. Older antebellum markets for Tennessee leaf at New Orleans and Clarksville were "paralyzed" while alternative markets at "Saint Louis and Louisville swelled into the largest tobacco markets in the West, a position they have maintained to the present time [1879]." Furthermore, Tennessee did not recover its antebellum tobacco production until 1889, when it produced over 45 million pounds of tobacco on over 67,000 acres and fetched over $3.6 million. Tennessee was still ranked third in the nation in tobacco production behind Kentucky and Virginia. However, Virginia, which produced over 20 million more pounds of tobacco than Tennessee on nearly double the acreage, only fetched the slightly higher figure of $3.8 million for its major cash crop.[32]

The postbellum tobacco economy of Tennessee was primarily located in three districts in the far northwest bordering on southeastern Kentucky. The leading district of Clarksville consisted of Montgomery, Robertson, Cheatham, Humphreys, Dickson, Houston, and Stewart Counties, which alone accounted for 55 percent of all state production and acreage and 58 percent of the value of the total state crop in 1879. Its primary product was called the Clarksville leaf described as "tough and strong, large, fine fibred, silky and oily" and "blackish brown or chestnut color." Its main consumers were in Germany, Austria, Switzerland, England, Italy, and France—the traditional export destinations for the dark leaf produced in Virginia. The second major leaf region, the West Tennessee tobacco district, lay between the Mississippi and Tennessee Rivers and embraced Benton, Carroll, Dyer, Henry, Obion, and Weakley Counties. Over 50 percent of its tobacco was dark and was exported, while the product of outlying areas was often used for domestic consumption. The third and smallest leaf region of northwestern Tennessee was the Upper Cumberland River district and consisted of Smith, Trousdale, Macon, Clay, Jackson, and Putnam Counties, with parts of Sumner, Wilson, and Overton Counties. A decade earlier, dark leaf had dominated its production, but consistently depressed prices had prompted a switch to more productive types of leaf "suited to domestic consumption."[33]

In short, the traditional tobacco economy of Virginia was very quickly caught up in the maelstrom of prolonged depression and a burgeoning new leaf industry. The tobacco market, much like social relations of agricultural production, was moving toward freedom; in the process it exerted even greater dominion.

Freedom's form seemed to be lurking throughout the Virginia tobacco region during the 1870s. Emancipation had freed labor from its traditional moorings of slaveholders, landholdings, and dependency. This process of dissolution had entered its second decade. Financial freedom during the early 1870s had inaugurated a depression that hung over the entire decade. One result was increased freedom of exchange in marketing cash crops. This marketing process was less unique than qualitatively different in postemancipation conditions. Along with free labor and market competition, tobacco sales were freed from state regulation. This withering away of the tobacco state contributed to the postemancipation depression of former masters and planters.

It is ironic that the origins of the postemancipation tobacco inspection system lay within a similar context of depression and class conflict, albeit during early eighteenth-century Virginia. The failure of both urban development and crop diversification to stem periodic price declines stimulated colonial state regulation of tobacco production and exports. Earlier attempts to forbid the selling of poor tobacco, to legislate mandatory inspection at public warehouses, and to reduce exports through setting production limits all proved ineffective. In 1730 Governor William Gooch, along with his allies, passed the Virginia Inspection Act, which systematized state regulation of tobacco marketing. All tobacco was to be marketed at public warehouses where it was to be inspected by public officials. Only good tobacco was approved and passed; the rest was destroyed. The good leaf was weighed, and notes of receipt were given to the planter. These notes, because they guaranteed value, became legal tender for debts and taxes. Although this legislation provoked angry responses, ranging from plant-cutting riots to warehouse arson, from many small tobacco planters, the tobacco inspection act remained statutory legislation.[34]

Between the early national decades and the antebellum period, the tobacco inspection system underwent several changes. These included geographical shifts along with specialization and concentration of market points. In 1797–98 there were 72 official inspection warehouses in the state, located mostly in the tidewater region. By 1860 these inspection stations had become 26 much larger warehouses mostly located in the piedmont. Furthermore, the state assumed even greater control over the business of tobacco inspection. In 1852, during Governor Joseph Johnson's administration, the appointment of inspectors shifted from county court recommendation to that of the governor's office. Annual salaries for inspectors ranged from $100 for small warehouses to $330 for large sites and $360 for state-owned warehouses. The process of inspection was straightforward: the two appointed inspectors broke open the tobacco hogshead, examined its contents, passed it if sound, and provided a receipt that was given to the owner. Tobacco inspection fees were threefold: 50 to 60 cents per hogshead rent to the warehouse owner, 75 cents per hogshead service charge to the inspector, and an inspection tax to the state of $1.65. This inspection system was often marked by abuses ranging from negligence to dishonesty, including short weights, advance listing, and stolen samples.[35]

The nature of such abuses, along with changing features of the tobacco market, prompted increasing challenges to the inspection system. The 1837 panic, for instance, destroyed local warehouses in Danville. The state inspection system went with it. This curtailed foreign exports because these would have been illegal. An impetus was provided for newer marketing methods, especially loose leaf auctions and street auctions. Different challenges emerged in Richmond. The warehouse auction sales system was inconvenient to commission merchants and buyers because of citywide scattered sales and inspectors acting as commission merchants. Consequently, on Wednesday, May 26, 1858, the Richmond Tobacco Exchange opened for business on Thirteenth and Cary Streets. It became a central locale where buyers and commission merchants could meet to sample tobacco. A number of commission merchants agreed to sell only at the tobacco exchange. Some Richmond papers commended the reform, but there was strong opposition to this promise of trade control. Meanwhile, tobacco inspectors at Shockoe, Public, and Seabrooks warehouses in Richmond publicized their continuance of the old inspection system.[36]

Rural producers also voiced their support for the traditional inspection system and protested these reforms. The lead was taken by the Bush and Biery Agricultural Club of Prince Edward County. On May 22, 1858, at a meeting in the home of John A. Scott, the club passed several resolutions in support of "the long established usage of this country" and against the imposition of commission merchants in tobacco marketing. Ten days later the tobacco planters of Prince Edward County assembled at the local courthouse to organize their opposition to the Richmond Tobacco Exchange. A committee of twelve headed by F. T. Wootton prepared a report that condemned the exchange as an attempt to abolish the inspection system and replace it with a monopolistic board of trade controlled by commission merchants devoid of planter influence. The resolutions against the exchange and its commission merchants and for legislative pressure were unanimously adopted. They also called for support from other agricultural clubs as well as the state agricultural society.[37] This emergent conflict over tobacco marketing was temporarily halted by the advent of war. It resumed a decade after emancipation and in the teeth of depression.

The old inspection system appears to have survived in the immediate aftermath of the Civil War. At the close of 1871 the Virginia general assembly approved for each warehouse one tobacco inspector, to be approved by the governor and the owner(s) of the warehouse. The inspector's tasks were specifically designated by law. The tobacco hogshead or cask was to be uncased and broken and then inspected

THE CONTESTED TOBACCO STATE

for quality to ensure it was "good, sound, well-conditioned, merchantable, and clear of trash." It was then to be weighed, measured, and either marked or branded with the warehouse name, the tare of the cask or hogshead, and its quality. The net weight was to be determined by weighing the hogshead or cask before it had been uncased and then deducting the hogshead/cask weight. For their services to the state these tobacco inspectors were to be paid either a proportion of hogshead, box, or cask proceeds or, if it was loose leaf, eight cents for every hundred pounds by each warehouse owner and buyer. Tobacco inspectors were also required to follow additional procedures, including quarterly accounting for money received by them as well as providing annual accounts to the state auditor. Warehousemen were held responsible for insurance on their warehouses, while various penalties were threatened against either fraudulent marketing or the failure to insure tobacco.[38]

Despite the passage of such laws, the tobacco inspection system became the subject of increasing debate. Planters and farmers were concerned at favoritism toward the middlemen by some inspectors. Buyers were concerned about the practice and potential of unfair sampling, packing, and weighing. Commission merchants were antithetical to what they perceived to be an unnecessary, burdensome, and antiquated system of state regulation. New forces, however, had been unleashed that increasingly challenged the existing system. One was the evolving auction system that had demonstrated its marketing efficacy in prewar Danville and continued to do so in the postwar period. Another was the marketing of yellow bright leaf that challenged older, simpler methods of classification. This new leaf varied tremendously in quality, was sold in small piles on the warehouse floor rather than packed in hogsheads or casks, and was bought for domestic manufacture rather than foreign export. Open inspection by domestic buyers along with declining tobacco exports simply reduced the need for state inspection. Finally, the political activities of tobacco warehousemen proved to be more efficacious in the climate of emancipation and depressed agricultural conditions.[39]

The clash over tobacco inspection came to a head in 1874. A new law was passed that allowed all loose tobacco to be sold without the need for state inspection and regulation. Warehousemen seized on this legislation as the thin edge of the wedge in a campaign to abolish state inspection altogether. Planters and farmers expressed their antipathy toward tobacco merchants' gaining control over the inspection of their rural produce.[40] Governor James L. Kemper responded to these rural demands in his end-of-year address by asking the general assembly to extend state inspection to all tobacco warehouses engaged in marketing activities.[41] Editorials in the *Southern Planter and Farmer* titled "Tobacco Inspections" endorsed this message and called for governor-related tobacco inspectorships reminiscent of the early 1850s.[42]

Throughout the following year planters and farmers waged a united campaign on several fronts to save the inspection system and resist market domination threatened by warehousemen and merchants. In the *Southern Planter and Farmer* there were repeated calls for legislative control of the tobacco trade. One editorial called for tobacco "inspection in the legislature."[43] Major R. L. Ragland, a prominent tobacco planter from Halifax County, called for state ownership and regulation of all tobacco warehouses.[44] In September 1875 the *Southern Planter and Farmer* reported on a convention of planters at Burkeville, Nottoway County, that highlighted the conflict between planters and merchants, especially at the Richmond exchange.[45] Elsewhere public meetings were held in at least fifteen counties in the Virginia tobacco region, which denounced the Richmond merchant cabal and called for legislative pressure to support the old inspection laws.[46] This extrapolitical pressure proved to be temporarily successful, as state tobacco inspection was retained.

This legislative victory, however, proved to be ephemeral. State inspection of tobacco was deemed an anachronism by legislators such as John W. Daniel. Others supported abolition because of antistatism as well as its irrelevance for the new bright tobacco. But most importantly, the warehousemen proved too strong, organized, and influential among state legislators. Abolition succeeded in the legislature of 1877–78 when state inspection was abolished altogether. The tobacco trade was freed to choose its own inspectors and charge its own prices. On April 4, 1877, the general assembly approved lengthy legislation that repealed all existing tobacco inspection laws. Its fifty sections dealt with an array of trade features, including warehouse erections, appointment of samplers and their duties, fees and charges, and penalties for infractions. Its most important section converted public warehouses into private warehouses, thus abolishing a controversial marketing distinction. The *Southern Planter and Farmer* condemned this legislation but to no avail. This tobacco laissez-faire was consolidated by additional legislation passed in early 1878.[47]

The old system of state inspection of tobacco had emerged out of class conflict and depressed agricultural conditions. A similar constellation of factors ended it. A system that had been codified since 1730 folded comparatively quickly. The seeds had been sown in the waning antebellum decades; postemancipation and depression nourished its fate. There were subsequent calls for the reintroduction of state inspection. N. W. Hazelwood promoted bills on behalf of rural interest during the 1881–82 general assembly. Similarly in 1889 the influential Farmers' Alliance periodical the *Progressive Farmer* called for regulation, since rural tobacco producers had experienced a tripling of warehouseman charges.[48] But these efforts were tantamount to plug chewing without spitting. The harsh reality was the triumph of tobacco warehousemen and merchants over rural interests, the unstoppable emergence of the laissez-faire market, and the end of the old state system of tobacco regulation. The free market and free labor were postemancipation cousins opposing an older dominion.

There had been, of course, extensive opposition to tobacco state abolitionism. The Patrons of Husbandry never amounted to a significant rural protest movement in postemancipation Virginia compared with states in either the Deep South or the Midwest. The Grange organization was, however, relatively strong in the Virginia tobacco region. Its popularity was spurred partially by emancipation and prolonged agricultural depression. It was also propelled by the controversy over tobacco inspection as well as consistent opposition to federal tobacco taxes. This opposition represented an important feature of the region's political economy during the mid-1870s. It also suggests important links to the politics of Reconstruction as well as future rural protest movements. These tobacco Granges proved to be short-lived rural organizations that eventually failed to achieve their legislative goals. Most significantly, they point to the depression of the tobacco state.[49]

Following hard upon the heels of emancipation, and under the impetus of consistently low agricultural prices, the Patrons of Husbandry became increasingly popular in the Virginia tobacco region. In

July 1872 the Patrons were organized and by the end of the following year were sweeping through the western and southern states.[50] The Patrons also rushed tobacco Virginia. At the statewide organization of the Grange in Richmond on December 29, 1873, around 45 percent of the subordinate Granges hailed from the tobacco belt.[51]

During the following twelve months this rural protest movement spread rapidly throughout the region. This growth was undoubtedly promoted by existing hard rural times. But its regional prominence can only be explained by the particular challenges facing tobacco producers for whom free labor, depressed prices, and a contested legislature made collective organization imperative. In March 1874 there were forty-two Granges in the state, many of which were located in tobacco Virginia.[52] In April the establishment of the Patrons of Husbandry was reported from Louisa County.[53] By the end of the spring there were ninety-two Granges in the state headed by local deputies and divided into distinct districts. The following months saw further local Grange organization in Prince Edward, Buckingham, and Appomattox Counties. In August 1874 increased Grange activity was reported from Pittsylvania and Henry Counties.[54]

Regional Grange organization continued unabated the following season. On January 1, 1875, at the zenith of the movement, around one-quarter of local Granges in the state were located in the tobacco southside. There were more Granges in Halifax and Pittsylvania Counties than in any other Virginia counties except Augusta in the central valley region.[55] Some proponents of the Grange did not appear averse to learning from the cooperative actions of the freedpeople. H. W. Cosby wrote "A Letter from Halifax," which was subsequently published in the *Southern Planter and Farmer*. After reiterating the various ills facing Virginia farmers, such as "Does Farming Pay?," "The Labor Question," "The Dog Question," and the "Fence Law" question, Cosby proposed that the solution lay in organization. The organization was the "Grangers"; the collective example was provided by the Negro. "We have," Cosby wrote, "long *begged* for our rights— let us now in *solid column demand* them! 'In Union there is strength!' This is the colored man's secret. Let them agree on any measure, and they are *one* for that measure. Let us take a lesson. Let us but *unite*, let us resolve to put our hands to the plow, to have more confidence in each other, and to make our old mother state the 'State of States' she used to be."[56] Meanwhile the *Southern Planter and Farmer* continued to report as well as encourage Grange activity. By January 1876 there were some 685 Granges in Virginia with a membership of 18,783.[57]

One of the indisputable points concerning the Virginia Grange was its planter leadership. This was hardly surprising, considering that planters had provided the state's political and cultural leadership for so long. Prominent early members were J. W. White, William Taylor, and Lewis E. Harvie. In 1875 M. W. Hazelwood of Richmond became secretary. Other active members were Franklin Stearns, W. H. Mann, C. T. Sutherlin, B. B. Douglass, Mann Page, J. M. Blanton, R. R. Farr, and William Ambler.[58] Frank G. Ruffin was a member of this patrician elite; he also edited the *Southern Planter and Farmer* during the Grange's zenith year of 1875. Planter leadership was particularly strong from the tobacco belt. During the spring of 1874 Robert Hubard, one of the most influential tobacco planters in Buckingham County, became an official of the Farmville Grange in Prince Edward County; he later went on to assume the leadership of the Buckingham County Grange.[59] In August 1874 leading tobacco planter Peter Hairston became master of the Grange in Henry County. Other prominent tobacco planters who played leading parts in local and state Granger activities included R. V. Gaines from Charlotte County as well as leaf planter/manufacturer William T. Sutherlin from Pittsylvania County.[60]

Less comment has been made concerning the rank-and-file majority of those 18,000 Grange members. Many were cast into the circulating net of the *Southern Planter and Farmer*. They constituted the backbone of the Grange and were probably exemplified by George Hunt. Born on April 27, 1836, Hunt went on to pursue small-scale farming before the war. On March 12, 1862, he enlisted at York as a private in Company K of the Third Virginia Calvary. He was captured soon after, spent the remainder of the war at the Union prison camp of Fort Delaware, and eventually was paroled on June 26, 1865. He managed to buy some 240 acres of cheap land. By the early 1870s he was engaged in small-scale farming. He hired one freedboy and employed occasional wage labor on an annual basis. Throughout the agricultural season he regularly contracted with numerous freedpeople to work his fields for daily, weekly, or monthly cash. Hunt was hard hit by the 1873 financial panic because both cash and hired labor were scarce. He received reduced prices for his 1873 tobacco crop. This was the context for Hunt joining his local Grange.[61]

According to his daily diary Hunt attended his first local Grange meeting at the residence of J. J. Homer on December 17, 1873. His membership fee was $3.00. Ten days later he attended another Grange meeting at the home of Mr. Butcher. For the next three years Hunt was a regular, often monthly, member of the Spring Creek Grange meetings held at numerous locations, including Farmville, Prospect Depot, and members' homes throughout Prince Edward County. It is hard to learn what went on at those Grange meetings because Hunt's most frequent recordings were brief: "Went to meeting of the Spring Creek Grange" (August 25, 1875) or "Went to Grange meeting this evening" (July 21, 1877). It seems, however, that many discussions revolved around farming improvements. On April 26, 1876, members discussed ways to improve corn cultivation. Broader issues were also occasionally broached. When Dr. J. M. Blanton, master of the Virginia State Grange, and Captain J. W. White, past master of the state Grange, addressed the Spring Creek Grange meeting on February 9, 1876, they undoubtedly addressed the agricultural crisis that was approaching its third consecutive season.[62]

On March 22, 1876, Sallie Hunt accompanied her husband to a meeting of the Spring Creek Grange. Both her role and her participation went unrecorded. Clearly, males dominated the local Grange's rank and file. This was expected in a household economy that designated men as the arbiters of public, or agricultural, affairs. Women still participated in the Grange in various ways. Occasionally wives attended. Often spouses acted as local officials. Mrs. Stokes, Mrs. Edmunds, Miss Stokes, and Mrs. Meredith all officiated for the Bush and Sandy Grange in Prince Edward County. All four Grange women were probably related to male Grangers. Similarly, Mrs. Ligon, Mrs. Anderson, and Mrs. Drumeller all worked for the Farmville Grange in the same county.[63]

The Virginia Grange was primarily a rural protest movement against languishing agricultural conditions that had been sparked by the financial panic of 1873. At state and local meetings, committees were formed to pressure the general assembly for the passage of favorable transportation and immigration policies along with the regulation of fertilizer and tobacco marketing. (Presumably, these types of issues constituted the mainstay of Blanton's and White's comments at Hunt's Grange meeting.) Many of these matters were discussed and argued at local meetings. Also at these convocations various immediate attempts were made to improve agricultural conditions, including the manufacture of fertilizer along with the pursuit of cooperative selling in order to circumvent the middleman and his profits. Meetings were also occasions for the dissemination of advice literature. It is not improbable that extracts were read from the *Southern Planter and Farmer*. George Hunt listened to a discussion of corn culture at the Spring Creek Grange. The Cuckoo Grange of Louisa County drew up plans for immigration and insurance for its members. The Prospect Grange in Prince Edward County called for a bridge over the Appomattox River at Beazley's Ford to facilitate transporting farm products to market. A cooperative store opened in Farmville to reduce the price of sugar, although it was soon closed for unexplained reasons.[64]

A specific collective concern of these Granges was opposition to what one authority referred to as the "oppression of unequal legislation, both state and national." This inequality was particularly apparent in the postemancipation and depressed tobacco economy. Many Granges, for instance, opposed the demise of the state tobacco inspection system. We have already seen how numerous public meetings were held in tobacco Virginia to rally against the iniquities of the Richmond merchants. The Farmville District Grange publicly recorded its support of the inspection system. It also opposed the conversion of public into private warehouses, since this would increase sales charges, and criticized hazy legislation that facilitated such transfers. Similarly, at the planters' convention at Burkeville, Nottoway County, held in September 1875 to discuss the inspection laws, members expressed a clear animus toward free tobacco marketing in general and the Richmond tobacco exchange in particular.[65]

This expression of Grange opposition to burgeoning marketing arrangements was especially apparent in southern tobacco Virginia. During the early 1870s the tobacco warehouse interests of Danville, Pittsylvania County, had established uniform sales charges. Particularly influential in setting this rate was the Tobacco Association, an umbrella organization loosely representing Danville warehousemen. This new collective became an obvious target in the prevailing antimonopoly climate. Between March and September 1874 the local Grange forced a reduction in warehouse sales commissions from 3 percent to 2.5 percent. This success was temporary, however, since the Tobacco Association managed to reestablish the old rate. Only Graves's warehouse, one of the earliest and presumably more established Danville leaf dealers, successfully resisted the Tobacco Association's regulations.[66]

It was directly out of this conflict between tobacco planters and dealers over commission rates that the Patrons of Husbandry decided to circumvent the middlemen through the creation of their own institutions. On March 25, 1875, the general assembly granted a charter to the Border Grange Warehouse and Supply Company of Danville. This leaf marketing organization was started by eighteen Grangers and led by prominent tobacco planter and manufacturer William T. Sutherlin. Its capitalization ranged from $5,000 to $120,000 and was issuable in transferable shares of $20 each. Sutherlin was also instrumental in the creation of the Border Grange Bank of Danville, whose capital stock ranged between $50,000 and $500,000 and was geared exclusively toward providing credit and independent funding for planter and farmer interests in southern tobacco Virginia.[67]

If some Grange members struggled to retain a benevolent state tobacco inspector, those same Grangers consistently supported the legislative struggle for the reduction of the federal tax on tobacco. During the Civil War manufactured tobacco had been taxed by Congress as an emergency revenue measure. Its lucrativeness, along with weakened southern political opposition in Congress, ensured its postwar continuation. On June 2, 1872, Congress enacted a new tobacco tax of $25, which was to be levied on all tobacco dealers effective July 1. Thus, virtually every aspect of the tobacco economy was under taxation.[68]

The contours of planter and farmer opposition to the federal tobacco tax followed the axis of tobacco Republicanism. This opposition was multidimensional and was expressed in several major arenas. The *Southern Planter and Farmer* was in the forefront with a concerted press campaign against the tax. In an 1872 editorial, "The New Tobacco Tax," John W. Rison and L. R. Dickinson criticized this new burden on an already overburdened tobacco Virginia.[69] In a long article published in the early fall of 1876, Virginia congressman John R. Tucker provided an "explanation of what it [the tobacco tax]" meant to *Southern Planter and Farmer* readers. He placed the inequalities of the tobacco tax on planters within a national context of revenue seeking by interests hostile to tobacco Virginia.[70] A year later an editorial examined another aspect of the tobacco tax that was destroying poor-grade tobacco manufacturing in Richmond.[71] *Southern Planter and Farmer* editorials continued to bemoan the deleterious effects of the infamous tax on tobacco.[72]

This opposition to the federal tobacco tax found its most public expression in the general assembly. Fueled by Jeffersonian republicanism, which differentiated between the benign state (which included militias and inspections) and the malign state (which included taxes and federal agencies), the general assembly called for a reduction of the tobacco tax for rural producers.[73] Two years later the state legislature called for a uniform tobacco tax in place of the existing graded tobacco tax.[74] (This latter measure was presumably strongly supported by warehousemen, who could use it to facilitate the eventual abolition of inspection.) This legislative pressure, however, was further fueled by depressed agricultural conditions. During the mid-1870s a systematic legislative campaign was waged through the general assembly that was dominated by the call for either reduction or repeal of the federal tax, especially on manufactured tobacco. In 1875 the general assembly issued a call to prevent the increase in the tax on manufactured tobacco from twenty cents to twenty-four cents per pound.[75] In 1877 there was a call for the reduction of the federal tax on manufactured tobacco from twenty-four cents to twelve cents per pound.[76] In 1879 the call was for tobacco tax reduction to sixteen cents per pound.[77] By 1882 the demand was for the abolition of the tax on manufactured tobacco altogether.[78] The important point about this state opposition to federal tobacco tax was that although it was representative of broader tobacco interests in the state as suggested by its legislative language of "culture & manufacture," the ultimate beneficiaries were the warehousemen rather than the planters and farmers.

The anti–tobacco tax campaign was even waged through the hallowed halls and smokeless committee rooms of Congress itself. In 1876–77 a congressional committee chaired by John R. Tucker of Virginia investigated the tobacco economy and delivered an exhaustive report on the federal tobacco tax. The committee identified a shift in the imposition of the federal tax from northern manufacturers to western and southern tobacco-growing states. It argued that Virginia's federal tax burden had shot from $1.9 million in 1867 to $7.6 million in 1872. In the mid-1870s the current federal tax on tobacco was twenty-four cents per pound. The committee endorsed the state legislature's call for a reduction to sixteen cents per pound. This would aid, it was argued, the manufacturer, producer, and consumer especially in such times of agricultural distress.[79]

The success of this systematic protest in tobacco Virginia was certainly mixed. Virginia Grangers did assist in some legislative successes: the appointment in 1873 of a state chemist to inspect fertilizer quality, the appointment in 1877 of a railroad commissioner to regulate transportation, and the creation of the Virginia Department of Agriculture, also in 1877. The Grange movement was less successful in its other objectives for regulating the tobacco economy. It did not succeed in saving state tobacco inspection. Furthermore, the reduction in the federal tobacco tax benefited urban more than rural tobacco concerns.[80] Indeed, rural protest from the Grange had all but declined by 1877, although it sputtered on somewhat afterward. George Hunt halted his regular attendance in 1878 when he only attended the Spring Creek Grange twice during the entire year. His last recorded meeting was in early 1879; he simply noted, "Went to Grange."[81]

While George Hunt joined his local Grange in an attempt to ameliorate postemancipation and depressed agricultural conditions, a very different response was being articulated some fifty miles away in Richmond. During the mid-1870s John Ott, the secretary of the SFC, wrote several pamphlets on the tobacco economy. This corpus of work provides a veritable mine of information on related themes: the historical significance of tobacco to Virginia; the existing global, national, and regional tobacco trade; modern tobacco farming methods; and the nature of postemancipation social conditions. The pamphlets also explore the adaptation of scientific analysis to tobacco cultivation. Their most interesting feature, however, is their intersection between past thoughts, contemporary challenges, and future projections. They were particularly eloquent on the ideological significance of the dialectic between emancipation, agricultural depression, and a changing tobacco economy.[82]

John Ott, a native of Maryland, was formerly employed by the federal treasury until 1861. When war broke out between the states, he resigned and joined the Confederate treasury. After the war he worked for a bank in Richmond. Ott joined the SFC as its secretary in 1872. This fertilizer company had set up shop in Richmond in February 1866, the same month the state agricultural society reconvened. Hoping to cash in on the "demoralized" nature of postemancipation farming, the SFC specialized in the production and promotion of fertilizers for cash crops such as tobacco, cotton, and wheat. Its key product was the Anchor Brand of fertilizer. Ott became this particular product's promoter as well as company salesman. He might also have served temporarily as the associate editor of the *Southern Planter and Farmer*. It was from such commanding heights that Ott produced his corpus during the mid-1870s.[83]

On February 27, 1875, the SFC published a thirty-two-page pamphlet laboriously titled *Tobacco: The Outlook in America for 1875; Production, Consumption and Movement in the United States, the German Empire, Hungary, Turkey, Cuba, Brazil, Japan, and the other Tobacco-growing Countries*. It offered some basic statistical generalizations concerning the U.S. tobacco trade over the previous four years that pointed to global tobacco domination by the United States, the country's prolific export business, its important but smaller manufacturing consumption of leaf, and the primacy of plug and chewing among indigenous tobacco manufacturers. The pamphlet further provided a remarkable sketch of the global tobacco economy, including the activities of thirty-seven countries and the extent of their production, tobacco prices, leaf types, export/import returns, and general marketing practices. Although it concluded that U.S. global tobacco leadership remained intact, it also pointed to some disturbing trends on the horizon. These included global competition as well as shifting consumer choices.[84]

Most disturbing was the problem of free labor. Ott concluded his account with a "FEW WORDS to our YOUNG MEN" on the "Question of Farm Labor." There are some encouraging words on the potential of postemancipation Virginia, especially to those prepared to work. He left the central advice to Major Robert L. Ragland on the best way to manage free labor on the farm. Ragland advocated a series of proposals. The proprietor must provide "vigilant supervision." There should be close management of Negro labor. Annual hiring of "good, steady men with families" was best. Paternal management whereby kindness and firmness "begets a *home* interest and local attachment" was deemed the most efficacious. The old squad system of labor under the foreman worked well. He concluded, "When properly hired and paid, when justly treated, efficiently managed, and judiciously worked, [the Negro] IS THE BEST LABORER we can get on the plantations formerly cultivated by slave labor." The science of craniology was enlisted to support the necessity of Negro management: Negroes had smaller brains, were backward, and had no history. The notion of comparative emancipation was also invoked in which the freeing of the Russian serfs compared favorably to the more recent Negro emancipation. The former "being disenthralled and of white blood, this arrangement at once developed in him self-respect as well as self-interest."[85] Clearly, the Old Dominion was not dead, at least in the minds and hearts of some of its fond recollectors.

It is important not to forget the marketing nature of Ott's pamphleteering. This was made more evident just over a year later when he followed up his first pamphlet with a second twenty-two-page brochure tendentiously titled *The Position Tobacco Has Ever Held as the Chief Source of Wealth to Virginia*, published on March 20, 1876. It began with a "review of tobacco in old times," sketching the origins, management, regulation, currency, and marketing of tobacco from colonial settlement to the Revolution. The second section traced the story from the Revolution until 1875. Special emphasis here was on statistical generalizations about the extent of the export trade. The concluding section dealt with the "Present Outlook." Tobacco's importance to Virginia was stressed throughout—from the leaf's earliest days as legal tender to the state's contemporary "chief reliance" on it as the leading cash crop. Indeed, the tobacco leadership of both the United States and Virginia seemed to be confirmed from sources as diverse as London operator Bremner, whose work showed "American tobacco has emphatically been 'king,'" to the U.S. Internal Revenue Service, whose figures promised "remunerative returns." Tobacco was still king. It defined the life and culture of the Old Dominion and continued to do so into the postwar decade.[86]

But Ott's second pamphlet also pointed to some worrisome trends. The old town/country conflict still plagued postemancipation Virginia, as did its colonial status. Virginia was still "too much the vassal of the people north of the Potomac." Furthermore, burgeoning western tobacco competition had reduced the state's former unrivaled position: "Whereas Virginia, less than a century ago, produced the bulk of tobacco produced in this country, now she has a rival in Kentucky, Tennessee, Missouri, and the country north of the Ohio, not only respectable in the matter of quality, but exceedingly so in the direction of quantity." All was not lost, however. If Virginia provided the human seeds for western tobacco cultivation after the Revolution, it could also learn from their more efficient progeny. "When we consider," Ott noted,

> the efforts being made in Kentucky, Tennessee and Missouri, to produce an article equal to that of Virginia and North Carolina, we cannot flag in our resolution to bring ours "fully up to the standard." We must not allow our strong fortress to be taken; so what we plant this Spring, let it be cultivated and manured so thoroughly as to command its just due, the "very top of the market." We speak, of course, to white men. Since the negroes have been freed, too many of them refuse to work as laborers, but desire to take land "on shares." This has had, and will continue to have, the effect of throwing on the market innumerable small crops; and nothing but the most careful and faithful assortment by warehousemen will keep the general range on a basis of reasonable uniformity. Without this is [*sic*] done, the market is bound to be demoralized.[87]

These words provide an eloquent link between western competition, quality production, and the challenge of emancipation. Ott's final words were positively Shakespearean as he invoked the historical memory of "those ties of brotherhood that should characterize men who stood shoulder to shoulder in a struggle, by the side of which the Revolution was as 'child's play.'"[88] Of course, demoralized markets, just like demoralized labor, were postwar realities that no amount of contrary wishful thinking could obviate—not even that of marketers of Anchor fertilizer.

Ott's final contribution was a thirty-nine page pamphlet simply called *Tobacco in Virginia and North Carolina*, published in 1877. Its several sections described the global tobacco trade, the iniquitous federal tax system, and cigar cultivation and included numerous tobacco planter endorsements for Anchor Brand fertilizer. Most importantly, emancipation, free labor, and the Negro tenant's poor tobacco production had glutted the marketplace. "With so much of our crop now in the hands of negroes, as tenant farmers," Ott argued, "the market is bound to show a considerable quantity of indifferent Tobacco, but the white men, whether large or small farmers, having the requisite intelligence and skill, have it in their power, the season all favoring, to bring a handsome result." Yet Ott's own analysis eloquently demonstrated that the changing nature of the tobacco economy, especially western competition and transportation developments, was primarily responsible for declining tobacco prices in the region. Freedpeople's tobacco farming had little to do with crop quality and all to do with emancipation. Its limitations could best be explained by an older dominion.[89]

The seeds of the *Southern Planter and Farmer* and SFC emancipation critique sprouted in the pages of subsequent federal investigations into the Virginia tobacco economy. In his thorough 1879 special report, federal investigator Joseph B. Killebrew stated that "the tobacco grown in most sections of this state has deteriorated in quality." The general reasons were simple enough: the "agricultural depression, low prices, and the scarcity of skilled labor have discouraged farmers; less fertilizers are used; less pains are taken, and the condition of the soil has been steadily declining for several years." Free labor, however, was the major culprit. "The old 'hands,'" Killebrew wrote, "trained in the operations of priming, topping, assorting, and the various details of cultivation and management, are dying out, and the younger generation is decidedly inferior to the old as trained and skilled laborers." One major problem was tenancy. "Tenants, the majority of whom are negroes, raise as a rule, an inferior grade, which is forced into market through local dealers in an unfit condition." The problem was especially acute in Lunenburg County, where the bulk of the tobacco crop was "grown by colored people, inexperienced and unskilled, who pay but little attention to the management of their tobacco."[90] Much like Ott before him and Benjamin Arnold after him, Killebrew claimed that emancipation was the primary cause of the decline of tobacco Virginia.

The real problem, of course, was more complex. Emancipation had subtly shifted social relations from the subordination of slavery to the semiautonomy of free labor. This entailed a reduction in labor supervision that was antithetical to those reared on the necessity of close Negro management. Tobacco Virginia's depression during the 1870s only seemed to confirm these traditional views. What was needed was the readjustment of free labor to meet these twin pressures. It is that legal-political struggle, both within and outside the tobacco fields, to which we now turn.

CHAPTER SIX

Readjusting Free Labor Relations, 1873–1889

Deed: Thomas Flournoy to Sills & Son: "crop of tobacco"
Lien: Sam White (col.) to J. W. Green: "all crops 1877."
—Brunswick County Court, 1875–77

Where land owner contracts with one to crop his land
and to give him part of the crop after paying all advances, and the crop has not been divided, such cropper
is not a tenant, but a mere employe, and the ownership
of the entire crop is in the landowner, and if cropper forc-
ibly, or against consent of land owner, takes the crop
from the possession of the latter, such taking is larceny,
robbery, or other offence, according to the circumstances
of the case.—Virginia Supreme Court, 1884

Synor Johns, on the 6th day of October 1885, in the said
county [Lunenburg] three hundred pounds of tobacco of
the value of five dollars of the goods and chattels of one
Zebulon Williams, then and there being found, un-
lawfully did steal, take and carry away.
—Lunenburg County Court, 1886

On Saturday afternoon, November 3, 1883, a major altercation occurred on the politically tense streets of Danville, Pittsylvania County,
in the tobacco southside. The ensuing race riot resulted in the deaths
of four black men and one white man. This was the bloody climax to a
decade-long political struggle over payment of the state's public debt
between the Funders, who desired immediate payment, and the Read-

justers, who wanted partial settlement. The riot also marked the end of the four-year reign of a Readjuster-Republican coalition that had attempted to reconstruct state politics since 1879. The Conservative Democrats, much as in 1869, were once again ushered in to redeem the Old Dominion.[1]

Just over a year later, on November 28, 1884, the Virginia Supreme Court sitting in Richmond delivered its majority opinion in *Parrish v. The Commonwealth.* The state's highest appellate court had to decide a crop settlement dispute originating some twenty months earlier that had resulted in a farmer's death and a lower court's indictment of the landlord for murder. Property owners, the supreme court ruled, had the ultimate right of protection over their own property. Furthermore, landlords were determined to be independent managers who had priority ownership of their crops until settlement time. Finally, sharecroppers were neither tenants nor share managers but simply employees who were to be compensated by their employer at his discretion after the division of the crops.[2]

The quiet deliberations of the Richmond court have attracted far less attention from historians than the more tumultuous events in Danville. Yet this legal decision had an important impact on the evolution of free labor relations, particularly in the Virginia tobacco region. Rather than posit some scale of importance for either riot or law—a ranking both specious as well as impossible to substantiate—this chapter argues that the 1884 state supreme court decision capped a decade-long struggle to readjust the law of free labor in favor of landlords and employers. Crop lien laws, together with legal distinctions between tenants and laborers, attempted to shackle free labor to the land with its profits to landlords and employers. The *Parrish* appeal was attractive in the tobacco region, especially the bright belt, which was disproportionately characterized by tenant relations and problematic relationships between capital and labor. Free laborers in the Virginia tobacco region, however, did not desist in protesting against these new regulations.[3]

The Funder/Readjuster debate in Virginia during the 1870s did highlight an important postwar reality—namely, that Civil War, defeat, devastation, and abolition wrought a credit crisis for the state. Planter capital, especially land whose value had been largely determined by slave ownership, had been significantly reduced. (Although there was

READJUSTING FREE LABOR RELATIONS

not an immediate cash lacuna, since tobacco sold quite well after the war, this was soon terminated by prolonged agricultural depression.) The tobacco economy was marked by a credit shortfall because much like other staple crop regions in the postemancipation South, its traditional collateral basis had been destroyed. Consequently, there emerged a system of engaging in a lien on the prospective crop as a means of encouraging agricultural production. The freedpeople would provide landlords and employers with a season's labor in exchange for supplies, tools, and some form of compensation; landlords and employers obtained a lien on this future crop produced by agricultural laborer. What began simply enough under the BRFAL soon evolved into a struggle over the control and dispensation of the crop and especially the control of free labor.[4]

Although the crop lien system emerged out of specific postemancipation conditions, it is important not to forget its broader historical dimensions. Chattel slavery had been an old system of involuntary human credit; nascent postemancipation free labor arrangements invariably entailed the freedpeople crediting their employers with a season's labor before they were eventually remunerated.[5] It was the resulting tensions over the dispensation of this burgeoning credit system that drew extensive commentary in BRFAL official's monthly reports from the field. If labor contracts offered one form of federal lien, landlord-employer duplicity occasionally merited the BRFAL suggestion that liens be passed that favored protection of the freedmen's labor. Similarly, chaotic free market conditions encouraged some employers to pursue provision debt peonage as a way to retain control over the real and potential mobility of "their" free laborers. The seasonal climax of this tension occurred during settlement time.[6]

Even the federal government's withdrawal did not ease free labor relations and address the difficulties of agricultural reorganization. An anonymous report on Virginia agriculture published by the USDA in 1870 summarized, "Throughout the tobacco region the crop is cultivated on nearly every farm, to a large extent by freedmen on rented land or on shares."[7] Lien arrangements, credit provisions, and share and crop disputes continued to earmark the agricultural calendar. The literature of agricultural advice highlighted these tensions.[8] As one *Southern Planter and Farmer* editorial opined in early 1873, "So much has been written and said about farm labor during the past four or five years, that, but for the fact that the subject is brought home to every one almost every day, we would let it rest for the present." It added, "The season of the year is approaching, when, if we intend to do anything, we must have help." The *Southern Planter and Farmer*'s immediate solution was prompt payment of the "colored population."[9] Such seemingly sensible advice, however, was undermined by the postemancipation realities of credit shortage, the freedpeople's potential mobility in an emergent free labor market, and older ideas of strict labor management. In short, the early 1870s continued to reflect unsettled free labor relations in Virginia.[10]

The first crop lien law of Virginia was passed on April 2, 1873. It consisted of three parts. The opening section described the nature of the crop lien: "Any person or persons" who "shall make any advance or advances, either in money or supplies," to anyone "engaged in, or . . . about to engage in the cultivation of the soil . . . shall be entitled to a lien on the crops which may be made during the year upon the land in cultivation." A written agreement had to be entered "before any such advance is made" and duly recorded in the "clerk's office of the county." Section 2 guaranteed the lien against premature settlement by the laborer. Persons who received such advances who "sell or dispose of said crops, without having paid or secured to be paid such advance or advances" or in any way "defeat the lien herein-before provided for" would be liable to the legal jurisdiction of either the county court, "any judge thereof in vacation," or "courts of equity." The final section prioritized the landlord's rent over the crop lien. The lien would not affect "in any manner the rights of landlords to their proper share of rents, or rights of distress, nor any liens existing."[11]

Many of these written agreements were recorded in the clerk's office of Brunswick County court in the tobacco southside. Their making became especially marked with the onset of agricultural depression. For the 1875 season the county clerk recorded ten "lien deeds" in which laborers received some form of credit or supplies from creditors in exchange for either "all his crops" or the "crop of tobacco." In June George Pelham gave the lien of "all his crops" to Valentine K. Allen, while the following month Thomas Flournoy legally promised his "crop of tobacco" to Sills and Son.[12] These lien deals doubled in number to twenty the following season. In the spring of 1876 O. A. Harrison signed over his tobacco and corn crops to Christopher

Jameson, while in September William Hellagner promised his tobacco crop to E. A. Christopher. Some liens were even greater. Freedman Ben Johnson signed a lien with W. F. Hobbs Sr. for his kitchen furniture as well as his crop.[13] The link between hard times and lien arrangements became acute during the difficult season of 1877. The county clerk recorded forty-seven "lien deeds" for the year. These included freedman Lewis Thrower to J. P. Wray for "all crops 1877" and freedman Sam White to J. W. Green for "all crops 1877." Lien making was especially prevalent around settlement time. There were sixteen lien deeds made in September for the 1877 crop, suggesting that the need for credit and its availability were strongest in the face of the impending harvest.[14]

This crop lien law was primarily designed to control free labor in the interests of landlords. It was, however, ambiguous enough to allow for the protection of alternative claims, especially those of merchant suppliers. Several months after the law's passage, the New York financial system collapsed, ushering in prolonged depression. The subsequent financial squeeze further justified the necessity for some means of collateral exchange. But it also paved the way for alternative credit sources. These were provided by local country merchants. The first section of the 1873 crop lien law legally protected the rights of merchant suppliers. If the landlord did not write out the lien agreement or have it recorded in the local court, then a merchant who had supplied the tenant gained prior access to the lien. Because of postemancipation conditions whereby credit was scarce, the law understandably did not stipulate that landlords were to be the sole source of credit.[15]

Unlike other cash crop plantation regions in the postwar South, landlords and employers in the Virginia tobacco belt do not appear to have faced either mercantile territorial monopolies or organized merchant challenges to their power during the 1870s.[16] Indeed, the *Southern Planter and Farmer*'s virtual silence on rural mercantilism greatly contrasts with its indictment of the challenges wrought by urban tobacco merchants. The prevalence of tenancy and the seriousness of the credit shortage nevertheless entailed the movement of some rural merchants and country stores into the lien business. Some of the lien deeds made in Brunswick County during the mid-1870s were probably with merchants.[17] Indeed, the eastern tobacco southside had many stores.[18] H. W. Taylor, from Brunswick County, received one half-ton of fertilizers worth $21.25 from Allison & Addison of Petersburg in exchange for a "lien upon all crops upon the land upon which said fertilizer used." The legal guarantee was the 1873 lien law.[19] These alternative credit suppliers posed the potential struggle between landlords and merchants for control over free labor.

One landlord from Fluvanna County explained the nature of this local conflict. Anonymous planter C.S.T. wrote to the *Southern Planter and Farmer* strongly castigating the omnipresent tenant system for being "radically wrong." Tenant farming required skills that "every negro thinks he can do, and the landowners concede it, or admit their inability to do better, by allowing them to try it." The result of "negro tenancy" was poor farming, neglected fields, and "ragged, worm-eaten, bruised, broken and badly handled" tobacco worth little at market. Negroes were fit for only laboring and not management. They were a "lazy, shiftless set," inhabiting "lonely hollows" whose primary activities were subsistence and stealing. Their theft was facilitated by avaricious country merchants blamable for "much of the petty pilfering" because they traded for anything and with anyone.[20]

Of course, this criticism provided eloquent commentary on a landlord used to stricter labor management; it also inadvertently outlined a different agenda pursued by the freedpeople. Hard agricultural times facilitated theft, which itself was facilitated by the trading activities of local rural merchants. It was, however, the relationship between tenancy and mercantilism that proved especially conflictual. C.S.T. employed two to four "tenants" who controlled six to ten "good average hands." The landlord provided all the provisions because the laborers had only their labor power. The arrangement seemed to have worked well. In 1876 the laborers "made bargains with a merchant to open accounts with them." Soon, C.S.T. reported, the laborers ran up "pretty large accounts" and began "to take things into their own hands." Although a settlement was eventually made at the end of the season, C.S.T. complained that the laborers "have made accounts with merchants without any reference to me, and have shown little regard for me in any way." Worse still, "they are disposed to run as long accounts as possible on it; while by a disregard of the management and system by which it was secured they fail to meet their obligations as before."[21]

Negro improvidence was the traditional explanation. BRFAL officials

FIG. 6.1. Crop lien for fertilizer, 1882 (Lunenburg County Court Judgments, 1885–89, box 1, VL)

had drawn attention to this unfortunate trait of the freedpeople, as did C.S.T. But this *Southern Planter and Farmer* article captures an important point about the specific nature of the contestation over credit. The freedpeople utilized the credit relationship between landlord and merchant to seek semiautonomy from their employers' control. In the process their semiautonomy became a wedge opening older systems of control. Thus "improvident negroes" became freedpeople struggling for autonomy through their use of the credit system. If improvidence was the landlords' problem, it could also be the freedpeople's solution to their free labor problem.[22] This was a much quieter rural version of the urban struggle over marketing between planters and warehousemen in the postemancipation Virginia tobacco region.

The tobacco landlords lost their battle with the warehousemen, but they won the struggle over credit arrangements in the countryside. Any concerted effort on the part of merchants for protection of their supplies was thwarted by the passage of the second crop lien law in early March 1882. If the first crop lien law protected landlords against tenants, the second further buttressed their position with additional protection against the claims of merchants. Unlike its earlier cousin, Chapter 230 of the *Acts of the General Assembly* had only one section. It stipulated that "any person or persons, being owners or occupiers of land," who made advances "either in money or supplies, to such person or persons so contracting to cultivate such land," would be "entitled to a lien on the crops which may be made during the year." This "lien shall be prior to all other liens on such a crop." The law prioritized the landlord's lien and dropped the requirement for written contracts (and presumably the need for registration in the local county court). The merchant's lien was inferior to the landlord's for both rent and advances even if it had been entered before that of the landlord. The legally recorded contract, while favoring landlords, at least left some basis for dispute and legal redress. The verbal contract, however, closed this option altogether.[23]

The efficacy of this legislation was the merger of mercantilism with landlord interests especially through the consolidation of the plantation store in tobacco Virginia. Philip A. Bruce, in his 1889 publication *The Plantation Negro as a Freeman*, noted the importance of this merger in the tobacco southside. Negro improvidence, he observed, was catered to by the merchant "who has a store in the immediate neighborhood" and acts "as the disbursing agent of the property-owners of the community." This role was critical to the smooth operation of the plantation, especially in establishing control over free labor relations. "The storekeeper," Bruce continued, "who is lax in granting credit to the negroes, is not only considered by the planters to be ignorant of the requirements of his business, but is also regarded as more or less an undesirable member of the community, since his conduct is likely to increase the restlessness of the laborers by creating a definite reason why they should wish to leave the neighborhood." In short, the landlord's territorial monopoly was legally protected by crop lien laws.[24]

If crop lien laws were much to the landlord's credit, the landlord's

READJUSTING FREE LABOR RELATIONS

property in the crop was still contested terrain with laborers. The appeal of *Parrish* settled, at least legally, this thorny free labor problem.

In January 1882 Andrew J. Mitchell, his wife Zanee Mitchell, and their five young children moved onto land belonging to Alexander L. Parrish in Goochland County in central Virginia.[25] The Mitchell household owned only one cow and two hogs. Their new landlord, a farmer and schoolteacher by profession, furnished the virtually propertyless Mitchells with corn to eat, wool with which to make clothes, and hay for their livestock. On February 3, 1882, Parrish and Mitchell engaged in a written contract for the ensuing agricultural season. The landlord agreed to "furnish land and team and give said Mitchell half of the crops he cultivates." In exchange the tenant was to take good care of the team and tools, "cultivate and secure the crops well," and maintain the pasture fence for "the pasturage of his cow." All the supplies and extra labor that "Parrish may employ in the cultivation and securing of said crop," along with one shilling costs for boarding "hands so employed," were to be met by the landlord and deducted from the tenant's share of the crop. Parrish was to be responsible for marketing the crop, keeping his half of the crop and "pay[ing] him [Mitchell] the balance." The landlord also agreed to provide Mitchell with corn for his family at $4 per barrel as well as oat and corn seed. The contract was signed by Parrish, thumbmarked by Mitchell, and witnessed by Virginia A. Parrish, the landlord's wife.[26]

The 1882 agricultural season was the usual demanding one for rural producers such as the Mitchell household. There was corn to plant, harvest, and shuck; tobacco to hill, transplant, top, worm, sucker, cut, and house; and sundry other tasks, including tending livestock, repairing fencing, and stocking the icehouse. Since the Mitchell household was free to labor only without any additional means of support, they were forced to rely on their landlord for the provision of a constant stream of supplies. In a special ledger Parrish kept a meticulous account of these supplies and other items along with their prices. Basic subsistence items such as corn, wheat, peas, potatoes, and oats were regularly furnished. On March 30 the Mitchell household received one-third of a barrel of corn costing $1.33, while on August 16 the family obtained bacon for 36 cents. Other items were recorded in Parrish's account book, including the work of casual day laborers on the crop. For instance, laborer William Yancey, who "was the only person on besides the family," did 25 cents worth of work on April 8, 20 cents on May 19, and 30 cents on July 19. Yancey's boarding bill was 20 cents on May 31 and 17 cents on July 12. Mitchell was also charged for processing his cereals "going to the mill twice" on May 27, costing 25 cents. Other expenses were incurred for washed wool, honey and coffee, oat seed, and carting. Mitchell's tobacco (chewing) cost him 8 cents on July 15. By November 8, 1882, Parrish had carefully tabulated that Mitchell owed him $84.86, plus 20 cents for medicine. Most of this amount was for corn and meal ($37.82), labor on the crop ($10.34), wheat and flour ($9.81), and cash and orders ($9.50).[27]

The landlord's meticulous credit accounting was perhaps a little too precise for the likes of his tenant. Sometime during the second week of November 1882, when Mitchell was busy shucking the corn, Parrish presented him with the itemized account. Mitchell's response was later recorded as being that he "would be damned if he would pay it." He thought the account was too high and that the landowner should pay it out of his own share of the crop. Mitchell was probably particularly incensed that the season's hard labor promised little actual return and the possibility of debt. The situation was exacerbated by the incompatibility between the cost of supplies and limited agricultural production that did not cover the expenses. The total corn crop amounted to around 31 barrels, while 7,500 tobacco plants raised on 1.5 acres produced 898 pounds whose eventual market price was $18.86. Clearly, both the supplies and labor costs exceeded the crop value; the point in dispute was whose share was to be affected.[28]

Over the next several days both parties appear to have consulted lawyers as to their best course of action. Parrish was counseled to take out either a peace or distress warrant against Mitchell because it was later recorded "he anticipated some trouble." The local constable, J. J. Cheatwood, was unable to meet the request because the local justice of the peace, R. S. Saunders, was not available to sign the warrant. Meanwhile, Mitchell had been advised by Mr. Fleming, his attorney, "to get a cart to go after his corn." Following this counsel, Mitchell went after the corn, putting twenty barrels in Parrish's corn house and ten barrels in the tobacco barn and taking the last barrel for his family.

Since he had the key to the tobacco barn for hanging the tobacco, he locked the door to prevent Parrish's access. Parrish subsequently barred the door to Mitchell by nailing a plank and slat across it.[29]

The impasse reached a climax on the evening of November 18, 1882. Mitchell visited the homes of freedmen Charles Nuckols and Archer Dandridge and offered them cash to help cart the corn from the tobacco barn. Nuckols, unsure of the task at hand, visited the Parrish place to verify if the removal of the corn was legitimate. Parrish told him it was otherwise, adding that he would have Nuckols arrested if he helped Mitchell. Meanwhile Mitchell had left his house, which was about three-quarters of a mile from the tobacco barn. On the path he was met by Nuckols, holding a torch in one hand and an axe in the other. Nuckols warned Mitchell that an armed Parrish was on his way to the tobacco barn. Meanwhile Parrish, armed with a single-barrel fowling gun, went to head off Mitchell. He met Archer Dandridge, the other cartman, on his way to help Mitchell. The freedman was warned off by Parrish, his sister Virginia, and cousin Margaret. Cousin Margaret reportedly encountered Mitchell "in a violent passion, with a torch of lightwood in one hand and an *axe* in the other, and his wife and his sister-in-law *hanging on to him*," trying to restrain him. All four women attempted to dissuade him, but Mitchell declared his intention "of going into that house and getting, then and there, his corn *or die*." This invocation suggests how passionate Mitchell felt about what he considered to be his just rights of labor. His action was clearly an attempt to readjust free labor in favor of his own family.[30]

Mitchell arrived at the tobacco barn door, which he attempted to break open. Parrish, who was standing a little way off, heard the women remonstrating with Mitchell. He also heard the cracking of boards being ripped from the door. By now the torch had gone out; it was a dark night. Believing Mitchell was armed, Parrish fired in his general direction, hitting him cleanly through the armhole of his vest. Mitchell "walked from tobacco house and to where he fell" and eventually bled to death. Parrish went to his neighbor's house and explained what had happened. The neighbor, James Aldhizer, advised Parrish that he should have let Mitchell take the corn and retrieved it the next day, although Parrish thought this plan was unworkable because Mitchell already owed him some corn.[31]

The case was subsequently tried in Goochland County court,

where Parrish was indicted for murder. On December 18, 1882, a special grand jury of nine decided that the defendant "feloniously, willfully, and of his malice aforethought, did kill and murder against the peace and dignity of the Commonwealth of Virginia." Parrish was found guilty of murder in the second degree and sentenced to seven years in the penitentiary. The defendant appealed the verdict and requested a new trial in the county circuit court. After a series of delays caused by a hung jury and the difficulty of obtaining new jurors, Parrish was eventually retried in early April 1884. The original conviction was upheld, and Parrish was transported to the county jail, where he awaited the beginning of his seven-year sentence.[32] On May 27, 1884, however, the legal team of W. B. Pettit, A. K. Leake, and W. W. Cosby submitted a petition on Parrish's behalf to the Supreme Court of Appeals of Virginia based on the belief "that there is error in the judgment complained of."[33] The opinion of the state's highest judiciary finally settled *Parrish v. The Commonwealth*.[34]

It is clear that these local county jurors decided the case primarily in terms of it being an act of unlawful murder. It is also conceivable that these jurors saw the case in terms of the legal rights of a hard-working tenant deserving of the fruits of his labor. One witness for the commonwealth, Aldhizer, testified that when Parrish had visited him after killing Mitchell, the defendant had talked about "the corn,—not his [Parrish's] corn." Aldhizer added that the "Prisoner did not say it was his corn." In other words, other rural producers decided that this case amounted to more than unlawful killing. It was also about fair compensation. What is fascinating about these jury verdicts at the lower court level is that local people clearly supported Mitchell against the landlord. Their view informed their subsequent position; perhaps they were even using the legal system to readjust the law in the laborer's favor for future contractual disputes. (This makes an interesting parallel to the BRFAL's previous adjudicatory role.) Of course, the reflections of five wise men in Richmond suggest that they were very much aware of the ultimate stakes involved in this case.[35]

After six months of careful deliberation, the Virginia Supreme Court finally passed down its decision. Its summary of the case makes for interesting reading. It excluded the original testimony upon which the conviction was based and drew exclusively from the petitioners' appeal. While it provided a succinct summary of events on Parrish's place, the account is peppered with tendentious and colorful language. Parrish failed to obtain a warrant, for instance, because Mitchell "designedly and cunningly" allayed his fears. The landlord "was remote," "surrounded by a helpless family of delicate females" and aged relatives. Mitchell was in a "violent passion." It was a "dark and chilly night" when Mitchell "rushed to the tobacco door as if he would tear Parrish to pieces." The supreme court's summary also contained some dubious reasoning. Why would Parrish arm himself with a gun when Mitchell had never physically threatened Parrish? Even if he had and the threat was so great, why would Parrish then entrust his wife and cousin to prevent Mitchell from coming to the tobacco barn? Why not simply take the advice of his neighbor and wait until the morning, when he could either retrieve his corn or start legal proceedings? The court, however, decided that Parrish committed justifiable homicide in defense of himself, his house, and his property. Accordingly, the court ruled that "he acted in justifiable defense to his property, and under reasonable apprehension of the necessity to shoot the deceased to prevent great injury both to his person and his property, and that the *verdict of the jury* was not warranted by the evidence and is against the law of the case." Having spent a sleepless night after killing Mitchell, several months traipsing in and out of lower courts, and two years on remand, Parrish was free at last.[36]

More to the point was the Supreme Court's legal rationalization protecting the landlord's right to defend his property through force even to the point of justifiable homicide. The court's central proposal was its ruling for a social distinction between cropper and tenant. The contract, they argued, made Mitchell a "mere employe or cropper." Parrish had credited Mitchell with a house and land free of charge. (The farmer had not credited his employer with a season's labor.) Mitchell was entitled to nothing until Parrish was fully reimbursed. Mitchell "was therefore no *tenant*." Parrish "was to pay him for his services, and the arrangement was only a mode of paying for Mitchell's labor." The tenant was free to labor only.[37]

This finding—that the tenant was simply a laborer with no interest in either the soil or the crop and that the landlord held exclusive property in the crop—was codified with a series of supporting evidence. The work of John B. Minor, professor of law at the University of Virginia, was invoked to explain that during crop divisions, the "occupant of the land, in such a case has no *interest in the soil*, (which is necessary in order to make him *a tenant*)." The land was in the sole possession of the landowner, the parties were "*tenants in common* of the crops produced," and the arrangement was "only a mode of *paying for the labor* or services of the occupant." Theirs was not a partnership but an employer-employee relationship. The tenant's non-ownership in the crop was further substantiated through recourse to John N. Taylor's voluminous *Treatise on the American Law of Landlord and Tenant*, which clearly stated that "if land is agreed to be cultivated upon shares, it does not amount to a lease with rent to be paid in produce; for the possession of the land remains in the owner, and the parties are merely tenants in common of the crop."[38]

Along with postbellum decisions made both in and out of the state, the Virginia Supreme Court drew on antebellum cases to support its argument for readjusting free labor law. In *State v. Elias Gay*, decided in the South Carolina Supreme Court in December 1833, it was decided that the crop sharer was "not a joint tenant" since the crop was "exclusively the property of the employer." A similar decision was reached by the North Carolina Supreme Court, which ruled four years later (1837) that "the property in the entire crop is in the employer until the share of the overseer or cropper is separated from the general mass."[39] In short, the 1884 ruling determined that the crop belonged to the landlord, its management was controlled by the landlord, and its protection by the landlord was legally guaranteed by any means necessary. The legal protection of private property had a venerable past, honed in earlier periods of more stability and efficient labor management and justified by current unsettled conditions.[40]

Parrish v. The Commonwealth may be seen in many lights. Mitchell lost his life; his family lost him. What happened to Zanee and her five children? The Mitchells' neighbors, including the freedpeople, presumably continued to labor. The defendant Parrish was eventually acquitted; he rejoined his family. What about the broader significance of the case? Possibly it can be seen as an eloquent example of exploitation that went too far and cost the tenant his life. Maybe it was simply a series of unique circumstances. Undoubtedly, it offers a glimpse into the nature of contested agricultural relations. These revolved around contracting and the credit system, the nature of tenant and wage labor, and settlement disputes over crops resulting in extralegal and legal actions. Local citizens thought murder had been committed; the state supreme court decided otherwise. The case suggests the jurors were right; the justices were probably wrong in terms of simple justice but undoubtedly right in terms of protecting property with law as the ultimate legitimization of disturbed social relations. This Virginia Supreme Court decision of 1884 was the legal reflection of the politics of anti-Readjusterism and redemption that had surfaced a year earlier.[41] Most importantly, it settled the question of the protection of property and determined managerial control strictly in favor of landlords. This paved the way for the legal consolidation of a rural proletariat in the Virginia tobacco region. This was the *real* Parrish appeal.

The passage of crop lien laws together with the state supreme court ruling ensured that out of free labor relations there emerged the legal consolidation of an agricultural proletariat in the Virginia tobacco region. These new laws readjusted free labor as a social relationship of exploitation whereby rural laborers, whether working for cash or shares, were reduced to employees engaged in exchanging their labor for some form of compensation. Some historians have restricted their definition of modern or capitalist agriculture to cash compensation. This one-dimensional definition of capitalist agriculture as simply laboring for cash is jettisoned here for a broader definition in which law was used to fashion a new rural proletariat consisting of wage laborers, share laborers, and, increasingly, tenant farmers in the Virginia tobacco belt.[42]

Wage labor relations were not insignificant in 1870s Virginia. According to the third annual report of the state commissioner of agriculture, published in 1879, agricultural laborers received wages averaging around $100 annually or $7–$8.50 monthly in most counties. The lowest wages were paid by employers in the southside area, where rural workers often received around $60 for their season's labor or as little as $5 monthly.[43] Federal investigator Joseph Killebrew reported that field workers in the tobacco area received $5 to $10 monthly with board, while during the busy season these laborers earned from 40 to 60 cents daily.[44] These wages for agricultural work were among the lowest in the state; they also compared unfavorably with national standards.[45]

Many landlords and employers engaged in various annual, monthly, weekly, and daily cash arrangements with agricultural laborers in the Virginia tobacco region. Planter Samuel P. Wilson employed numerous freedpeople to work his tobacco plantation, "Cascade," in the far southwest corner of Pittsylvania County in the tobacco southside.[46] At least twenty-three freedpeople, including seventeen men, four women, and two girls, were hired by Wilson between 1870 and 1883. Twenty-one of the surviving pay receipts in his personal papers were marked with an "X," and three were signed. Based on these flimsy scraps from the past, it is possible to resurrect these freedpeople as well as reconstruct a crude wage scale for a tobacco plantation. On July 26, 1871, freedman Moses Daniel received $8 for one month's work. This was probably the rate for male laborers during the busy season. The following spring freedman James Cousins "received of Samuel P. Wilson twenty-five dollars *in full* of work done up to this day, this the 27th day of April 1872." Cousins's pay probably reflected the average winter monthly wage of $6.25 for January through April. Over a decade later freedman Sam Chilton received $19.50 for "all work done to this day, this 22 of March 1883." This suggests that the average winter monthly rate of $6.25 in the early 1870s had increased by a mere 25 cents to $6.50 by the early 1880s.[47]

The freedmen's compensation for a year's work also appears to have increased only marginally. Charles Campbell received $90 on November 17, 1877, presumably post-harvest pay for the preceding year's work. Tom Ely Hairston on February 9, 1880, "received of [*sic*] Samuel P. Wilson $92.20 in part payment of money due for one year's work." In just over two full seasons the annual wage scale for freedmen had increased from $90 to $93. Freedman Robert Hambleton received $22.75 on January 14, 1871, "in full of work done to the 1st of January"; a decade later, on Christmas day 1882, he received $157.48 "in part of work to this day." The little information extant on freedwomen on Wilson's plantation suggests that their agricultural labor was linked to that of their children, and they only rated half as much as freedmen in the fields. Thus, freedwoman Milly Daniel, probably related to Moses Daniel, received $41.60 for her labor and that of her daughter Mary for the year 1870; Ann Reece received $54.00 for her own labor and that of her daughter Marinda for the year 1873.[48] These wage rates for freedpeople on Wilson's plantation were similar to the wage scales reported by both state and federal investigators.[49]

Many smaller farm owners also employed wage laborers in the tobacco region. The compensation received by freedpeople working on George Hunt's small farm in the Darlington Heights district of Prince Edward County was exemplary. In 1873 Hunt's total wage bill reached $132.16 for casual laborers working daily, weekly, and monthly. This included $15 for the services of twelve-year-old Ryland Ford, who was hired out by his mother, Mandy Ford. In late January 1874 several freedpeople were compensated at 25 cents daily for stripping tobacco. In September 1874 several freedwomen were paid 25 cents daily for worming and suckering tobacco. In January 1876 nineteen-year-old field laborer Harry White contracted with Hunt for a season's labor at $85. In late November 1876 several freedpeople stripped tobacco for 25 cents a day. Not all this wage work was on the farm or in the fields. Ryland Ford did odd jobs around the house, while Lucy Watkins received $3.50 for some domestic work.[50]

A decade later Hunt continued to farm with wage labor. On March 12, 1887, Hunt recorded in his diary paying out $5.74 for "stripping tobacco and other labor." A month earlier thirty-five-year-old field laborer Dock Venable received $1.75 for some rural labor. In the opening three months of 1887 Hunt's agricultural wage bill was $18.47. There were, however, some important changes over the decade on Hunt's farm. The wage bill of 1887 was only half that of 1873, suggesting a cutting back on the wage labor bill under the duress of prolonged agricultural depression. Furthermore, there appears to have been a high turnover of rural laborers at Hunt's place. There were nineteen entries for agricultural wage labor in Hunt's expenses for 1887. Many of these were anonymous, but of those laborers named, only Dock Venable had been around since the mid-1870s.[51] He was married to twenty-nine-year-old Clementine, who was listed in the manuscript census as a domestic worker with two children, thirteen-year-old Green and eight-year-old Lizzie. Clementine was also paid for her "work in onions."[52] Meanwhile, H. Johnson, Tom, Jeff Ed, Lewis, Willis Gilliam, and Peter Davenport were all new casual wage laborers. Ryland Hunt, who had worked many previous seasons for George Hunt, was last mentioned in early 1881.[53]

Working for shares, much like wage labor, constituted an important part of agricultural relations in the Virginia tobacco region. Landlords and employers made payments in exchange for the agricultural work of laborers. This arrangement was different from that of tenancy, whereby the tenant paid the employer for renting and working a piece of land.[54] Working such land was usually difficult without the employment of rural laborers. Several seasons earlier, freedman Dillard had employed other freedmen and their families to help him work another's land in exchange for shares of the crop.[55] Writing from Fluvanna County during early 1877, employer C.S.T. reported similar labor arrangements: "Have had every year from two to four tenants, controlling a force of from six to ten good average hands."[56] Federal investigator Killebrew noted those "croppers" who were employed by tenants and were paid a share of the crop in exchange for their season's labor in the tobacco belt.[57] Charles Bruce wrote a long letter to the *Southern Planter and Farmer* editor describing conditions in "Southside Virginia" concerning those "engaged mainly in the production of tobacco suitable for shipping." In the process of castigating those planters who used "hired labor," Bruce distinguished between wage labor, the "crop share plan," and the "tenant system."[58] In short, those working the crop share plan resembled those receiving wages for their seasonal labor: they were being compensated for exchanging their labor power, the form of which was largely determined by postemancipation and depressed agricultural conditions.

Laboring for shares or cash was altogether different from the tenant system. Rather than simply receiving compensation, tenant farmers rented land from landowners in exchange for which they either paid a cash rent or handed over a share of the year's crops. These were primarily renters who were described as tenants by planters such as C.S.T. and Bruce and federal investigators such as Killebrew in the tobacco region.[59] These renters were also employers who made arrangements with other rural laborers to work the season in exchange for some form of compensation. Writer G. F. Harrison provided a clear (if harsh) description of the nature of this tenancy. Harrison attacked what he deemed "the one sided, unjust and absurd *terms* upon which farms are rented." Renters, he argued, merely subsisted on landlords' property for the portion of the crop they paid. They did not pay taxes on the farm, and they did not pay proportions of other things raised on the farm. Most problematic was the unequal relationship: "The one party firmly bound to surrender entire possession of his farm and dwelling for a year and pay the taxes on it; the other bound to *nothing*, but at liberty to make any use he chooses of it, and if he happens to fancy making, or pretending to make, with the most slovenly work, a little corn, wheat, etc., he delivers you one fourth of them; and even that, dependent upon the question of his honesty."[60]

Despite his clear views regarding postwar renting, Harrison failed to appreciate the significance of a burgeoning tenancy in the tobacco southside that actually indicated increasing rural proletarianization and immiseration. Indeed, it is difficult to separate the 1884 *Parrish* decision from the proliferation of confusing free labor relations, especially in Virginia's cash crop regions. Tobacco salesman John Ott had pointed out in the mid-1870s the proclivity of "freed negroes" for taking land on " 'shares.' "[61] Federal investigator Killebrew had pointed out in his 1879 report that a great deal of tobacco produced in Virginia was cultivated on the share system, the proportions ranging from one-half to three-fourths depending on land fertility, variety grown, and curing costs.[62] It is important, however, not to forget that it was during the ensuing decade of the 1880s, after the successful passage of the two crop lien laws and the 1884 court ruling, that tenant farming expanded especially in the tobacco southside.

During the 1880s Mecklenburg, Halifax, Pittsylvania, Henry, and Franklin Counties along the North Carolina border underwent some major transformations. Although the black population remained at around 99,000, suggesting some emigration, the white populace increased from 72,587 to 83,846.[63] These southsiders represented the heart of the tobacco belt. While production fell from 30 million pounds to 22.4 million pounds over the decade, the region's share of the state's total tobacco production rose from 37 to 46 percent.[64] According to the federal census returns, much of this tobacco was increasingly produced on the share farming system. In 1879 3,497 share farms in the five counties accounted for 6 percent of all share farms in the state. This regionally high tenant farming expanded even further during the 1880s. Share farming in Halifax County remained at around 40 percent; however, it was an island in a rising sea of tenancy. In Mecklenburg County share farms increased to 870 (36 percent of all farms), while in Henry County these increased to 836 (52 percent) and

TABLE 6.1. Share Tenancy in the Bright Tobacco Belt, 1880s

County	Farms Rented for Shares				Tobacco Production (in thousands of pounds)	
	N		%			
	1879	1889	1879	1889	1879	1889
Franklin	422	642	17	22	3,529	1,748
Halifax	952	963	39	40	7,653	5,432
Henry	538	836	38	52	2,953	2,533
Mecklenburg	373	870	22	36	3,436	2,737
Pittsylvania	1,212	1,979	35	47	12,271	10,024
Totals	3,497	5,340	16	24	29,842[a]	22,474[b]

Sources: USBC, *1880, Agriculture*, 94–97, 318–21; USBC, *1890, Agriculture*, 190–92, 454–55.

[a] 37 percent of state production.
[b] 46 percent of state production.

in Pittsylvania County to 1,979 (47 percent.) By 1890 these combined 5,340 share farms in the region accounted for nearly one-quarter of all share farms in the state.[65] (See table 6.1.)

If it is important not to reduce capitalist agriculture simply to relations of wage labor, similarly we should not reduce this process to share tenancy. After all, small farmers such as George Hunt were not engaged in tenancy but were very much caught up in the throes of capitalist agriculture. Although Alexander Parrish might have pursued tenant relations, many rural producers in Virginia's central piedmont did not engage in tenant relations. During the 1880s the number of farms and plantations in the state working on shares hovered at around one-fifth, while many traditional tobacco-producing counties in the central piedmont often registered small tenancy declines hovering between one-sixth and one-fourth of their farms. Thus, rural producers in Appomattox County worked 257 farms on shares in 1880; this fell slightly to 220 a decade later but still represented one-fifth of all county farms. In Powhatan County the number of farms worked on shares fell from 137 to 119, from 20 percent to 16 percent. In George Hunt's Prince Edward County 259 share farms (24 percent) decreased to 179 (16 percent). Interestingly enough, despite the overall decline in tenant farming in the central piedmont, Goochland County registered an increase in

READJUSTING FREE LABOR RELATIONS

TABLE 6.2. Share Tenancy in the Dark Tobacco Belt, 1880s

County	N 1879	N 1889	% 1879	% 1889	Tobacco Production (in thousands of pounds) 1879	Tobacco Production (in thousands of pounds) 1889
Albemarle	353	273	17	14	2,466	557
Amelia	266	188	26	20	1,726	933
Amherst	349	243	21	18	3,111	1,953
Appomattox	257	220	26	26	1,965	1,554
Bedford	585	488	21	17	5,315	2,812
Brunswick	358	411	25	22	1,538	1,075
Buckingham	412	273	25	22	2,136	881
Campbell	353	264	25	19	3,927	1,973
Caroline	329	432	20	20	991	364
Charlotte	267	188	25	20	3,226	1,762
Chesterfield	218	94	12	6	523	83
Cumberland	130	189	18	19	1,814	1,649
Dinwiddie	248	324	15	18	1,540	964
Fluvanna	107	181	12	20	917	406
Goochland	179	289	17	23	656	280
Louisa	216	306	12	18	1,921	632
Lunenburg	206	176	18	14	1,976	1,474
Nelson	389	301	30	25	2,660	1,131
Nottoway	177	259	18	24	1,582	725
Powhatan	137	119	20	16	914	519
Prince Edward	259	179	24	16	2,462	1,633
Totals	5,790	5,357	27	24	43,368[a]	23,305[b]

Sources: USBC, 1880, Agriculture, 94–97, 318–21; USBC, 1890, Agriculture, 190–92, 454–55.
[a] 54 percent of state production.
[b] 48 percent of state production.

share farms from 179 (17 percent) to 289 (23 percent) over the decade.[66] In short, there was a clear correlation between the expansion of tenant farming in the tobacco southside and its decline elsewhere in the Virginia central piedmont during the 1880s (see table 6.2).

It would be futile to reduce these different expressions of free labor relations to one pattern.[67] As other scholars have pointed out, the limitations of the evidence, especially federal census materials, make it next to impossible to clearly differentiate between tenant farmers and sharecroppers because the difference was not reported until the 1920 federal census.[68] The argument here is that this differentiation, which was of limited significance to the federal enumerator but of great importance to rural producers in the South, was already being made in conditions of emancipation and agricultural depression. The laws of free labor had readjusted property toward the interests of the landlord and employer. Share farmers, much like casual wage laborers, were simply rural proletarians exchanging their labor for some form of compensation. The racial sides of this transformation were clear. The transition to tenancy mostly occurred in the bright tobacco region along the border and engaged young, white, landless farmers. The freedpeople became mired in sharecropping throughout the tobacco region but especially in the tobacco southside. In this leaf area the freedpeople worked for tenants as well as planters. All these rural producers were part of an agricultural proletariat forged during postemancipation and depressed conditions and consolidated by political and legal redemption.[69]

Of course, if it is important to demonstrate the social nature of law, it is no less crucial to illustrate the social limitations of that law. The crop lien laws attempted to settle the potential conflict between landlord and merchants over the dispensation of credit. The 1884 state supreme court ruling legally clarified the confusing nature of employer-employee agricultural relations. These laws guaranteed the fruits of labor to landlords and employers and fashioned an agricultural proletariat. They did not, however, remove social conflict between employers and laborers. The tragic consequences of Andrew Mitchell's actions only highlighted a more mundane form of everyday rural protest. Other rural workers simply left. This was the central theme behind all that paternal management advice in the *Southern Planter and Farmer* calling for the fair treatment of the freedpeople and nurturing their strong "local attachment."[70]

Along with transiency, rural laborers in the Virginia tobacco region resorted to other forms of rural protest. These included theft. In early February 1877 farmer George Hunt went in search of 1,000 pounds of tobacco that had been stolen from his neighbor in the Darlington Heights district of Prince Edward County.[71] Synor Johns was accused

READJUSTING FREE LABOR RELATIONS

of stealing 300 pounds of tobacco worth $5 from Zebulon Williams on October 6, 1885, in Lunenburg County.[72] Local lawyer Beverley Mumford, who practiced in the court of Pittsylvania County, recollected the actions of landlord Philip Hardcastle, who sued his tenant Jasper Jenkins for stealing tobacco without paying his rent.[73]

Striking was another form of rural protest. On Tuesday, September 4, 1877, fourteen farm laborers walked off the job at Hawfield plantation in Orange County because, according to manager William Green, "there was no corn meal, nothing but potatoes and bacon." This absence of provisions violated the food supply arrangements that had been made at the beginning of the season.[74] Incidents such as these might well have been simply idiosyncratic, local, and isolated disputes. But their specific timing, at the end and the beginning of the agricultural season, suggests an extralegal dimension over settlement disputes in the fields. They also occurred within a broader context of agricultural depression.[75] This was the stuff of rural resistance by the unpropertied who engaged in their own less spectacular attempts to readjust free labor in their own interests.[76]

Readjusterism was everywhere in Virginia during the 1870s. Free labor readjusted itself to hard agricultural times. The Readjusters provided a political challenge to an older dominion. Legislation, along with judicial decisions, readjusted property rights in favor of landlords and transformed agricultural producers into rural proletarians. Rural Readjusterism was the logical consequence of proslave ideology. Meanwhile, these rural proletarians attempted to readjust to the new conditions as well as struggle for the fruits of their labor, especially around settlement time.

Other forms of social protest included freedpeople voting with their feet as their emancipatory aspirations became depressed by the vicissitudes of prolonged agricultural depression as well as readjusted free labor laws. Their social movement was a link between the antebellum Underground Railroad, wartime self-emancipation, and postemancipation mobility in the search for freedom. This latter process is explored more fully in the final chapter, which details the dissolution of the Virginia tobacco region. But first we need to complete the explanation for the regional nature of tobacco tenancy. Why, exactly, did tenancy predominate disproportionately in the tobacco southside along the North Carolina state border? This question can only be addressed by temporarily leaving the local fields and examining broader transformations in the tobacco economy emanating from southern towns, northern cities, and overseas markets.

CHAPTER SEVEN

The Highest Stage of Tobacco Alliance, 1890–1892

> The largest tobacco factories are gathering under one roof the manufacture of practically everything that contributes to the tobacco industry.
> —Federal reporter John H. Garber

> We respectfully demand of our Senators and Representatives in Congress to use their best efforts to enact some laws to protect the farmers in the bright tobacco belt from the oppression of the American Tobacco Company.
> —Mecklenburg County farmers

> Organized against the deadly fangs of monopoly, and rings, and trust companies.
> —The Virginia Colored Farmers' Alliance

The pressures wrought by emancipation, prolonged depression, and a changing tobacco economy sowed the seeds for the emergence of unique tobacco combinations from the late 1880s onward. Tobacco manufacturers in the cigarette industry quickly consolidated to form the American Tobacco Company, which soon monopolized this dynamic and profitable new branch of the tobacco economy. This monopoly was almost immediately challenged by tobacco producers in the field who organized against this anticompetitive "trust." The resulting rural combination drew on older Republican traditions against centralization; it also joined together planters, farmers, and even rural proletarians in a unique fashion that challenged older ideas of domination and subordination. The evils of the ATC momentarily replaced unschooled laborers, profligate tenants, and exploitative landlords in the Virginia tobacco region.

The format of this chapter is as follows: We begin with the rapid growth of the cigarette industry. This is explained by linking modes of production and consumption through changing demand and transformed technology.[1] We then turn to the rise and consolidation of control over the new tobacco industry by the ATC. This successful monopoly capitalism is explained through the notion of articulation. Danville in the tobacco southside became the regional entrepôt for the marketing of bright tobacco; towns such as Durham and Winston in the North Carolina piedmont became the machine eaters of this rural product; and ATC shareholders consumed the surplus value produced by rural and urban proletarians.[2] Unique expressions of collective rural protest against this new industry and its domination are the subject of the final section. These were the highest stages of tobacco combinations. It was the success of the ATC and the failure of the opposition to it that furthered the breakdown of the Virginia tobacco region.

Although the bright tobacco industry took off in the postwar years, its origins lay in the immediate antebellum period. Bright tobacco got its name from the light and yellow hue of its leaf. Its major requirements included siliceous soils, a regular and mild climate, and careful curing or drying methods. Along the Virginia–North Carolina border otherwise poor soils for agricultural production proved to be fertile ground for bright tobacco leaf. The major curing methods ranged from elementary wooden flues to charcoal firing. The latter curing method was rather serendipitous. Stephen, a slave owned by Abisha Slade of Caswell County, North Carolina, was minding tobacco drying over a charcoal fire one evening in 1839 when he fell asleep. Suddenly awakening and noticing the dying embers, he quickly threw extra logs onto the fire. The result was a tobacco leaf that dried to a unique and glorious yellow hue. Stephen's accident was heralded far and wide—albeit under the auspices of slaveowner Slade's expertise in tobacco management. Slade continued to popularize curing methods for bright tobacco until the early 1870s, when the mantle of expertise was assumed by Major Robert L. Ragland. His Hyco plantation in Halifax

County became the center of bright seed production. Ragland further popularized quality bright leaf production for meeting the free labor problem as well as depressed tobacco prices.[3]

Bright tobacco production thrived in postemancipation conditions and quickly spread southward throughout the Carolina piedmont. During the 1870s dark tobacco leaf production dropped from around 36 percent to 15 percent of North Carolina's production.[4] Federal investigator Killebrew explained the reasons for the expansion of bright tobacco: "The chief reason given for the great change in the character of the tobacco grown is the decline in price for shipping leaf, coinciding with the demand for fancy leaf at high prices."[5] Bright tobacco also replaced other cash crops, especially cotton, fetching low market prices. In the doggerel of one bright populist: "Cotton was once king, And produced Carolina's cracker; But now we have a better thing—The glorious Bright Tobacco."[6] Its glory was evident in tobacco's takeoff in the Carolinas. During the 1890s North Carolina's tobacco production exploded from 36 million to over 127 million pounds. There was a similar expansion in South Carolina, whose minimal tobacco production of under 250,000 pounds in 1889 had jumped to nearly 20 million pounds a decade later. Most of this increased tobacco production was bright leaf.[7]

Bright tobacco production also spread northward into the Virginia piedmont. It was originally restricted to the three counties of Pittsylvania, Henry, and Halifax along the North Carolina border, where conditions of soil and climate were most favorable. But emancipation, prolonged price declines for traditional dark export tobacco, and bright's marketers such as Ragland, Ott, and the *Southern Planter and Farmer* promoted the spread of the light leaf from the 1880s onward. Its contiguous area in the tobacco southside included Mecklenburg, Nottoway, Dinwiddie, Brunswick, and Lunenburg Counties, although expansion was limited because of inadequate soil types that did not favor a quality product. Bright tobacco assumed increasing importance in Virginia's regional economy. In 1859 bright tobacco could not have exceeded the 18 million pounds returned from Halifax, Pittsylvania, and Henry Counties. By 1899 these three counties had been joined by the other five counties, returning over 54 million pounds, much of which was bright leaf. This increase of bright tobacco in Virginia was up from approximately 14 percent to over 40 percent.[8]

The rise of this new tobacco monarch made the readjustment of free labor relations imperative.[9]

Bright tobacco prices fluctuated throughout the postemancipation decades. Between 1869 and 1873 they remained consistently high at 12 to 13.5 cents per pound. This was mainly because of the prolonged suspension of tobacco production during the war years. In 1874 bright producers received record high returns exceeding 20 cents per pound, primarily because of that year's very small tobacco crop. From 1875 to 1881 prices fell from around 13 cents per pound to just over 9 cents. Bright leaf prices picked up in the first part of the 1880s, fell during the mid-1880s, and picked up again during the late 1880s. These price fluctuations were explainable by specific conditions, including hornworm attacks (1873), increased manufacturing demands for bright leaf (early 1880s), and unfavorable seasons (late 1880s).[10]

These bright price fluctuations were significant for rural producers in the Virginia tobacco belt for two reasons. First, bright tobacco generally fetched higher market prices than traditional Virginia tobacco. In 1869 the new leaf averaged 12.25 cents per pound on the Danville market; this compared with an average warehouse or auction price of nearly 6.5 cents for dark tobacco. (The estimated average price of tobacco received by Virginia producers was just over 10 cents per pound, presumably a conflation of these two prices.) In 1881 while bright prices had dropped to 9.41 cents per pound, Virginia tobacco producers received 8.6 cents while dark leaf only fetched 5.85 cents per pound. In 1890 the respective market prices were 11.95 cents for bright, 8 cents for Virginia producers, and 4.87 cents for dark leaf. The other point was that even though bright prices remained higher than Virginia tobacco prices, even these experienced a rapid fall throughout the 1890s. In 1889 bright fetched 13.22 cents per pound in Danville; by 1895 it had fallen to 7.79 cents and, by 1899, to 6.76 cents. This price drop was due to the expanded production of bright leaf as an antidote to the price falls of other cash crops. It was also strongly identified by producers with the monopolistic activities of the ATC, which provided an identifiable culprit.[11]

With the advent of bright leaf and its expanded production came the development of the smoking industry, which transformed the tobacco economy from the 1880s onward. During the antebellum and immediate postbellum years tobacco manufacturing was dominated by the plug and chewing industry. Consumers either chewed, pipe-smoked, or sniffed the manufactured product. Both Virginia and North Carolina led the nation in this industry. In 1859 these two states accounted for 61 percent of national tobacco manufacturing. Despite wartime devastation, these two states maintained their national pre-dominance (41 percent in 1879), while the national total had increased to 35 percent. The major product was the light, sweet wrapper for plug and chewing, especially North Carolina bright and Kentucky burley leafs. With increased demand for cigarettes, however, manufacturing demand switched from leaf wrappers for plug and chewing products to leaf for cigarettes. Despite earlier forays in the cigarette industry during the mid-1870s in Richmond and later in New York City, not until the early 1880s did the smoking industry take off. Its essence lay in changing production and consumption patterns, while its growth lay in the control of cigarette-making machinery. The control of this technological transformation provided the basis for the monopoly cap-italism of the ATC.[12]

The roots of monopoly were grounded in a generation of competi-tion over emerging markets in a changing tobacco economy. The cen-ter of this conflict occurred south of the tobacco southside around Durham, North Carolina. Its earlier phase was marked by the rise of Bull Durham smoking tobacco under the entrepreneurial spirit of Julian Carr. Carr's expansion and business success soon became clear. By 1884 the Blackwell Durham Tobacco Company shipped 5 million pounds of brand smoking leaf and employed nearly 1,000 workers. The town had grown to 5,000 people, while the factory whistle was heard for thirteen miles around, presumably by the kin of those who stayed to labor on the land. This horn was also heard by the compet-ing firm of W. Duke, Sons & Co. Much like a more famous political executive, Duke had some log cabin roots that were subsequently immortalized. After the war he peddled and processed tobacco and eventually moved to Durham. By the early 1880s his business was capitalized at $100,000 with a factory workforce of sixty. Duke could not profitably compete with his rivals in the smoking industry, so he was forced to enter the burgeoning, risky, and untrusted cigarette industry.[13]

The key to the eventual success of Duke in the cigarette industry was utilization, consolidation, and monopoly of advanced technology for the manufacture of a new smoking product that was in heavy demand. Duke began with the hand-rolling labor of young men and then turned to that of young women. One expert could hand-roll 40 cigarettes a minute. Rising demand, however, required a speedier manufacturing process. A young Virginian, James A. Bonsack, after exhaustive intellectual effort promising great rewards, finally patented a cigarette-making machine on September 4, 1880. By 1884 one machine was doing the work of 48 hand rollers. Two years later the Dukes of Durham were using 15 Bonsack machines doing the work of 1,200 workers. Production increased from 9 million cigarettes in July 1885 to 60 million in August 1887. By 1889 24 Bonsack machines were turning out over 2 million cigarettes daily, amounting to approximately 823 million cigarettes for the year.[14]

Through technological monopoly, however, the new tobacco industry was transformed. Duke controlled the means of production through special agreements with Bonsack. These included lower royalty charges for machine hires in 1885, restricted access to Bonsack by other tobacco companies in 1888, and the provision of 25 percent competitive advantage in 1889. The control paid off handsomely. By 1888 those companies with Bonsacks controlled around 86 percent of the U.S. cigarette industry. There was a similar technological monopoly across the Atlantic. In May 1883 British cigarette manufacturers W. D. & H. O. Wills secured absolute rights to the Bonsack machine in the United Kingdom; by 1888 the Wills company was using eleven Bonsacks at its Bristol, England, plant with a daily output of 85,000 to 100,000 cigarettes. Such technological monopolies sealed Wills's and Duke's control of new national markets.[15]

Duke's success also stemmed from innovative marketing techniques that included women drummers, prizes, picture cards, and signboards. By 1889 intense competition among the five largest tobacco companies had emerged. Unlike the Bonsack machine, advertising methods were neither patentable nor monopolizable. This was the free marketplace, with its potential of ruinous competition. Consequently, Duke suggested a merger between the largest cigarette companies. On January 31, 1890, Allen & Ginter of Richmond; F. S. Kinney of New York and Richmond; W. S. Kimball of Oxford, North Carolina, and Rochester, New York; and Goodwin & Company of New York received a charter from the New Jersey legislature to form the ATC. The new company was capitalized at $25 million and headed by James Duke. Its concrete assets amounted to a mere $3.1 million, while 86 percent of company stock was in the less tangible form of patents, trademarks, and potential earning power. It nevertheless provided the mass financial capital with which to dominate the U.S. tobacco industry in the late nineteenth and early twentieth centuries.[16]

Before describing the nature of this domination and its impact, it is important to examine the transformed tobacco economy. Tobacco consumption had always been high in the United States. During the eighteenth century, colonial consumption was estimated to have averaged between two and five pounds per capita.[17] Consumers in the postbellum United States, however, increasingly demanded smoking products in the form of cigarettes. This rise in demand emerged among rural dwellers as well as a growing urban populace.[18] The technology needed to meet this new demand inspired a scramble by regional inventors to design a machine that would be more efficient as well as easy to operate. Manufacturers used and monopolized this technology for the tobacco industry from rising tobacco towns in the North Carolina piedmont. The demands of the smoking industry encouraged planters and farmers to engage in bright tobacco production, especially in the context of falling prices for traditional dark tobacco and, more generally, cotton. The result was a new tobacco dominion stretching from southern Virginia through South Carolina.[19]

The regional entrepôt for the marketing of this new product was Danville in Pittsylvania County, several miles from the North Carolina border. The roots of its articulation lay in antebellum marketing and manufacturing processes. One local historian explained that as "the plantations in the surrounding country multiplied in number and increased in acreage, more and more tobacco was bought and brought to Danville to feed the many tobacco factories there."[20] During the depression years of the mid-1870s this articulatory role took off. According to one contemporary expert, licensed tobacco dealers increased from 52 to 96, while other merchant enterprises grew from 203 to 594 between 1873 and 1878. Danville blossomed as the regional tobacco exchange. Prior to 1867 Neals had been the sole tobacco warehouse; by 1879 there were seven others. Between October 1, 1874, and September 30, 1875, these warehouses marketed over 14 million pounds of tobacco valued at over $3 million. Three years later these leaf merchants nearly doubled their sales to over 27 million pounds, although depressed prices meant they only received $2.4 million. There was simultaneous growth in tobacco factories. In 1879 it was estimated there were twenty plug and twist factories, two smoking-leaf factories, one stripping and stemming factory, and seventy-three factories for reprising and buying tobacco on order.[21]

Despite this impressive tobacco manufacturing, Danville's major role was in its marketing of the product cultivated in the nearby hinterland. This role increased with the expansion of the cigarette industry. In 1879 SFC secretary John Ott generalized that Danville served the surrounding region by "furnishing a market at home for the products of all kinds raised by the farmer." This relationship, Ott added, was reciprocal, since the hinterland boosted Danville's tobacco interests, the "country [being] tributary to Danville" because "the chief attention of the farmers is paid to the tobacco crop." The term *tributary* was particularly precise because of the increased power of tobacco merchants over tobacco planters consolidated by the late 1870s. This link between town and countryside was enhanced as the cigarette industry became more entrenched.[22]

Danville's importance as the primary regional marketing entrepôt was consolidated during the 1880s. In 1870 13 million pounds of tobacco were sold there; by 1890 over 40 million pounds of leaf were marketed.[23] It is important to recall that most of this bright leaf was produced by free labor on surrounding farms and plantations in both southern Virginia and northern North Carolina. Edward Pollock, one of Danville's town boosters, summarized this regional articulation during the mid-1880s. "By far," he wrote, "the greater portion of the tobacco brought to this market still comes by wagons, direct from the neighbouring plantations, but that grown in more remote districts also comes in considerable quantities over the lines of the several Railroads centering here, and this latter class is increasing very rapidly."[24] This increase was due to the emergence of smaller tobacco exchanges at various railroad depots. These were capillaries to Danville's artery. As Pollock went on to explain, "In many of the smaller towns and villages along the Railroads that penetrate the tobacco-growing counties, warehouses and re-prizing factories have been established, and much

THE HIGHEST STAGE OF TOBACCO ALLIANCE

of the tobacco so collected is forwarded in hogsheads to Danville (*which holds a sort of metropolitan relationship to the whole section*) to be re-sold."[25] This leaf metropolis continued to grow. By 1893 Danville had become the greatest bright tobacco market in the world. Pollock was not inaccurate in his prediction "that for generations to come it will hold the leading place among local industries, and that all others will remain to some extent tributary to it, and dependent for their success upon its prosperity."[26] He would have been even more accurate if he had noted the impact this huge market had on tying free labor to the surrounding countryside.

The ATC gained monopoly control over the U.S. tobacco industry almost immediately. In its first year the corporation accounted for 90 percent of all cigarette sales in the nation, with profits exceeding $40 million. These profits, along with a consolidated base, enabled the ATC to dominate quickly other aspects of the tobacco manufacturing industry. In 1891 the ATC's share of U.S. production of all smoking products was 13.5 percent; the same year, it bought two major smoking firms in Baltimore, paving the way for domination in this branch of the industry. During the mid-1890s the ATC bought the Bull Durham Company. By the late 1890s the ATC controlled around two-thirds of the smoking-tobacco industry. Similar monopolies were exerted over plug, twist, and snuff products. In 1891 the ATC had 3 percent of the market share of these products. By 1907 this had risen to between 80 and 90 percent. Only the cigar industry remained immune to the ATC's monopoly of the tobacco industry, although not for lack of valiant efforts by the ancillary American Cigar Company. According to the ATC's official history, by 1906 the business was capitalized at $235 million, of which $78.7 million was in preferred stock, $40.2 million in common stock, and $116.1 million in bonds. Of this common stock, $35.5 million was owned by fifty-two shareholders, with the ten largest, including six directors, owning 63 percent.[27]

The ATC consolidated the U.S. tobacco industry primarily in terms of centralization, small manufacturer decimation, and product specialization. New York City became the center of the tobacco business. Duke had already transferred his headquarters there in 1884, while three of the other four companies that later merged to become the ATC (Kinney, Kimball, and Goodwin) were either located or had factories

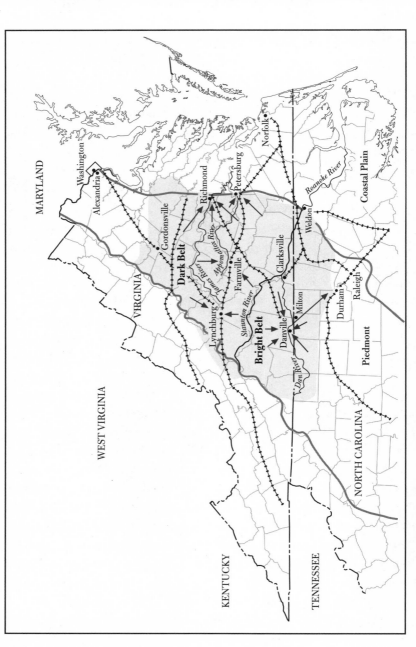

MAP 7.1. Tobacco Virginia's regions and articulation (adapted from E. H. Mathewson, "Summary of Ten Years' Experiments with Tobacco," Virginia Agricultural Experiment Station Bulletin 205 [June 1914]. 8; Robert, *Tobacco Kingdom*, 16–17)

in New York City. After the merger the company established its headquarters there. In 1901 Benjamin Duke left Durham and joined his
brother in the North.[28]

With corporate relocation the ATC furthered the destruction of the
small-scale manufacturer in the tobacco industry. According to federal
census returns, the total number of tobacco factories in Virginia fell
from 296 in 1890 to 212 in 1900. The annual reports from the Internal
Revenue suggest an even more dramatic business closure rate. Between
1889 and 1904 the number of smoking and plug factories in Virginia
virtually halved from 174 to 87. This failure of small-scale plug manufacturers was exemplified by J. H. Hargrave & Son in Chatham, Pittsylvania County. In 1889 the company produced 251,520 pounds of
chewing tobacco and sold 256,305 pounds. By 1892 shipping tobacco
was down to a few thousand pounds, consisting mainly of sales to
larger suppliers for manufacturers in Richmond. The following year
the business was listed as "the leaf tobacco firm of Chatham, Va.," and
by 1900 had become a "sash, door, and blind factory." There were
similar closure rates in adjoining North Carolina. The number of factories listed fell from 234 in 1889 to 86 by 1904. The passing of these
small tobacco manufacturers was the direct result of prolonged depression, a transformed tobacco economy, and the ATC's monopoly.[29]

Specialization was the flip side of decimation and the third feature
of this consolidation. As small factories dropped out, larger factories
took over. Even though the number of tobacco factories in Virginia
declined during the 1890s, their combined product value registered
only a slight fall from nearly $22 million to just over $21 million. This
process of specialization was most pronounced in smoking and plug
manufacture, the leading branch of the Virginia tobacco industry. In
1890 its 93 factories had a capital investment of over $6.8 million with
a product valued at over $11.8 million; a decade later 69 factories were
invested with over $5.7 million in capital with a final product worth
over $10.7 million. Similar specialization occurred in smaller branches
of the state's tobacco industry. In stemming and rehandling 101 factories with over $1.8 million in capital investment with a product worth
$6.4 million decreased to 54 factories with over $2.4 million with a
product of over $5.7 million. In the cigarette branch the number of
factories declined from 102 to 89, with capital investment down from

over $1.8 million to just over $700,00, while the product value increased from over $3.7 million to over $4.8 million.[30]

Incremental specialization in the tobacco industry drew comments from various contemporaries. One writer for the *Southern Tobacco Journal* observed that there were "fewer plug factories in the South today than there were several years ago." This had less to do with either declining consumption or declining output, "but the large factories are growing larger while the little ones are dropping out."[31] Federal enumerator John H. Garber prepared a special report on tobacco manufacturing that paid particular attention to specialization and its consequences. "The largest tobacco factories," he observed, "are gathering under one roof the manufacture of practically everything that contributes to the tobacco industry. Factories are now fully equipped for manufacturing the tin, paper, cloth, and other packages in which the products are packed for market, as well as boxes or cases in which they are shipped. Equipment for printing and lithographing labels and advertising posters is also an adjunct of a modern factory, so that there is little demand to be supplied by outside establishments."[32] One writer for the *Richmond Times Dispatch* gloomily declared that the "country factory has about passed out of existence," while the progeny of "these famous old-time tobacco makers have moved their plants to the towns and cities." He went on to describe wistfully the local loss in southern tobacco Virginia, where the "trust has swallowed up Farmville, Boydton and Clarksville, and the songs of the factory hands are no longer heard in those towns."[33]

The combination of depressed agricultural conditions and the rise of the cigarette industry paved the way for the making of the ATC's colonial economy.[34] This was most obvious in the ATC's consolidation and monopoly over the national tobacco industry. It centralized finance capital with a shifting manufacturing base. Corporate headquarters were established in New York City, while the production center shifted southward toward the source of bright tobacco materials and cheap factory labor. In 1880 workers in New York City accounted for 72 percent of U.S. cigarette production; by 1888 Duke & Sons' record cigarette production of 744 million was being accomplished by proletarians in factories in both New York City and Durham. After the formation of the ATC, more factories were moved southward and made more concentrated, while the cheaper labor of women increasingly feminized the workforce. Indigenous colonial capitalism affected Virginia no less. Between 1890 and 1900 women workers in cigarette factories increased from 1,355 to 1,791, representing the state's largest group of industrial tobacco workers, compared with men and children.[35]

The ATC's colonial economy also girdled the earth. Its global expansion was the logical consequence of technological domination, domestic overproduction, and the hunger for new consumers in order to maintain profits and corporate power. The Duke company originally pursued limited foreign sales. In 1889 most of its cigarettes were consumed domestically, while it exported only 34,123 pounds of smoking tobacco. However, massive expansion into foreign markets followed fairly quickly after the formation of the ATC. In 1893 the ATC shipped 12 million cigarettes to Japan in one load. Over the next four years the ATC's total sales to Japan amounted to 985 million cigarettes. In response to this prolific commercial expansion into its home market the Japanese government passed a high tariff to protect the indigenous cigarette industry. The ATC's response was to double exports as well as to invest heavily, eventually gaining 60 percent of the controlling interest in Murai Brothers Company, which had been formed during the 1890s, the largest cigarette firm in the nation. In 1901 the ATC produced about 8 million cigarettes in Japan. The following year Duke's company realized profits worth $500,000 on its Japanese tobacco interests. In response to this aggressive corporate aggrandizement the Japanese government eventually nationalized the cigarette industry, encouraging the ATC to shift its attentions elsewhere.[36]

The ATC's move southward extended to Cuba and its lucrative cigar trade. One year after the 1898 Spanish-American War, the Havana Commercial Company bought one cigarette and twelve cigar factories in Havana. In 1901 the ATC moved into Havana and combined around twenty factories to form the American Cigar Company, which absorbed the Havana Commercial Company the following year. Much like other business monopolies such as Bethlehem Iron, Havermeyer Sugar, and United Fruit, the ATC took full advantage of the recent war and moved into Cuba to seize control of this lucrative part of the tobacco industry. By 1902 the ATC controlled around 90 percent of the cigar export trade. Still, it ran into difficulties and eventually registered deficits in this branch of the tobacco industry.[37]

The most succinct expression of the ATC's global expansion came with the formation of the British-American Tobacco Company (BAT). The British company Wills mirrored the Dukes in dominating the national tobacco market through technological advantage, aggressive advertising, and eventual monopolizing of all facets of the industry. Duke entered the British market by buying up Ogden's, Wills's major rival. This led to the formation of the International Tobacco Company, which consisted of Wills and twelve other tobacco manufacturers. The ATC now had a transatlantic rival. A trade war broke out that reached its climax in 1901. Nightmares of potentially destructive competition were fairly recent; these had been assuaged through company consolidation. The following year an agreement was brokered whereby corporations agreed to keep out of one another's territory. The BAT was to control the rest of the global tobacco trade outside the United Kingdom and the United States, along with Cuba and Puerto Rico. The ATC was to have two-thirds control of the BAT located in London. The result was the international division of the global marketplace that diverted ruinous competition. The BAT was, in Sherman Cochran's succinct words, "the two former rivals' international division."[38]

The ATC turned its attention to China after its failure to seize the Japanese market. This Asian human mass promised a huge market. More specifically, the ATC developed a monopoly over the Chinese tobacco industry through replication of its domestic methods of building and consolidating an integrated business of mass cigarette production and distribution under the auspices of the BAT. This foreign arm emulated the ATC policy of gaining monopoly through consolidation of the tobacco industry and increased capital investment. By 1902 ATC cigarette exports to China had reached 1.25 billion, and they multiplied eightfold within the decade.[39] Under the auspices of the BAT, Duke reached deep into the Chinese market. James A. Thomas, also from North Carolina, was the managing director of the BAT in 1905. Thomas provided a revealing comment on colonial business in explaining reasons for overseas assignments. "It was the chance, the life that drew me," he explained. "As a missionary of this new American industry I went out to the East. . . . I knew not a soul." The best missionaries, of course, did not have to.[40]

Out of this capital monopoly of the U.S. tobacco industry emerged the seeds of the ATC's dissolution. While the 1890 Sherman Antitrust

Act did not affect the ATC, signs of growing discontent culminated in legal disputes during 1906–7. These led to the 1911 U.S. Supreme Court decision effectively dissolving the ATC because it was deemed in restraint of free trade. The ruling countenanced an important breakup of the tobacco monopoly. Although the monopoly was replaced by the oligopoly of the four biggest tobacco companies, the principle of capital's domination was never at issue.[41] More pertinently, this legal ruling against the tobacco trust had been anticipated by rural producers in the fields from the outset, and it is to their social protest, especially in the Virginia tobacco region, that we now turn.

The historiographical contours of agrarian protest in late nineteenth-century Virginia have remained remarkably resilient over the decades. Organized rural protest was both weak and insignificant. Its unique patrician leadership was stamped, in C. Vann Woodward's words, with "the traditional sobriety of the Upper South." This elite-led, weak, rural organization produced a tepid populism that finally foundered on the hard rock of white racism. Broader studies of agrarian protest in other areas of the American South and West have confirmed the relative insignificance of rural rebellion in Virginia. This view of moderate discontent, dignified leadership, and conservative politics also supports the popular image of the Old Dominion as the exceptional state.[42]

Our focus on the Virginia tobacco region challenges this traditional portrait. Although agrarian protest was limited statewide, rural combinations were particularly evident in the tobacco region. These local alliances were forged through long-term socioeconomic dislocation wrought by emancipation, depressed market conditions, and the ATC's monopoly. Ripples from strong rural organizations in bordering North Carolina also promoted combinations in tobacco Virginia. Furthermore, these regional farmers' alliances did not suddenly spring up. They were anticipated by previous expressions of collective protest against the machinations of the tobacco warehousemen and the iniquities of the federal tax on manufactured tobacco. The *Southern Planter and Farmer* and its various contributors had represented a more discreet form of protest against existing conditions through calls for agricultural reform. Additionally, the focus on leadership has detracted from the rank-and-file membership of these local alliances. These were often tenant farmers and, occasionally, rural laborers. They also included freedpeople whose protest was the culmination of previous expressions for the realization of emancipatory desires. These local members of the Colored Farmers' Alliance (CFA) have also suffered from the condescension of posterity. Indeed, it is suggested here that one of the aspects of this highest stage of tobacco alliance in the fields was the momentary suspension of ideologies informed by the old dominion. The ATC, not wasteful Negro tenants or avaricious proslave landlords, was revealed to be primarily responsible for hard rural times. Finally, organized rural protest did not simply rise and fall and disappear; it was linked to the broader dissolution of free labor from tobacco Virginia that was its corollary.

There was a direct correlation between the successful formation of the ATC and the growth of rural combinations in tobacco Virginia. The Farmers' Alliance initially appeared in Virginia during 1887, but with a slow start. By January 1888 there were 28 suballiances, all located in Rockbridge, Page, and Rappahannock Counties in the Shenandoah Valley. Partly inspired by the depression of agricultural prices and the tireless proselytizing of *Progressive Farmer* editor Leonidas L. Polk in adjoining North Carolina, rural combinations spread throughout Virginia. By August 1889 the alliance claimed 460 lodges with 8,000 members in 32 counties. The following year, after the successful incorporation of the ATC, the alliance took off in tobacco Virginia. By August 1890 there were alliances in some 90 counties, with 1,113 suballiances and over 30,000 members. By August 1891 alliances had been formed in 96 counties, with 20 county alliance stores and 5 district exchanges, each capitalized at $2,000. Farmers' Alliance membership in the state peaked at around 35,000.[43] It would be foolish to attribute all these rural combinations to anti-ATC sentiment, but it would also be mistaken to ignore the link between legislative struggles over possible market monopolies and the growth of rural alliances in tobacco Virginia.

In December 1889 the Allen & Ginter Company requested a charter for the ATC, into which it wished to incorporate. The general assembly agreed. During the Christmas recess, however, while legislators were in their home constituencies, they were exposed to strong sentiments of opposition from both rural tobacco producers and small manufacturers. They feared the negative effects of monopoly on the tobacco market especially at a time when leaf prices were already low. Tobacco prices, for instance, appear to have been only between 5.25 and 6.5 cents per pound in December 1889. After they returned to Richmond, the legislators repealed the charter with a vote of 69 to 18 in the House and 19 to 8 in the Senate. The ATC subsequently obtained legal incorporation from the Trenton assembly in New Jersey.[44]

The repeal of the proposed charter in Virginia did not stop the ATC's formation; neither did it terminate collective expressions of rural discontent against the "trust." After the general assembly's reversal, Richmond tobacco manufacturer William E. Dibrell observed that country members continued to be "opposed to any trust measures and see but little difference in one company or capitalists and another." The *Lynchburg Advance* reported tobacco growers' increasing animosity toward the ATC for reducing prices for the crops they produced but not for the finished product they consumed.[45]

Rural combination became marked throughout the tobacco belt during the ensuing year. County alliances were organized throughout the region by the early fall of 1890. A county alliance directory listing the name, post office, and county of various officials was first published in the *Southern Planter and Farmer* in October 1890. The tobacco southside was represented by local officials including J. D. Hankins at Basses P.O., Halifax County; T. Y. Allen at Skipworth P.O., Mecklenburg County; P. C. Keesee at Keeling P.O., Pittsylvania County; and J. A. Browder at Smoky Ordinary P.O., Brunswick County. Central tobacco Virginia was represented by W. W. Haskins at Buckingham Court House P.O., Buckingham County; H. J. Harris at Apple Grove P.O., Louisa County; and George Dunn at Nottoway Court House, Nottoway County. These were the local leaders of the Farmers' Alliance in tobacco Virginia. They were also the delegates, along with others from agricultural Virginia, that passed the Declaration of Principles at the Lynchburg annual convention in August 1890. Its eleven resolutions called for a combination of deflationary measures, reduced and equitable taxes, and railroad regulations. These demands were important to tobacco producers because they faced low leaf prices, high tobacco taxes, and expensive transportation costs. One other demand called for "the destruction of all trusts and the withdrawal of all favors in the shape of subsidies and bounties."[46] The following annual meeting in August 1891 was attended by delegates from ninety-six counties who endorsed the National Alliance program issued at the Ocala, Florida, meeting as well as reendorsed the state alliance program at Lynchburg. The delegates also called for fertilizer regulation, which was particularly salient to members from tobacco Virginia because of their special reliance on this product. The delegates also called for pressure on the general assembly to enact some of the alliance principles.[47]

Such pressure was expressed in legislative struggles against the most blatant organizational expression of the ATC's tobacco market monopoly. The 1891–92 general assembly session was packed with planter/farmer delegates, with about forty alliance legislators in both houses. Several bills were introduced, but all were eventually voted down. On January 23, 1892, a resolution of the farmers in Mecklenburg County clearly articulated this rural resentment: "We respectfully demand of our Senators and Representatives in Congress to use their best efforts to enact some laws to protect the farmers in the bright tobacco belt from the oppression of the American Tobacco Company." The manifestation of their political opposition came with a February 2, 1892, bill introduced into the House to prevent ATC operations in Virginia. Although it eventually failed, it did highlight the extent of local rural protest from tobacco Virginia.[48]

These legislative battles were only the most spectacular collective expression of rural protest from tobacco Virginia. Their failure suggests the limitations of rural protest in the state. However, this protest was often more discreet and localized. On May 11, 1889, local 314 of the Farmers' Alliance was organized at Rice in Prince Edward County. It provided a cooperative store designed to thwart the middlemen whose high prices were deemed so deleterious. The alliance acquired property for the store with J. Y. Phillips and wife conveying a lot 44 feet wide and 102 feet deep to trustees H. E. Watkins and W. H. Hubbard. Meanwhile, Major A. R. Venable was elected state business agent for the alliance in 1890, while W. A. Barrow attended the Richmond convention in August 1891 as county delegate. In Prince Edward County the cooperative store appears to have been in operation on this property for a number of years.[49] Its protest against the iniquities of the prolonged depression, while quiet, were no less important.

One problem with equating rural activity with the Farmers' Alliance during the early 1890s is that it ignores all other manifestations of rural protest. As we shall see in the final chapter, there were several other features that characterized the regional dissolution of tobacco Virginia. However, expressions of rural protest also emanated from local organizations and clubs that do not appear to have been officially affiliated with the Farmers' Alliance. These reflected the same kind of collective expression of rural discontent. One such expression came from the heart of the tobacco southside.

Just before noon on a hot and humid August 16, 1890, representatives from twenty-three local alliances convened at Chatham Court House in Pittsylvania County. The meeting had been called in response to a circular issued by nineteen alliancemen for the establishment of a countywide organization. Along with these county representatives, the official journal recorded "many other visiting bothers" in attendance. Officers were duly elected, with T. N. Williams as president, G. S. Norman as secretary, and eight other directors. The delegates' call for unity was met with the resolution to form the Pittsylvania Central Alliance Trade Union (PCATU), to be capitalized from $2,000 to $50,000 with shares at $10 each, with no stockholder owning more than fifty shares. The new alliance organized several committees and drafted a series of bylaws. Its constitution consisted of ten articles and nineteen sections modeled in classic republican fashion. This encompassed election rules, duties, and responsibilities of board members and a constitutional amendment provision based on a two-thirds quorum of stockholders. The PCATU's "business shall be to conduct a general mercantile & manufacturing business." After an enthusiastic convocation, the meeting adjourned.[50]

The PCATU subsequently met on the morning of October 10, 1890, with representatives from eighteen suballiances in attendance. The committee responsible for obtaining a future space for the mercantile and manufacturing business reported an available factory rentable for $250 on warehouse company land. Chatham was agreed upon as the future location for all company business. It was also decided that one representative from each suballiance would "solicit stock to the above named company" from their local membership.[51] The following month the Location Committee presented several options on where best to set up the alliance store. Mr. Christian was offering one acre of land on the railroad for $300. There was Mr. Hargrove's factory. Mr. Carter's storeroom adjoining the hotel was available for $10 monthly, while Mr. Giles's storeroom, "now occupied by Moses," was rentable for $200 per annum. The Committee on Subscriptions reported thirty-eight subscribers from eight suballiances who had contributed a combined $1,195 to company stock. Since this was less than the full figure required, representatives were urged to go back to their suballiances and obtain more stock subscriptions from their rural members.[52]

The actual membership of the PCATU appears to have been mostly planters and farmers, with a sprinkling of tenants. Taylor L. Shields was a thirty-eight-year-old white farmer married to thirty-six-year-old Camelia, who kept house with Martha Baines, a twenty-year-old freedwoman domestic. Shields represented the Spring Garden suballiance, located several miles southeast of Chatham.[53] B. C. Rover was a sixty-one-year-old planter married to forty-eight-year-old Emma. He had a large household consisting of fourteen members, with five sons in their twenties who were all farmers. Rover also headed the Oak Hill suballiance, located several miles west of Danville southwestern Pittsylvania County.[54] Samuel B. Blair was a fifty-two-year-old white farmer married to forty-five-year-old Emily; they had three teenage children. Blair represented the Hollywood suballiance in the Callands District west of Chatham. The Hollywood suballiance was very supportive of the PCATU, with seventeen of its members raising $465 in subscriptions to company stock. These were led by delegate Blair with $100; other members contributed more modest sums. Thirty-nine-year-old white farmer John Foust bought $10, thirty-eight-year-old white farmer William H. J. Foust paid $10, and thirty-seven-year-old white farmer Bedford O. Foust contributed $20. Samuel H. Dodd, a seventy-two-year-old white farmer, paid $10. Frank Fuller, a thirty-year-old white "farm hand" who boarded with the Dodds, does not appear to have been a member of the suballiance.[55]

The fourth meeting of the PCATU had a small turnout because of bad weather. Still, the Subscription Committee reported eleven stock subscribers from the three suballiances of Green Rock, Harpin Creek, and Dry Fork, with a total of $590 raised. C. R. Mitchell from Harpin Creek was particularly successful soliciting eleven subscribers who bought from one to three shares of $10 to $30 each.[56] One month later, at the next meeting, $580 in subscriptions to stock were presented, amounting to roughly one-quarter of the minimum $2,000 capitalization required for official company formation. The board of directors decided to proceed as soon as the requisite $2,000 had been collected. Furthermore, a committee was set up to confer with representatives from a fertilizing company as well as the state agent of the Border Alliance that was scheduled to meet in Danville on February 18, 1891.[57] By early 1891 the PCATU appeared to be well on its way to achieving countywide support and financial security as well as setting up shop.

The next meeting of the PCATU was held on February 23, 1891. Members continued to discuss rental arrangements for the company store, whether it was to be Giles's storehouse or Carter's stable and lot. The director's compensation of $2.50 a day for services was decided. More importantly, the Committee on Fertilizers reported meeting with the president of the Durham Fertilizer Company (DFC). This fertilizer manufacturer had begun business in 1881 under Samuel Tate Morgan. He drew on John Ott's marketing techniques with the SFC of Richmond with great success. The DFC befriended the Farmers' Alliance, with the president agreeing to store fertilizers with the PCATU. It was resolved by the PCATU secretary to order one carload of fertilizers from the DFC immediately and to store it in Chatham for selling at cost to Farmers' Alliance members.[58] At the following meeting it was resolved that the secretary "be instructed to allow all alliancemen a discount not to exceed 10% on all goods which in his discretion would bear such a discount."[59]

During the spring of 1891 the PCATU began to experience difficulties collecting subscriptions from stock buyers. The organization had only been in existence for a year, but the depression of agricultural prices, especially for tobacco, continued to plague planters and farmers. At the May 18 meeting a list of delinquent stockholders was read to those members in attendance. Representative C. R. Mitchell of the Harpin Creek suballiance motioned to strike from membership D. A. Jefferson and J. R. Yeatts, which was approved. T. A. Parrish was also struck from the list on the motion of D. A. Cooper. This latter representative further proposed "to give notice to all Delinquents to pay the amounts due the company on or before the 1st day of June next—if not legal steps will be taken to collect the same." The motion was adopted, and the secretary was instructed to act accordingly after June 1.[60]

Delinquent business was the first priority at the subsequent meeting in June 1891. C. R. Mitchell motioned to strike T. W. Kendrick from the list of subscribers. Others were granted extensions. J. N. Williams requested sixty days for the Caddo suballiance and indefinite extensions for E. Prewett, which was approved. Brother Cooper sought time for T. W. Dodd, which was also granted. The alliance also finalized the renting of Giles's storeroom for $170 annum.[61] The board further agreed on prices for goods to be sold at the store: bulk meat and meal and groceries at 10 percent, with no discount; store goods such as tin and domestic plaid along with shoes at 20 percent, with a discount of 10 percent. They also resolved that "our agent sell all goods out of season at prime cost," adding that goods for alliancemen merit only 2 percent extra "if ordered in Bulk and money is deposited before goods are ordered."[62] These reduced charges were an important means of undercutting existing exorbitant prices at a time when tobacco producers were receiving low payments for their cash crops.

Just as the organization was getting under way by the end of its first season, serious difficulties began to undermine its best efforts. On July 21, 1891, the full board met to settle an outstanding account with the DFC, which was owed $1,382.89 for guano fertilizer. There was a company cash flow problem. The amount from cash sales to members had "been used for the benefit of this company in discounting bills for merchandise." Some stockholders held notes to the DFC with 8 percent interest. J. L. Tedway, company lawyer, suggested that stockholders buy bonds in the PCATU that could then be used to pay back the debt to the DFC and credited to the stockholder. The PCATU sent the following telegram to the DFC: "We cannot get the parties bonds to whom we sold your goods—will you take our company note payable 1st May 1892—we are anxious to settle." It was also decided to form a four-member committee "to take an inventory and make settlement with secretary & treasurer." The latter settlement had become necessary because amid a seemingly chaotic financial situation, original allianceman and long-term company treasurer G. S. Norman had tended his resignation. This was accepted pending settlement with the DFC.[63]

Three weeks later the board reconvened in Chatham. They elected N. A. Hall as the new secretary and treasurer. The report into the company's inventory revealed assets worth $3,715.54. The meeting then turned to the unresolved DFC business. The issue of extra bonds was met with disapproval by J. E. Taylor, who consequently resigned. The directors then proceeded to issue two bonds, one to Chatham Savings Bank for $450 and one to the DFC for $450. The board also upped the prices of goods purchasable at the company store from 20 to 25 percent.[64] Despite these setbacks several directors returned in November, when "the financial standing of the Co was discussed and a motion to continue as a business was adopted." A new board of directors was also voted in with 981 votes cast. Their mandate was to meet in the near future "for the purpose of receiving bids for clerk for store."[65] The following meeting in early December was attended by only five directors, forcing postponement of the election until there was a fuller attendance. At the last meeting of the year, on December 27, 1891, seven members were present. Brother Nuckold was chosen as salesman for the following year at a salary of $600. Meanwhile, Brother Hodge tended his resignation.[66]

The writing was clearly on the wall. By the spring of 1892 the PCATU was in the process of disbanding. At the Chatham meeting on March 9, attended by seven members, President Williams read an agreement between himself and Brother Venable, who was the state agent for fertilizers. The meeting also approved Daniel Nuckold's request for an assistant clerk "during the fertilizer season." Most importantly, the company agreed on a resolution "to issue a call for a meeting of the stock holders." On May 6, 1892, six members convened. The president reported "no business was transacted at the call[ed] meeting of the stock holders there being no quorum present." On the motion of D. A. Cooper, "it was agreed to advertise all goods (except groceries) to be sold for ninety day[s] at cost the object of this being to close out the business as soon as possible." The final business was with Nuckold, who agreed to work for $40 a month until company affairs wound down.[67]

What was the significance of the PCATU? Most obviously, it arose in response to hard agricultural times for tobacco producers. These hard times were exacerbated by the monopoly alliance of the ATC. Its control reduced leaf prices and exemplified the trust. Furthermore, the PCATU represented a local rural organization that was widespread throughout the county. It had little chance of affecting crop prices, but it could lower consumer prices through a cooperative store with reduced prices. It could also provide much-needed fertilizer at cost. It might even have been able to store nonperishable tobacco for higher market prices at propitious times. Still, such a county organization, impressive though it was, was simply no match for the new forces unleashed by prolonged agricultural depression, a transformed tobacco economy, and capital monopoly.[68] This tobacco alliance represented a fleeting recognition that emancipation and the free labor "problem" could not explain all the postwar woes of planters and farmers in the Virginia tobacco region.

This highest stage of local organization and consciousness also characterized the activities of rural freedpeople. The advent of emancipation had wrought individual and collective struggles by the freedpeople: protesting with their feet against slavery during the war, reconstructing households in the image of freedom, voting collectively for Republicanism or Readjusterism against the Democrats' old dominion, and pursuing seasonal mobility to fulfill emancipatory aspirations. These were the ripples that flowed into the broader stream of the CFA.[69]

The CFA had begun through the organization of a local alliance in Houston County, Texas, on December 11, 1886. Richard M. Humphrey, a white Baptist preacher, was elected local superintendent. By March 1888 the CFA's organizing activities had become successful enough to call for the making of a national organization, which was convened at Lovelady, Texas.[70] By October 1890 there was a large membership in the CFA with 175 alliances in the southern states. Twenty-five of these, or one-seventh, were located in Virginia. The editor of the *Southern Workman* estimated there were "over one million white and colored members in the U.S."[71]

In August 1890 the first annual meeting of the CFA in Virginia was held in Richmond. It was addressed by Humphrey, who spoke of postemancipation progress and the efficacy of the CFA.[72] There were important regional variations to the state CFA. Norfolk, in the southeastern peninsula, quickly became the center of the regional rural protest movement. This was understandable given Norfolk's historic role as a coastal entrepôt linking northern and southern as well as foreign and domestic markets. It was also an important federal navy base. In the fall of 1890 the CFA claimed 5,000 members; their hub was Norfolk. Joseph J. Rogers, the CFA agent responsible for North Carolina and Virginia, also managed the CFA exchange at Norfolk. The exchange had been organized by Humphrey during early 1888 with stock at $2 a share and over $700 collected.[73] This financial collective

THE HIGHEST STAGE OF TOBACCO ALLIANCE

alliance resembled the PCATU in providing a cooperative store for cutting out external and expensive merchandising. It appears to have been even more successful in obtaining support from small shareholders, although whether this was because of more entrenched corporate identity or smaller member subscriptions remains unclear.

The second annual meeting of the state CFA was held in Richmond during August 1891. One of the resolutions of the delegates favored protecting members against "the deadly fangs of monopoly, and rings, and trust companies." This was a clear echo of the Lynchburg Declaration issued by the state Farmers' Alliance against all monopolies, including the ATC. Since Rogers was unable to attend, Humphrey declared the state superintendentship vacant. The CFA delegates subsequently elected William H. Warwick, an African Virginian state lecturer and local organizer. He was elected unanimously over Rogers because of the latter's perceived mismanagement of the Norfolk exchange along with the self-determinationist aspirations of the freedpeople.[74] The latter struggle was a hallmark of freedpeople's politics stretching back into Republicanism and Readjusterism. It might be added that during this second meeting, it was claimed that there were around 20,000 members of the CFA in Virginia, hailing from forty-two counties.[75]

Although the state CFA revolved around Norfolk, its activities were no less evident farther westward in tobacco Virginia.[76] These rural actions were marshaled by local county leaders. Harry C. Green, a tax official and landholder of 107 acres in Brunswick County, along with Frank B. Ivy, a Hampton alumnus from Mecklenburg County, served on the CFA's board of directors. Edward Austin Jr., a preacher from Appomattox County, was the local representative to the CFA August 1891 meeting, while D. C. Beasley, a landholder with 110 acres, represented Dinwiddie County.[77] Although it is difficult to determine the precise nature of all the rank-and-file members represented by these local leaders, it is probable that they were mostly farmers or tenants. According to the federal census and the state tax books, there were between 1,722 and 2,053 freedpeople in these four counties who had obtained some landholdings by 1900.[78] It is likely that many of these black landholders belonged to local alliances headed by county delegates such as Green, Ivy, Austin, and Beasley. They would oppose hard agricultural times as well as capital monopolies such as the railroads and the ATC. But it is also probable that freedwomen were members of the CFA. They were rarely listed as "farmers" but often appeared as "servants." Their role in the cash economy as either rural domestics or petty traders guaranteed the payment of regular subscriptions and made them especially attractive to the CFA.[79] Black farm laborers, much like white farm laborers, were unlikely to have been members of the CFA.

Such rural protest does not appear to have met with the complete approbation of Hampton Institute despite the membership activities of alumnus Frank Ivy. In an article published in the *Southern Workman* just after the second state CFA meeting, contributor W. T. Fuller criticized the unworkability of such alliances. After briefly surveying the origins of the Farmers' Alliance, Fuller described its ten-point program. Most of it he found to be hopeless: deflationary measures "would soon sink [the country] into financial ruin"; switching silver for gold would adversely affect foreign currency exchange, while railroad regulation would entail only more burdensome government. Fuller added that although it "was not the object of the organization to go into politics," it was forced in that direction because both major political parties had ignored the "farmers' cause."[80] Although Fuller never referred to the Virginia CFA, as an important contributor to the leading journal devoted to the freedpeople, he can hardly have been unaware of its existence. Indeed, the *Southern Workman* was deafeningly silent on the CFA, with only a single reference besides Fuller's general observations.[81] We can only assume that the *Southern Workman* approved of the cooperative aims of the CFA but was less enthusiastic about the politicization of its alliance programs.[82]

The Virginia CFA did not hold a meeting in August 1892. The historian of the state's CFA has attributed this collapse to a combination of internal weakness and failure of an economic program.[83] Both factors probably played a part; these mirrored the decline of the PCATU at the same time and in a similar context. But it was also true that the political potential of this rural organization was dashed upon the hard realities of Democratic politics. During the 1892 state elections Colonel J. Thomas Goode, the Populist candidate for the Fourth District embracing much of the eastern tobacco southside, came within a few hundred votes of unseating the incumbent Democratic congressman. He had received a great deal of support from the freedpeople. Goode appealed the decision to the House of Representatives. He failed, despite enough evidence of destroyed ballots and rejected bundles to suggest that fraud had taken place. As was pointed out many years ago, "Fraud had deprived Colonel Goode of the opportunity to be the only Populist to serve in Congress from Virginia, but [General William] Mahone's negro votes were the principal basis of his possible honor."[84] The sarcasm of the latter part of this observation should not detract from the accuracy of the first part; neither should it gloss over the freedpeople's generational political agency since emancipation. It should also not be forgotten that political power sealed the fate of this rural organization.

Rather than suggest some sort of remarkable class alliance symbolizing the highest stage of consciousness, our focus has been on the self-determinationist organization of freedpeople in relation to their own emancipatory aspirations. This contrasts with normative definitions of a race and class alliance that remain the dominant historiographical paradigm.[85] The CFA in southside Virginia was an expression of the freedpeople's agrarian protest that was linked to older patterns of regional politics, including Republicanism and Readjusterism. It was a black rural protest movement with a tradition and efficacy rather than a weathervane pointing to possibly better race relations. That it failed to meet either its own expectations or those of subsequent commentators is an unfortunate but inescapable historical reality.[86]

The CFA, the Farmers' Alliance, and the ATC represented the highest stage of tobacco alliances during the early 1890s. These unique combinations were fueled by prolonged agricultural depression along with a transformed tobacco economy, especially the cigarette industry. One alliance proved to be remarkably successful; it helped pave the way for broader corporate domination. Although the success of the ATC proved ephemeral, the cigarette industry at large was remarkably successful, only recently facing some fundamental challenges. The other alliances failed to achieve their primary objectives, but they undermined older ideas honed during the reign of the old dominion. The central component in this undermining, however, was the freeing of labor, or shifting human terrain, and is the subject of our concluding chapter.

CHAPTER EIGHT

Shifting Terrain

I have been growing tobacco all my life and for myself for the last 30 years and I have a good experience in grow-ing tobacco for 27 years. I also work a farm of my own and has been for 9 years.—Farmer Sampson W. White

Black labour, for which there was no substitute, has practically disappeared from the country districts, and flocked into big cities, to mines, and to public works. —Traveler Arthur G. Bradley

Sums of money are sent in by children working in the northern cities.—Investigator Carl Kelsey

During the 1890s freedpeople began to accumulate land at unique rates as well as leave the countryside in record numbers. Unique landholding and record emigration seem strange bedfellows. Why would freedpeople leave the land just when such land was becoming available as a means to fulfill their long-awaited emancipatory aspirations for social autonomy? This concluding chapter seeks to explain this seeming paradox through a focus on land, labor, and generational change among the freedpeople in the Virginia tobacco region. It argues that both landholding and exodus were the culmination of emancipation, prolonged agricultural depression, and a transformed tobacco economy. Furthermore, these two processes were twin aspects of the erosion of older social relations. This dissolution occurred not simply between former slaves and former masters, but also among younger and older generations of freedpeople as each pursued their freedoms in very different terms.

We begin with an examination of freedpeople's landholdings in the

Virginia tobacco belt. While numerous historians have noted black land acquisition in tidewater Virginia, far less attention has been given to the interior regions. We then turn to the mass exodus of the freedpeople from the countryside to villages, towns, cities, and other states. This exodus is further linked to landholding as freedom's younger generation helped provide the funds for the realization of the emancipatory aspirations of freedom's older generations. This familial cooperation was part of a broader tradition of welfare provision traceable to the communal actions of slaves in the tobacco fields. Most importantly, these seeming opposites of old and young, land and urbanization, country and city, were part of an emergent agrarian capitalism that was transforming the American South in general and tobacco Virginia specifically.[1]

In French novelist Emile Zola's *La Terre*, the Fouan men give eloquent expression to the rural cultivator's passionate embrace of the land. To the family patriarch old Fouan, a "single piece of land would represent months of a bread-and-cheese existence, spending whole winters without a fire and summers drenched in sweat, with no respite from his toil save a few swigs of water." His son Buteau was "proud at having his roots in his own patch of land, bound to it like a stubborn hardy tree." Meanwhile, Hourdequin's landed ruminations were even more organic, bordering on the orgasmic: "God, how he had come to love that land, with a passion which went far beyond the grasping avarice of a peasant, with a passion that was sentimental and almost intellectual, recognizing in it the Great Mother who had given him life and sustenance and to whose bosom he would return." For the five Fouan men overlooking the Beauce, this "flat, fertile plain, easy to cultivate but requiring continuous care, has made its inhabitants cold and reflective; their only passion is for the earth." The last word lay with old Fouan. "The peasant," he pondered,

> who had for so long cultivated the land for the benefit of the lord of the manor yet who was beaten and stripped like a slave, not even owning his own skin; who had made the land fruitful by his efforts; then the constant, intimate link with the land which makes him love and desire it with a passion such as you might feel for someone

else's wife whom you care for and take in your arms but can never possess; that land which, after you have coveted it in such sufferings for centuries, you finally obtain by conquest and make your own, the sole joy and light of your life.[2]

It is tempting to view the freedpeople's struggle and desire for landownership in covetous terms similar to those of their rural counterparts of the 1860s French countryside. After all, the freedpeople had historically slaved in the land, made it fruitful from their repeated labors, and literally invested their lives in its produce. This intuitively appealing analogy, however, is not completely accurate since landownership for the freedpeople represented an important emancipatory aspiration whose primary feature was autonomy in a postslave society.[3] Their passion for the land was undoubtedly bound up with the fruits of their labor, but it also had to do with the desire to live outside the dictates of control defined by a social system of slavery. In this historical conjuncture, landholding served a specific rather than a general social function. Its ideological implications of autonomy were the same during the 1890s as they had been during the late 1860s. What was different, however, were rural conditions that had undergone prolonged agricultural depression and a transformed tobacco economy. The freedpeople's quest for landownership was an older generation's ambition for liberation forged during the transition from slavery to freedom.

The freedpeople's quest for land stretched back to the opening years of emancipation. It has been estimated that black people in Virginia accumulated between 80,000 and 100,000 acres by the late 1860s and early 1870s.[4] During the 1870s some freedpeople in the Virginia tobacco region managed to obtain land. In Brunswick County the county clerk recorded several land transactions during the mid- 1870s. Farmer T. Taylor sold 171.75 acres to freedman Henry Field in 1876. Freedpeople J. N. and J. W. Greene bought 7.5 acres from George B. Malone the following year, while R. A. Kidd sold 20 acres to freedman George Harrison in March 1878.[5] During the 1870s and 1880s Hampton Institute alumni wrote letters to the editor of the *Southern Workman* reporting land acquisitions by freedpeople in the Virginia interior. Hampton alumnus H wrote from Bedford County in late 1878 that as "many as twelve families within a mile of my school have homes of their own, owning from five to two hundred and fifty acres of land."[6] Alumnus E noted freedpeople landowners in the tobacco southside during the mid-1880s.[7] Some of the county land tax books also identified freedpeople who owned rural real estate. For instance, in the Dan River district of Pittsylvania County there were listed thirty-seven freedpeople who owned 1,160 acres with land and buildings worth $580 in 1880.[8] During the 1880s several freedpeople accumulated large landholdings in adjoining Mecklenburg County.[9] Luther Porter Jackson's pioneering study of postwar black officials in Virginia thoroughly documented their property gains accumulated through political and communal leadership.[10] It has been estimated that by 1900 African Virginians had acquired 1,031,331 acres divided into 25,566 farms with buildings worth a combined total of $12,915,931.[11]

This impressive landownership has been the hallmark of much African American pioneering scholarship.[12] These insights have formed the basis for much subsequent scholarship on property accumulation among African Virginians.[13] Much of this historical literature, however, has focused almost exclusively on the tidewater region. The Virginia interior, especially the tobacco region, has been generally ignored.[14] In this staple crop region, it is assumed, planters persisted while the freedpeople and their descendants remained mired in immutable poor agricultural conditions either as tenants, sharecroppers, or day laborers. As we have seen, many rural producers were tied to tobacco lands, especially through the readjustment of free labor law.[15] Furthermore, prolonged agricultural depression made life hard for many people living from the land. However, many freedpeople also began to gain unique access to landownership during the 1890s. The otherwise commendable social history of African Virginian landownership has not only ignored the interior region; it has also failed to explain the timing of this landownership beyond attributing it to a simple stubbornness on the part of the freedpeople—they desired land, and it eventually came. Freedpeople's landholding obviously preceded the 1890s, but its takeoff during that decade can only be explained by the broader context of prolonged agricultural depression, a transformed tobacco economy, the failure of rural combinations, and the resulting shift of white landowners from the countryside to the towns and elsewhere.[16]

During the 1890s numerous freedpeople began to accumulate land in the Virginia tobacco region. According to the 1900 federal census there were approximately 9,416 "Negro" farm owners registered in twenty-four tobacco-producing counties.[17] The Virginia land tax books, which recorded taxable real estate in the rural districts, listed over 10,000 "colored" landholders from the same region.[18] Over four-fifths of these landholding freedpeople resided in the traditional dark tobacco belt that had experienced emancipation, prolonged agricultural depression, and a changing tobacco economy. In contrast, there were far fewer landholding freedpeople in the newer bright tobacco southside. This regional difference was largely due to the declining significance of the older tobacco economy in contrast to the emergent cigarette economy whose demand for an available rural proletariat precluded the sale of rural real estate to those free laborers who might be tempted through landholding to withdraw from the tobacco economy. Even so, some freedpeople managed to obtain landholdings in the flue-cured region, especially Mecklenburg County.[19]

These raw numbers listed in the federal census and state tax records cloak the familial nature of freedpeople's landholding. There were around 211,488 freedpeople reported from these twenty-four counties in 1900.[20] According to the federal census most of the freedpeople in the Virginia tobacco region lived in family households of at least five.[21] Farmer Sampson W. White, for example, headed a six-person household that included his wife, Martha; daughters Mary Betti, Pup, and Leathy; and brother Green in the Dan River district of Pittsylvania County.[22] The most recent historian of postwar Louisa County estimated a mean family size of 5.5.[23] Assuming a minimal norm of five-person households and that each listed landowner belonged to a different family, then over one-fourth of all freedpeople households owned some land in the dark tobacco belt. Indeed, nearly half of all freedpeople households in Amelia, Fluvanna, and Goochland Counties owned land, while over three-quarters in Louisa County were landowners. In contrast, fewer freedpeople households owned land in the bright tobacco southside. Indeed, only one family in ten owned land in the region, while in Henry and Pittsylvania Counties the figure was probably even lower. This latter area was the closest to the conventional stereotype of Negro tenancy, sharecropping, and laboring in the Virginia tobacco region (see tables 8.1 and 8.2).

The households of landholding freedpeople also owned a great deal of acreage. In 1870 it was estimated that the freedpeople owned some

TABLE 8.1. Freedpeople's Landholdings in the Dark Tobacco Belt, 1900

County	Black Population N	%	Black Farm Owners[a]	Black Landowners[b]	Black Households as % of Black Population[c] Farm Owners	Landowners	Tobacco Production (in millions of pounds)
Amelia	5,985	66	475	612	40	51	3.1
Amherst	7,057	39	242	356	17	25	5.2
Appomattox	3,931	41	213	238	27	30	4.0
Bedford	9,739	32	458	—	23	—	6.9
Brunswick	10,842	59	483	366[d]	22	—	3.7
Buckingham	7,851	51	419	217[d]	27	—	3.3
Campbell	9,615	41	293	336[d]	15	—	5.4
Caroline	9,042	54	657	—	36	—	1.8
Charlotte	8,545	56	297	451	17	26	5.5
Cumberland	6,205	69	364	388	29	31	3.4
Dinwiddie	9,500	62	482	583	25	31	3.0
Fluvanna	4,011	44	321	398	40	50	1.2
Goochland	5,558	58	452	589	41	53	1.0
Louisa	8,621	52	912	1,317[e]	53	76	1.7
Lunenburg	6,572	56	393	458	30	35	4.6
Nelson	5,672	35	234	166[d]	21	—	2.9
Nottoway	7,400	60	381	561	26	38	2.2
Powhatan	4,481	65	233	516	26	57	1.7
Prince Edward	9,769	65	462	734	24	37	4.9
Totals	140,396	51	7,771	8,286[f]	28	29	65.5[g]

Sources: USBC, *1900, Population*, 561–62; USBC, *1900, Agriculture*, pt. 1, 190–91, 133–35, and pt. 2, 576–77; Virginia Land Tax Books, Goochland County (1899), Amelia, Amherst, Appomattox, Bedford, Brunswick, Buckingham, Campbell, Caroline, Charlotte, Cumberland, Dinwiddie, Louisa, Lunenburg, Nelson, Nottoway, and Powhatan Counties (1900), Fluvanna and Prince Edward Counties (1901). Some 1900 land tax books were unavailable. For the dark-fired district in 1909, see E. H. Mathewson, "Summary of Ten Years' Experiments with Tobacco," Virginia Agricultural Experiment Station Bulletin 205 (June 1914), 7–8.

[a]From 1900 federal census.

[b]From 1900 state land tax books.

[c]Of at least five persons.

[d]Statistics for one county district.

[e]Shifflett, *Patronage and Poverty*, 18, estimates 1,314.

[f]The total of freedpeople landholders listed in the state land tax books is higher because it includes all districts in Brunswick, Buckingham, Campbell, and Nelson Counties as well as returns from Bedford and Carolina Counties.

[g]This amounts to 53 percent of Virginia's tobacco production in 1900.

TABLE 8.2. Freedpeople's Landholdings in the Bright Tobacco Belt, 1900

County	Black Population N	Black Population %	Black Farm Owners[a]	Black Landowners[b]	Black Households as % of Black Population[c] Farm Owners	Black Households as % of Black Population[c] Landowners	Tobacco Production (in millions of pounds)
Franklin	5,947	23	250	187	21	16	3.2
Halifax	19,275	52	543	543	14	14	13.0
Henry	8,383	43	89	42[d]	5	—	3.6
Mecklenburg	16,198	61	544	866	17	27	7.3
Pittsylvania	21,289	45	219	89[d]	5	—	17.0
Totals	71,092	46	1,645	1,727[e]	11	12	44.1[f]

Sources: USBC, *1900, Population*, 561–62; USBC, *1900, Agriculture*, pt. 1, 190–91, 133–35, and pt. 2, 576–77; Virginia Land Tax Books, Franklin, Halifax, Henry, Mecklenburg, and Pittsylvania Counties (1900). For the flue-cured district in 1909, see E. H. Mathewson, "Summary of Ten Years' Experiments with Tobacco," Virginia Agriculture Experiment Station Bulletin #205 (June 1914), 7–8.
[a]From 1900 federal census.
[b]From 1900 state land tax books.
[c]Of at least five persons.
[d]Statistics for one county district.
[e]The total of freedpeople landholders listed in the state land tax books is higher because it includes all districts in Henry and Pittsylvania Counties.
[f]This amounts to 36 percent of Virginia's tobacco production in 1900.

80,000 to 100,000 acres in the state; a generation later the freedpeople in the tobacco region alone had quadrupled their landholdings to nearly 400,000 acres. This land was located especially in the dark tobacco region, where freedpeople owned over 300,000 acres worth nearly $1 million with buildings worth nearly $400,000. This acreage pointed to the class dynamic of autonomous landholding freedpeople; their independent farming also refuted the adage of incompetent Negro farming. Despite the fact that freedpeople were either a majority or a large minority of the population, however, their landholdings paled in size and monetary value compared with those of traditional landholders. The freedpeople in Louisa County, for instance, owned the most acreage, yet this amounted to only 12 percent of all county real estate. The least acreage was held by the freedpeople in the bright tobacco belt. Apart from Mecklenburg County, the freedpeople owned far smaller amounts of land, ranging from 3 to 4 percent, in spite of the

TABLE 8.3. Freedpeople's Acreage, Land Values, and Building Values in the Dark Tobacco Belt, 1900

County	Black Population N	%	Land Owned by Freedpeople Acreage	%	Value ($)	%	Buildings Owned by Freedpeople Value ($)	%
Amelia	5,985	66	21,412	9	72,062	11	32,958	11
Amherst	7,057	39	10,281	3	35,161	3	21,293	5
Appomattox	3,931	41	10,683	5	26,745	5	12,342	6
Bedford	9,739	32	—	—	—			
Brunswick	10,842	59	34,203	9	86,686	10	26,356	7
Buckingham	7,851	51	13,304	5	26,149	6	10,115	7
Campbell	9,615	41	10,838	3	96,038	5	61,916	6
Caroline	9,042	54	—	—	—			
Charlotte	8,545	56	13,937	5	57,074	6	18,204	4
Cumberland	6,205	69	15,722	8	52,231	10	15,469	6
Dinwiddie	9,500	62	26,880	8	70,498	7	24,045	7
Fluvanna	4,011	44	10,489	6	22,897	5	9,295	5
Goochland	5,558	58	16,382	9	65,290	8	28,430	10
Louisa	8,621	52	37,030	12	107,084	10	37,928	8
Lunenburg	6,572	56	23,407	9	39,335	9	9,178	6
Nelson	5,672	35	10,795	4	36,815	4	13,280	4
Nottoway	7,400	60	18,994	10	45,857	10	29,478	14
Powhatan	4,481	65	11,460	7	33,108	7	24,135	8
Prince Edward	9,769	65	22,832	10	48,113	6	15,621	4
Totals	140,396	51	308,649	8	921,143	7	390,043	7

Sources: USBC, *1900, Population*, 561–62; Virginia Land Tax Books, Goochland County (1899), Amelia, Amherst, Appomattox, Brunswick, Buckingham, Campbell, Charlotte, Cumberland, Dinwiddie, Louisa, Lunenburg, Nelson, Nottoway, and Powhatan Counties (1900), Fluvanna and Prince Edward Counties (1901). Some 1900 land tax books were unavailable. Statistics for Bedford and Caroline Counties were not collected.

fact that they constituted either a demographic majority or large minority. The shifting terrain of landholding economy was less pronounced in the bright belt.[24] (See tables 8.3 and 8.4.)

This land owned by freedpeople in tobacco Virginia was worth a great deal. The total market price for the freedpeople's combined landholdings of 398,019 acres was nearly $1.2 million. Although this averaged over $3 per acre, some land was worth more than other land,

TABLE 8.4. Freedpeople's Acreage, Land Values, and Building Values in the Bright Tobacco Belt, 1900

County	Black Population N	%	Land Owned by Freedpeople Acreage	%	Value ($)	%	Buildings Owned by Freedpeople Value ($)	%
Franklin	5,947	23	14,977	3	28,120	2	10,003	3
Halifax	19,275	52	21,452	4	82,047	4	43,461	6
Henry	8,383	43	7,999	3	9,105	2	2,780	4[a]
Mecklenburg	16,198	61	29,476	7	62,189	7	29,604	8
Pittsylvania	21,289	45	15,466	2	96,232	4	44,745	6
Totals	71,092	46	89,370	4	277,693	4	130,593	6

Sources: USBC, *1900, Population*, 561–62; Virginia Land Tax Books, Franklin, Halifax, Henry, Mecklenburg, and Pittsylvania Counties (1900).
[a]Building value for one district.

because of either its fertility, its improvement, or its proximity to an urban environment. Freedwoman Elberta Anderson owned one-eighth of an acre worth $50, while G. W. Thorton owned 121 acres worth $15.36 an acre in Prince Edward County. While Thorton's acreage was three miles east of Farmville Court House, Anderson's tiny plot nestled a mere quarter-mile south of the courthouse.[25] In the Brookville district of Campbell County, freedpeople's landholdings amounted to only 3,024 acres; these were, however, worth $52,485 because of their close proximity to the city of Lynchburg.[26] Furthermore, some rural real estate was worth less because it was poorer land. In Henry County the freedpeople's land was worth an average of $1.14 per acre, while in Lunenburg County it was valued at a mere $1.68 per acre.[27] These poor lands were probably either river bottoms, over-cropped soils, or even wastelands. Such poor lands were a red flag to agricultural reformers or efficiency-minded economists. To an older generation of freedpeople, however, these paltry plots betokened freedom. Their arability might well have been limited, but they were an important symbol of shifting terrain toward freedom.

These freedpeople landowners also owned numerous small and large buildings on their lands. In 1900 freedpeople landowners owned over $500,000 worth of rural buildings in the Virginia tobacco region.

These ranged from log cabins and wooden huts to barns and farmhouses. Of particular note was the Brookville district of Campbell County, where freedpeople owned buildings worth $50,661. Their high value is explained by their proximity to Lynchburg.[28] In Halifax County freedpeople owned $43,461 worth of buildings, while in Louisa County the figure was $37,928.[29] Unlike those in Brookville, the buildings in the latter counties were primarily rural structures. Some buildings increased land values because of improvement. Albert Cox's buildings on his 33.5 acres were worth $200, which represented half of the value of his real estate in the Dover district of Goochland County.[30] These relatively high building values stood in marked contrast to the Dan River district, Pittsylvania County, in the bright tobacco belt, where freedpeople owned only $3,655 worth of buildings, constituting a mere 1 percent of the district's building values.[31] Indeed, the value of these buildings paled into insignificance when compared overall with the buildings owned by planters. The highest proportion of building values held by freedpeople landowners was reported from Nottoway County at around 14 percent ($29,478).[32] This percentage was about the same in Gloucester County.[33] It is hard to say whether this reflected the freedpeople's wealth or the region's poverty. In virtually all other tobacco counties, freedpeople owned less than one-tenth of the building values even though they often constituted either demographic majorities or large minorities. Nevertheless, it is important to reiterate the symbolic meaning of owning a shed or a barn in a postemancipation society that contradicted the postulates of an older dominion.

Local land tax records paint an impressive statistical picture of freedpeople's landholdings in the Virginia tobacco region during the 1890s. Within the broader context of a postemancipation society, these landowning freedpeople can be seen as an emergent peasantry or small farmer class who eventually realized their emancipatory aspirations. Such a conclusion is surely grist for the progressive's mill.[34] These were all freedpeople landholders in Virginia who obtained land in the generation following emancipation. However, there are also some crucial social distinctions within this emergent peasantry. Elberta Anderson's one-eighth of an acre in Prince Edward County obviously meant something very different from the thirty-three acres owned by Albert Cox in Goochland County.[35] The latter represented a degree of independence, property, and social standing; the former stood for semidependence, subsistence, and survival. Small landholders often gained simple symbolic meaning away from slavery and toward freedom; these certainly were not the basis for subsistence living. It was even likely that patches of worthless land possessed by land-hungry freedpeople reflected the power of landowners concerned with retaining free labor, especially in the bright tobacco southside.

If the emancipatory and regional dialectic resulted in freedpeople owning land, it also encouraged rural class formation. Approximately 195 freedpeople landholders were registered as owning over 50 acres in ten counties in the dark tobacco belt. Cohorts of large landholders were especially prevalent in parts of Brunswick and Louisa Counties. In the Sturgeon district of Brunswick County, Ruffin Callis and Alexander Hill owned, respectively, 326 and 172 acres of rural real estate worth $815 and $519.[36] Elsewhere, freedpeople owned large tracts of land. Frank Barnes owned 300 acres with land valued at $450 and buildings at $150 at Buffalo Ridge in the Court House district of Amherst County.[37] In the Jackson district of Amelia County, Berthie Mann owned 181.5 acres worth $635 fifteen miles southeast of the county courthouse.[38] In the southside district of Appomattox County, J. Hancock owned 233.75 acres worth $640 nine miles southwest of the courthouse.[39] Some of these large landholdings were truly remarkable. In the Lovingston district of Nelson County, Emily R. Thomas reportedly held eight tracts totaling 2,040 acres worth $8,768 six to eight miles south of the courthouse.[40] There were even some major landholders in the flue-cured tobacco southside. In the Reed Creek district of Henry County, J. M. Dapper held 288 acres worth $1 per acre on Turkey Cock Mount twelve miles northeast of the courthouse, and J. W. and G. Fuller owned 137.5 acres evaluated at $3 per acre at Sandy River sixteen miles northeast of the courthouse.[41] These large landholdings conferred independence, stability, and local power on their owners.

From their ranks local political and communal leadership was plucked. Sometime before the early 1880s freedman Samuel P. Bolling accumulated 925.5 acres (some of which belonged to his former master) in the Randolph district of Cumberland County. In 1883 Bolling was elected to the House of Delegates as the representative for Cumberland and Buckingham Counties, where he served until 1887. In

1900 this resilient eighty-one-year-old former slave, freedman, farmer, mechanic, and politician died. Although his landholdings had decreased in size, they were still exceptionally large. According to the 1900 land tax book for Cumberland County, Bolling died owning 748.6 acres worth $4 per acre totaling $2994.40 adjacent to the Buckingham road twelve miles south of the courthouse.[42] In short, Samuel P. Bolling was among an older generation of freedpeople representing the landed talented tenth.[43]

Unlike this rural talented tenth, the vast majority of freedpeople landholders owned more modest-sized tracts in the tobacco region. Most freedpeople landholders in the various counties held fewer than 50 acres. Agnes Wade, for instance, held 40.75 acres worth $81.50 at Snow Creek fourteen miles south of the courthouse in District One, Franklin County.[44] Many freedpeople held considerably less than 50 acres. Approximately three-quarters of the landholders in the Court House district of Amherst County owned 20 or fewer acres.[45] Mary Cottrell owned 20 acres worth $3 per acre on David's road fourteen miles west of the courthouse in James River district of Buckingham County, and Patrick Woodson owned 20 acres worth $60 at Salem four miles northeast of the courthouse in Palmyra, Fluvanna County.[46] The importance of land can be determined by the recording of even the smallest measurement, such as William Walker's 18 43/100 acres worth $96 adjoining the Petersburg Railroad twelve miles east of the courthouse in Rowanty, Dinwiddie County.[47]

Most freedpeople landholders owned even fewer than 10 acres. This was the case in both Lunenburg and Prince Edward Counties.[48] In the Brookville district of Campbell County, around 90 percent of landholders owned 10 or fewer acres.[49] William Johnson owned 3 acres worth $120, and M. A. owned 6 acres worth $84.[50] In Amelia County, George Perkinson owned 2 acres worth $50, while in the Leigh district of Prince Edward County, Louisa Smith owned 1 acre worth $25 at Green Bay twelve miles southeast of the courthouse.[51] These differences in land values were largely due to differences in arability, building conditions, and proximity to urban areas.[52]

Of course, there were many freedpeople whose ownership of less than an acre hardly qualified them for the title of landed proprietor. In a world where economic efficiency or land accumulation was a measure of success, these tiny plots meant very little. They were insuffi-

TABLE 8.5. Distribution of Freedpeople's Landholdings by Size in the Dark Tobacco Belt, 1900

County/District	Black Landowners	Acres (and % of Total County Acreage)			
		10 or Fewer	20 or Fewer	50 or Fewer	More than 50
Amherst/Court House	136	—	104 (76%)	—	—
Brunswick/Sturgeon	55	—	14 (25%)	22 (40%)	19 (34%)
Buckingham/James River	120	—	—	102 (85%)	18 (15%)
Buckingham/Marshall	228	—	—	209 (92%)	19 (8%)
Campbell/Brookville	620	556 (90%)	—	—	—
Dinwiddie/Darville	62	—	—	—	9 (14%)
Fluvanna	398	—	—	383 (96%)	15 (4%)
Goochland/Dover	185	—	—	173 (93%)	12 (7%)
Louisa/Louisa	380	—	—	335 (88%)	45 (12%)
Louisa/Jackson	151	—	—	109 (72%)	42 (28%)
Lunenburg/Loch Leven	34	—	—	27 (79%)	7 (21%)
Nelson/Lovingston	60	—	—	51 (85%)	9 (15%)
Totals	2,429	556 (23%)	118 (5%)	1,411 (58%)	195 (8%)

Sources: Virginia Land Tax Books, Brunswick and Nelson Counties (1890), Goochland County (1899), Amherst, Buckingham, Campbell, Dinwiddie, Fluvanna, Louisa, and Lunenburg Counties (1900). Some 1900 land tax books were unavailable.

cient to support a family. Such landholding was undoubtedly supported by either rural proletarianization or urban work. But in terms of a postemancipation society in which land provided some independence, the symbol of freedom, and removal from the managerial eye of neoslavery, it meant a great deal. This was the meaning behind H. R. Hancock's otherwise pitiful one-half acre with a land value of $15 and buildings worth $60 near Evergreen eleven miles northwest of the courthouse in Clover Hill, Appomattox County.[53] Similarly with Ammon Nowlin's ⅜ acre worth $75 half a mile from the courthouse in District One, Franklin County, and Ella Christopher's half-acre worth $5, adjacent to William Christopher's place, thirteen miles southeast of the courthouse in the Bellafonte District of Nottoway County.[54] These modest rural hearths and homes provided some autonomy for growing food, tending gardens, and living relatively free[55] (see table 8.5).

These small plots only superficially resembled slave gardens because they stood for the distance traveled from servitude. It must be emphasized that there is a complex dialectic between the material na-

ture of small landholding—such as usage, reproduction, and subsistence—and the ideological significance of such landholding in a postemancipation society. For the freedpeople it entailed distance from supervision and the embodiment of past labor's fruits as well as material
contribution to reproduction.[56] For former slaveowners, landlords,
planters, and employers, freedpeople's landholding meant the clearest
refutation of a proslave ideology of natural African dependency. It also
raised more immediately troublesome issues such as employee scarcity
in agricultural production, especially labor-intensive tobacco cultivation. For the Hampton Institute guardians of free labor, this landholding suggested the workability of freedom as long as the right values of
hard work, thrift, and strict household control were pursued. In short,
these small landholders were the untalented nine-tenths living on
the land.

The ownership of rural real estate was clearly an important index of
freedom for independent freedpeople's households. This was no less
true of the broader communal nature of freedpeople's landholding.
Numerous freedpeople held the trusteeship of certain lands for free
institutions, especially churches, benevolent societies, and schools.
Hal Cymes was the trustee of half an acre for an unnamed church in
Pleasant Grove, Lunenburg County.[57] H. Morris and others acted as
trustees for 17.5 acres belonging to Peterville Church at Phelps Union
in Marshall, Buckingham County.[58] Albert Sears was the trustee for 2
acres of the Baptist Union Church in the same region. Although the
land was only worth $3, we can safely assume that it meant far more for
the congregation in terms of providing a space for communal worship.
In addition, some of the older members of the congregation probably
recalled Baptist Union's secession from the Buckingham Baptist
Church in 1868 in response to the maltreatment of the black deacon
during the first flush of freedom.[59]

Communal landholding was especially pronounced in Dinwiddie
County. The Independent Order of St. Lukes held several small tracts
of land in trust, including 2 acres on Squirrel Lock road and .75 acres at
adjoining Sutherland, both twelve miles northeast of the county courthouse at Namozine. Another freedpeople's benevolent society, the
Good Samaritans, held 1.5 acres on the Pluck road two miles away.
These friendly societies were enhanced by other communal endeavors
including schools, fraternities, and churches. In the Rowanty district

the Zion Church held 1 acre on the Hawkins road; the Gula Star Church also held 1 acre on the Scotts road.[60] It might be added that these communal landed expressions of freedom were somewhat cheaper than individual holdings. According to the legal provisions of the *Code of Virginia*, all "real estate used for divine worship" would be "exempt from taxation."[61] This appears to have applied equally to freedpeople's churches since the state's tax assessor did not return a tax bill from these premises. The most important point, of course, is that such institutions provided useful expressions of the collective meaning of freedom in the countryside.[62]

Having explored the extent, nature, and meaning of freedpeople's land-holdings in the Virginia tobacco region, let us turn to the social process of land accumulation during the 1890s. Both contemporaries and historians have commented extensively on postemancipation landholdings, but few have provided explanations for both the quantitative and qualitative transformation in freedpeople's landholding, especially during this period. The key explanation for the emergence of freedom's land-holding generation concerned the structural transformation of agrarian life in postemancipation Virginia. The combination of emancipation and prolonged agricultural depression changed rural relations through-out the state. In the tobacco region the decline of the traditional dark leaf shipping economy and the rise of the new bright leaf cigarette industry encouraged shifting terrain. This loosening of old bonds to the land was particularly salient in the older tobacco regions. During the postemancipation decades, consistently low prices for dark leaf tobacco together with competition from western cereal production and the rise of bright leaf production boded poorly for many traditional rural pro-ducers. Between 1891 and 1894 wheat prices for Virginia producers nearly halved from 100 cents to 56 cents per bushel. Tobacco prices also plummeted from 7 cents to 5.2 cents per pound in 1896.[63] These con-sistently low prices, together with the failure of rural combinations to combat the slide effectively, forced many traditional landowners to sell small parcels of their land. Some sold their landholdings altogether and emigrated to the local town or city or left the state. The emancipatory aspirations of an older generation of freedpeople provided a humble but consistent demand for this land.

Land sales caused by depressed agricultural conditions constituted the primary source for the freedpeople's landholdings from the 1890s onward. According to the state land tax books there were several hundred land transfers in the Virginia tobacco region during the 1890s. The actual nature of these land transfers was often unclear: Were these market transactions, property gifts, or inheritances? It is clear, however, that numerous freedpeople purchased land from traditional landowners. Unlike some more complicated agrarian societies, these land transactions were fairly straightforward. Fee-simple sales predominated whereby real estate was bought for a cash sum. Such market transactions were especially pronounced in Campbell County during the 1890s. Freedwoman Mary Alexander bought 6 acres worth $132 from white landowner Frank Nelson in the Rustburg district, while freedman Stonewall J. Graves purchased 51 acres worth $154.07 from white landowner John Thornhill, who owned 336 acres.[64] Freedman William P. Tweedy was recorded as obtaining 55 acres worth $131.40 from M. M. Tweedy (white) in Rustburg.[65] Similarly, there were numerous land transfers recorded in the Brookville district that resulted in large numbers of freedpeople owning land.[66] In the Buffalo district of Prince Edward County at least eleven white landowners sold some land to freedpeople. A. L. Robinson, who owned 78.25 acres, was recorded as giving "off" 26.75 acres to freedwoman Margaret Allen.[67] There was, in short, a clear connection between traditional landowners selling their land because of prolonged depression and older freedpeople buying small lots in order to achieve their long-term emancipatory aspirations.

Contemporaries also commented on the dialectic between depressed agricultural conditions, land sales, and freedpeople's landholdings. The alarmist *Petersburg Weekly-Index-Appeal* urged "our native white people to be content with their country and *remain here.*" "Don't let," the editorial continued, "your freehold in this fair land slip from you, to be grasped and held by foreign or colored settlers. Hold on to the old Southside."[68] Mr. F. M. Fitch, Hampton Institute's field missionary, reported from Charlotte and Appomattox Counties that "the people are flocking to the cities," including "the white boys." Consequently, "land is cheap, and the colored people should be induced to stay and buy it."[69] Writing on Prince Edward County at the turn of the century, Carl Kelsey noted the link between the "decadence

TABLE 8.6. Land Transfers in the Dark Tobacco Belt, 1900

County/District	Black Landowners	Transfers[a]
Amelia	612	numerous "deeds from" and "deeds to"
Amherst	356	numerous
Appomattox	238	30
Brunswick/District 1	366	numerous to railroad
Buckingham	655	numerous
Campbell	956	numerous
Charlotte	451	numerous
Cumberland	388	several "deeds from" and "deeds to"
Dinwiddie	583	several through will
Louisa	1,317	numerous
Nelson/Lovingston	60	11
Prince Edward/Buffalo	734	148

Sources: Virginia Land Tax Books, Nelson County (1890), Amelia, Amherst, Appomattox, Brunswick, Buckingham, Campbell, Charlotte, Cumberland, Dinwiddie, Louisa, and Prince Edward Counties (1900). The 1900 land tax book for Nelson County was unavailable.

[a]Recorded under "Comments" in the final column of the land tax books.

of agricultural conditions, affording at the same time a chance for many Negroes to become land owners."[70] Dr. Charles W. Dabney Jr., president and professor of economics at the University of Tennessee, also noted this process. Testifying before the 1901 Industrial Commission, he noted that his old home of Prince Edward County "has been very much abandoned by the whites, not because Negroes were there, but because the land was very poor and remunerating crops could not be made now, and the Negro bought land and settled there."[71] In sum, freedpeople's landholding was directly tied to the broader structural context of emancipation, agricultural depression, and emigration (see tables 8.6 and 8.7).

It is also evident that some landownership by freedpeople resulted from a dying paternalist ideology. The most vocal advocate of this explanation has been Crandall Shifflett, who traced some freedpeople's landholdings to local patron Thomas Watson's largesse in Louisa County.[72] It is probable that some of the several hundred land transfers recorded in the state land tax books were likewise the result of the

White Landowners	Sold to Black Farmers	Land Tax Delinquents	Off[a]	Rem[b]	Deed[c]
107[d]	11	3	42	8	34

Black Landowners	Bought from White Landowners	Land Tax Delinquents	Off[a]	Rem[b]	Deed[c]
41[e]	11	8	—	—	15

Source: Virginia Land Tax Book, Prince Edward County (1900), 1–83.
[a]Land transfer described as "off," meaning sale, gift, will, etc.
[b]Land transfer described as "formerly," meaning remarried landholder.
[c]Land transfer by deed.
[d]9 miscellaneous entries.
[e]7 miscellaneous entries.

vestiges of paternalism in the postemancipation Virginia countryside. This certainly seems to have been the case around Whipping Creek in the Falling River district of Campbell County. According to the land tax book for 1900, Mary Hubbard owned 375.25 acres worth $4.50 per acre. Her white neighbors included Sallie Moore and Clara Moore with 50 acres apiece worth $2.50 per acre and Bettie Mosley with 215.25 acres worth $4.10 per acre. Hubbard's black neighbors included Delphy Buck and Diner Young with 25 acres apiece at $2.50 per acre and Jennie Lin and Alice Hubbard with 5 acres each also worth $2.50 per acre.[73] Much of this land had been willed to the owners by Hubbard sometime during the late 1890s. Thus, the Moores and Mosley received their land from Hubbard, as did the four freedwomen.[74] This points to a combination of familial and paternal obligation from an older dominion.[75]

While it is important not to ignore this paternalist explanation, it is equally important not to reduce the complex process of land transfers between traditional landowners and freedpeople simply to planter largesse. Broader structural agrarian changes *forced* many traditional landowners to sell some or all of their land even if some might have been tempted to see their actions in terms of benevolence. Furthermore, some traditional landowners might well have sold their land to retain the freedpeople's field and domestic labor besides earning some hard cash. George V. McGehee once owned 70 acres at Reedy Creek in the Louisa Court House district, but he subsequently transferred 10.25 acres to freedman Thomas H. Hughson, 1 acre to freedwoman Lucy Appleby, and 10 acres to freedman Jefferson Wright, leaving McGehee with 48.75 acres. Freedman Willie Cole in the Bacon district of Charlotte County obtained 6 acres from William G. Friend, who owned 100 acres, and 52.75 acres from F. Emerick. Freedman Tweedy gained 55 acres from another Tweedy in Campbell County.[76] These land transfers were undoubtedly prompted by market forces and perhaps labor retention along with a strong dose of paternalism.[77] Most importantly, this paternal explanation for landholding detracts from the agency of the freedpeople themselves in realizing their emancipatory aspirations at a particularly propitious moment.[78]

The experience of Beverly Jones, a former slave in Gloucester County, exemplifies the freedpeople's agency in purchasing land along with its potential difficulties. Jones recalled buying 12 acres of land at $12 per acre from a white man named Perrin Kemp. "It wasn' much good," Jones said, "for farm-land, that's why he sold it, but it was cheap." He then described in detail the difficulties black landholders might encounter once they had bought land. Jones had "an awful ruckus gittin' the deed fo' my property, though. I hadn' had much schoolin' but I knew that when you bought any land, you was suppose to get a deed with it. At that time when any land was transferred, it had to go through the Constable's hands. Well, ole man Perrin Kemp went to the Constable to collect for the lan' an' the Constable come to me." Jones asked the constable for the deed and told him he would pay the money once he received the deed. The constable "went back to the white man an' tole him an' ole Perrin Kemp sent along a bill an' tole him to tell me to write on this bill 'Deed is due.' I took the bill an' looked at it, then I tole the constable, 'I'm goinna pay the money when I get the deed.'" A few days later Jones "was walkin' in to town an ole Perrin Kemp come along drivin' his team." Kemp asked Jones "effen I want to ride. I got in wid him. Then he slapped me on the back an' laughed. 'Beverly, you black rascal you, here's yo' deed.' An he give me the deed an' I reached in my pocket an' give him the payment on the property. Never had no more trouble wid that white man."[79] This freedman desired some land; the traditional landholder sold a few acres of limited arability to a seemingly desperate landless ex-slave.

The local constable was to oversee the transaction presumably in favor of the landholder. The freedman, however, insisted on receiving the deed before handing over the cash for the land. The landholder recognized that this land sale was unlikely without his providing the deed. The final transaction, despite its paternal dress, could not camouflage this freedman's agency in buying land.

This agency was clear from the actions of other freedpeople who transferred land independent of planter paternalism. Archie Scott owned 10 acres, of which he transferred 2 acres worth $30 to Mary Fogus near Mount Airy in the Court House district of Amherst County.[80] Similarly, George H. Banks transferred 10 acres to Margaret Fautaine in the Marshall district of Buckingham County.[81] Other freedpeople landholders willed rural real estate to either friends or relatives. R. Hill willed 60 acres worth $180 to freedwoman Maria L. Johnson, 30 acres to Susun Goodwyn, and 10 acres to Martha Goodwyn in the Sapony district of Dinwiddie County.[82] Other freedpeople landholders willed rural real estate to their surviving family members. Calvin Beverley transferred 1 acre worth $50 to Eliza B. Beverley, while Martin Freeman deeded 10 acres worth $3 per acre to Robert Freeman.[83] Samuel P. Bolling, who died in 1900 owning 748.6 acres, passed his rural real estate to his family in Cumberland County, who retained it for decades.[84]

Land transfers among freedpeople were not always successful. Beverly Jones's story outlines some of the pitfalls that might beset a potential landholder. Furthermore, small landholdings that resulted from hard agricultural times and took so long to accumulate could easily disappear during subsequent times. Some freedpeople, for example, sold small plots of land to railroad companies during the 1890s. The Petersburg Railroad bought one-fourth of an acre from John Wright, who owned 6 acres worth $30, and $1^{57}/_{100}$ acres from William Walker, who owned $18^{43}/_{100}$ acres worth $96 in Dinwiddie County.[85] Freedpeople who were delinquent in paying their land taxes risked forfeiture of their land. According to the state treasurer's reports there were around sixty "colored" landholders who owed back taxes on land in Prince Edward County. Peter Scott and his wife were recorded as owing tax on their 10 acres in the Farmville district.[86]

Land tax delinquency among freedpeople appears to have been especially prominent in Louisa County. In the Court House District 56

SHIFTING TERRAIN

delinquents were recorded. Three of these, including Samuel Baker (21 acres), Mary Johnson (4 acres), and Robert Tyree (62 acres), had their land "redeemed" to the "commonwealth." In the Green Spring district there were 175 delinquent "colored" land taxpayers listed, of whom 20 had their land redeemed. Margaret Bloomer had owned 7 acres, while Nelson Harris and James Hackney, who owed 63 cents in state tax and 77 cents in county tax, lost 100 acres. The Cuckoo district had 39 land tax delinquents recorded; 8 had their land redeemed, including Dabney and Henry Kenney's 24 acres for back taxes of 46 cents to the state and 56 cents to the county. In Jackson district there were 11 delinquents, of whom 3 had their land redeemed, including Dick, Susan Hope, and their children.[87]

Other freedpeople forfeited their land because they died intestate, leaving the state in possession. Washington Martin owned 379 acres worth $568.50 in 1890; by 1900 he had added 185 acres worth $1 per acre, but he was listed as deceased. Ammon Nowlin owned ⅜ of an acre worth $75 in 1890; this had increased to 2 acres worth $185 by 1900, but he too had died.[88] This land could be assumed by relatives along with its county and state taxes, or the county land commissioner, according to the state code, could "ascertain who are the heirs of the intestate, and charge the land to such heirs." In addition, where "the owner has devised the land absolutely, the commissioner may charge the land to such devisee."[89] Undevised land could be seized by the state tax assessor, who then resold it. These land reversals can be seen as the socioeconomic side of an earlier political redemption.

There were, however, numerous instances of freedpeople persisting in their landholding over the years in the Virginia tobacco region. The Bollings retained their land in Cumberland County for decades.[90] Susie Burns, a former slave, proudly recalled how her family obtained and retained their piece of land in Brunswick County. Her family's landholdings were traceable to the Civil War. "A Yankee soldier—one o' de generals," she recalled, "tole Father de land was our'n an tole us we could have a piece effen we paid de taxes." The Burnses appeared to have paid their taxes because Susie "still own a piece of dat lan'." Indeed, she added, "Colored people still livin' on most of it, down to de third and fo'th generation, I guess."[91] Both Ruffin Callis and Alex Hill retained their land in the Sturgeon district of Brunswick County during the hard times of the 1890s; they even increased its value.[92]

The same was true of Mary Alexander and Stonewall Graves in the Rustburg District of Campbell County.[93] Agnes Wade held on to her 40.75 acres despite the misfortunes of other freedpeople landholders in Franklin County.[94] Similarly, hundreds of freedpeople maintained their small acreages despite the large amount of redeemed land in Louisa County.[95]

More examples of freedpeople's landholding persistence could no doubt be added though systematic examination of the all the state land tax books over a generation. Such research would no doubt reveal the making of a black peasantry in the tidewater and piedmont regions whose small landholdings challenge the view that the freedpeople were simply mired in immutable poor sharecropping or wage labor conditions. Even this finding, however, might have to be qualified. Pioneering African Virginian sociologist Harry Roberts once argued for black agency over white paternalism as an explanation for landholding: the "amount of land inherited by Negroes from their masters was a small fraction of the land which Negroes have acquired." He also added that this process was quick and soon unraveled. By the 1940s, "such land has passed back to white families as a result of the white heirs contesting wills or rejecting verbal agreements between a white donor and negro beneficiaries."[96] Such fascinating research questions, however, are outside the purview of this work. The point is to establish the actions of the freedpeople themselves in the social process of landholding as being an important feature of a recently formed African Virginian peasantry in fin de siècle tobacco Virginia.[97]

This black peasantry in tobacco Virginia was characterized by farming knowledge, household labor, and a landed definition of freedom. According to 1910 supplemental census schedules returned from Louisa County in the dark tobacco belt, Ralph A. Dabney, J. Ballard Fleming, James H. Jackson, Alexander Minor, John N. Mitchell, and J. E. Morris headed households that engaged in tobacco production. All cultivated sun-cured tobacco of the "orinoco" variety, fertilized from 300 to 400 pounds per acre with brands such as Venables, Star-Brand, Eureka, Hugh, and National. Their average tobacco yield per acre over the preceding five years ranged from a high of 1,000 pounds by the Minor household to a low of 630 pounds by the Morris household.[98]

This farming expertise was also reported from the bright tobacco belt. Black tobacco farmers Caesar Alexander, Ben Bennett, Thad Carter, Jennie Crowder, Richard Dodson, Rebecca Floyd, Scott Gillespie, Ransom F. Jiggett, George Revis, James R. Talley, and Samuel Taylor all produced flue-cured tobacco, supplemented with cigar binders, wrappers, and fillers. These tobacco types were variously fertilized at rates ranging from as low as 200 pounds per acre to as high as 2,000 pounds with nitrogen-phosphate-potash mixtures of either 2-8-2 or 3-8-3. Tobacco yields varied from 400 to 600 pounds over the preceding five years.[99] The farming knowledge of these black tobacco producers challenges older notions of freedom's untrained generation.

Much of the labor on these tobacco farms was performed by younger members of the household. According to the Louisa County census, nineteen-year-old Arthur Dabney, eighteen-year-old Edmond Dabney, twenty-nine-year-old Henry Fleming, fifteen-year-old Lloyd Fleming, eighteen-year-old Roxie Jackson, fifteen-year-old Sherman Jackson, eleven-year-old Gilliam Jackson, eighteen-year-old Aubrey Mitchell, thirteen-year-old Melville Mitchell, sixteen-year-old Loga Mitchell, and fifteen-year-old Charley Morris all labored on the "home farm."[100] This laboring on the home farm by younger family members was also reported from Mecklenburg County: twenty-four-year-old Rebecca, twenty-two-year-old Willie, and twelve-year-old Eliza in the Alexander household; eighteen-year-old Thad, sixteen-year-old Lennon, and thirteen-year-old Paul of the Carter family; fourteen-year-old Charlie Crowder; nineteen-year-old George Dodson; twenty-five-year-old Robert, twenty-two-year-old Della, twenty-year-old Bessie, nineteen-year-old Allen, sixteen-year-old Charlie, and fourteen-year-old Augustus in the Floyd household; and seventeen-year-old Isaiah and fourteen-year-old Ezekiel of the Taylor family all helped with the farmwork.[101] These young rural laborers often worked all season long, with no unemployment recorded during 1909.[102] This familial farming stretched back to an older dominion of cooperation begun during slavery and forged with emancipation.[103]

Many of the black tobacco households exhibiting this extensive household labor and farming knowledge were headed by older freedpeople. Of the total of sixteen supplemental schedules returned by black farmers from Louisa and Mecklenburg Counties in 1910, four did not specify tenure, two were from tenants, two by part-owners, and nine from landowners. Of these owners, only thirty-year-old Alexander Minor and forty-one-year-old J. E. Morris had been born before the Civil War. The other seven landowners, and their wives, were born during or before the war. The youngest of these was forty-seven-year-old James R. Talley, born in 1863; the eldest, sixty-three-year-old Caesar Alexander, born in 1847.[104] This was freedom's older generation. As Ransom F. Jiggett put it in concluding his schedule, "I am my person."[105]

A lucid example of this postemancipation black peasantry was provided by the White household in the heart of the tobacco southside. According to the 1880 county census, Sampson W. White was a forty-year-old freedman married to fifty-year-old Martha White in the Dan River magisterial district of Pittsylvania County. They had three children, eighteen-year-old Mary Betti, fifteen-year-old Pup, and ten-year-old Leathy. Rounding out the White household was thirty-seven-year-old brother Green. All were reported to "work on farm," except Martha, who was "keeping house."[106] By the early 1900s Sampson White owned 107 acres worth $535, while Martha owned 7 acres a few miles distant worth $140.[107]

The Whites grew tobacco, especially the Warn variety of bright tobacco that was fertilized "from 800–1000 lbs" per acre at mixtures of "8-3-3 and 9-3-3" and the costs of which were split between the landowner and his free laborers. In 1909 White produced 1,049 pounds per acre although his average was around 722 pounds per acre. White did not rent out his land for cash; he usually paid his employees a fourth share of the tobacco crop.[108] In addition to filling out the supplemental census schedule, Sampson W. White wrote a letter to the census enumerator that summarized his own personal history in the tobacco fields. He stressed his expertise: "I have been growing tobacco all my life," he wrote, "and for myself for the last 30 years and I have a good experience in growing tobacco for 27 years." He was independent: "I also work a farm of my own and has been for 9 years." He was, furthermore, an employer: "I work men for a part of the crop they pay ½ the fertilizer bill and gets ½ of the crop." Finally, he took pride in his work: "I would like to meet you in person and tell you all about it."

The testimony of Sampson White and these other black tobacco farmers, otherwise buried in dusty folders in a federal archive, provide an important challenge to contemporary notions of emancipation's being a failure. This evidence of farming expertise, household organization, and independent landownership also calls into question more recent assertions that black farmers in the postbellum tobacco South were all poor, paternalized, and hopeless.

As I have demonstrated, postbellum tobacco Virginia was far removed from the plodding lore of a genteel Ellen Glasgow novel. During the immediate postwar years federal troops temporarily occupied regions of the defeated Confederacy, while freedpeople and old masters struggled over competing definitions of freedom honed in an older dominion. Rather than being a temporary tempest, these emancipatory struggles were part of a vortex of prolonged agricultural depression and a transformed tobacco economy. The consequence of this long-term dialectic was the erosion of older forms of social relations, especially in the century's waning years. If one part of this process entailed freedpeople's landholding as freeing labor from dependency, the other side of the paradox was the freeing of labor from the land, and it is to that complementary social process that we now turn.[109]

During the late nineteenth century many Virginians began to leave the Old Dominion. In the final decade the population of the state increased only from 1,655,980 to 1,854,184. This addition of 198,204 residents was a mere 12 percent; only six states in the nation had smaller percentage increases, and these were either lowly populated New England states or large midwestern states.[110] The freedpeople made up a large part of this exodus. In 1860 forty-three counties had slave majorities; by 1900 only thirty-five counties had freedpeople majorities.[111] During the 1890s the black populace in the state increased by only 25,284 (4 percent), while the white populace increased by 172,733 (15 percent).[112] At the same time approximately sixty counties registered losses in their numbers of black inhabitants.[113] The primary explanation for these limited demographic gains was outmigration. It has been estimated that 74,000 blacks (11.5 percent) emigrated from Virginia during the 1890s. This constituted the highest emigration rate of all the southern states. The following decade witnessed only a slight drop, to 59,000 black emigrants (9 percent),

TABLE 8.8. Freedpeople's Exodus from the Dark Tobacco Belt, 1890s

County	Total Population 1890	Total Population 1900	Black Population 1890	Black Population 1900	White Population 1890	White Population 1900
Amelia	9,068	9,037	6,045	5,985	3,023	3,052
Amherst	17,551	17,864	7,628	7,057	9,923	10,807
Appomattox	9,589	9,662	4,335	3,931	5,254	5,731
Bedford	31,213	30,356	11,149	9,739	20,064	20,617
Brunswick	17,245	18,217	10,584	10,842	6,661	7,375
Buckingham	14,383	15,266	7,597	7,851	6,786	7,415
Caroline	16,681	16,709	9,322	9,042	7,359	7,667
Charlotte	15,077	15,343	9,361	8,545	5,716	6,798
Cumberland	9,482	8,996	6,622	6,205	2,860	2,791
Fluvanna	9,508	9,050	4,457	4,011	5,051	5,039
Goochland	9,912	9,519	5,874	5,558	4,083	3,961
Louisa	16,997	16,517	9,805	8,621	7,192	7,896
Lunenburg	11,372	11,705	6,736	6,572	4,636	5,133
Nelson	15,366	16,075	6,303	5,672	9,033	10,403
Nottoway	11,582	12,366	7,623	7,400	3,959	4,966
Powhatan	6,791	6,864	4,433	4,481	2,358	2,343
Prince Edward	14,694	15,045	9,924	9,769	4,770	5,276
Totals	236,511	238,591	127,798	121,281	108,728	117,270

Sources: USBC, *1900, Population*, 561–62; USBC, *1900, Abstract*, 172 n. 11, 173 n. 16.

Note: Campbell and Dinwiddie Counties have been excluded because the urban incorporation of Lynchburg and Petersburg during the 1890s complicates the statistics.

and Virginia ranked second behind South Carolina, which had 87,000 emigrants. Thus a record 133,000 blacks left Virginia within the short span of twenty years.[114]

This was an emigrant tide compared with past rivers, streams, and rivulets of freedpeople flowing from the land. It also ran from the Virginia tobacco region. In 1870 twenty counties had black demographic majorities; by 1900 there were only fifteen such counties.[115] More specifically, the black populace in the tobacco region fell by some 4 percent during the 1890s. This was especially apparent in the dark tobacco belt, where the regional population fell from 127,748 in 1890 to 121,281 in 1900 (5 percent). Even the bright tobacco belt with its proportionately larger population was affected; its black populace

TABLE 8.9. Freedpeople's Exodus from the Bright Tobacco Belt, 1890s

County	Total Population		Black Population		White Population	
	1890	1900	1890	1900	1890	1900
Franklin	24,985	25,952	6,248	5,947	18,737	20,005
Halifax	34,424	37,197	19,416	19,275	15,008	17,922
Henry	18,298	19,274	8,283	8,383	9,925	10,881
Mecklenburg	25,359	26,551	16,030	16,198	9,329	10,353
Totals	103,066	108,974	49,977	49,803	52,999	59,161

Sources: USBC, *1900, Population*, 561–62; USBC, *1900, Abstract*, 173 n. 6.
Note: Pittsylvania County is excluded because the urban incorporation of Danville during the 1890s complicates the statistics.

remained level at around 49,000 throughout the decade, suggesting regional emigration[116] (see tables 8.8. and 8.9).

This exodus of freedpeople elicited much contemporary comment. During the early 1880s one local correspondent in Prince Edward County attributed a neighbor's farming apathy to a labor scarcity caused by emigration to the coal fields of southern West Virginia.[117] Twenty years later investigators Dabney and Kelsey reported that the labor problem still had not abated in that county.[118] This process was also reported farther south in the bright tobacco belt. From the late 1880s onward there were consistent complaints of a shortage of free labor.[119] During 1904–5 tobacco cultivation was reportedly curtailed because of the limited availability of free labor. Indeed, J. W. Gregory, the state delegate for Pittsylvania County, introduced an anti-enticement bill.[120] Its failure reflected the decline of planter political power in the state legislature. It also suggests the longevity of free labor struggles honed during the first flush of emancipation decades earlier.[121]

Who was leaving the Virginia tobacco region? It seems clear that a younger generation of freedpeople was increasingly pushed off the land because of the prolonged depression as well as the transformation of the tobacco economy. This younger generation was also pulled by higher-paying wage work in extractive industries, transportation improvements, and factory and domestic employment in towns and cities. Their emigration was part of a longer tradition of freedpeople's protest: self-emancipation during the Civil War, short-term migration and "enticement" during the earliest days of emancipation, and seasonal mobility during the 1870s and 1880s. These migratory ripples fed a broader stream that eventually flowed into the river of the Great Migration.[122] What was different, however, about freedom's second and third generations was that small landholding did not define their emancipatory aspirations. These younger freedpeople were after a different kind of freedom altogether.[123]

Where did freedom's second and third generations go? There was a large shift from the countryside to the town during the late nineteenth century. In Virginia in 1890 there were twenty-seven towns and cities with 282,693 inhabitants representing 17 percent of the populace. Richmond dominated with nearly one-third of urban Virginia's inhabitants. Ten years later these towns and cities had increased their populations by 57,374, or one-fifth. Richmond's urban lead was cut to one-fourth. The key urban growth occurred on the periphery of the tobacco region. Richmond's populace increased by 3,662, while Danville's went up by 6,215. The most spectacular growth was in the southwestern and southeastern regions. Big Lick's 669 inhabitants in 1880 grew to Roanoke's 21,495 residents twenty years later, while Newport News went from a mere crossroads in Warwick County to 19,635 inhabitants. This spectacular urban growth was evident in other parts of the southeastern peninsula: Norfolk and Portsmouth expanded from 21,966 to 46,624 and 11,390 to 17,427, respectively, during the last two decades.[124] This urbanization was directly attributable to the fundamental dislocation wrought by postemancipation and agrarian transformation as freedom's second and third generations flocked to factory and mill, port and dock, and shop and house[125] (see table 8.10).

Let us briefly examine this social process of urban proletarianization in the state. Its most important aspect was spectacular growth. During the 1890s the ten principal manufacturing centers in Virginia increased their number of factories by nearly half, tripled their capitalization, nearly doubled their wage earners to over 45,000, doubled their costs, and doubled the total value of their products. The leading industries of the state, ranked by value, were tobacco processing, flour and grist mill products, lumber and timber, iron and steel, railroad cars and shop repair, foundry and machinery, textiles, fertilizer, and planing

SHIFTING TERRAIN

TABLE 8.10. Urban Population Growth in Virginia, 1890s

Place	1890	1900
Alexandria	14,339	14,528
Berkley	3,899	4,988
Bristol	2,902	4,579
Charlottesville	5,591	6,449
Clifton Forge	1,792	3,212
Covington	704	2,950
Danville	10,305	16,520
Fredericksburg	4,528	5,068
Hampton	2,513	2,764
Harrisonburg	2,792	3,521
Lexington	3,059	3,203
Lynchburg	19,709	18,891
Manchester	9,246	9,715
Newport News	4,449	19,635
Norfolk	34,871	46,624
Petersburg	22,680	21,810
Pocahontas	2,953	2,789
Portsmouth	13,268	17,427
Pulaski	2,112	2,813
Radford	2,060	3,344
Richmond	81,388	85,050
Roanoke	16,159	21,495
Salem	3,279	3,412
Staunton	6,975	7,289
Suffolk	3,354	3,827
Winchester	5,196	5,161
Wytheville	2,570	3,003

Source: USBC, *1900, Abstract*, 148.

mill products. There was a racial division of labor, especially between black tobacco proletarians and white textile proletarians. Tobacco workers operated in Richmond, Lynchburg, Danville, and Petersburg and served the inner, crop-producing region. Richmond was still the major proletarian city, with workers in old plug and chewing factories and new cigarette factories alongside 5,000 to 6,000 workers at the Tredegar Iron Works during the 1890s. There were also new urban centers. Roanoke, in southwestern Virginia, had 2,688 workers in 120 factories largely engaged in machine manufacturing, with a total prod-

TABLE 8.11. Manufacturing Growth in Virginia, 1890s

City	Manufacturing Establishments		Capital (in millions of dollars)		Wage-Earning Proletarians		Cost of Materials (in millions of dollars)		Product Value (in millions of dollars)	
	1890	1900	1890	1900	1890	1900	1890	1900	1890	1900
Richmond	966	763	16.7	20.8	16,891	16,692	14.0	13.1	27.7	28.9
Danville		139		5.8		5,143		5.1		8.1
Norfolk	374	445	3.4	6.4	2,391	4,334	2.5	5.2	5.1	9.3
Newport		123		14.9		5,675		3.3		6.9
Petersburg	271	225	3.9	3.9	5,108	4,730	4.3	3.7	7.1	6.4
Roanoke		120		2.0		2,688		3.7		5.7
Lynchburg		168		3.4		2,452		2.3		4.5
Berkley		48		1.7		1,186		1.4		2.3
Alexandria		172		1.7		1,065		0.7		1.8
Portsmouth		103		1.1		1,154		0.9		1.8
Totals	1,611	2,306	24	61.7	24,390	45,119	20.8	39.4	39.9	75.7

Source: USBC, 1900, Abstract, 357–58, 361–81.

uct worth nearly $6 million. These new manufacturers were especially prominent in the southeast. In Newport News, Norfolk, and Portsmouth over 11,000 wage workers engaged in shipbuilding, including some 2,000 workers at the massive federal navy yard in Norfolk.[126] These industries were fed by increasing emigration from the surrounding countryside[127] (see table 8.11).

This movement from field to factory was noted by numerous contemporaries. Investigator Carl Kelsey generalized about declining agricultural conditions in Prince Edward County, where "the labor force [was] attracted to the towns and the North by higher wages."[128] Tobacco share tenant J. S. Dawdy provided a precise appraisal of this social process in his region of Belona, Powhatan County, in a personal letter to federal census enumerator E. Dana Durand. Although there was a local tobacco economy, he explained, "generally the prices of dark tobacco grown [in] this county are not satisfactory and are not profitable considering the expense of production since labor has become scare." Consequently, Dawdy explained, "labor is almost beyond reach and our sons have [sic] very dissatisfied on the farm

SHIFTING TERRAIN

growing tobacco."[129] Such a labor scarcity was traditionally attributable to the exodus of ex-slaves; it was compounded by the emigration of freedom's second and third generations deserting the countryside. This movement was part of the same social process that induced landowners in Campbell County to sell their land and emigrate from the countryside to either Lynchburg, Danville, or Roanoke.[130]

Addie Luck Williams recalled the specific nature of her family's emigration from the countryside to the city in the tobacco southside. Williams was born on February 20, 1874, in King's Old Field to Jerry and Luvenia Smith Luck. Her parents were former slaves who worked as tenants raising tobacco and corn. Williams recalls her hard-working youth when there was "nothing but work on the farm." She recalled having "to work in the field, but I had to milk two cows . . . and just scrub the churn and everything before I went to the field to work, every day of my life." "We worked," Addie continued, "from sunup until sundown, and in planting tobacco time, when there was much rain, we'd plant tobacco all day long in the rain." When Addie was thirteen, the Lucks moved to Danville, apparently because Luvenia "wanted to leave the country." Jerry ended up getting work at the gas house, while Luvenia "didn't work at all when they moved here to my knowledge." Addie Luck Williams went on to become a local schoolteacher in Pittsylvania County for the next fifty years.[131]

This exodus went even farther afield and was often defined by either region or gender. In 1900 there were nearly 17,000 black residents in West Virginia who had been born in Virginia.[132] Between 1890 and 1910 over 25,000 blacks left the state to work in the coal mines of West Virginia. They hailed mostly from areas along the Norfolk and Western Railroad stretching from the rural tidewater through the central piedmont via Richmond and Lynchburg. African American recruiters were often persuasive in their talk of abundant opportunities. (Their oratorical skills found fertile ground in depressed agricultural conditions.) Usually the new miners were men between twenty and their mid-forties (freedom's second generation) who arrived without their families and boarded either separately or with extended kin. Between 1887 and 1910 their labor contributed to the extraction of 5 million tons of coal, which increased to forty million tons. In 1893 the Woodson family emigrated to West Virginia, where Carter G. Woodson, another of Virginia's famous sons, came up from freedom. Woodson climbed from the coal face of West Virginia to perform doctoral work at Harvard University and on to pioneer the study and propagation of African American history.[133]

Women were also proletarianized in Virginia. According to the 1900 federal census there were 12,197 women over sixteen earning nearly $2 million in the state. This amounted to nearly one-fifth of all wage earners.[134] Most of these proletarians worked in either textile mills or tobacco factories.[135] By 1900 there were 1,791 women workers in cigarette factories.[136] Black women worked especially in the tobacco factories. Their experience was captured by longtime tobacco proletarian Elviry Magee, who also revealed an expertise and moral acumen on exploitation. "I knows tobacco," she explained:

> I knows all de grades an' blends. I knows bright tobacco an' burley tobacco an' Kaintucky tobacco an' all de rest. You 'members Old Man Hughes what built all dese here schools an' hospitals in town? Well, I learnt Mister John how to grade tobacco when he first come in de factory. Yes, Jesus, I give Mister John his start. I'm po' now an' I was po' den but he come to be a rich man. But it didn't do him no good. De Lawd called him away wi' Bright's misery. I believes one reason was case he didn't pay niggers nothin'. I was his best hand— he say so hisse'f—an' he didn't never pay me no mo'n fifty to sebenty-five cents a day.[137]

Magee explained her experience to fellow Danville resident Julian R. Meade, and in doing so she touched on the dialectic of expropriation and judgment that was central to the freedpeople's postemancipation experience. Along with the desire for just compensation for hard work, one can also hear faint echoes of an admonition of exploitation that stretched back to an older dominion.

Despite this proletarianization of black women emigrants, most freedwomen pursued domestic work. Historian Jacqueline Jones has painted a broad canvas of this domestic work in the postwar urban South and North.[138] Of course, black familial emigration was as important as either male or female individual migration. Addie Luck Williams's story was part of this process in the tobacco southside.[139] So was the story of Patience and Frank Gnomes, who migrated to the Fulton district of Richmond in 1906. Frank worked as a laborer for the Chesapeake and Ohio Railroad, and Patience engaged in domestic work as well as some small-scale marketing.[140] Orra Langhorne, a local Lynchburg journalist, described both individual and familial emigration from the Virginia interior. In one conversation with a local businessman, she recalled encountering hundreds of black men going to work on the railroads and mines; she had another conversation with a freedwoman domestic who was on her way to join her husband in Pittsburgh.[141] This social process of black emigration by freedom's younger generation was indissolubly linked to the structural transformation of the Virginia countryside by the late nineteenth century.

It is, of course, difficult to provide aggregate information on the age, sex, and nature of many black emigrants from Virginia. This would require systematic linking of the county census with the urban census. Still, some broad generalizations can be made. According to the 1900 census over 450,000 Virginia-born individuals resided in fourteen other states in the Union. Many of these former Virginians lived in bordering states such as West Virginia and Maryland or nearby cities such as Washington, D.C., Baltimore, or Philadelphia. While many white Virginians emigrated to the rural Midwest, most blacks headed for the urban Northeast. There were 22,736 Virginian-born residents in New York City; although not demarcated by race, around three-fourths of all Virginia-born emigrants to the state were black, which suggests the city as a major destination.[142] The same is true of Philadelphia; most of its 20,688 Virginia-born residents were probably black.[143] This is confirmed by one of the few local studies of black emigration by sex and age to Philadelphia during the 1890s. In the Seventh Ward there were 1,951 Virginia-born blacks, of which 1,012 were women and 939 were men. Furthermore, of the 4,401 black emigrants to the Seventh Ward in Philadelphia who had been born in the Upper South including Virginia, 2,714 (62 percent) were between twenty-one and forty years old.[144] These were the roots of the later Great Migration (see table 8.12).

The historical analysis of the Great Migration has become much richer over the last decade or so. The earliest studies published during the 1920s focused on the basic causes and effects of northward migration.[145] The civil rights and black power movements of the 1960s encouraged a different approach that stressed the making of a collective racial consciousness synonymous with black nation-building.[146] During the 1980s historians focused on the role of migration in class forma-

TABLE 8.12. Virginia-Born Residents in Other Locations by 1900

Location	Total	Black		White	
		N	%	N	%
West Virginia	61,508	16,944	28	44,564	72
Pennsylvania	54,260	40,870	75	13,388	25
Philadelphia	20,688	—	—		
District of Columbia	46,807	28,029	60	18,778	40
Maryland	40,553	18,391	45	22,162	55
Baltimore	23,633	—	—		
Missouri	35,376	4,391	12	30,985	88
New York	32,404	24,118	74	8,274	26
New York City	22,736	—	—		
Ohio	32,342	9,983	31	22,358	69
Tennessee	25,953	8,152	31	17,799	69
North Carolina	25,619	8,499	33	17,120	67
Kentucky	22,223	3,614	16	18,609	84
Texas	21,832	7,158	33	14,673	67
New Jersey	19,453	15,965	82	3,488	18
Illinois	19,218	3,473	18	15,745	82
Indiana	14,673	1,235	8	13,438	92
Totals	452,221	190,822	42	261,399	58

Source: USBC, *1900, Population*, pt. 1, 688–89, 692–93, 704–5, 709–13.

tion, especially proletarianization, in response to an earlier school that had focused on urban living and ghettoization.[147] Most recently historians have concentrated on the diversity of emigration, its age and gender differences, and its cultural expression.[148] The focus remains, however, on the war years and just after, movement from the rural South to the urban North, and the fact that migration was one-way only.[149]

Much of this recent literature is of limited significance for understanding the exodus from fin de siècle Virginia.[150] It is especially important not to see this social process of migration and class formation simply in terms of a one-way ticket. Many of freedom's second and third generations retained their links to the Virginia countryside through frequent visits and winters spent with older family members who stayed behind. Most importantly, younger members who were engaged in the cash economies of either extraction, construction, in-

SHIFTING TERRAIN

dustry, or domestic work often remitted their wages for familial usage in Virginia. This extended household economy helped families survive. It also played a vital role in facilitating the freedpeople's landholding. Coal miners, railroad workers, factory operatives, and domestic servants used their cash earnings to buy and maintain farms and land in Virginia. Local investigator Kelsey reported from Prince Edward County that large "sums of money are sent in by children working in the northern cities."[151] At the 1904 annual summer conference held at Hampton Institute, presenter J. Thomas Hewin drew attention to the "Negro race" that was "returning from the slums of the city to the county districts, purchasing lands, acquiring homes, and engaging in some thrifty business where parents can educate their children and become property owners."[152] Others went back home to assist in agricultural duties at planting and harvest time or to join in familial and communal celebrations.[153] Some recent historians have also hinted at this link, arguing that the emigration of young women to domestic work "might be a strategy to enable a family to hold on to its land and remain where it was."[154] This nexus suggests a more complex relationship between migration and landholding than is traditionally portrayed.[155]

The notion of extended kinship is hinted at in the 1910 county census returns for black households. Alongside the wife of the household head were listed reproduction rates, including the number of children born and those still living. Thus, for example, Lucy Dabney had given birth to twelve children, of whom nine were living, while Alice Alexander had had eleven children, nine of whom were alive.[156] However, only six of the nine Dabney children and three of the nine Alexander offspring lived in their respective households. Some might have branched out locally to make their own families.[157] But given hard rural times, emigration rates, and changing definitions of freedom, it is more likely that this was freedom's younger generation, which sought newer dominions.

The social process of emigration and return worked as follows: Freedom's younger generation went off to waged work; they might return periodically with some of their savings, or they might remit some of their earnings in classic migrant fashion. Clearly, remittance had a long tradition in the region. During the late 1860s and early 1870s numerous former slaves left the barren fields of Fluvanna County for higher wages in the sugar fields of the Louisiana delta, from where they remitted their sweated earnings back to families including wives, brothers, daughters, and sons.[158] Younger blacks continued to bring or send small amounts of money home from the local town or quarry or from farther afield. Occasionally remittances would be sent to the local post office, where they would be picked up in the form of postal orders by family members.[159] This extended household economy was simply part of a much longer familial tradition of providing for the young and the elderly. It is what linked the cooperative action of slaves in the tobacco fields with their descendants several decades later. Perhaps this was one final act of the black familial tradition of caring for the elderly. The young helped the old gain a plot of land that the former had no desire to inherit or live on because their definition of freedom was different.

Much of the literature on early twentieth-century tobacco Virginia depicts slow, sluggish rural rhythms of living. Whether an Ellen Glasgow novel, a planter memoir, or a federal census return, the picture is one of seemingly inescapable immutability. The broader canvas of emancipation, prolonged depression, and tobacco transformation, however, points to a paradoxical social breakdown. Both landholding and rural exodus, while seemingly antithetical, were indissolubly linked in the erosion of traditional social relations.

What about the notion of progress? Surely landholding and exodus constituted movement toward freedom and away from slavery both materially and ideologically. Many older freedpeople were eventually successful in gaining some land, only to realize its limitations included poor soil, low crop prices, and legal/political obstacles. This latter problem was compounded by the revision of the state constitution in 1902 effectively ending a generation of sustained black political representation. Alternatively, a younger generation lured by the urban promise of freedom moved to the towns and cities, only to find hard work, low wage labor, poor living conditions, and hostility from existing residents. This movement from the land to the city was conceptualized at the time as a problem; its recent echoes ring down the broken roads, abandoned factories, and rundown neighborhoods of modern cities. Perhaps the longest-lasting legacy concerns the notion

SHIFTING TERRAIN

of advancement. Its historiographical and political roots are traceable to this period. There are, however, more complex directions and ways of judging it. Perhaps the only true progress will come from those freedpeople's descendants whose struggle can thrive, much like the bright tobacco leaf, in the most seemingly inhospitable environment.

What did the Virginia tobacco region look like a generation after emancipation, prolonged depression, and a transformed economy? Geologically, the region remained relatively unchanged. The rocks were fractionally smoother, the rivers a little lower, and the soils slightly less nutritious. The foothills still gently undulated under seasons of cool winters and hot summers. Tobacco still reigned as the region's major cash crop; it still required slavish devotion from its retainers throughout the growing season. Indeed, the last season of the century produced around 122 million pounds of tobacco worth just over $7 million; this matched the poundage and market price of forty seasons earlier.[1]

This immutable tobacco world, however, had been fundamentally transformed by the postwar generation. Slavery, tobacco, and an older dominion were being increasingly replaced by free labor relations, newer tobacco regions, and the aspirations of a new generation. A central part in this erosion of traditional social relations was played by the freedpeople. With the advent of emancipation, they struggled to shape free labor in their own image; their struggle was sometimes assisted but often impeded by northern versions of free wage labor and a southern slaveholding *mentalité* of an older slave management. Prolonged depression provided many freedpeople with a semiautonomy associated with rural proletarianization, while others remained tied to the tobacco region through tenancy, crop lien, and new labor laws. Both depression and economic transformation further loosened the bonds of the freedpeople. By the century's turn, the first generation of freedpeople sought the fruits of their free labor through small landholdings, while subsequent generations emigrated in search of an altogether different kind of freedom. Both actions were aspects of the same process of social dissolution linking the countryside to the town and city. The ending of unfree labor prolonged the crisis of former masters and new employers; unlike the freedpeople, they seemed less prepared for freedom.

If the Long Depression of the nineteenth century had a major impact on freedom's first and second generations, the same was true of the Great Depression and the third and fourth generations. Under the impetus of harsh weather conditions and a drastic drop in tobacco prices during the 1930s, planters, farmers, and rural producers petitioned the federal government for support. The result was a federal agricultural program legislating reduced production for guaranteed prices. The combination of depressed agricultural conditions and federal support programs encouraged the further breakdown of the Virginia tobacco region as the freedpeople's descendants continued to emigrate. Black landholding also came under increasing pressure. The number of black farm owners fell from 30,908 registered in 1920 to 22,238 two decades later. If the Long Depression had once partially contributed to the rise of black landownership, the Great Depression ensured that it would be temporary.[2]

The most recent generations of freedpeople have seen the transformation of tobacco farming into an agribusiness. During the 1960s machines replaced labor in the tobacco fields in much the same way as machines had replaced labor in the cotton fields a generation earlier. This technological revolution of traditionally labor-intensive crop production led to the decline in the number of black landholders. Between 1950 and 1974 the number of black farmers in Virginia fell from 18,957 to 3,482. By 1982 only 2,459 black Virginians owned their own farms.[3] Meanwhile, many black Virginians continued to move cityward. Their descendants can be found in many northern, midwestern, and western cities today.[4]

In July 1994 I visited Roger Edwards's farm in central Pittsylvania County. The county highway, lined with numerous tobacco plants, wound north from Danville past a sleepy Chatham. I was immediately struck by the beauty of the region: its curvaceous, undulating hills; gleaming white fences; rich, reddish-brown soil; and tall, sturdy tobacco leaves of strong green hue. It all seemed so pure and natural. The human labor on Edwards's farm was provided by five Mexicans whom the employer had hired through a state work permit, which was on proud display. They were paid by the hour. They are "good workers," explained Edwards; "I can't find anyone else." There "used to be black sharecroppers," but these had long gone.[5] The long historical struggle over free labor finds its echo in this innocuous comment. Meantime, the newest free laborers continue to work Virginia's old tobacco fields.

Colonel Brown's Address to the Freedmen of Virginia

Bureau of Refugees, Freedmen and Abandoned Lands.
Head Quarters Asst. Commissioner, State of Virginia.
Richmond, Va., July 1st, 1865

TO THE FREEDMEN OF VIRGINIA

Having been appointed Assistant Commissioner in the Bureau of Refugees, Freedmen and Abandoned Lands for the State of Virginia, it becomes my duty to look after all matters that pertain to your welfare, to endeavor to teach you how to use that freedom you have so earnestly desired, and to prevent the abuse of it by yourselves or others.

The difference between your former and your present condition is this: formerly your labor was directed, and the proceeds of it taken by your masters, and you were cared for by them, now you are to direct and receive the proceeds of your own labor and care for yourselves.

Can you do this is the question you must now answer to the world. Your friends believe you *can* and *will*. The Government and charity will aid you, but this assistance will be of little advantage unless you help yourselves. To do this you must be industrious and frugal. You have now every inducement to work, as you are to receive the payment for your labor, and you have every inducement to save your wages, as your rights in what you possess will be protected. You have now no masters to provide for you in sickness and old age, hence you must see the necessity of saving your wages while you are able to work for this purpose.

While it is believed that most of you will feel the responsibilities of your new condition, and will do all in your power to become independent of charity and of government aid, it is feared that some will act from the mistaken notion that Freedom means liberty to be idle.

This class of persons, known to the law as *vagrants*, must at once correct this mistake. They will not be allowed to live in idleness when there is work to be had.

You are not to suppose that your former masters have become your enemies because you are free. All good men among them will recognize your new relations to them as free laborers: and as you prove yourselves honest, industrious and frugal, you will receive from them kindness and consideration. If others fail to recognize your right to equal freedom with white persons, you will find the Government through the agents of this Bureau as ready to secure to you, as to them, Liberty and Justice.

Schools, as far as possible, will be established among you, under the protection of the Government.

You will remember that in your condition as *freedmen*, education is of the highest importance, and it is hoped that you will avail yourselves, to the utmost, of the opportunities offered you.

In the new career before you, each one must feel the great responsibility that rests upon himself, in shaping the destinies of his race. The special care that the Government now exercises over you as a people, will soon be withdrawn, and you will be left to work and provide for yourselves.

It is then of the greatest importance that you take immediate advantage of the protection and assistance now afforded you to place yourselves in a position in which you can do so. All officers and employees of this Bureau will aid you in doing this. If you are in a location where work is to be obtained at fair wages, it is much better for you to remain than to be looking for something better. You must remember that, owing to the unsettled state of the country, work is scarce, and the chances are against finding constant employment at high wages.

Be quiet, peacable, law abiding citizens. Be industrious, be frugal and the glory of passing successfully from Slavery to Freedom, will, by the blessing of God, be yours.

O. BROWN
Col. and Assistant Commissioner.

Source: Letters and Orders Received, 4056, Louisa County, RG 105, NA.

Captain Sharp's Report to Colonel Brown

Office Asst. Supt. of Freedmen
Dinwiddie Court House, Virginia
February 28, 1866

Col. O. Brown
   Asst. Comm. State of Virginia

Colonel

In obedience to Circular no. 6 [?] Asst. Commissioner State of Virginia dated Richmond Va., January 29, 1866. I have the honor to make the following Report of Freedmen's affairs in the County of Dinwiddie.

To a casual observer, or to one who felt but little interest in the matter I presume everything here in this relation would look bright and promising. There are but ten freedmen who draw Government rations and these are all old and infirm; most of the young and able-bodied are working for the whites at either remunerating wages in money or for a share of the crop. There are no apprehensions of insurrection and, in general, mutual good feeling exists between the whites and the blacks; many trivial cases have indeed been presented to me, but few differences have been considered worthy of a hearing before the Freedmen's Court and of these some were withdrawn and the remainder easily adjusted and since my [?] in the County on the 28th of last January there has been no established charge of abuses here brought by any Freedmen against any white citizen and during that time I have placed but one freedmen in confinement.

Such is the superficial view but to one who feels a deep interest in the welfare of the county and the future prospects of the Freedmen, and who seeks to understand the true state of affairs, things do not look so promising.

Just freed from slavery and infactuated with the new and dazzling idea of liberty, many of the blacks have settled on miserably poor lands in the fallacious hope of making a crop. These lands have been rented or leased to them for the one fourth of their product by persons who realize that an ear of corn is better than nothing—for, without these settlers, the land is valueless. In most cases, the freedmen have to build a cabin to live in, fence the land, and clear so much land; and all this without a supply of provisions, without money, without wagons, ploughs or harrows—in some cases with and in others without an old and worthless horse, the former being much the better off, as they have no horse to feed. Some of the inevitable results of this pernicious system, the full effects of which are seen in Jamaica, have already developed themselves here, and others equally baleful remain to be developed in the future.

One of the consequences is the fact that many honest and reliable farmers offering from five to ten dollars a month and board, have not so many laborers as they desire and others have none at all—and, of course, their lands will remain untilled or be so much the less productive. Then again, these would-be planters must resort to theft to eke out a subsistence, and grievous complaints against them reach me every day from the neighborhoods where many of them are located; and thus although I by no means believe that in all cases the freedmen are guilty—ill will and bad feeling are generated in the minds of the whites which of course produce the same feeling in the blacks and so they mutually act and react on one another.

The prospective evil most to be dreaded is that they will not raise enough of corn and meat to support them and will become dependents on the charity of the Government in the course of the year or perish of want and the deseases thereby engendered.

But I do not wish the above remarks to be understood as applying to all the Freedmen who have located on lands, for a few of them have good lands, have provisions, teams and money enough to make a crop, and are thriving so handsomely that it makes me feels proud and glad when I visit them.

I had proposed to make a rigorous examination into the cases of some of those settlers and to break up the worst of them—those most destitute and most egregiously misled by their improvidence and folly—and insisting on these parties hiring with farmers who will treat and pay them well, these conditions being carefully supervised by the office and agents of the Bureau—but the Superintendent of the district informed me that this cannot be done, and I would respectfully ask what can be done, or must the evil go on getting worse and worse every day?

The few cases of injustice towards the blacks have almost invariably originated with one of the three following classes—first: disreputable men who never had any character in the county—second: old men whose ideas have become crystalised and who cannot accommodate themselves to changed circumstances—third: idle women whose tongues are busier than their hands.

One of the difficulties I encounter is a propensity the freedmen have to break their contracts. In some cases they wander about the county either idly or seeking employment but very often they go directly to a neighbor of the person by whom they had been employed, which neighbor I am very frequently inclined to believe, has persuaded them to come to live by promising them higher wages, though the person who promises unusually high wages I have found are the worst to pay—a fact which few of the Freedmen can yet appreciate.

In conclusion, I must state that as far as my experience has gone, the oft quoted remark that "the nigger won't work" is false, and that under proper regulations I believe he will become an honest, good, and useful member of society—but that locating at his pleasure and that of unprincipled whites on poor lands—subject to no control but the indolence and gross appetites engendered by slavery—will make him a thief, a pauper, and a curse to the country.

Very Respectfully
[?]
J. W. Sharp
Capt. & Asst. Supt. of Freedmen
Dinwiddie co., Va.

Source: Captain J. W. Sharp to Colonel Orlando Brown, Feb. 28, 1866, Monthly Report, Dinwiddie County, BRFAL, RG 105, NA.

APPENDIX TWO

Sampson White's Letter to Federal Census Director E. Dana Durand, September 1910

Dear Sir

Regarding the tobacco questions [?] I answered as well as I could with them in the blank. Would you have me in person. I can give a fair better information than I can write. I have been growing tobacco all my life and for myself for the last 30 years and I have a good experience in growing tobacco for 27 years. I have been renting land and pay ¼ for rent. The owner pays ¼ of fertilizer bill. I also work a farm of my own and has been for 9 years. I work men for a part of the crop they pay ½ the fertilizer bill and gets ½ of the crop. I work land of my own and rent land and rent out land to others the above is the terms. Well I have said all I have time now. I would like to meet you in person and tell you all about it.

Sampson White.

Source: Sampson White to E. Dana Durand, September 1910, attached to USBC, *1909, Agriculture, Supplemental Schedule: Tobacco*, Pittsylvania County, Virginia, NA.

NOTES

ABBREVIATIONS

In addition to the abbreviations used in the text, the following abbreviations appear in the notes:

Acts	Virginia General Assembly, *Acts of the General Assembly* (1860–1900)
AGLL	American Genealogical Lending Library, Bountiful, Utah
MR	Monthly Report by BRFAL official, in RG 105
NA	National Archives, Washington, D.C.
RG	Records of the Bureau of Refugees, Freedmen, and Abandoned Lands,
105	1865–69, Record Group 105, microfilm 1048, NA
SPF	*Southern Planter and Farmer*
SUP	Superintendent, BRFAL
SW	*Southern Workman*
USBC	U.S. Bureau of the Census
UVA	University of Virginia, Charlottesville
VHS	Virginia Historical Society, Richmond
VL	Virginia Library, Richmond
VSLL	Virginia State Law Library, Richmond

INTRODUCTION

1. Bradley, *Other Days*, 272–73.

2. The works of J. H. Plumb and G. M. Trevelyan provided the classic Whiggish statements; the British Marxist historians popularized the radical critique.

3. For an eloquent statement of Virginia exceptionalism, see Dabney, *Virginia*.

4. The historical literature is huge and growing. Useful surveys include Vaughan, "Slavery and Racism in Seventeenth Century Virginia"; Treadway, "New Directions in Virginia Women's History"; Schwarz, "Recent Writings on Black Virginians."

5. For this earlier black historiographical challenge, see Woodson, *Rural Negro*; Alrutheus A. Taylor, *Negro in the Reconstruction of Virginia*; Jackson, *Negro Office-Holders*; Roberts, "Life and Labor of Rural Virginia Negroes." For useful contextual commentary on this challenge, see Meier and Rudwick, *Black History*; Goggin, *Woodson*.

6. Engs, *Freedom's First Generation*; Jordan, *Black Confederates*. For older statements of the superior Virginia Negro, see Olmsted, *Journey in the Seaboard Slave States*, 89, and Phillips, *American Negro Slavery*, 276.

7. See the April 1995 edition of the *Virginia Magazine of History and Biography*, titled " 'Play the Bitter Loser's Game': Reconstruction and the Lost Cause in the Old Dominion." Between January and October 1996, the VHS hosted a touring Reconstruction exhibition.

8. Ayers and Willis, *Edge of the South*.

9. The major expression of this view is Barbara J. Fields, *Slavery and Freedom*. (The arresting metaphor is also hers.) A recent application to Civil War Virginia is provided by Lynda J. Morgan, *Emancipation*. These works build upon earlier excavations of Upper South contradictions unearthed by, among others, Russel, *Economic Aspects*; Genovese, *Political Economy*; Fox-Genovese and Genovese, *Fruits of Merchant Capital*. For studies of the precapitalist Chesapeake and its transformation, see Kulikoff, *Tobacco and Slaves* and *Agrarian Origins*.

10. Lynda J. Morgan, *Emancipation*, stops in 1870, while Shifflett, *Patronage and Poverty*, is a county study. The Virginia tidewater continues to hold sway in studies of nineteenth-century Virginia at the expense of the interior regions. Similarly, Civil War transitions continue to dominate over later decades and transformations.

11. Both Lynda J. Morgan, *Emancipation*, and Shifflett, *Patronage and Poverty*, say very little about the world of tobacco, while Barbara J. Fields, *Slavery and Freedom*, equates tobacco production with backward southern regionalism.

12. This opening section is lengthy, partly because of the richness of the documentary record, but also because of the establishment of the contours of freedom's struggle, which so influenced life in postemancipation Virginia.

13. Wright, *Old South, New South*, 18.

14. Ransom and Sutch, *One Kind of Freedom*, 169.

15. Behind recent calls for reparations lurks a long historical memory of work without just reward. This has little to do with simple accumulation but everything to do with moral judgment.

16. Thus, in Glasgow, *The Deliverance*, the characters plod along to the timeless rhythms of the old, dull, tobacco calendar, while in Tilley, *Bright Tobacco*, the new entrepreneurial spirit of planters, salesmen, and manufacturers reflects the new bright cigarette industry. Recent echoes of this monocrop determinism can be found in Siegel, *Roots of Southern Distinctiveness*.

17. Raymond Williams, "Culture Is Ordinary," 4. For this definition at work in eighteenth-century Virginia, see Sobel, *World They Made Together*. How easily this perspective glides into the liberal contributionism and restored canvas of Jordan's recent work on African Confederates.

18. Thompson, *Customs in Common*, 7.

19. Shanin, *Awkward Class*.

20. For rational slaves and masters, see Fogel and Engerman, *Time on the Cross*. For their postwar descendants, see Higgs, *Competition and Coercion*. For the argument that hiree slaves became used to wage labor relations that prepared them for the postemancipation marketplace, see Lynda J. Morgan, *Emancipation*. For a recent comparative statement on slave wage labor that probably overstates its case, see Mary Turner, *From Chattel Slaves to Wage Slaves*, esp. O. Nigel Bolland, "Proto-Proletarians?," 123–47.

21. For an opposing view, see Sharon Ann Holt, "Making Freedom Pay."

22. Marx, *Eighteenth Brumaire*, 15. This telling phrase captures the notion of past

traditions affecting future generations that became especially salient in postemancipation Virginia.

23. Much of the recent literature emphasizes culture and community at the expense of work. While adding vitally to our understanding of the slave and free experiences, it also poses the danger of diluting the specific historical struggles of a people who have always *had* to work. For a useful corrective in slave studies, see Berlin and Morgan, *Cultivation and Culture*.

24. Woodward, *Origins*; Barbara J. Fields, "Slavery, Race, and Ideology"; Arnesen, *Waterfront Workers*, x.

25. For a different view, see Schwalm, "Meaning of Freedom."

26. The growing field of comparative emancipation studies is making the salient point that processes of abolition and postemancipation cannot be sufficiently understood outside the contemporaries' own knowledge and ideologies.

27. Chakrabarty, *Rethinking Working-Class History*, 6. For a similar approach in the field of U.S. labor history, see Kenny, *Molly Maguires*, esp. 6.

CHAPTER ONE

1. For useful surveys of this transatlanticism, see Blackburn, *New World Slavery*, chap. 6; Walvin, *Fruits of Empire*, chap. 5.

2. USBC, *1860, Agriculture*, 154–59; Shanks, *Secession Movement*, 5, 215–16; Lynda J. Morgan, *Emancipation*, 24; Peterson, *Historical Study of Prices*, 101, 73; Booker and Perry in Purdue, Barden, and Phillips, *Weevils*, 53, 223–24.

3. USBC, *1860, Manufacturers*, 638–39; Shanks, *Secession Movement*, 5–6, 215–16; Lynda J. Morgan, *Emancipation*, 24, 60–71; Robert, *Tobacco Kingdom*, 161–226; Woodman, *King Cotton*, pt. 1. We await a historical analysis of antebellum tobacco factorage comparable with Woodman's work on the cotton economy.

4. Killebrew, "Culture and Curing of Tobacco in the United States," 42; USBC, *1860, Agriculture*, 109.

5. Tilley, *Bright Tobacco*, 3–36.

6. William H. Brewer, "Cereal Production," 62.

7. Robert, *Story of Tobacco*, 116; Eaton, *Southern Confederacy*, 233; Wiley, *Southern Negroes*, 45.

8. Berlin et al., *Destruction of Slavery*, 745–46.

9. Evans and Govan, "Belgian Consul," 489.

10. These processes of social dissolution are traced, respectively, through prolonged agricultural depression (Chapter 5), the takeoff of the cigarette industry and transformation of the tobacco economy (Chapter 7), and shifting human terrain (Chapter 8).

11. Morgan and Nicholls, "Slaves in Piedmont"; Siegel, *Roots of Southern Distinctiveness*, 16–17, 92, 106.

12. Philip D. Morgan, "Slave Life"; Morgan and Nicholls, "Slaves in Piedmont." See also Kulikoff, *Tobacco and Slaves*, for comparative comment on the eighteenth-century Chesapeake region.

13. Lynda J. Morgan, *Emancipation*, 1–76 (quote, p. 17). I of course argue that the modernization of the Virginia tobacco belt was essentially a much later postwar

phenomenon associated with emancipation, agricultural depression, and a changing tobacco economy. I also wonder whether these hiree slaves faintly echo the exceptional Virginia Negro.

14. USBC, *1860, Agriculture*, 243–45; Shanks, *Secession Movement*, 5–8, 215–16; Maddex, *Virginia Conservatives*, 6–7; Lynda J. Morgan, *Emancipation*, 19–22; Jordan, *Black Confederates*, 7–12.

15. Lynda J. Morgan, *Emancipation*, 57–76.

16. Lynda J. Morgan, *Emancipation*, 57, sees slave hirees "as cultural and economic go-betweens and interpreters for those who remained on the plantations." I agree, except these slave hirees were probably more akin to human veins or capillaries than arteries of freedom pulsating from the tobacco piedmont, a view that Morgan's own sparse evidence substantiates. The classic comment on slave hirees posing an internal contradiction is Genovese, *Political Economy*, chap. 9, and more recently Barbara J. Fields, *Slavery and Freedom*, chap. 3.

17. Tadman, *Speculators and Slaves*, 12; Lynda J. Morgan, *Emancipation*, 36. It is probable that slave trading, much like slave hiring, occurred less in the piedmont than in the tidewater because of the constant seasonal demand for labor in the tobacco fields. It is nevertheless striking that virtually all of the ex-slaves interviewed in Purdue, Barden, and Phillips, *Weevils*, made some personal, anecdotal, or historical reference to Virginia's slave trade.

18. Dew, "Abolition of Negro Slavery," *American Quarterly Review* 12 (1832), reprinted in Faust, *Ideology of Slavery*, 61. It should not be forgotten that Nat Turner also drew on the Bible for his antislavery actions. See Greenberg, *Confessions of Nat Turner*.

19. Dew, "Abolition of Negro Slavery," in Faust, *Ideology of Slavery*, 66. For a more critical understanding of exploitative slavery underpinning "the magnificent achievements of classical civilization," see Croix, *Class Struggle*, 40.

20. Hammond, "Letter to an English Abolitionist," Jan. 28, 1845, *South Carolinian*, reprinted in Faust, *Ideology of Slavery*, 186.

21. Fitzhugh, "Southern Thought," *De Bow's Review* 23 (1857), reprinted in Faust, *Ideology of Slavery*, 295.

22. I have, of course, lumped together a complex set of ideas under the term *proslavery*. For further details, see Genovese, *World the Slaveholders Made*; Tise, *Proslavery*. For the provocative role played by abolitionists, see Genovese's most recent work, esp. *Slaveholders' Dilemma* and *Southern Tradition*.

23. Craven, *Soil Exhaustion*; Robert, *Tobacco Kingdom*; Gates, *Farmer's Age*.

24. Stampp, *Peculiar Institution*; Genovese, *Political Economy*.

25. Mullin, *Africa in America*, chap. 5.

26. The *Southern Planter* was the premier agricultural advice journal in antebellum Virginia. The problem of slave management lurked behind many of the otherwise mundane entries on agricultural improvement. I explore this question more fully in Chapter 4.

27. Robert, *Tobacco Kingdom*, 18; Gates, *Farmer's Age*, 104; Tilley, *Bright Tobacco*, 37–88.

28. Olmsted, *Journey in the Seaboard Slave States*, 76.

29. The most eloquent collective statement on this sowing is in Berlin and Morgan, *Cultivation and Culture*.

30. Hunt, in Purdue, Barden, and Phillips, *Weevils*, 148.

31. Ibid. Of course, Hunt learned his farming knowledge after emancipation. But this does not refute the point that slaves/freedpeople could competently farm free from master/planter management. Such competency, and its potential, was to become a problem for a free regime weaned on a proslave ideology.

32. Bell, in Purdue, Barden, and Phillips, *Weevils*, 26.

33. In other words, the likes of Hunt, Bell, Perry, and Booker all "developed ideas about the importance of labor, the role of property, and the relation of both to their own being; such ideas eventually stood at the center of the slaves political cosmos" (Berlin and Morgan, *Cultivation and Culture*, 7).

34. Lynda J. Morgan, *Emancipation*, 87–123; James H. Brewer, *Confederate Negro*; Jordan, *Black Confederates*.

35. Earlier works on slave self-emancipation during the Civil War include Du Bois, *Black Reconstruction*, chap. 4; Wiley, *Southern Negroes*, pt. 1. More recent works on slave self-emancipation in Virginia include Engs, *Freedom's First Generation*, pt. 1; Lynda J. Morgan, *Emancipation*, chap. 5. The Freedmen Southern Society Project, begun at the University of Maryland in the fall of 1976 under the directorship of Ira Berlin, provides the definitive documentary record of slave self-emancipation during the Civil War.

36. Spiece to Secretary, Dec. 4, 1861, in Berlin, Reidy, and Rowland, *Black Military Experience*, 782–83.

37. Minor to Secretary, Spring 1862, in ibid., 698.

38. This captivating phrase was employed by Genovese to describe the denouement of the South's paternalist ideology of slaveholding as a result of slave self-emancipation during the Civil War. See Genovese, *Roll, Jordan, Roll*, 97–112.

39. Kevin Conley Ruffner, "Civil War Desertion from a Black Belt Regiment: An Examination of the 44th Virginia Infantry," in Ayers and Willis, *Edge of the South*, 81–82.

40. There were around 17,789 slaveholders listed in 26 Virginia piedmont counties. Of these, 11,993, or 67 percent, were yeoman slaveholders who owned fewer than 10 bondspeople each. They probably provided the backbone of the Confederate military effort from the Old Dominion. See USBC, *1860, Agriculture*, 243–45.

41. Pollard, in Purdue, Barden, and Phillips, *Weevils*, 228.

42. Payne to Clendenin, June 20, 1866, Sarah P. Payne Letters, 8668, UVA.

43. Wiley, *Southern Negroes*, 51.

44. Eaton, *Southern Confederacy*, 237–39.

45. Lynda J. Morgan, *Emancipation*, chap. 5, is the best recent study of this process in the Virginia interior.

46. Pollard, in Perdue, Barden, and Phillips, *Weevils*, 228; Isaac Petty, Pittsylvania County, Virginia, *Allowed Claims*, box 384, claim 13,734, RG 56, NA.

CHAPTER TWO

1. Captain J. W. Sharp to Colonel Orlando Brown, Feb. 28, 1866, MR, Dinwiddie County. All following quotes by Sharp are from this document. It is reprinted as Appendix 2.

2. Our focus on the freedpeople's emancipation supports the view that masters had failed to paternalize their slaves. The recent musing of one prominent historian of the antebellum slavocracy, "I may have gotten the answers wrong for the slaves," is essentially correct. See Genovese, *Southern Front*, 12. For a lucid critique of the limitations of paternalism as an analytical tool because it is too broad, top-down, and backward looking, see Thompson, *Customs in Common*, 21–24. Of course, we shall not lose sight of the likes of those "old men" described by Captain Sharp. Suffice to say, slavery prepared them poorly for emancipation.

3. Bentley, *Freedmen's Bureau*, 1–49; Foner, *Reconstruction*, 68–70.

4. Howard, *Autobiography*, 2:215; McFeeley, *Yankee Stepfather*, 15; Alderson, "Freedmen's Bureau," 8–10; Brown, Circular Order 6, Jan. 29, 1866, in Captain John W. Barnes to Captain J. F. P. Crandon, Feb. 28, 1866, MR. These monthly reports from the field provide the documentary basis of this chapter. Unless otherwise noted, monthly reports are drawn from reels 44–49, microfilm 1048, RG 105.

5. Hopkins to Brown, Dec. 31, 1868, MR, Orange County. This monthly report has been reprinted as an addendum in Mugleston, "Diary of Hopkins," 101–2.

6. Howard, *Autobiography*, 2:366.

7. The benevolent school includes Bentley, *Freedmen's Bureau*; Alderson, "Freedmen's Bureau"; Lowe, *Republicans and Reconstruction*, 30, 206 (quote).

8. The racialist school includes McFeeley, *Yankee Stepfather*; Litwack, *Been in the Storm*; Wiener, *Social Origins*, 47–58; Engs, *Freedom's First Generation*, 99–136; Lynda J. Morgan, *Emancipation*, 133–42.

9. The free labor school includes Barbara J. Fields, *Slavery and Freedom*, chap. 6; Reidy, *Agrarian Capitalism*, chap. 6; Thomas Holt, *Problem of Freedom*, pt. 1; Foner, *Reconstruction*, chap. 4; Cohen-Lack, "Free Labor in Texas." Jaynes, *Branches without Roots*, chap. 2, offers a Benthamite twist to this free labor ideology.

10. Foner, *Free Soil*.

11. Howard, *Autobiography*, 2:212–25.

12. Alderson, "Freedmen's Bureau," 19.

13. Brown, "To the Freedmen of Virginia," July 1, 1865, in Letters and Orders Received, 4056, Louisa County, RG 105. It is reprinted as Appendix 1.

14. Ibid.

15. George W. Julian, *Speeches and Political Questions* (1872), quoted in John Ashworth, "Free Labor, Wage Labor, and the Slave Power," 145 n. 26, in Stokes and Conway, *Market Revolution*.

16. For the heart of the argument, see Hobsbawn, *Age of Capital*. For its British colonial arteries in the Caribbean and East Africa, see Thomas Holt, *Problem of Freedom*, and Cooper, *Slaves to Squatters*.

17. Despite the wealth of historical research lavished on the freedpeople, much less attention has been devoted to the freedpeople's labor theory of value and their moral values.

18. Alderson, "Freedmen's Bureau," 52, 141–42, 156–57; Howard, *Autobiography*, 2:231–32; Oubre, *Forty Acres*, 37. The county acreage held by the BRFAL in the Virginia piedmont was as follows: Dinwiddie County, 275 acres; Brunswick County, 1,006 acres; Nottoway County, 1,900 acres; Powhatan County, 60 acres; Halifax County, 400 acres. See Monthly Reports on Confiscated & Abandoned Lands, Aug. 1865 through Dec. 1868, RG 105, reels 50–51.

19. Jordan to Captain Stuart Barnes, May 31, 1866, MR, Prince Edward and

Cumberland Counties. See also Jordan to Barnes, July 31, 1866, MR, Prince Edward and Cumberland Counties.

20. In contrast to planter persisters and forty-acres-and-a-mule purists for whom rapid restoration irrevocably settled the land issue, the argument here is that the struggle over land and free labor continued to be an inescapable part of the postemancipation landscape in the Virginia tobacco region.

21. Howard, Circular Order, Contracts, 4057, Louisa County, RG 105.

22. Freedmen with Goode, Labor Contracts, Short Family Papers, 1SH818/5a, VHS.

23. Freedmen with Baskerville, Labor Contracts, Baskerville Family Papers, 1B2924a–d/28b, VHS.

24. Freedmen with Harvie, Labor Contracts, Harvie Family Papers, 1H2636b–d, VHS.

25. Freedmen with Langan, Labor Contracts, May 11, 1865; Freedmen with Pendleton, Labor Contract, May 1865; Freedmen with Waddy, Labor Contract, May 1865; 183 freedmen with 23 employers, Labor Contracts, May 1865–Sept. 1865—all in 4057, Louisa County, RG 105. A thorough search of the BRFAL files for counties in the Virginia tobacco region revealed only around seventy extant labor contracts for the entire 1865 agricultural season. Thirty-two of these, or nearly half, were from Louisa County alone. Shifflett, *Patronage and Poverty*, a postwar study of Louisa County, does not appear to have consulted these contracts. Digging around in planter records and archives, however, suggests that far more labor contracting went on than the limited BRFAL records suggest. Indeed, the paucity of the extant records does not detract from the reality of the BRFAL's influential presence at the local level in the immediate postemancipation years—one of the central arguments of this chapter.

26. Freedmen with Goode, Labor Contracts, Short Family Papers, 1SH818/5a, VHS.

27. Freedmen with Baskerville, Labor Contracts, Baskerville Family Papers, 1B2924a–d/28b, VHS.

28. Craddock with Harvie, Labor Contracts, Harvie Family Papers, 1H2636b–d, VHS.

29. See source in n. 25.

30. Ibid.

31. It is salutary never to forget that the freedpeople were invariably presented through someone else's spectacles. This does not render such spectacles the only sights of history as some postmodernists would have it, but it does require careful scrutiny of the sources.

32. William Overton, July 22, 1865, 4057, Louisa County, RG 105. This letter was buried among the labor contracts.

33. Freedmen with employers, Contracts, May 1865–Sept. 1865, 4057, Louisa County, RG 105. Rental arrangements also produced free labor tensions. On October 10, 1865, John S. Cammack and freedmen Stephen Hiton and Joseph Perkins entered an agreement. Both Hiton and Perkins rented arable land near Louisa Court House for "halves" of all crops, "three fourths" of the fruit, and "four fifths" of the grapes. Each party to the contract had to provide necessary livestock, while the freedmen had to provide their own board. There was an equal forfeiture of $25 and an annulment clause. Tensions soon emerged. On March 26, 1866, a new contract was entered into which stated that the "said parties are now desirous of altering said contract." Hiton

and Perkins were to relinquish all land in the past contract except about five acres. The land and the house continued to be provided although they were responsible for the upkeep. See ibid.

34. Descriptions of these actions simply in terms of *homo economicus* miss the crucial context of the transition from slavery to freedom in which they occurred.

35. Liny to Henderson, July 24, 1865, Letters and Orders Received, 3944, Cumberland County, RG 105.

36. Lieutenant Thomas M. Butler adjudicated a settlement dispute between Mr. G. F. Cralle and the freedpeople in Nottoway County. It is unclear whether this dispute was fueled by either employer subterfuge or freedmen squabbles. Either way, it highlights the BRFAL's adjudicatory role during a particularly disputatious time in the agricultural season. See Lt. Butler, Orders Received, Aug. 25, 1865, 3911, Nottoway County, RG 105. Employers like Henderson and Cralle cannot have been pleased with such detailed interference in their customary supervisory rights.

37. Thompson to Wilcox, Jan. 24, 1866, Letters Received, 3948, Pittsylvania County, RG 105. To reiterate the point: these freedmen's actions, motivated by a sense of just compensation, played on the free labor agenda of the BRFAL. For squatting as freedpeople's rights in other postemancipation societies, see Thomas Holt, *Problem of Freedom*, chap. 8; Rebecca J. Scott, *Emancipation in Cuba*, chaps. 10 and 11; Cooper, *Slaves to Squatters*, chaps. 6, 7.

38. Gilliam, Holman, and Spencer to Col. Jordan, Oct. 16, 1865, Contracts, Bonds, Court Records, and Miscellaneous Reports and Lists, 3905, Buckingham County, RG 105; Charles W. White, *Hidden and Forgotten*, 113, where the letter is printed in its entirety.

39. Freedmen with Harvie, Contracts, Harvie Family Papers, 1H2636b–d, VHS. In this case and the one in Buckingham County the BRFAL apparently supported the claims of the employers.

40. Howard, *Autobiography*, 2:248.

41. Lowe, *Republicans and Reconstruction*, 47.

42. Barnes to Captain J. F. P. Crandon, Feb. 28, May 31, 1866, MR, Orange County; BRFAL Labor Contracts, 4014, Orange County, RG 105.

43. Wilcox to Captain R. S. Lacey, Jan. 22, Feb. 5, 1866, and Wilcox to Colonel O. Brown, Feb. 12, Mar. 1, 14, 30, 1866, MR, 3948, Pittsylvania County.

44. Lieutenant J. M. Kimball to Captain Stuart Barnes, Feb. 28, 1866, MR, Brunswick County; Lieutenant J. A. Yeckley to Captain James A. Bates, Feb. 28, 1866, MR, Lunenberg County.

45. Freedmen with Harvie, Labor Contracts, Harvie Family Papers, 1H2636b–d, VHS.

46. Shifflett, *Patronage and Poverty*, 30–34.

47. Jaynes, *Branches without Roots*, 45–46, 53, 345–46.

48. Lynda J. Morgan, *Emancipation*, 188, chap. 11.

49. These labor contracts are drawn from various sources, including 3894, Bowling Green, Caroline County; 3905, Buckingham Court House, Buckingham County; 3950, Danville, Pittsylvania County; 3946, Cumberland Court House, Cumberland County; 3953, Dinwiddie Court House, Dinwiddie County; 3975, Farmville, Prince Edward County; 4052, Liberty, Bedford County; 4057, Louisa Court House, Louisa County—all in RG 105; Allen Family Papers, 1AL546a; Hannah Family Papers,

1H1956a3032; Harvie Family Papers, 1H2636c; Short Family Papers, 1SH8185a; Skipworth Family Papers, 1SK366a—all planter papers at VHS; Bremo Recess Papers, 9513; Hannah Family Papers, 1H1956a—both planter papers at UVA.

50. Freedmen with Brent, Labor Contracts, Bremo Recess Papers, 9513, UVA.

51. Freedmen with Allen, Labor Contracts, Allen Family Papers, 1AL546a, VHS.

52. Thompson, *English Working Class*, 215.

53. Freedmen with Harvie, Labor Contracts, Harvie Family Papers, 1H2636c, VHS; Freedmen with McKinney, Labor Contracts, Hannah Family Papers, 1H1956a 3032, VHS.

54. Freedmen with Skipworth, Labor Contracts, Skipworth Family Papers, 1SK366a, VHS; Edmund Burke, Labor Contracts, 4052, Bedford County, RG 105.

55. Freedmen with Haskins, BRFAL contracts, 3905, Buckingham County, RG 105. For the notion of free labor as freeing dependency, see Barbara J. Fields, *Slavery and Freedom*, chap. 6, for the Upper South, and Reidy, *Agrarian Capitalism*, chap. 6, for the Lower South.

56. Yeckley to Captain James A. Bates, Feb. 28, 1866, MR, Lunenburg County. The Virginia general assembly did pass an antienticement bill on February 20, 1866, but it appears to have had little impact.

57. Connelly to Captain Stuart Barnes, Apr. 1, 1866, MR, Prince Edward and Cumberland Counties.

58. I think the values of freedom after slavery are a more useful guide here than rational economic assumptions that would posit that the freedpeople's enticement was simply the search for the highest wages.

59. Lyon to Brown, Apr. 30, 1866, MR, Charlotte County. The seven completed planter surveys were attached to this report. Needless to say, there are certain limitations to these surveys: only planters responded, the BRFAL set questions that could beg the answers, and freedpeople were described rather than consulted. Still, this source adds detail to earlier generalizations, while earlier generalizations help plug the gaps here.

60. Ibid.

61. William E. Spaulding to Lyon, Apr. 16, 1866; Spencer to Lyon, Apr. 17, 1866; Dr. Dennis to Lyon, Apr. 25, 1866; Dr. Spraggins to Lyon, n.d.; J. R. Watkins to Lyon, May 1, 1866; W. A. Smith to Lyon, May 1, 1866; William L. Scott to Lyon, May 18, 1866—all in ibid.

62. See n. 61, above.

63. Sharp to Colonel Orlando Brown, Feb. 28, 1866, MR, Dinwiddie County.

64. See n. 61, above.

65. For this useful metaphor, see Raymond Williams, *Country and City*, chap. 1.

66. William E. Spaulding to Lyon, Apr. 16, 1866; W. A. Smith to Lyon, May 1, 1866; J. R. Watkins to Lyon, May 1, 1866—all in Lyon to Brown, Apr. 30, 1866, MR, Charlotte County. Presumably, Lieutenant Lyon's monthly report was sent to Richmond sometime after mid-May in order to include the later questionnaires.

67. William L. Scott to Lyon, May 18, 1866, in ibid.

68. Edmund S. Morgan, *American Slavery*; Kulikoff, *Tobacco and Slaves*; Siegel, *Roots of Southern Distinctiveness*, 16–21; Berlin and Morgan, *Cultivation and Culture*, chap. 7.

69. Lynda J. Morgan, *Emancipation*, chap. 10, examines freedom's institutional

building in the Virginia interior while Engs, *Freedom's First Generation*, chap. 7, does the same for the southeastern peninsula. Our focus is different: how did freedom work (or not) in the fields during the day and throughout the season?

70. For freedwomen's withdrawal from agricultural production, see Ransom and Sutch, *One Kind of Freedom*, 44–47, 232–36; Litwack, *Been in the Storm*, 244–47; Jaynes, *Branches without Roots*, 229–32; Jacqueline Jones, *Labor of Love*, 58–68. For a critique of this token comment on freedwomen's work, see Schwalm, "Meaning of Freedom," 318–49. Presumably, all these works include freedchildren in their observations. We focus on the struggle over the household economy within the broader context of former slaveowner control and proslave ideology, BRFAL ideals of the nuclear family unit, and freedpeople's attempts to realize their local autonomy.

71. Dr. Dennis to Lyon, Apr. 25, 1866, in Lyon to Brown, Apr. 30, 1866, MR, Charlotte County.

72. J. R. Watkins to Lyon, May 1, 1866, in ibid.

73. William E. Spaulding to Lyon, Apr. 16, 1866, and Spencer to Lyon, Apr. 17, 1866, in ibid.

74. W. A. Smith to Lyon, May 1, 1866, and Dr. Spraggins to Lyon, n.d, in ibid.

75. Planter surveys, in ibid.

76. Willliam L. Scott to Lyon, May 18, 1866, in ibid. Scott's comment about idle freedwomen recalls Captain Sharp's later complaint about "idle women whose tongues are busier than their hands."

77. William E. Spaulding to Lyon, Apr. 16, 1866, in ibid.

78. W. A. Smith to Lyon, May 1, 1866, in ibid.

79. Dr. Dennis to Lyon, Apr. 25, 1866, in ibid.

80. William L. Scott to Lyon, May 18, 1866, in ibid.

81. J. R. Watkins to Lyon, May 1, 1866, in ibid. Some employers did attempt compulsion by apprenticing orphaned freedchildren. Freedpeople often resisted by assuming extrafamilial responsibilities. For the "proper government" exercised by freedwoman Sallie Harris for "Cousin Wilson" and by freedman Wister Miller for seven-year-old "Charles Ganaway," in Amelia County, see Berlin and Rowland, *Families and Freedom*, 236–39. For apprenticeship struggles elsewhere, see Barbara J. Fields, *Slavery and Freedom*, 148–56; Reidy, *Agrarian Capitalism*, 153–55.

82. Slavery as schooling has earmarked the historiography. For the benign school, see Phillips, *American Negro Slavery* and *Life and Labor*. For the harsh school, see Stampp, *Peculiar Institution*. For the contradictory school, which seems to have fooled both the masters and the slaves, see Eugene D. Genovese, intro. to Phillips, *American Negro Slavery*; Genovese, *World the Slaveholders Made* and *Roll, Jordan, Roll*.

83. Lyon to Brown, Apr. 30, 1866, MR, Charlotte County.

84. A conservative might read this evidence as historical validation for the continuation of the pathological black family from slavery through freedom to the modern period. The modern black family continues to face devastating blows, but these have absolutely nothing to do with emancipation. Indeed, the fairer conservative might even note the difference between past criticisms of poor "parenting" and modern invective toward mass "matrifocality."

85. Lieutenant George Buffum to Major General Alfred H. Terry, July 31, 1866, MR, Halifax County.

86. USDA, *Annual Report* (1866), 55. The exact returns were 114,480,516 pounds on 159,444 acres and worth $15,683,830.

87. Shaun to General A. H. Terry, July 31, 1866, MR, Bedford County.

88. Lieutenant Jacob Roth to Major William R. Morse, Aug. 18, 1866, MR, in Letters Received, 4056, Louisa County, RG 105.

89. Buffum to Terry, July 31, 1866, MR, Halifax County.

90. Captain Jerome Connelly to Brown, Aug. 1, 1866, MR, Nottoway and Lunenburg Counties.

91. White to Brown, July 31, 1866, MR, Amelia County.

92. Knight to Brown, Sept. 30, 1866, MR, Franklin County.

93. Tidball to Bates, Aug. 31, 1866, MR, Albemarle County.

94. Connelly to Brown, Oct. 1, 1866, MR, Franklin County. Other reports of employers breaking contracts and refusing to fulfill payment obligations were reported in the fall of 1866 in BRFAL monthly reports from Nelson, Goochland, and Powhatan Counties.

95. Lieutenant Jacob Roth to Major William R. Morse, Aug. 18, 1866, Letters Received, 4056, Louisa County, RG 105.

96. Tidball to Bates, Aug. 31, 1866, and Tidball to Brown, Jan. 31, 1867, MR, Albemarle County.

97. Lieutenant Jacob Roth to Major William R. Morse, Aug. 18, 1866, Letters Received, 4056, Louisa County, RG 105; Connelly to Brown, Oct. 1, 1866, MR, Nottoway and Lunenburg Counties.

98. Jordan to Major J. R. Stone, Sept. 30, 1866, MR, Prince Edward, Cumberland, Buckingham, Charlotte Counties. The freedpeople's usage of the BRFAL was analogous to the actions of self-emancipated slaves embracing invading Union armies during the war: active agency pursuing emancipatory aspirations.

99. Stevenson to Brown, Jan. 31, 1867, MR, Lynchburg, Campbell County. Such bitter complaints suggest complicated urban-rural relations among freedpeople. Here, black Lynchburgers appear to have advised the BRFAL.

100. Jordan to Major J. R. Stone, Jan. 31, 1867, MR, Prince Edward, Cumberland, Buckingham, Charlotte Counties. This BRFAL antipathy toward the freedpeople's urban migration resurfaced later in Hampton Institute's stay-on-the-farm movement. See Chap. 8.

101. Stevenson to Brown, May 31, 1867, MR, Lynchburg, Campbell County.

102. Tilley, *Bright Tobacco*, 97.

103. Lieutenant G. F. Cook to Major J. R. Stone, Jan. 24, 1867, MR, Mecklenburg County.

104. Captain A. J. Connelly to Brown, Feb. 28, 1867, MR, Lunenburg and Nottoway Counties. Du Bois, *Black Reconstruction*, 538, estimated that 200,000 freedpeople emigrated between 1865 and 1867 because of economic oppression, although his estimate is unsourced.

105. Cook to Stone, Jan. 24, 1867, MR, Mecklenburg County; Connelly to Brown, Feb. 28, 1867, MR, Lunenburg and Nottoway Counties. This tension also challenges the neoclassical assumptions of economic historians of postemancipation. The debate is extensive, but for a lucid summary, see Woodman, "Sequel to Slavery."

106. Spencer to Lyon, Apr. 17, 1866, and Dr. Dennis to Lyon, Apr. 25, 1866, in Lyon to Brown, Apr. 30, 1866, MR, Charlotte County.

107. For the explanation of "idle wanderers," see Eckenrode, *Political History*. For old and new emancipatory explanations, see, respectively, Alrutheus A. Taylor, *Negro in the Reconstruction of Virginia*, chap. 5, and Lynda J. Morgan, *Emancipation*, chap. 10.

108. Connelly to Brown, Nov. 1866, MR, Lunenburg and Nottoway Counties. For earlier reports of freedmen debts, see Lieutenant J. A. Yeckley to Captain J. A. Bates, Feb. 28, 1866, MR, Lunenburg County, and Lieutenant G. Buffum to General J. M. Schofield, Aug. 31, 1866, MR, Halifax County. This latter report also contains some free labor lessons: "Comparatively few will have one cent coming to them, and in many instances they will be indebted to the employer, and in their ignorance will naturally feel that they have been defrauded." Lieutenant G. Buffum anticipated difficulties during settlement time, but he thought the lesson useful: "Many who will not take advice will learn a lesson from bitter experience this year, which I feel satisfied will be of benefit to them in the future." It does not appear to have crossed Buffum's mind that some of the freedmen used credit as their payment system precisely because of their employers' past duplicity at settlement time. This strategy was double-edged because it could lead to debt peonage through increased consumption.

109. These 1867 labor contracts were drawn from the following sources: 3905, Buckingham Court House, Buckingham County; 3946, Cumberland Court House, Cumberland County; 3950, Danville, Pittsylvania County; 4005, Goochland County; 4057, Louisa Court House, Louisa County—all in RG 105; Dabney Family Papers, 1D1124b-3135; Hannah Family Papers, 1H1956a-3002; Short Family Papers, 1SH8185a, sec. 9—all in VHS; Alexander & Alexander contract, Feb. 18, 1867, 10015-2; Hannah Family Papers, 1H1aSGa—both in UVA.

110. Freedmen with Hannah, Jan. 1, 1867, in Hannah Family Papers, 1H1956a 3002, VHS.

111. Freedman Gregory with Goode, Dec. 24, 1866, in Short Family Papers, 1SH8185a, sec. 9, VHS.

112. Freedman Fontaine with Hunter, Sept. 15, 1866, in 4057, Louisa County, RG 105.

113. Lieutenant J. M. Kimball to Major J. R. Stone, Sept. 30, 1866, MR, Brunswick and Greensville Counties.

114. Lieutenant Robert Cullen to Brown, Oct. 19, 1866, MR, Mecklenburg County.

115. Freedman Scott and Powell, Feb. 1, 1867, 4005, Goochland County, RG 105. The reduced number of written contracts for 1867 might be explained by freedpeople's cynicism, employer resistance, or BRFAL apathy. Alternatively, there might be thousands of contracts still undiscovered. However, the BRFAL monthly reports indicate that many contemporaries realized that free labor struggles were simply too great to be contained by legal documents that reflected rather than resolved ambiguities.

116. Connelly to Brown, Dec. 31, 1866, MR, Lunenburg and Nottoway Counties.

117. Stevenson to Brown, Dec. 31, 1866, MR, Nelson and Amherst Counties.

118. Stevenson to Brown, July 31, 1866, MR, Nelson County.

119. Ibid.

120. USDA, *Annual Report* (1866) 55. Also Buffum to Barnes, June 1, 1866; Buffum to Schofield, Aug. 31, Sept. 30, Oct. 25, 1866—all MR, Halifax County.

121. Captain William L. Tidball to Brown, Dec. 31, 1866, MR, Albemarle County, and Lieutenant F. W. Knight to Brown, Jan. 31, 1867, MR, Franklin County.

122. Lieutenant J. B. Clinton to Brown, Jan. 31, 1867, MR, Amelia and Powhatan Counties.

123. Buffum to Schofield, Oct. 25, 1866, MR, Halifax County.

124. It is also important to note that Buffum meant *bargain* as *haggle* rather than simply *contract* or a favorable sale. For the word's etymology, see *The Concise Oxford Dictionary of Current English*, 5th ed., 1964, 94; *Webster's Ninth New Collegiate Dictionary*, 1991, 131.

125. Freedmen with Goode, Labor Contracts, Dec. 24, 1866, in Short Family Papers, 1SH8185a, sec. 9, VHS.

126. Freedmen with Hannah, Jan. 1, 1867, in Hannah Family Papers, 1H1956a 3002, VHS.

CHAPTER THREE

1. Shanks, *Secession Movement*; Maddex, *Virginia Conservatives*, 5–45, 67–85; Du Bois, *Black Reconstruction*, 537.

2. Maddex, *Virginia Conservatives*, 46–66; Lowe, *Republicans and Reconstruction*, chap. 6; Du Bois, *Black Reconstruction*, 537.

3. Alderson, "Freedmen's Bureau," 140; Lynda J. Morgan, *Emancipation*, 139.

4. Schofield, *Forty-Six Years*, 400.

5. Maddex, *Virginia Conservatives*, 45; Foner, *Reconstruction*, 271–80; Lowe, *Republicans and Reconstruction*, 72–81.

6. Our purpose here is twofold: to trace the role of politics in collectivizing free labor struggles, and to link these politics with older ideas of social redistribution (ex-slaves) and radical antebellum tendencies (ex-masters).

7. Lowe, *Republicans and Reconstruction*, 74–77. Howard, *Autobiography*, vol. 2, chap. 55, is silent on the BRFAL's political work.

8. Colonel G. B. Carse to Captain R. S. Lacey, SUP, 7th District, June 1, 1867, MR, Pittsylvania County; Lieutenant G. Buffum to Colonel O. Brown, Aug. 31, Sept. 30, 1867, MR, Halifax County.

9. Colonel J. W. Jordan to Major J. R. Stone, Aug. 31, 1867, MR, Prince Edward, Cumberland, Buckingham, Charlotte Counties; Lowe, "Convention." For brief comments on the Union League in Virginia during this period, see Lowe, *Republicans and Reconstruction*, 125–28.

10. Foner, *Reconstruction*, 283.

11. Captain A. J. Connelly to Captain Garrick Mallory, June 30, 1867, MR, Nottoway and Lunenburg Counties; Lieutenant J. M. Kimball to Major J. R. Stone, July 31, 1867, MR, Brunswick County.

12. Dwyer to Brown, Aug. 31, Sept. 30, 1867, MR, Caroline County.

13. Jordan to Stone, Sept. 30, 1866, MR, Prince Edward, Cumberland, Buckingham, Charlotte Counties.

14. Lowe, *Republicans and Reconstruction*, 119. These cooperative activities, in the face of hostile emancipatory conditions, transcended gender conflict espoused by some recent historians. See Schwalm, "Meaning of Freedom," which conflates familial conflicts with fractured class identities.

15. Saville, *Work of Reconstruction*, 163. Given went on to address "a multitude" in southeastern Virginia.

16. Saville, *Work of Reconstruction*, 166. Saville's work on South Carolina Reconstruction is excellent on grassroots activism with wider ripples of communication and politicization among the freedmen.

17. Foner, *Reconstruction*, 304; Lowe, *Republicans and Reconstruction*, 77.

18. Foner, *Freedom's Lawmakers*, 12–13, 108, 185.

19. Colonel Jordan to Major Stone, Oct. 31, 1867, MR, Prince Edward, Cumberland, Buckingham, Charlotte Counties; Lieutenant J. B. Clinton to Stone, Oct. 31, 1867, MR, Amelia County; Agent Alex D. Bakie to Stone, Oct. 31, 1867, MR, Mecklenburg County; Agent John Burke to Stone, Oct. 31, 1867, MR, Dinwiddie County; Lieutenant J. F. Wilson to Colonel Orlando Brown, Oct. 31, 1867, MR, Goochland County; Lieutenant Louis W. Stevenson to Brown, Oct. 31, 1867, MR, Campbell, Appomattox, Nelson, Amherst Counties; Lieutenant B. F. Shaun to Brown, Oct. 31, 1867, MR, Bedford County; Agent Mahoney to Captain R. S. Lacey, Oct. 31, 1867, MR, Pittsylvania County.

20. Lowe, *Republicans and Reconstruction*, 122–29; Morton, *Negro in Virginia Politics*, 111.

21. Lowe, *Republicans and Reconstruction*, 126–27, 199–200; Lynda J. Morgan, *Emancipation*, 161–62; Alrutheus A. Taylor, *Negro in the Reconstruction of Virginia*, 227–28.

22. Lowe, "Convention."

23. Lowe, *Republicans and Reconstruction*, 131–32, 138, 199.

24. Lowe, "Convention"; Foner, *Freedom's Lawmakers*, 225. It might be added that General Schofield was a moderate Republican whose negative racial views of the freedmen often endeared him to Virginia conservatives. See Lowe, *Republicans and Reconstruction*, 75–76.

25. Foner, *Freedom's Lawmakers*, 12–13, 19, 38, 42, 125, 155–56, 159–60, 185, 209, 225. For rare photos of these lawmakers in the tobacco region, see ibid., 19, 25, 59, 69, 94, 134, 169, 217. It should not be forgotten that Jackson, *Negro Office-Holders*, provided the first historical sketches of these Black Republicans. For a more critical view of the role of freedom's lawmakers in South Carolina, see Thomas Holt, *Black over White*.

26. Foner, *Freedom's Lawmakers*, 19; Du Bois, *Black Reconstruction*, 541–42.

27. Foner, *Freedom's Lawmakers*, 19, 52, 134, 209–10.

28. Ibid., 13–14; Lowe, *Republicans and Reconstruction*, 91–92, 95–96; Du Bois, *Black Reconstruction*, 541.

29. Foner, *Freedom's Lawmakers*, 233–34.

30. Ibid., 134.

31. Lowe, "Convention," 351; Jackson, *Negro Office-Holders*, 29; Alrutheus A. Taylor, *Negro in the Reconstruction of Virginia*, 228; Foner, *Freedom's Lawmakers*, 155–56; Charles W. White, *Hidden and Forgotten*, 118–20.

32. Charles W. White, *Hidden and Forgotten*, 118–19. It is conceivable that Moss was using the presence of Union troops as a defense for his radical public utterances. Whatever the case, it is clear that his politicking posed a threat to traditional social relations that was far from ridiculous.

33. See n. 31, above.

34. We skirt the emancipatory import of those like Moss when we view them singularly, as either individuals or representatives, rather than dialectically, as freedmen.

35. It should be noted that some freedmen representatives were more moderate in their political views of emancipation. These included men such as Fields Cook and Joseph Cox. They complicate simple class or race divisions as pointed out by Robinson, "Beyond the Realm." However, it should be noted that many of the freedmen were far from quiescent or moderate in the fields, as this chapter has tried to show.

36. A classic expression of this opposition to freedmen politics was provided by Sarah P. Miller of Campbell County. Commenting on the constitutional convention assembled at Richmond in December 1867, she informed her cousin Mary in Maryland, "The radical speakers sent south have been a great disadvantage to the negroes[,] and of all ridiculous and mischievous legislating, that of giving an ignorant, uninformed class of people the right to vote and the chance of being set over the whites of the land, takes the lead" (Miller to Clendenin, Dec. 12, 1867, Miller Letters, 8668, UVA). Note the congruence with the proslave view that slaves were happy except when interfered with by outsiders. The complaint against freedmen politics became the seed of "Negro" disfranchisement that flowered in both the 1902 constitution and anti-Reconstruction historiography like Eckenrode, *Political History*, and Morton, *Negro in Virginia Politics*.

37. Connelly to Captain Garrick Mallory, June 30, 1867, MR, Nottoway and Lunenburg Counties; Knight to Colonel Orlando Brown, June 30, 1867, MR, Franklin County.

38. Carse to Captain R. S. Lacey, June 1, 1867, MR, Pittsylvania County; Colonel Jordan to Major J. R. Stone, May 31, 1867, MR, Prince Edward, Cumberland, Buckingham, Charlotte Counties; Lieutenant A. F. Higgs to Brown, July 31, 1867, MR, Albemarle County; Lieutenant L. W. Stevenson to Brown, Oct. 31, 1867, MR, Campbell, Appomattox, Nelson, Amherst Counties; Lieutenant B. F. Shaun to Brown, Oct. 31, 1867, MR, Bedford County. We can only assume the political involvement of those freedmen squatters in Dinwiddie County, freedmen supporters of Representative Moss in Buckingham County, and those troublesome freedwomen in Charlotte County.

39. Kimball to Major J. R. Stone, July 31, 1867, MR, Brunswick County.

40. Jordan to Stone, Aug. 31, 1867, MR, Prince Edward, Cumberland, Buckingham, Charlotte Counties.

41. Agent John Burke to Stone, Oct. 31, 1867, MR, Dinwiddie County; Lieutenant J. F. Wilson to Brown, Oct. 31, 1867, MR, Goochland County; Mahoney to Captain R. S. Lacey, Oct. 31, 1867, MR, Pittsylvania County.

42. Shaun to Brown, Oct. 31, Nov. 30, 1867, MR, Bedford County. This conflict over the political dimensions of free labor became a generational hallmark of postemancipation politics as witnessed during readjusterism, populism, and disfranchisement. It might be added that few historians have mined the BRFAL records for the postemancipation activities of either yeoman farmers or poor whites. But see Lynda J. Morgan, *Emancipation*, chap. 9.

43. Connelly to Brown, Oct. 31, 1867, MR, Nottoway and Lunenburg Counties.

44. Kimball to Stone, Oct. 31, 1867, MR, Brunswick County.

45. Stevenson to Brown, Nov. 30, 1867, MR, Campbell, Appomattox, Nelson, Amherst Counties.

46. Shaun to Brown, Dec. 31, 1867, MR, Bedford County.

47. Higgs to Brown, July 31, 1867, MR, Albemarle County.

48. Whitten to Brown, Dec. 31, 1867, MR, Franklin County.

49. Buffum to Brown, Aug. 31, 1867, MR, Halifax County.

50. Jordan to Major J. R. Stone, May 31, Aug. 31, Oct. 31, 1867, MR, Prince Edward, Cumberland, Buckingham, Charlotte Counties. For other examples of BRFAL officials' concern at this clash, see Dwyer to Brown, Sept. 30, 1867, MR, Caroline County, and Lieutenant A. F. Higgs to Brown, Jan. 31, 1868, MR, Albemarle County. It is not inconceivable that employers complained to BRFAL officials about this clash because they believed it would be efficacious. Although this question is difficult to resolve, the point remains that all parties saw the connection between politics and free labor, albeit from conflictual positions.

51. Kimball to Major Rollen, Nov. 30, 1867, MR, Brunswick County.

52. Lieutenant N. Whitten to Brown, Nov. 30, 1867, MR, Franklin County.

53. Stowell to Brown, Apr. 30, May 30, 1867, MR, Lunenburg County.

54. Mahoney to Captain R. S. Lacey, Jan. 31, May 30, 1868, and Agent William Leahy to Lacey, July 16, 1868, MR, Pittsylvania County. To reiterate the point, these compensatory claims cannot be reduced simply to wage claims. Rather, they suggest that the freedmen utilized free labor ideology to resist the continuation of exploitation they associated with slavery. This was their antislave ideology grounded in emancipation.

55. Morse to Brown, Mar. 31, 1868, MR, Goochland County.

56. Stowell to Brown, May 30, 1868, MR, Lunenburg County.

57. USDA, *Annual Report* (1867), 82. That season Virginia rural producers also harvested over 18 million bushels of corn worth nearly $16 million and nearly 7 million bushels of wheat worth over $14 million.

58. Rutherford to Brown, Feb. 29, 1868, MR, Nottoway and Lunenburg Counties.

59. Bakie to Major J. R. Stone, Sept. 30, 1867, MR, Mecklenburg County.

60. Egbert to Brown, Jan. 31, 1868, MR, Franklin County.

61. Rutherford to Brown, Jan. 31, 1868, MR, Nottoway and Lunenburg Counties.

62. Clinton to Stone, Jan. 31, 1868, MR, Amelia County.

63. Lieutenant J. M. Kimball to Major J. R. Stone, Mar. 31, 1868, MR, Brunswick County; Agent Thomas Leahey to Brown, May 31, 1868, MR, Prince Edward and Charlotte Counties.

64. Morse to Brown, Feb. 29, 1868, MR, Goochland County.

65. Puryear with Goode, Short Family Papers, 1SH8185a, sec. 9, VHS.

66. Freedmen with Allen, Allen Family Papers, 1AL546a, VHS.

67. BRFAL contracts, 3905, Buckingham County, RG 105.

68. Lowe, *Republicans and Reconstruction*, 148–55.

69. Leahey to Brown, July 31, 1868, MR, Prince Edward and Charlotte Counties.

70. Stowell to Brown, July 31, 1868, MR, Halifax County.

71. Rutherford to Captain W. D. Coulter, July 31, 1868, MR, Lunenburg County. It should be noted that in spite of the numerous challenges to the implementation of the new free labor system caused by the freedmen's politicking and white antipathy, none of the BRFAL officials actually opposed the extension of suffrage to the freedmen.

72. Colonel G. B. Carse to Captain R. S. Lacey, Mar. 28, 1867, Letters Received, 3948, Pittsylvania County, RG 105.

73. Dillard with Taylor and Womack, Jan. 5, 1866, Contract, Indentures, and Court Records, 3950, and Lt. Colonel Carse to Captain Lacey, Mar. 28, 1867, Letters Received, 3948, RG 105.

74. Leahy to Captain R. S. Lacey, July 16, 1868, MR, Pittsylvania County; Leahy to Brown, Aug. 1, 1868, MR, Pittsylvania County.

75. Leahy to Captain R. S. Lacey, Sept. 1, 1868, MR, Pittsylvania County.

76. Ibid. Freedman Wicker's actions echoed Black Republican Lewis Lindsay's 1867 speech in which God was thanked since "the negroes had learned to use guns, pistols and ram-rods." See Foner, *Freedom's Lawmakers*, 134. For numerous examples of attacks on freedpeople and subsequent acquittals or penalties, see Register of Complaints, May 1867–July 1868, 3949, Pittsylvania County, RG 105.

77. Register of Court Cases, June–Oct. 1868, Letters Sent, 3947, Pittsylvania County, RG 105.

78. Alvord, "Semi-Annual Reports on Schools for Freedmen," no. 7, Jan. 1869, 3; Lynda J. Morgan, *Emancipation*, 211–12; William Leahy to Brown, Aug. 1, 1868, MR, Pittsylvania County.

79. Mugleston, "Diary of Hopkins," 94.

80. Kimball to Brown, Nov. 30, 1868, MR, Brunswick County.

81. Thomas Leahey to Brown, Dec. 31, 1868, MR, Prince Edward and Charlotte Counties.

82. USDA, *Annual Report* (1868), 26–27.

83. Leahy to Lacey, Dec. 1, 1868, MR, Pittsylvania County.

84. Kimball to Brown, Dec. 31, 1868, MR, Brunswick County.

85. Morse to Brown, Dec. 31, 1868, MR, Goochland County.

86. Stowell to Brown, Nov. 30, Dec. 31, 1868, MR, Halifax County.

87. Lynda J. Morgan, *Emancipation*, 214–15; Lowe, *Republicans and Reconstruction*, chap. 8.

88. Alrutheus A. Taylor, *Negro in the Reconstruction of Virginia*, 257.

89. Ibid., 259; Du Bois, *Black Reconstruction*, 545–46.

90. Major Marcus S. Hopkins to Brown, Dec. 31, 1868, MR, Orange County. This monthly report has also been reprinted as an addendum in Mugleston, "Diary of Hopkins," 99–102.

CHAPTER FOUR

1. USBC, *1860, Agriculture*, 154–62; USBC, *1870, Wealth and Industry*, 266–70; Janney, "Virginia," 26–33.

2. *SPF*, Apr. 1869, 214.

3. See n. 1, above.

4. See n. 1, above. The calculations for determining land values were worked out by dividing the cash value of farms by the acreage of the state or county.

5. The leading propagator of postbellum planter persistence has been Wiener, especially his *Social Origins* and "Class Structure."

6. For planter persistence in Virginia, see Shifflett, *Patronage and Poverty*; Townes, "Effects of Emancipation"; Burdick, "From Virtue to Fitness"; Susannah H. Jones, "Labor and Landownership."

7. *SPF*, Jan. 1874, 14.

8. For some salient critiques of planter persistence that emphasize labor as land's real value, see Barbara J. Fields, *Slavery and Freedom*, chaps. 6 and 7; Wright, *Old South, New South*, 17; Lynda J. Morgan, *Emancipation*, 205–6.

9. USBC, *1860, Agriculture*, 154–59; USBC, *1870, Wealth and Industry*, 268–72.

10. USBC, *1860, Agriculture*, 154–59; USBC, *1870, Wealth and Industry*, 268–72; USBC, *1870, Compendium*, 700–701.

11. See n. 10, above.

12. See n. 10, above. It should be recalled that West Virginia had seceded, which affected cereal and livestock returns but not tobacco production.

13. USBC, *1860, Agriculture*, 154; USBC, *1870, Wealth and Industry*, 267.

14. Shifflett, *Patronage and Poverty*, 15; USBC, *1860, Agriculture*, 159; USBC, *1870, Wealth and Industry*, 271.

15. Townes, "Effects of Emancipation," 405 n. 10.

16. "Meteorology of 1867," in USDA, *Annual Report* (1867), 431–64; "Meteorology of 1868," in USDA, *Annual Report* (1868), 614–51; "Meteorology of 1869," in USDA, *Annual Report* (1869), 640–81; *SPF*, Oct. 1870, 607.

17. *SPF*, Sept. 1869, 541.

18. *SPF*, Jan. 1870, 55. Tobacco production per acre usually averaged around 600 pounds.

19. Alvord, "Semi-Annual Reports on Schools for Freedmen," no. 9, Jan. 1, 1870, 15. Alvord concluded his report on a tendentious note: "The fact that they are actually carrying this burden is much to their credit, and should command both admiration and pity."

20. *SPF*, Oct. 1870, 607.

21. Phillips, *Life and Labor*, 3.

22. In their study of the postbellum cotton South, Ransom and Sutch argue that "historians and economists [like contemporaries] have also been misled by the 1870 Census." The deficient 1870 census, they claim, makes the decreases from the 1860 census all the more exaggerated: "In particular, census figures on the population and the level of agricultural output of the South in 1870 are substantially below their true values." See Ransom and Sutch, *One Kind of Freedom*, 53. Townes, "Effects of Emancipation," 405 n. 10, further notes statistical discrepancies between the 1870 unpublished manuscript census and published census returns.

23. This barefaced explanation does not ignore war devastation, drought conditions, or even census undercounting, but it does insist on the centrality of emancipation in accounting for postwar agricultural decline. Lynda J. Morgan, in *Emancipation*, 203, writes, "The root causes of postwar depression in a commodified market were the combined pressures of depression, restricted credit, and freedpeople's initiatives on the plantations." This is unfortunately phrased; the former factors can only be explained by the latter.

24. Handy, "On the Tobacco Plantation" (1872), 655.

25. King, *Great South*, 650.

26. The sighs of old tobacco planters were particularly revealing.

27. Arnold, *Tobacco Industry in Virginia*, 21.

28. Ibid., acknowledgments. The historical significance of this 1897 survey should not be forgotten. It was published as part of the Johns Hopkins University Studies series in historical and political science and has reigned for a century as the only regional study of postwar tobacco Virginia. Tilley's *Bright Tobacco* (1948), despite its acuity, was primarily concerned with North Carolina and only Halifax, Pittsylvania, and Henry Counties in southside Virginia.

29. Arnold's title, *History of the Tobacco Industry in Virginia from 1860 to 1894*,

obviously referred to production, marketing, and manufacturing in postwar Virginia. But regarding the impact of emancipation, Arnold was really writing about nonindustriousness.

30. It is crude because other factors did contribute to this decline in cash crop production.

31. In 1788 African slaves in French Saint Domingue produced over 163 million pounds of sugar and 68 million pounds of coffee; fourteen years after emancipation, Haitian freedpeople produced under 2 million pounds of sugar and just over 20 million pounds of coffee. In the coastal lowlands of South Carolina and in Georgia, rice production fell from nearly 172 million pounds in 1859 to just over 54 million in 1869. In the cane fields of southern Louisiana, production fell from an average of 161,000 metric tons annually between 1857 and 1861 to 77,000 metric tons in 1870. See Lacerte, "Land and Labor," 449, 455 n. 22; Clifton, "Postbellum Rice Culture," 146; Rebecca J. Scott, "World of Cane," 72, 76.

32. The VAS proceedings were reproduced in *SPF*, Feb. 1867, 21–51. All quotations are from this account.

33. Ibid. Sutherlin's comments suggest that even those reconciled to the new realities of emancipation insisted on older forms of labor management.

34. Arnold, *Tobacco Industry in Virginia*, 46–47. This legislation was to prove incapable of addressing the challenges wrought by emancipation.

35. Riley, *Magazines*, 250–55. The immediate postwar run of editors included Charles B. Williams (1867–70), James T. Johnson and John M. Allan (1870–71), John W. Rison (1871–72), and Rison and L. R. Dickinson (1872–73). It is interesting to speculate on the magazine's name change: Did it indicate planter decline? Was it an attempt to hegemonize? Or was it simply a marketing ruse to broaden the paper's appeal? Or all three? We shall never know for sure. However, there are hints of the broad appeal of the magazine. Its Civil War peak was around 5,000; by 1881 it was being posted to 300 post offices in the Virginia–North Carolina tobacco region; and by 1893 circulation approximated 20,000. See Riley, *Magazines*, 253; Tilley, *Bright Tobacco*, 159 n. 18. If BRFAL monthly reports offered one free labor conduit into the Virginia interior, the *SPF* provided another albeit very different conduit.

36. *SPF*, Mar. 1867, 125–26.

37. H, "Hints," *SPF*, Sept. 1867, 510–11.

38. H, "Hints," *SPF*, Oct. 1867, 573–74. H was either silent or oblivious to the contradictory nature of his own position. If Negroes had such strong local attachment, then why the need for inducements to stay? How could the employer control the Negro's household economy if the Negro was induced to control his own household economy?

39. Ibid., 574. The BRFAL reports suggest the freedpeople's agenda was more concerned with balancing their emancipation aspirations with subsistence needs.

40. The Goodwyn Club met on August 26, 1871. Its minutes were subsequently published in *SPF*, Nov. 1871, 656–61.

41. This planter preoccupation with labor's freedom to move clearly distinguished it from antebellum "Negro Management" literature.

42. Ruffin, "Address," *SPF*, Dec. 1867, 641–58. Ruffin served as *SPF* editor for spells encompassing a quarter of a century: 1851–58, jointly with Williams in 1870, and again in 1875. See Riley, *Magazines*, 255.

43. Ruffin, "Address," *SPF*, Dec. 1867, 641–58.

44. Other land-labor ratios were mentioned in *SPF*. One writer identified 59,475 Virginia farms with the same number of laborers as found by Ruffin. See *SPF*, June 1867, 315–18; *SPF*, July 1867, 375–76; *SPF*, Sept. 1869, 566. The exact ratio is less important than the point it is trying to serve, namely, rural employers' calls for white immigrants to stem the power of former slaves' labor due to an adverse land-labor ratio. The possibility that immigrant labor might soon buy up cheap land, thus removing it from the ranks of employer to employee, seems to have mattered less to planters and employers. For an uncritical attempt to place the land-labor debate at the heart of postemancipation struggles in the British Caribbean, see Engerman, "Economic Change," in Richardson, *Abolition*.

45. There has been a vigorous debate over slave planter ideology: Was it modern, capitalist, and forward-looking, or was it traditional, feudal, and backward-looking? The debate does not concern us here, but postwar contributions to *SPF* suggest that many planters advised older forms of slave control for free labor management. For a recent contribution to the debate that argues confusedly and unconvincingly for antebellum plantation rationalization, see Mullin, *Africa in America*, chap. 5.

46. *SPF*, Jan. 1868, 42–43.

47. *SPF*, Jan. 1868, 43.

48. Of course, questions of values, property ownership, and access to the means of production were ignored by these contributors to *SPF*. They also conveniently forget that the Old Dominion was based on slavery. Incidentally, one wonders if this farming experiment involved those freedmen and their employers in Charlotte County identified by Lieutenant Lyon in the spring of 1866.

49. Richardson, "White Labor," *SPF*, May 1868, 283–87.

50. *SPF*, June 1868, 354–59; *SPF*, July 1868, 422–23; *SPF*, Aug. 1868, 504–5.

51. *SPF*, Dec. 1867, 678–82.

52. *SPF*, May 1867, 245.

53. *SPF*, Dec. 1867, 658–66.

54. *SPF*, Sept. 1868, 565. This call of machines for men in the direct aftermath of emancipation highlights the modernizing impulse of some postwar employers. Its roots lay in an antebellum critique, emancipation was its fillip, and it later flowered into the program of the New South propagandists. For the progressive credentials of Sutherlin, see Siegel, *Roots of Southern Distinctiveness*, 140–61. For New South modernizers, see Gaston, *New South Creed*.

55. Advertising sheet, *SPF*, May 1867. Throughout this period the Watt company of Richmond ran regular advertisements for its plows, emphasizing their superiority over other machines and labor-saving devices. See Advertising sheets, *SPF*, June–Dec. 1867.

56. Advertising sheet, *SPF*, May 1867.

57. For tobacco's labor intensity, see Tilley, *Bright Tobacco*, chap. 2. Siegel, *Roots of Southern Distinctiveness*, takes this argument one step further and argues that distinct material conditions for tobacco production precluded its capitalist takeoff. This argument begs the question of planter choice: Why produce such a cash crop in the first place? It also ignores the modernizer's proslave foot, which was squarely in the camp of the Old Dominion. Our central point, though, is to identify some of the contradictions engendered by emancipation especially through the actions (and potential actions) of the freedpeople themselves. These *SPF* comments should always be read in the shadow of free labor struggles described in the previous chapter.

58. There has grown over the years a fairly extensive literature on what might be called the condition of Virginia debate. Two schools have emerged. The first, the soil optimists, argue that the Old Dominion's exhausted lands underwent a major agricultural renaissance during the 1850s. They include Craven, *Soil Exhaustion*, 127–52; Gray, *History of Agriculture*; Robert, *Tobacco Kingdom*; Gates, *Farmer's Age*. Revisionists have argued that the antebellum Upper South experienced serious agricultural decline. These soil pessimists include Tilley, *Bright Tobacco*; Genovese, *Political Economy*, 124–53; North, *Economic Growth*, 123; Siegel, *Roots of Southern Distinctiveness*; Matthew, *Edmund Ruffin*, 195–213; Lynda J. Morgan, *Emancipation*, 23–24, 238. Our focus on the immediate postwar period suggests that agricultural reform, especially crop fertilization, was not marked in the Virginia tobacco region.

59. Janney, "Virginia," 24.

60. *SPF*, Mar. 1868, 143–45; *SPF*, May 1868, 279–83; *SPF*, Aug. 1868, 457–59. Contrast the "wandering freedmen" of G. C. Gilmer with the Negroes of "local attachment" of H.

61. *SPF*, Oct. 1871, 578–82.

62. *SPF*, Nov. 1871, 645–47.

63. Tilley, *Bright Tobacco*, 168.

64. Advertising sheet, *SPF*, May 1867, 5, 16.

65. Ibid., 18.

66. Advertising sheet, *SPF*, Sept. 1867, 483–84.

67. Advertising sheet, *SPF*, Mar. 1868, 143–45.

68. Advertising sheet, *SPF*, Oct. 1868 and Sept. 1869, 32.

69. *SPF*, Aug. 1867, 411–14.

70. Ibid.

71. *SPF*, June 1867, 297.

72. *SPF*, Apr. 1867, 167–69.

73. "Cultivation of the Peanut," in USDA, *Annual Report* (1868), 221–24. It is feasible that some of the freedpeople in these counties switched to peanut cultivation since it was less labor-intensive, promised a fair return, and provided some autonomy away from the close supervision associated with tobacco production.

74. *SPF*, May 1868, 268–75. Tilley, *Bright Tobacco*, 118, criticized the H article because its labor costs were unreliable and it failed to consider land, building, and equipment costs. Even if such criticisms were valid, the point remains that specialized crop production was being promoted in response to the impact of the freedpeople's actions.

75. *SPF*, May 1871, 265.

76. Bowie, "Culture," 179–84.

77. Ficklin, *SPF*, Dec. 1870, 743–44.

78. Shelton, "Culture," *SPF*, Feb. 1867, 1–12. For the gradual spread of bright tobacco in the antebellum period, see Tilley, *Bright Tobacco*, chap. 1; Siegel, *Roots of Southern Distinctiveness*, chap. 7.

79. *SPF*, Nov. 1868, 661–71.

80. *SPF*, Oct. 1869, 591–94.

81. *SPF*, Mar. 1868, 187–89.

82. There is a danger of overdeterminism here—that is to say, reducing all agricultural production and advice literature to the question of contested free labor relations.

Still, this is preferable to arguing that the *SPF* was simply a practical advice magazine wedded to agricultural improvement.

83. For Armstrong and the Hampton idea, see Engs, *Freedom's First Generation*, 111, 144, 147–48; Harlan, *Washington*, 58–64; Anderson, *Education of Blacks*, 38–42; Maddex, *Virginia Conservatives*, 215. For a useful insight into the mind and mission of Armstrong, see Armstrong, SUP, 9th District, to Brown, June 30, 1866, Monthly Report, Elizabeth City County, Armstrong Collection, Hampton Institute.

84. Washington, *Up from Slavery*, 62.

85. Ibid., 51–62. The metaphor of dark and light, the juxtaposition of rural simplicity and urban complexity, and the leitmotiv of pilgrim's progress all resonated in late nineteenth-century Virginia. See Chapter 8.

86. *Acts*, 1871–72, 237, 466–67; Alrutheus A. Taylor, *Negro in the Reconstruction of Virginia*, 168–70; Maddex, *Virginia Conservatives*, 215; Engs, *Freedom's First Generation*, 89, 104–5, 148, 153, 159; Foner, *Freedom's Lawmakers*, 19, 162. I think the focus on the freedpeople's initiative here (Taylor, Engs, and Foner) is warranted but incomplete, while Anderson, *Education of Blacks*, inexplicably ignores this key political moment that supports his broader argument of the education of blacks for socialization.

87. Anderson, *Education of Blacks*, 36–37. Engs, *Freedom's First Generation*, 139–60, argues persuasively for the fund-raising nature of Armstrong's activities.

88. In recent years scholars have devoted a great deal of attention to the educational endeavors of the freedpeople. Hampton Institute has come in for its fair share of attention, including a vigorous debate over whether it represented education for liberation or education for socialization. Engs, *Freedom's First Generation*, argues for unintended liberation, while Anderson, *Education of Blacks*, argues for deliberate social control. What has drawn less attention are those links between the BRFAL's Republican free labor ideology and Hampton's program as well as the *SW*'s missionary forays into the Virginia countryside. Indeed, reading through the *SW*, it is hard not to be reminded of analogous European penetration into the African continent beyond the coastal regions, an advanced imperial mission that was already getting under way and was confirmed by the Berlin Conference of 1884–85.

89. *SW*, Jan. 1872, 2.

90. *SW*, Feb. 1877, 10.

91. Engs, *Freedom's First Generation*, 153, notes General Howard's trusteeship.

92. Anderson, *Education of Blacks*, chap. 2, in an otherwise commendable critique, misses this crucial distinction. To reiterate: unlike proslave notions, BRFAL ideas did not preclude the possibility of the successful independence of the freedpeople.

93. By early 1878 the *SW* reported 123 Hampton alumni, from the classes of 1871 through 1877, serving in the Virginia interior. See *SW*, Jan. 1878. For extended comment on these missionary activities, see Kerr-Ritchie, "Freedpeople and Schooling."

94. *SW*, Mar. 1880, 27.

95. *SW*, Jan. 1878, 5. Compare the advice to diversify crop production in the *SPF*.

96. *SW*, Apr. 1874, 3–4; Brown letter, *SW*, Sept. 1872. We may fairly assume that the goal of stability met with the approval of *SPF* planters and farmers, but the freedpeople's schooling efforts also exacerbated the problem of free labor because they continued to reconstruct the household away from cash crop production.

97. See following chapter.

98. *SW*, Feb. 1873.

99. *SW*, June 1875.

100. T.B. letter, *SW*, Sept. 1875, in Link, *Hard Country*, 30.

CHAPTER FIVE

1. Rezneck, "Depression," 494; Foner, *Reconstruction*, 512.

2. Rezneck, "Depression," 495; Foner, *Reconstruction*, 512–24.

3. Hobsbawn, *Age of Capital*, 46; Hobsbawn, *Age of Empire*, 34–35, chap. 2.

4. Hunt Diary, Sept. 29, 1873, VHS.

5. Reidy, *Agrarian Capitalism*, chap. 9; Hahn, *Roots of Southern Populism*, chap. 4.

6. Barbara J. Fields, *Slavery and Freedom*, chap. 7, epilogue.

7. Ferleger, *Agriculture and National Development*, 354.

8. Ibid.

9. "Average Prices," *Journal of the Royal Agricultural Society of England*, 3rd ser., 4 (1898): 422–23.

10. Hobsbawn, *Age of Empire*, 36. For the political significance of American prairie grain production on Irish agriculture during the late 1870s, especially resurgent nationalism, see Foster, *Modern Ireland*, 402–5.

11. Ferleger, *Agriculture and National Development*, 354–57. I used the 1876 returns for cotton because that was when the price series began. For the most thorough examination of the expanding vortex of the postbellum cotton economy and its implications, see Hahn, *Roots of Southern Populism*, chaps 4, 5.

12. Ferleger, *Agriculture and National Development*, 356.

13. Peterson, *Historical Study of Prices*, 182.

14. Ibid. It should be pointed out that barley was the exception to the fall in the price of Virginia cereal crops. Its price actually rose from 70 cents per bushel to 84 cents, although this too was to decline rapidly from the late 1880s. For useful summaries of national agricultural production and statistics in the late nineteenth-century United States, see Ferleger, *Agriculture and National Development*, 344–57; Lake, "Export, Die, or Subsidize," 88–89.

15. USDA, *Annual Report* (1876), 266; USDA, *Annual Report* (1890), 257. By 1900 global tobacco production exceeded 2 billion pounds. See USDA, *Yearbook* (1905), 714.

16. Ferleger, *Agriculture and National Development*, 356.

17. Bremner letter quoted in Ott, *Tobacco: Outlook in America*, 8. By 1900 the U.S. share of global tobacco production amounted to 40 percent. See USDA, *Yearbook* (1905), 714–15.

18. USBC, *1900, Agriculture*, 2:4, 507; USDA, *Annual Report* (1890), 258.

19. USDA, *Annual Report* (1874), 59; USDA, *Annual Report* (1890), 257; USBC, *1900, Agriculture*, 2:4, 507; Ferleger, *Agriculture and National Development*, 356.

20. USDA, *Annual Report* (1890), 257–58.

21. USBC, *1900, Agriculture*, 2:4, 507; Ferleger, *Agriculture and National Development*, 356. These federal investigations into the postwar tobacco economy reflect an emergent national interest arrayed against competing national economies.

22. This transformation in the tobacco economy is pursued in Chapter 7.

23. To stress the broader point, emancipation undid traditional social relations just at the moment when the roots of the modern global tobacco economy were being firmly planted.

24. USDA, *Annual Report* (1869) 34.

25. USDA, *Annual Report* (1889), 229. It should be noted that Virginia did increase its tobacco production later. However, this did not affect the major challenge from western tobacco. In 1900 the nation produced over 868 million pounds of tobacco on over 1 million acres worth nearly $57 million; Kentucky, Tennessee, and Ohio combined produced nearly 430 million pounds on over 528,000 acres worth over $26 million, or half the national production, acreage, and value. This was the sort of role formerly enjoyed by the Old Dominion. See USBC, *1900, Abstract*, 274. It should be added that some rural producers in northern states also switched to tobacco production during this period. Pennsylvania returned over 3 million pounds of tobacco in 1860; this had expanded to 41.5 million pounds on nearly 28,000 acres and brought nearly $3 million by 1900. See USBC, *1870, Compendium*, 701; USBC, *1900, Abstract*, 274.

26. Killebrew, "Tobacco in Kentucky," 42–44. Much of the following sketch of the postbellum U.S. tobacco economy is drawn from this exhaustive federal report specially prepared by Tennessee tobacco expert Joseph Buckner Killebrew. Its precision, detail, and expended effort were remarkable. It is especially useful for charting changes in the postwar tobacco economy although it is frustratingly sketchy on social relations in the tobacco fields fifteen years after emancipation.

27. USBC, *1870, Compendium*, 700–701; Killebrew, "Tobacco in Kentucky," 42–80; USDA, *Annual Report* (1869), 34; USDA, *Annual Report* (1889), 229.

28. Killebrew, "Tobacco in Kentucky," 44, 80. In contrast to these high yields, Virginia's average yield in 1879 was only 572 pounds. See Killebrew, "Tobacco in Virginia," 212.

29. Killebrew, "Tobacco in Kentucky," 74.

30. USDA, *Farmer's Bulletin*, no. 60, 1898, 9–10; Tilley, *Bright Tobacco*, 371–73, 560–61. For additional comment on Kentucky's tobacco districts, see Killebrew, "Tobacco in Kentucky," 44–63. There also existed intrastate as well as extrastate leaf competition. Kentucky's three other leaf districts encompassing twenty-nine counties grew various types of leaf that came under increasing pressure from white burley and also yellow bright. We still await an examination of postemancipation tobacco Kentucky.

31. Killebrew, "Tobacco in Tennessee," 167–68; USBC, *1870, Compendium*, 700–701.

32. Killebrew, "Tobacco in Tennessee," 168; USDA, *Annual Report* (1889), 229.

33. Killebrew, "Tobacco in Tennessee," 173–78. McKenzie, *One South or Many*, says little about one of Tennessee's major regional economies. This is ironic since his argument is for regional differences. One also wonders how significant changes in the postwar tobacco economy were for southern whites and freedpeople in Tennessee. Other burgeoning western tobacco economies that also challenged tobacco Virginia included Ohio and Wisconsin. For their potted histories, see Killebrew, "Tobacco in Ohio," and "Tobacco in Wisconsin," in USBC, *1880, Agriculture*, 11, 14, 126–47; USBC, *1900, Abstract*, 274.

34. Kulikoff, *Tobacco and Slaves*, 9–10, 104–17; Roberts, *Tobacco Kingdom*, 7–9.

35. Roberts, *Tobacco Kingdom*, chap. 5; Siegel, *Roots of Southern Distinctiveness*, 21, 29; Beeman, *Southern Backcountry*, 167–69, 182–83.

36. Tilley, *Bright Tobacco*, 197–99; Siegel, *Roots of Southern Distinctiveness*, 125, 149; Roberts, *Tobacco Kingdom*, 104–6; Bradshaw, *Prince Edward County*, 347.

37. Bradshaw, *Prince Edward County*, 347–49, 512; Roberts, *Tobacco Kingdom*, 106.

38. *Acts*, Dec. 15, 1871, 4–5; *Acts*, Feb. 11, 1873, 54 (quote); *Acts*, Apr. 2, 1873, 366–67; *Acts*, Apr. 15, 1874, 206–7. See also Arnold, *Tobacco Industry in Virginia*, 44–45; Tilley, *Bright Tobacco*, 253.

39. Arnold, *Tobacco Industry in Virginia*, 44–45; Tilley, *Bright Tobacco*, 253.

40. Arnold, *Tobacco Industry in Virginia*, 45; *SPF*, Nov. 1874, 217–18.

41. Maddex, *Virginia Conservatives*, 172–73.

42. *SPF*, Dec. 1874, 297–303, and Jan. 1875, 55–57.

43. *SPF*, Feb. 1875, 113–15.

44. Ragland, "Tobacco Inspections," *SPF*, Mar. 1875, 152–53.

45. "Convention at Burkeville," *SPF*, Sept. 1875, 524–25.

46. Tilley, *Bright Tobacco*, 403; Arnold, *Tobacco Industry in Virginia*, 47.

47. *Acts*, Apr. 4, 1877, 314–21; *Acts*, Feb. 20, 1878, 51–52; *SPF*, July 1877, 486; *Code of Virginia*, 1887, 467–74. See also Arnold, *Tobacco Industry in Virginia*, 44–45; Tilley, *Bright Tobacco*, 403–4; Maddex, *Virginia Conservatives*, 173.

48. Pearson, *Readjuster Movement*, 147; Arnold, *Tobacco Industry in Virginia*, 45; Maddex, *Virginia Conservatives*, 173.

49. For classic treatments of the Grange, see Buck, *Granger Movement*; Woodward, *Origins*, 82–94; Saloutos, *Farmer Movements*, 31–43. For more recent work, see Barns, *West Virginia Grange*; Woods, *Knights of the Plow*; Marti, *Women of the Grange*. There is no single study of the Virginia Grange. For scattered comments, see Pearson, *Readjuster Movement*, 59, 147; Sheldon, *Populism*, 23, 62; Blake, *Mahone*, 163; Woodward, *Origins*, 94–95; Maddex, *Virginia Conservatives*, 237–38; Moger, *Virginia*, 88. Most of this work draws from Pearson's brief comments and concludes that the Virginia Grange was insignificant, planter dominated, and preparatory for a tepid populism that only emulated its weakness. Our focus is different: to unearth local rural organizations in the Virginia tobacco region; to analyze their ideological thrust, especially in the context of a changing cash crop economy; and to explore the Grange as an extension of the conflict over agricultural reconstruction into the prolonged depression of the 1870s.

50. *SPF*, July 1872, 404–6.

51. *SPF*, Nov. 1873, 563–66; Tilley, *Bright Tobacco*, 397.

52. *SPF*, Feb. 1874, 77; *SPF*, Mar. 1874, 107–8, 149–57.

53. *SPF*, Apr. 1874, 197, 199–201.

54. *SPF*, May 1874, 260; *SPF*, June 1874, 275–76; *SPF*, Aug. 1874, 107.

55. *SPF*, Feb. 1875, 61–76.

56. *SPF*, Aug. 1875, 431. It is likely that Cosby's observation was prompted by the freedpeople's solidarity during emancipation's first decade. It also suggests an ironic link between the freedpeople's teaching and planter/farmer learning.

57. *SPF*, Oct. 1875, 586–90; *SPF*, Dec. 1875, 698–720; *SPF*, Jan. 1876, 74–76; Tilley, *Bright Tobacco*, 397; Pearson, *Readjuster Movement*, 59.

58. Pearson, *Readjuster Movement*, 59.

59. Bradshaw, *Prince Edward County*, 511–12; Burdick, "From Virtue to Fitness," 29.

60. *SPF*, Aug. 1874, 107; Tilley, *Bright Tobacco*, 404.

61. Hunt Diary, 1873–81, VHS; Nanzig, *Third Virginia Cavalry*, list of personnel. Hunt's diary, while obviously a personal memoir, also reveals a great deal about rural life in the postemancipation Virginia interior. Thus, his wartime activities freed slaves in the region from supervision, while emancipation facilitated his land purchases. Furthermore, there is a great deal of comment on the freedpeople's work and community in this diary. For further analysis, see Kerr-Ritchie, "Life in the Postwar Virginia Interior."

62. Hunt Diary, Dec. 17, 1873; Aug. 25, 1875; July 21, 1877; Apr. 26, 1876; Feb. 9, 1876, VHS.

63. Ibid., Mar. 22, 1876; Bradshaw, *Prince Edward County*, 511–12. For women in the Virginia Grange, see *SPF*, July 1875, 368. For other suggestive work on gender and the Grange albeit at different places and times, see Marti, *Women of the Grange*. Of course, one can only speculate as to whether or not these women Grangers were simply the indefatigable secretaries of lore, usually indispensable to local organization and regular functioning, while male Grangers sat around and spouted forth.

64. Pearson, *Readjuster Movement*, 59; *SPF*, Jan. 1875, 44–49 (Cuckoo Grange); *SPF*, Feb. 1875, 61–76; Hunt Diary, Apr. 26, 1876, VHS (Prospect Grange); Bradshaw, *Prince Edward County*, 512–13 (Farmville store).

65. Pearson, *Readjuster Movement*, 59, unidentified source for opening quote; *SPF*, 1874; Bradshaw, *Prince Edward County*, 512; *SPF*, Sept. 1875, 524–25.

66. *SPF*, Mar. 1874, 108–11; Tilley, *Bright Tobacco*, 397–99.

67. *Acts*, Mar. 25, 1875; Tilley, *Bright Tobacco*, 400–402.

68. *SPF*, July 1872, 442–43; Tilley, *Bright Tobacco*, 539, 202.

69. *SPF*, July 1872, 442–43.

70. Tucker, "Tobacco Tax," *SPF*, Sept. 1876, 597–615.

71. *SPF*, Nov. 1877, 739–40.

72. *SPF*, Dec. 1877, 811–13; *SPF*, Mar. 1878, 171; *SPF*, Oct. 1878, 574–75. These postwar arguments, much like those on free labor management, drew on antebellum tradition.

73. *Acts*, Feb. 21, 1870, 167–68.

74. *Acts*, Feb. 20, 1872, 5.

75. *Acts*, Feb. 18, 1875, 76–77.

76. *Acts*, Dec. 29, 1877, 7.

77. *Acts*, Feb. 1, 1879, 45–46.

78. *Acts*, Feb. 14, 1882, 109–10.

79. Ott, *Tobacco in Virginia*, 6–10; Tucker, "Tobacco Tax," *SPF*, Sept. 1876, 597–615. Taxing manufactured tobacco continued to be lucrative for the federal state. In 1889 the Internal Revenue collected nearly $34 million nationally, of which just over $3 million came from Virginia. See Tilley, *Bright Tobacco*, 620.

80. Sheldon, *Populism*, 62.

t81. Hunt Diary, Feb. 15, 1879, VHS. It is clear that most freedpeople were not part of this Grange movement. Those who worked as wage laborers for George Hunt, for instance, were not recorded as attending the Spring Creek Grange in Prince Edward County. Similarly, Lewis Harvie's free laborers in Mecklenburg County probably did not attend the Grange for which their employer was a leader. However, such freedpeople's membership was not altogether impossible. Both Robert Baker and Jerry Price were relatively successful black tobacco farmers and landholders from Louisa County. It is not inconceivable that they were affiliated with the county's Cuckoo Grange. See *SPF*, Apr. 1874, 197; Jan. 1875, 44–49.

82. Ott, *Tobacco: Outlook in America*; Ott, *Tobacco as Chief Source*; Ott, *Tobacco in Virginia*.

83. Tilley, *Bright Tobacco*, 157–58. Tilley claims Ott's associate editorship of *SPF* although there is no mention of Ott among the journal's editors listed in Riley, *Magazines*, 255.

84. Ott, *Tobacco: Outlook in America*, 9–25. Tobacco production was always part of the transatlantic marketplace of mercantile capitalism. In the waning decades of the nineteenth century, however, it became part of an expanded global economy. There are two additional points here. Global competition was to be countered by the organization of monopoly capital companies such as the ATC and its global expansion as traced in Chapter 7. Furthermore, Ott's observations of the mid-1870s offer a useful refutation of the banalities of present-day advertisers who claim that the world has only recently become a global marketplace in the 1990s.

85. Ott, *Tobacco: Outlook in America*, 27–31. The point on comparative emancipation is important, but it should not distract us from the pamphlet's theme of central interaction between emancipation, depression, and free labor management.

86. Ott, *Tobacco as Chief Source*, 2–22.

87. Ibid (extract, p. 22).

88. Ott's Civil War reference compares to King Henry's famous call for brotherly arms to his exhausted English troops in *Henry V*, act 3, scene 1.

89. Ott, *Tobacco: Outlook in America*, 10. Tilley, *Bright Tobacco*, 157–60, claims Ott was primarily a successful fertilizer salesman. I would not disagree, but I would argue that his written corpus provides rich ground for exploring tensions between emancipation, depression, and a changing tobacco economy.

90. Killebrew, "Tobacco in Virginia," 200.

CHAPTER SIX

1. For copious comment on Virginia politics during the 1870s, especially the Funders versus the Readjusters, see Pearson, *Readjuster Movement*; Blake, *Mahone*; Woodward, *Origins*, chap. 4; Moore, *Two Paths*; Maddex, *Virginia Conservatives*; Moger, *Virginia*, chap. 3; Moore, "Black Militancy."

2. *Parrish v. Commonwealth*, 81 Virginia 1 (1884), 1–16.

3. The conceptualization of this chapter has been strongly influenced by the work of Harold D. Woodman, especially his *New South—New Law*. A clear but uncritical review of this book is provided by Kantrowitz, "The Crop, the Rent." Our focus is slightly different from Woodman's. We examine the tobacco rather than the cotton South, trace legal change within the specific context of emancipation and depression, and explore extralegal rural resistance in relation to legal coercion.

4. Woodward, *Origins*, 180–84; Woodman, *King Cotton*, chap. 24; Woodman, *New South—New Law*, chap. 1.

5. Barbara J. Fields, "Capitalist Agriculture," 86–87.

6. See Chapter 2.

7. Secretary of Agriculture, "Status of Virginia Agriculture in 1870," 269.

8. See Chapter 3.

9. "Farm Hands," *SPF*, Feb. 1873, 72.

10. An older historiography argued for Virginia's early postwar agricultural redemption. This view uncritically reflected contemporary sources that often painted a calm rural scene in order to attract capital and immigrants to postwar Virginia (see Chapter 4). More recent versions of rapid rural redemption have crept in through the work of Jaynes, *Branches without Roots*, and Lynda J. Morgan, *Emancipation*, both of which depict emancipatory changes as having been concluded by the late 1860s.

11. *Acts*, 1872–73, 357–58; Woodman, *New South—New Law*, 60. This crop lien law has received scant attention from historians of postbellum Virginia, whether their emphasis be state politics (Maddex), local freedpeople (Engs), or a general survey (Dabney). Shifflett, *Patronage and Poverty*, does mention the lien but sees it simply as "the centerpiece of patronage capitalism" (p. 29), which perpetuated the "economic dependence of freedmen upon their landlords" (p. 34).

12. Brunswick County Court Order Books, vol. 41, 1875, VL.

13. Ibid., 1876.

14. Ibid., 1877.

15. Woodman, *New South—New Law*, chap. 1. It should be noted that many of these crop lien arrangements (much like labor contracts) were verbal rather than written. This attempt to maximize control over free labor ended up becoming a means of dispute over creditors' rights.

16. For mercantile territorial monopoly in the cotton South, see Ransom and Sutch, *One Kind of Freedom*, chaps. 7 and 8. For the merchant challenge in the Alabama black belt, see Wiener, *Social Origins*, pt. 2. For mercantilism in the Georgia upcountry, see Hahn, *Roots of Southern Populism*, chap. 5.

17. It is possible that creditors such as Sills and Son and Warwick and Bro. were local merchants in Brunswick County. See Brunswick County Court Order Books, vol. 41, 1875–77, VL.

18. For the location of stores in Brunswick County during the Civil War, see the map produced by General J. F. Gilmer for the Confederate Engineer Bureau reprinted at the VHS. For local merchants between 1847 and 1880, see R. G. Dun & Co., Virginia, vol. 7, Brunswick County, at the Baker Library, Harvard Business School, Cambridge, Mass. For the regionally high number of stores in Brunswick and adjoining Mecklenburg County in 1900, see county census map for the South, reproduced in Ayers, *Promise*, 82.

19. Taylor with Allison & Addison, Sept. 27, 1882, in Lunenburg County Court Judgments, 1885–89, box 1, VL.

20. C.S.T., "The Labor Question," *SPF*, Feb. 1877, 93–96.

21. Ibid. We can only guess as to why C.S.T. moved to merchant crediting: hard times? credit scarcity? freedpeople demands—which if unmet might result in their leaving?

22. Of course, freedpeople using extra provisions to realize the fruit of their labor easily elided into debt peonage. However, our challenge is alternatives to "negro improvidence," which are rarely suggested.

23. *Acts*, 1881–82, Mar. 6, 1882, 239–40; Woodman, *New South—New Law*, 60.

24. Philip A. Bruce, *Plantation Negro*, chap. 13, esp. 198–200. By 1900 there were only three to five stores per thousand people in the Virginia tobacco region, making it

the least mercantilist region in the state (calculated from Ayers, *Promise*, 82). For descriptions of plantation stores in other parts of the South, see Thanet, "Plantation Life in Arkansas"; Wharton, *Negro in Mississippi*, 71–73; Woodman, *King Cotton*, 308–11; Wiener, *Social Origins*, 78–79.

25. There are two major sources for *Parrish v. Commonwealth*. One contains transcripts of the county and circuit court proceedings along with Parrish's appeal. This is contained in an in-house bound volume of records filed with the Supreme Court of Appeal of Virginia, 1883–86, pp. 717–36, located at VSLL. The other source is the statement and opinion of the state supreme court published as *Parrish v. Commonwealth*, 81 Virginia 1 (1884), 1–16.

26. *Parrish v. Commonwealth*, VSLL, 23. For a contemporary description of Goochland County, see Hampton Institute alumnus Alexander Truatt, "Report on Goochland County," *SW*, Aug. 1881, 86.

27. *Parrish v. Commonwealth*, VSLL, 28–33. It should be noted that the landlord was in charge of the merchandising.

28. Ibid., 21, 33–34, 36. It is not inconceivable that Mitchell was also incensed at the prospect of another poverty-stricken year that was being instigated by his employer.

29. Ibid., 2, 28–29, 35. This postseason contractual dispute resembled earlier free labor struggles recorded by BRFAL officials.

30. Ibid., 19–22; *Parrish v. Commonwealth*, 81 Virginia 1 (1884), 5–7. The freedmen's roles are interesting. Neighbors Nuckols, Dandridge, and Sam Watson were close enough to Mitchell for him to attempt to enlist their support in retrieving his corn. Watson refused, Nuckols checked out the situation and then decided against it, while Dandridge showed up only to return home. The actions of these freedmen highlight their agency; they also suggest an alternative set of social relations beyond those with former masters.

31. *Parrish v. Commonwealth*, VSLL, 19–22; *Parrish v. Commonwealth*, 81 Virginia 1 (1884), 5–7.

32. *Parrish v. Commonwealth*, VSLL, 1–19; Goochland County Circuit Court, Common Law Order Book 5 (1863–83), 738–55, VL.

33. *Parrish v. Commonwealth*, VSLL, 1–19; Goochland County Circuit Court, Common Law Order Book 5 (1863–83), 738–55, VL.

34. Judicial review in Virginia between 1870 and 1902 was as follows: the justices of the peace and the magistrates courts handled petty offenses in the countryside and the town, respectively; these lower courts were superseded by county and corporation courts. Above these were sixteen circuit courts, and at the apex was the supreme court consisting of five judges serving for twelve years. See Nelson, *Judicial Review*, 235; "Virginia Judicial System"; Ray, Hart, and Kolbe, *Preliminary Guide*, 303–7.

35. *Parrish v. Commonwealth*, VSLL, 21. I have been unable to determine who the original jurors were. They were obviously not noted in the legal briefs. Presumably they are somewhere on the Goochland County manuscript census returns for 1880. Still, their location is less important than the significance of their original verdict.

36. *Parrish v. Commonwealth*, 81 Virginia 1 (1884), 3–9 (italics added). My point is less to retry the case (although I think the original decision was correct) than to suggest its broader political-legal dimensions. Incidentally, my own favorite colorful phrase from the court's summary is its gothic "dark and chilly night."

37. Ibid., 7–16. The court appears to have been less than sanguine about the crop

being the product of Mitchell's labor. Twice the summary referred to the nexus between crop cultivation and the tenant's labor in producing it. On one occasion it referred quite distinctly to "the crops, the results of Michell's [*sic*] labor." Of course, this was not the point, which was the protection of landlord's property and rights legally secured by this decision as well as previous crop lien laws.

38. Ibid., 7–16; Minor, *Institutes*, 1882, 182; John N. Taylor, *Landlord and Tenant*, 20–21.

39. *Parrish v. Commonwealth*, 81 Virginia 1 (1884), 7–16; *State v. Elias Grey*, 1 South Carolina (1833–37), 364–65; *State v. John Jones*, 19 North Carolina (1837), 544–46.

40. Woodman, *New South—New Law*, places the new laws of free labor within the broader context of unfolding capitalist social relations that encompassed the North and South as well as antebellum and postbellum periods.

41. More famous examples of influential court rulings emanating out of specific historical contexts include *Plessey v. Ferguson* (1896) during resurgent racism and *Brown v. Topeka* (1954) during emergent postwar liberalism. The recent legal rulings in California and Texas against affirmative action programs in universities reflect the resurgence of racial intolerance in the 1980s and 1990s.

42. For this one-dimensional capitalism for Virginia, see Irwin, "Farmers and Laborers." For the cotton South, see Mann, *Agrarian Capitalism*, and critique by Mooney, "One-Dimensional Mann." For the broader conceptualization, see Woodman, *New South—New Law*, 95–117; Reidy, *Agrarian Capitalism*, 235–41; Barbara J. Fields, *Slavery and Freedom*, 177–78.

43. Virginia Department of Agriculture, *Annual Report* (1879), 131–32.

44. Killebrew, "Tobacco in Virginia," 212.

45. These low wages, while betokening hard times for rural laborers, were propagated as advantageous by the Virginia Department of Agriculture for purposes of attracting either prospective immigrant employers or capital investors. For low wages as the key to understanding the South's regional poverty compared with the higher-waged North and West, see Wright, *Old South, New South*.

46. The following account draws on twenty-three receipts and one pay order for 1870 through 1883 in the Wilson Papers, 10721, UVA.

47. Wilson to Daniel, receipt, July 26, 1871; Wilson to Cousins, receipt, Apr. 27, 1872; Wilson to Chilton, receipt, Mar. 22, 1883, Wilson Papers, UVA.

48. Wilson to Campbell, receipt, Nov. 17, 1877; Wilson to Hairston, receipt, Feb. 9, 1880; Wilson to Hambleton, receipts, Jan. 14, 1871, Dec. 25, 1882; Wilson to Milly Daniel, receipt, n.d.; Wilson to Reece, receipt, n.d., Wilson Papers, UVA. The only receipt suggesting freedgirl/woman wage labor was between Wilson and Eliza for $6.33 for work completed at an unknown date and for an unknown period.

49. See sources in nn. 43 and 44, above. For annual wage contracting between planter Peter W. Hairston and more than twenty freedpeople at the Leatherwood and Camp Branch tobacco plantation in Henry County during the 1870s, see Tilley, *Bright Tobacco*, 97–99. Tom Hairston's work for Samuel P. Wilson suggests local mobility.

50. Ford with Hunt, Feb. 25, 1873; freedpeople with Hunt, Jan. 21–22, 1874; freedwomen with Hunt, Sept. 30, 1874; White with Hunt, Jan. 1876; freedpeople with Hunt, Nov. 29, 1876; Watkins with Hunt, Nov. 14, 1873, Hunt Diary, VHS.

51. Hunt Diary, 1887, pp. 168–70, 152–54, VHS. Dock Venable is consistently mentioned throughout the diary from Feb. 5, 1875, onward.

52. USBC, 1880, Prince Edward County Manuscript Census, Darlington Heights, household no. 226, AGLL.

53. Hunt Diary, 1887, pp. 168–70, 152–54, VHS. Tenants also employed wage laborers. Andrew J. Mitchell employed William Yancey as an occasional day laborer for the 1882 season. See *Parrish v. Commonwealth*, VSLL, 28–33.

54. Barbara J. Fields, *Slavery and Freedom*, 178.

55. Dillard with Taylor and Womack, Jan. 5, 1866, Contract, Indentures, and Court Records, 3950, Pittsylvania County, RG 105.

56. C.S.T., "The Labor Question," *SPF*, Feb. 1877, 93–96.

57. Killebrew, "Tobacco in Virginia," 212.

58. *SPF*, May 1887, 244–54.

59. C.S.T., "The Labor Question," *SPF*, Feb. 1877, 93–96; *SPF*, May 1887, 244–54; Killebrew, "Tobacco in Virginia," 212.

60. Harrison, "Renting Farms," *SPF*, Oct. 1889, 228–29.

61. Ott, *Tobacco as Chief Source*, 21–22.

62. Killebrew, "Tobacco in Virginia," 212.

63. USBC, *1900, Population*, 561. The majority of these tobacco southsiders were engaged in agricultural production. Danville, in Pittsylvania County, was the only major urban area, and its populace expanded minimally from 7,526 to 10,305. See USBC, *1890, Population*, 346–51, 483.

64. USBC, *1880, Agriculture*, 320; USBC, *1890, Agriculture*, 455.

65. USBC, *1880, Agriculture*, 95–97; USBC, *1890, Agriculture*, 190–92.

66. USBC, *1880, Agriculture*, 95–97; USBC, *1890, Agriculture*, 190–92.

67. It is the same problem with labor contracts: impossible to do and ultimately irrelevant.

68. Woodman, *New South—New Law*, 65–66 n. 86.

69. Tilley, *Bright Tobacco*, 93, sees the rise of tobacco tenancy as a "natural evolution." To reiterate the alternative view: new laws were passed to readjust disputed social relations caused by emancipation, agricultural depression, and a changing tobacco economy. These legal decisions were less discrete than class based. And white tobacco tenants increasingly were sucked into the exploitative production process.

70. Tilley, *Bright Tobacco*, 97–99, suggests that the shift to tenancy in the tobacco belt also resulted from employers attempting to stem black laborers' mobility. Conversely, Woodman, *New South—New Law*, 92, argues that annual movements "amounted to little more than labor turnover, inconvenient, perhaps, but not causing a dangerous shortage of needed laborers." Perhaps, except that the freedpeople's transiency reflected a form of rural resistance, especially in a postslave society formerly characterized by the strict control of work and movement.

71. Hunt Diary, Feb. 5–6, 1877, VHS.

72. Lunenburg County Court Judgments, 1885–89, box 1, VL.

73. Mumford, *Random Recollections*, 75–82.

74. Farm Diary, Sept. 4, 1877, Hawfield Plantation Account Book, 2198, Crenshaw Papers, UVA.

75. Historians have yet to come to terms with the nature of local rural crime in postbellum Virginia and the South at large. For planter condemnation of Negro

crime, see J. G. Tinsley, "The Labor Question," *SPF*, July 1876, 465; C.S.T., "The Labor Question," *SPF*, Feb. 1877, 93–96. For a fence-breaking and enclosure dispute in April 1888, see J. R. Skinner (plaintiff) versus John S. Hatchett, in Lunenburg County Court Judgments, 1885–89, box 1, VL. For a cereal dispute between Mrs. R. L. Crowder and M. P. Andrews in October 1888 that did not lead to murder, see Lunenburg County Court Judgments, 1885–89, box 1, VL. For comparative comments on rural crime, see Hay et al., *Albion's Fatal Tree*; Archer, *Flash and Scare*; Christopher Hill, *Liberty against the Law*. For a recent treatment of convict labor that is placed at the heart of postbellum modernity, see Lichtenstein, *Twice the Work*.

76. Incidentally, Hunt's neighbor's tobacco was never found, Synor Johns was found not guilty by a local jury, Jasper Jenkins won his case, and the Hawfield laborers eventually returned to work.

CHAPTER SEVEN

1. For conceptualization linking demand with manufacturing and production, see Karl Marx, *Introduction to The Grundisse*, in Tucker, *Marx-Engels Reader*, 222–46. My thanks to rural sociologist James Dickinson for this insight. This link is pursued in contrast to the recent emphasis on consumption in tobacco studies pursued by Kiernan, *Tobacco*, and Goodman, *Tobacco in History*.

2. For articulation in the American South, see Fox-Genovese, *Plantation Household*, 70–78; Barbara J. Fields, *Slavery and Freedom*, 17–18; Janiewski, *Sisterhood Denied*, 26.

3. Killebrew, "Tobacco in North Carolina," 110–12, 118; Tilley, *Bright Tobacco*, chaps. 1–2.

4. Tilley, *Bright Tobacco*, 123–41.

5. Killebrew, "Tobacco in North Carolina," 110–11.

6. Tilley, *Bright Tobacco*, 141–50 (quote, p. 196).

7. USBC, *1900, Abstract*, 274; Tilley, *Bright Tobacco*, 141–50; Reidy, "Slavery, Emancipation, and the Capitalist Transformation," 245 n. 8; Daniel, *Breaking the Land*, 31–32.

8. Tilley, *Bright Tobacco*, 16, 150–52, 395; USBC, *1860, Agriculture*, 155–63; USBC, *1900, Agriculture*, pt. 2, 576–77.

9. See Chapter 6.

10. Tilley, *Bright Tobacco*, 353–54; Peterson, *Historical Study of Prices*, 101, 182.

11. Tilley, *Bright Tobacco*, 353–54; Peterson, *Historical Study of Prices*, 101, 182. It is interesting to note the parallel between depressed bright prices and the ATC. Bright prices did not exceed their 1889 market return until 1911; these years marked the rise, domination, and fall of the ATC.

12. Tilley, *Bright Tobacco*, 489–592, 346, 373; Woodward, *Origins*, 129–31; Janiewski, *Sisterhood Denied*, chap. 5.

13. Janiewski, *Sisterhood Denied*, 67–69; Tracy Campbell, *Politics of Despair*, 21–22; Tilley, *Bright Tobacco*, 545–59. For older celebratory accounts of the rise of the Dukes of Durham, see Jenkins, *Master Builder*, 44–64 passim; ATC, "*Sold American!*," 17–34. Recent celebratory echoes can be heard in Billings, "*New South*," 113–20; Ayers, *Promise*, 105–7.

14. Roberts and Knapp, "Paving the Way"; Tracy Campbell, *Politics of Despair*,

22–23; Janiewski, *Sisterhood Denied*, 69–70; Stubbs, *Tobacco on the Periphery*, 3–4; Tilley, *Bright Tobacco*, 559, 568–76.

15. Roberts and Knapp, "Paving the Way"; Stubbs, *Tobacco on the Periphery*, 3–4.

16. Campbell, *Politics of Despair*, 23–24; Roberts and Knapp, "Paving the Way," 279; Janiewski, *Sisterhood Denied*, 70.

17. Shammas, *Pre-Industrial Consumer*, 78.

18. By 1900 per capita consumption of tobacco in the United States amounted to a record 5.3 pounds. See Goodman, *Tobacco in History*, 93.

19. The recent focus on different regional economies in the postemancipation South is a welcome challenge to the traditional sovereignty enjoyed by King Cotton. However, this regional focus poses the danger of creating newer and smaller fiefdoms that are local, discrete, and noninteractive.

20. Clement, *Pittsylvania*, 244.

21. Ott, *Danville*, 1–3.

22. Ibid. This articulation encouraged rural proletarianization on the surrounding farms and plantations. The legal groundwork was laid by the 1884 Virginia Supreme Court decision.

23. Tilley, *Bright Tobacco*, 353.

24. Pollock, *Sketch Book*, 126.

25. Ibid. (italics added).

26. Moger, "Industrial and Urban Progress," 320; Pollock, *Sketch Book*, 126. Descriptions of Danville's importance must be treated with caution since these were meant to boost Danville, a task made especially important in the wake of the bad publicity surrounding the November 1883 race riot. However, it remains a useful statement on Danville's tobacco articulation. It certainly seems more useful than the Democratic circular put out by Danville businessmen just prior to the November 1883 elections, which claimed "that hundreds of the North Carolina tobacco raisers who live within a few miles of the Town and used to sell their tobacco in our market now go five times as far to a market in their own State on account of negro rule in Danville" (Pollock, *Sketch Book*, 89). This was simply hyperbole since Danville dominated regional marketing. Indeed, in 1890 the next largest bright tobacco markets were Wilson and Winston with 1.5 million pounds and 16 million pounds sold, respectively. Compare this with Danville's more than 40 million pounds. Statistics from Tilley, *Bright Tobacco*, 355.

27. Tracy Campbell, *Politics of Despair*, 24–25; Stubbs, *Tobacco on the Periphery*, 4; Janiewski, *Sisterhood Denied*, 70; Tilley, *Bright Tobacco*, 594; ATC, *"Sold American!,"* 36–37. Compare this $35.5 million owned by fifty-two stockholders with the $93.4 million fetched by the 1906 tobacco crop for *all* U.S. tobacco producers. Computed from Ferleger, *Agriculture and National Development*, 356.

28. Tilley, *Bright Tobacco*, 594; Woodward, *Origins*, 308; Janiewski, *Sisterhood Denied*, 70.

29. USBC, *1890, Manufactures*, pt. 1, 312–13; USBC, *1900, Manufactures*, pt. 3, 664–66; Tilley, *Bright Tobacco*, 596–98; Woodward, *Origins*, 309; Ayers, *Promise*, 107.

30. USBC, *1890, Manufactures*, pt. 1, 312–13; USBC, *1900, Manufactures*, pt. 3, 664–66.

31. Tilley, *Bright Tobacco*, 600–601.

32. Garber, "Tobacco," in USBC, *1900, Manufactures*, vol. 9, pt. 3, 672.

33. Tilley, *Bright Tobacco*, 600–601. For an example of this concentration of manufacturing, see 1904 inventory of David Dunlap chewing company of Petersburg, Virginia, reproduced in Tilley, *Bright Tobacco*, appendix H, 690–96. The company had been taken over by the BAT the previous year.

34. On the South as a colonial economy, the classic statement is Woodward, *Origins*, chap. 11. On colonial Maryland, see Barbara J. Fields, *Slavery and Freedom*, chap. 7. On colonial North Carolina, see Janiewski, *Sisterhood Denied*, chap. 5. On colonial Kentucky and Tennessee, see Tracy Campbell, *Politics of Despair*, chap. 2.

35. Tilley, *Bright Tobacco*, 510; Roberts and Knapp, "Paving the Way," 276–77; Woodward, *Origins*, 309; USBC, *1890, Manufactures*, pt. 1, 312–13; USBC, *1900, Manufactures*, pt. 3, 664–66. See Janiewski, *Sisterhood Denied*, chaps. 4, 6, for women's proletarianization and its consequences in Durham, North Carolina.

36. Tilley, *Bright Tobacco*, 543–44; Cochran, *Big Business*, 40–41. For the classic statement linking the end of American isolationism, the stirrings of U.S. colonialism, and corporate expansionism overseas during the 1890s, see William Appleman Williams, *Tragedy of American Diplomacy*.

37. Stubbs, *Tobacco on the Periphery*, 22–26; ATC, *"Sold American!,"* 59–72. The former offers a critical view of the ATC's action, while the latter provides a more benign description of its Cuban policy. This is being written on the eve of the Pope's visit to Cuba in late January 1998 amidst media rumors of Fidel Castro's impending demise. One wonders if history will repeat itself should the five U.S. multinational tobacco companies gain influence in a post-Castro Cuba.

38. Stubbs, *Tobacco on the Periphery*, 5; Tracy Campbell, *Politics of Despair*, 25–26; Cochran, *Big Business*, 11–13; Tilley, *Bright Tobacco*, 544. The complete text of the BAT agreement can be found in Bureau of Corporations Report of the Commissioner of Corporations on the Tobacco Industry (Washington, D.C., 1909), pt. 1, 440–47.

39. In 1928 the Chinese were estimated to have consumed 87 billion cigarettes; by 1988, 1,500 billion. China remains the world's largest tobacco producer with 2,692,000 metric tons accounting for 38 percent of the world's share in 1990. See Goodman, *Tobacco in History*, 95, 8.

40. Cochran, *Big Business*, 1–38. The Thomas quote is on p. 15. For the efficacy of integrated business, see Chandler, *Visible Hand*. As Cochran's work demonstrates, U.S. business interests in the Asian Pacific rim are far from new.

41. Tracy Campbell, *Politics of Despair*, 24–25, 150–52; Janiewski, *Sisterhood Denied*, 71–72; Stubbs, *Tobacco on the Periphery*, 5. This oligopoly continues but not without contestation. In 1988 eight multinational tobacco companies—five of which are American, the other European—accounted for 35 percent of world cigarette output. State monopolies account for another 60 percent of output. See Goodman, *Tobacco in History*, 10–12. Perhaps one of the most disturbing consequences of U.S. tobacco companies settling recent lawsuits with state attorneys general is that the astronomical costs involved ($368.5 billion over 25 years) will simply be shifted onto the shoulders of Third World consumers in deadly fashion. Richard Peto of Oxford University argues that smoking-related deaths will rise from 3 million per year to 10 million within a generation, with most of these deaths occurring in the developing world. See *Washington Post*, in *Guardian Weekly*, Dec. 1, 1996, p. 15.

42. For Virginia, see Sheldon, *Populism*, ix; Moger, *Virginia*, 88–94, 109–11; Link,

"Cavaliers and Mudsills." For broader state studies, see Woodward, *Origins*, chap. 9 (quote, p. 245); Ayers, *Promise*, chaps. 9, 10; Goodwyn, *Populist Moment*.

43. Link, "Cavaliers and Mudsills," 43–44; Moger, *Virginia*, 89; Arnold, *Tobacco Industry in Virginia*, 48; Tilley, *Bright Tobacco*, 408.

44. Moger, "Industrial and Urban Progress," 312–13; Tilley, *Bright Tobacco*, 268; Peterson, *Historical Study of Prices*, 182.

45. Tilley, *Bright Tobacco*, 268; Moger, *Virginia*, 86.

46. *SPF*, Oct. 1890, 481–82; *SPF*, Nov. 1890, 533–34; *SPF*, Dec. 1890, 581–83; *SPF*, Feb. 1891, 90; *SPF*, Mar. 1891.

47. "News Notes," *SPF*, Sept. 1891, 504.

48. Sheldon, *Populism*, 70–71, 5 n. 14; Tilley, *Bright Tobacco*, 268–69.

49. Bradshaw, *Prince Edward County*, 513.

50. PCATU Journal, Aug. 16, 1890, accession 38-89, UVA. This maximum stockholding option was a familiar provision of many local alliances. It contrasts sharply with the unlimited stock options of ATC shareholders. Unless otherwise stated, all quotes come from the PCATU Journal.

51. PCATU Journal, Oct. 10, 1890, UVA.

52. Ibid., Nov. 7, 1890.

53. Ibid., Aug. 16, 1890; Manuscript Census, Virginia, Pittsylvania County, Banister District, 1880, AGLL; Pittsylvania Genealogical Map, 1909, Danville Public Library.

54. PCATU Journal, Aug. 16, 1890, UVA; Manuscript Census, Virginia, Pittsylvania County, South Pigg River District, 1880, AGLL; Pittsylvania Genealogical Map, 1909, Danville Public Library.

55. PCATU Journal, Aug. 16, Nov. 7, 1890, UVA; Manuscript Census, Virginia, Pittsylvania County, Callands District, 1880, AGLL; Pittsylvania Genealogical Map, 1909, Danville Public Library. There were some women subscribers, such as Mildred Johnson of the Caddo suballiance south of Chatham. It is also possible that freedmen were subscribers: one J. A. Hodnett was listed in the PCATU as paying $25 to the Hollywood suballiance; thirty-five-year-old black farmer Jessey Hodnett is listed in the manuscript census alongside the other Hollywood members in the Callands District. See PCATU Journal, Nov. 7, 1890, UVA; Manuscript Census, Virginia, Pittsylvania County, Callands District, 1880, AGLL.

56. PCATU Journal, Dec. 30, 1890, UVA.

57. Ibid., Feb. 2, 1891.

58. Ibid., Feb. 23, 1891. For the DFC, see Tilley, *Bright Tobacco*, 160.

59. PCATU Journal, Mar. 17, 1891, UVA.

60. Ibid., May 18, 1891. It is hard to explain why these local members were delinquent in their subscriptions. They might have been "free riders," although this economist's explanation still begs the question of why they would have joined such a cooperative in the first place. It might simply have been because of hard times.

61. Ibid., June 19, 1891. One wonders what happened to Moses, the previous occupant.

62. Ibid.

63. Ibid., July 21, 1891.

64. Ibid., Aug. 10, 1891.

65. Ibid., Nov. 4, 1891.

66. Ibid., Dec. 27, 1891.

67. Ibid., Mar 29, May 6, 1891. Link, "Cavaliers and Mudsills," 34–39, briefly notes the saga of the PCATU.

68. It might be added that the president of the DFC was a close friend of James Duke; indeed, the DFC subsequently served as a nucleus for fertilizer combination, adding eight Virginia companies and calling itself the Virginia-Carolina Chemical Company, formed in September 1895. While it seems unlikely that the DFC deliberately planned to ruin the PCATU, it soon became apparent that the latter's weakness would serve the former's interests. See Tilley, *Bright Tobacco*, 160.

69. This powerful metaphor of a black river of protest is provided by Harding, *There Is a River*.

70. Spriggs, "Virginia Colored Farmers' Alliance," 191–92.

71. "Farmers' Alliance in the South," *SW*, Oct. 1890, 103.

72. Spriggs, "Virginia Colored Farmers' Alliance," 193–94. For descriptions of this CFA meeting, see *Richmond Times*, Aug. 20, 22, 1890, and Aug. 9, 1891; *Richmond Dispatch*, Aug. 23, 1890; *Richmond Planet*, Aug. 30, 1890.

73. Sheldon, *Populism*, 35; Spriggs, "Virginia Colored Farmers' Alliance," 194; Goodwyn, *Populist Moment*, 122.

74. Spriggs, "Virginia Colored Farmers' Alliance," 199, 195–96. Sheldon, *Populism*, 36, argues that the state organizer absconded with the funds for planned cooperative ventures.

75. Sheldon, *Populism*, 35, claims this figure was "probably exaggerated."

76. Our focus is the Virginia interior; however, it is only fair to recall that the southeastern peninsula is rich in history of the black people of Virginia, with slave runaways in the dismal swamp, Nat Turner's rebellion, self-emancipated slaves at Fortress Monroe, Hampton Institute, Readjusterism, and the CFA.

77. Spriggs, "Virginia Colored Farmers' Alliance," 198–99.

78. USBC, *1900, Agriculture*, pt. 1, 190–91, 132–35; Virginia Land Tax Books, Brunswick, Mecklenburg, Appomattox, Dinwiddie Counties, 1900, VL. The broader social and ideological significance of these landholdings by blacks is pursued in the final chapter.

79. Spriggs, "Virginia Colored Farmers' Alliance," 199. There are numerous references to freedwomen who were listed as "servants" or "keeping house" in the manuscript census returns. It is likely that a number of them were either affiliated with or supported the CFA. Perhaps Martha Baines, the twenty-year-old black domestic in the PCATU Shields household, was one of these local subscribers to the CFA.

80. Fuller, "The Farmers' Alliance, Its Aims and the Means by which it Wishes to Accomplish Them," *SW*, Sept. 1891, 228.

81. "Farmers' Alliance in the South," *SW*, Oct. 1890, 103. This is all the more remarkable given the close proximity of Hampton to Norfolk.

82. The clash between rural freedpeople's activities and Hampton Institute's reform agenda is pursued in the final chapter.

83. Spriggs, "Virginia Colored Farmers' Alliance," 201.

84. Sheldon, *Populism*, 88–92.

85. For the race-class paradigm of southern Populism, see the debate over Tom Watson between Woodward, *Tom Watson*; Shaw, *Wool-Hat Boys*.

86. The debate has obvious contemporary resonance. The focus on black self-determination is different from that of race relations because it asserts agency over

white/moderate/liberal control. Indeed, some of the tensions over the CFA seem to have been precisely because of this difference. For a similar critique, albeit primarily concerned with race and labor in an urban setting, see Arnesen, "Black and White Workers."

CHAPTER EIGHT

1. I would like to thank Robert F. Engs, Harold Forsythe, and an anonymous reader for the *Virginia Magazine of History and Biography* for their insightful criticisms of a previous draft of this chapter.

2. Zola, *La Terre*, 38, 53, 85, 93, 112. This powerful rural story is dotted with numerous examples of the Fouans' pathological obsession with the land. Less evident is the rural labor theory of value felt by the Fouan women and the wage laborers, all of whom worked hard in the fields and probably believed in just remuneration of their toil with an equal passion.

3. The other crucial difference with *La Terre* is that it traces the dissolution of landholding, whereas our concern is with the accumulation of landholding. Still, there is a suggestive comparative meaning of landholding as constituting rural freedom.

4. Alrutheus A. Taylor, *Negro in the Reconstruction of Virginia*, 133; Du Bois, *Black Reconstruction*, 539.

5. Brunswick County Court Order Books, vols. 41–43, 1875–86, VL. It should be noted that these land transfers were probably not unrelated to existing hard rural times.

6. *SW*, Nov. 1878, 84.

7. *SW*, Oct. 1886, 104. For other reports of freedpeople landholding, see D, *SW*, Dec. 1878, 92; S, *SW*, Apr. 1880, 42; R, *SW*, June 1880, 66; CB, *SW*, June 1880, 66.

8. Pittsylvania County Land Tax Book, 1880, VL.

9. Lynda J. Morgan, *Emancipation*, 207.

10. Jackson, *Negro Office-Holders*.

11. Alrutheus A. Taylor, *Negro in the Reconstruction of Virginia*, 133; James S. Russell, "Rural Economic Progress."

12. Walker, "Development"; James S. Russell, "Rural Economic Progress"; Alrutheus A. Taylor, *Negro in the Reconstruction of Virginia*, 133; Jackson, "Free Negro Farmer"; Jackson, *Negro Office-Holders*. For a brief account of early African American historiography, see Meier and Rudwick, *Black History*, chaps. 1 and 2.

13. The intellectual progeny of these founding fathers of African Virginian landholding include Engs, *Freedom's First Generation*; Schweninger, "Vanishing Breed"; Lynda J. Morgan, *Emancipation*.

14. The exceptions are the works of Jackson and Russell that include the southside and other parts of the Virginia interior. Lynda J. Morgan, *Emancipation*, notes the process, but it falls outside the purview of her work.

15. See Chapter 6.

16. It might be added that black landholding histories remain trapped within a discourse of progress in which they are supposed to demonstrate the distance traveled by thrifty freedpeople from slavery to freedom. Despite its pioneering scholarship, this work often had more to do with the integrationist aspirations of an emergent

black bourgeoisie than of freedom's generations it purported to represent. Much of the recent scholarship repeats uncritically these aspirations. See n. 13, above.

17. USBC, *1900, Agriculture*, pt. 1, 132–35. This was the same source used by Alrutheus A. Taylor, *Negro in the Reconstruction of Virginia*, to estimate landholdings.

18. The following is drawn from the Virginia Land Tax Books, Amelia, Amherst, Appomattox, Bedford, Brunswick, Buckingham, Campbell, Caroline, Charlotte, Cumberland, Dinwiddie, Fluvanna, Franklin, Goochland, Halifax, Henry, Louisa, Lunenburg, Mecklenburg, Nelson, Nottoway, Pittsylvania, Powhatan, and Prince Edward Counties, 1900. (Some books were unavailable for 1900, hence the 1899 and 1901 books.) These large dusty ledgers housed in the vaults of the VL contain a mint of information. The state assessor recorded the name of the owner in freehold possession, the owner's acreage, the name of the land tract and its locale, the distance and direction from the courthouse, the value per acre, land and building values, the sum value of the real estate, and of course, the tax bill. These tax books also record land transfers, railroad developments, institution building, and landholder persistence or decline over the years. For the legal codification of these county land tax books, see *Code of Virginia*, 1860, T12, chap. 35, sec. 39–40, pp. 194–19; *Code of Virginia*, 1887, T13, chap. 23, pp. 167–69.

19. There were approximately 866 freedpeople landholders listed in the Mecklenburg County Land Tax Book, 1900.

20. USBC, *1900, Population*, 561–62.

21. USBC, *1900, Statistical Atlas*, plate 98.

22. Manuscript Census, Virginia, Pittsylvania County, Dan River District, 1880, household 45–45, AGLL.

23. Shifflett, *Patronage and Poverty*, chap. 6. Barbara J. Fields, *Slavery and Freedom*, 176, estimates an average family size of five in postwar Maryland.

24. It might be noted that freedpeople's landholdings in the dark tobacco belt compared favorably with those in the tidewater region. In Gloucester County the black populace was 6,608, or 51 percent of the total in 1900. In 1901 freedpeople landholders owned 14,020 acres, or 10 percent, worth $70,792, or 11 percent of land values, and $62,139 in building values. See USBC, *1900, Population*, 561; Gloucester County Land Tax Book, 1901, VL. For contemporary depictions of Gloucester County as the flagship of Negro landholding, see Walker, "Development."

25. Prince Edward County Land Tax Book, 1901, VL.

26. Campbell County Land Tax Book, 1900, VL.

27. Henry County and Lunenburg County Land Tax Books, 1900, VL.

28. Campbell County Land Tax Book, 1900, VL. Lynchburg, formerly in Brookville district, Campbell County, was independent by 1900. See USBC, *1900, Population*, pt. 1, 644–45 nn. 14–16.

29. Halifax County and Louisa County Land Tax Books, 1900, VL.

30. Goochland County Land Tax Book, 1899, VL.

31. Pittsylvania County Land Tax Book, 1900, VL.

32. Nottoway County Land Tax Book, 1900, VL.

33. Gloucester County Land Tax Book, 1899, VL; USBC, *1900, Population*, 561–62. It might be added that these freedpeople landholders paid $527.81 in Gloucester County and $751.11 in Nottoway County in real estate taxes in 1900. Apart from challenging the hoary old chestnut that white property owners paid for public ser-

vices that disproportionately served nontaxpaying Negroes, what public services did these rural freedpeople benefit from, especially during rising Jim Crowism and disfranchisement? For a useful overview of this latter contextual debate, see Rabinowitz, "Woodward Thesis."

34. For a consistent ideology of progress that linked Negro landholding with successful emancipation from slavery, see the numerous letters published in the *SW* from 1872 onward, the reports of Hampton's Annual Summer Conferences from 1897 bound as in-house proceedings at Hampton's Archives, and the first generation of historians of landholding noted in n. 12, above.

35. Prince Edward County Land Tax Book, 1901, and Goochland County Land Tax Book, 1899, VL.

36. Brunswick County Land Tax Book, Sturgeon district, 1900, VL. For a complete list of the minor civil divisions that also list county districts, see USBC, *1900, Population*, pt. 1, 396–402.

37. Amherst County Land Tax Book, 1900, VL.

38. Amelia County Land Tax Book, 1900, VL.

39. Appomattox County Land Tax Book, 1900, VL.

40. Nelson County Land Tax Book, 1900, VL.

41. Henry County Land Tax Book, 1900, VL.

42. Cumberland County Land Tax Book, 1900, VL; Jackson, *Negro Office-Holders*, 4.

43. Although W. E. B. Du Bois's notion of the talented tenth was constructed for different reasons and in a different context, I am invoking it as a means for understanding social differentiation among the freedpeople in the fin de siècle Virginia countryside. Landholdings were a crucial indicator of class power. Not only did many black politicians, preachers, and teachers own rural real estate, but the majority of freedpeople continued to live in the countryside.

44. Franklin County Land Tax Book, 1900, VL.

45. Amherst County Land Tax Book, Court House District, 1900, VL.

46. Buckingham County Land Tax Book, James River District, 1900, and Fluvanna County Land Tax Book, 1901, VL.

47. Dinwiddie County Land Tax Book, 1900, VL.

48. Lunenburg County Land Tax Book, 1900, and Prince Edward County Land Tax Book, 1901, VL.

49. Campbell County Land Tax Book, Brookville District, 1900, VL. I counted 64 of 620 landholders owning over 10 acres.

50. Campbell County Land Tax Book, 1900, 1901, VL.

51. Amelia County Land Tax Book, 1900, and Prince Edward County Land Tax Book, Leigh District, 1901, VL.

52. Many freedpeople landholders in the tidewater region also owned tiny plots. In the Ware district of Gloucester County in 1890 around 265 of 300 listed land taxpayers owned fewer than 20 acres (88 percent). This small acreage did not change during the 1890s although its value could. Simon Jones's 10 acres tripled its worth from $32.50 to $100, while Harriet Cosby's 2 acres remained at $12. See Gloucester County Land Tax Books, 1890, 1899, VL.

53. Appomattox County Land Tax Book, 1900, VL.

54. Franklin County Land Tax Book, 1890, and Nottoway County Land Tax Book, 1900, VL.

55. Unlike what appears to be the case in North Carolina described by Sharon Ann Holt, "Making Freedom Pay," the Virginia county land tax records allow us to trace even the smallest landholdings of freedpeople.

56. This contrasts with Moselle, "Allotments," which offers an economistic account of rural allotments as an alternative or supplement to wage labor for agricultural laborers in the different context of English postenclosure during the eighteenth and nineteenth centuries.

57. Lunenburg County Land Tax Book, 1900, VL.

58. Buckingham County Land Tax Book, 1900, VL.

59. Ibid.; Charles W. White, *Hidden and Forgotten*, 138–42.

60. Dinwiddie County Land Tax Book, 1900, VL.

61. *Code of Virginia*, 1860, T12, chap. 35, sec. 36, p. 194.

62. Some of these communal traditions are still practiced. During the 1980s the Reverend James H. Franklin served as pastor of Buckingham County's largest church, Baptist Union. It still thrives under the leadership of the Reverend Roy Foots. On June 1, 1996, they had an open store where indigent families and senior citizens were invited to shop free for men's, women's, and children's clothing. See Buckingham County's local black paper, *The Informant*, June 1996, 8. For urban Richmond's postemancipation communal efforts, see Brown, "Uncle Ned's Children."

63. Peterson, *Historical Study of Prices*, 182.

64. Campbell County Land Tax Book, 1890, VL.

65. Ibid., 1900.

66. Ibid.

67. Prince Edward County Land Tax Book, Buffalo district, 1900, VL.

68. *Index-Appeal* reprinted in *SPF*, July 1883, 320.

69. *SW*, Sept. 1897, 167–68.

70. Kelsey, *Negro Farmer*, 38. Bradshaw, *Prince Edward County*, chap. 17, which deals with the county's postbellum economy in exhaustive detail, is silent on freedpeople owning land.

71. Dabney in Roberts, "Life and Labor of Rural Virginia Negroes," 57 n. 7. Note how Dabney adds—presumably for the benefit of race relations—that white emigration was *not* caused by the Negroes being there.

72. Shifflett, *Patronage and Poverty*, 53, 132–33. It might be noted that Shifflett's paternal land transfers are drawn from Watson's papers and neither the county land tax book nor deeds of transfer.

73. Campbell County Land Tax Book, Falling River District, 1900, VL.

74. Deeds and Conveyances of Land, Campbell County, 1897–1900, VL.

75. The similarity in surnames between the traditional landholder (Mary Hubbard) and a freedwoman (Alice Hubbard) suggests an older dominion. While this implies Mary's paternalism, it does not necessarily mean that Alice shared this paternal spirit, although gaining land obviously meant a great deal.

76. Louisa County Land Tax Book, 1890; Charlotte County Land Tax Book, 1900; Campbell County Land Tax Book, 1900, VL.

77. The Virginia land tax books were, in Marc Bloch's catchy phrase, "witnesses in spite of themselves." They are also obviously mute on the possibility of land transfers prompted by paternalism. What is most essential is that the freedpeople's emancipatory aspirations, especially for land, are not draped in the mantle of planter largesse. We will never be exactly sure of Hubbard's motivations, but we can question the

contemporary ideological position, especially when it is uncritically reproduced by some historians.

78. It might be added that despite Shifflett's useful and detailed attention to black Louisans, his paternalist explanation fails to explain how those other 1,300-odd freedpeople managed to gain land in Louisa County by 1900. This was either an incredible degree of largesse or had more to do with the complex interaction between agrarian transformation and the actions of the freedpeople themselves. Perhaps systematic attention to the latter might have undermined the overall paternal model being proposed in the first place. In addition, paternal land transfers were unlikely in the tobacco southside because landholding by freedpeople withdrew them from a dwindling free labor pool as well as providing an autonomy contradictory to past views of racial dependency.

79. Purdue, Barden, and Phillips, *Weevils*, 183–84.

80. Amherst County Land Tax Book, 1900, VL.

81. Buckingham County Land Tax Book, 1900, VL. In his otherwise commendable attempt to reveal the hidden history of blacks in Buckingham County, local historian Charles W. White's *Hidden and Forgotten* is silent on the freedpeople's landholding and their transactions in the region.

82. Dinwiddie County Land Tax Book, 1900, VL.

83. Campbell County Land Tax Book, Brookville District, 1900, VL. The Freemans' family name says much about their emancipatory aspirations.

84. Cumberland County Land Tax Book, 1900, VL; Jackson, *Negro Office-Holders*, 4.

85. Dinwiddie County Land Tax Book, 1900, VL. Traditional landholders also sold their land to railroad companies. The Lynchburg and Danville Railroad bought 2 acres from William A. Hammersley and 10⅙ acres from S. C. Perron in the Stanton River District of Campbell County. See Campbell County Land Tax Book, 1890, VL.

86. Delinquent Land Sales, Treasurers Reports, Prince Edward County, 1902, VL. In Charlotte County there were numerous reports of freedpeople landholders selling their land to the commonwealth. These included T. Morrell's 2½ acres worth $18, Jimmie Elam's 8⁵³⁄₁₀₀ acres worth $103, Marshall Dow's 11¹³⁄₁₀₀ acres worth $83, L. Pollard's 20 acres worth $110, and William Dickerson's 26¾ acres worth $107. Were these sales encouraged by a landowning class supported by the county and state authorities who were opposed to such landholding, especially because of its prospect of independence and labor control in a tobacco region? Or were they simply a younger generation of freedpeople who wanted to leave the land? See Charlotte County Land Tax Book, 1900, VL.

87. Delinquent Land Sales, Treasurers Reports, Louisa County, 1900, VL.

88. Franklin County Land Tax Books, 1890, 1900, VL.

89. *Code of Virginia*, 1860, T12, chap. 35, sec. 24, p. 192.

90. Jackson, *Negro Office-Holders*, 4.

91. Purdue, Barden, and Phillips, *Weevils*, 64.

92. Brunswick County Land Tax Books, Sturgeon district, 1890, 1900, VL.

93. Campbell County Land Tax Books, 1890, 1900, VL.

94. Franklin County Land Tax Books, 1890, 1900, VL.

95. Louisa County Land Tax Books, 1890, 1900, VL. Freedpeople's landholding persistence was notable in Gloucester County. Simon Jones's 10 acres worth $32.50 in 1890 were improved to $125 by 1910, while Harriet Cosby's 2 acres worth $12 in 1890

were valued at $45 twenty years later. See Gloucester County Land Tax Books, 1890, 1900, 1910, VL.

96. Roberts, "Life and Labor of Rural Virginia Negroes," 111.

97. This idea of freedpeople persistence is deliberately juxtaposed with the more familiar notion of planter persistence in the postbellum South in general and post-bellum Virginia in particular. For long-term black landholding, see suggestive comments in Jackson, *Negro Office-Holders*. If the complete story of black landholding requires detailed investigation, then so does its unmaking, especially during and after the Second World War. It is also a strange coincidence (and another research topic) that rising black landowning was accompanied by political disfranchisement during the fin de siècle, while declining black landholding was accompanied by the struggle for political and civil rights during the 1960s.

98. Dabney, Fleming, Jackson, Minor, Mitchell, Morris, Louisa County, 1910 Supplementary Tobacco Schedules, Records of the USBC, entry 309, RG 29, NA; Manuscript Census, Virginia, Louisa County, 1910, AGLL.

99. Alexander, Bennett, Carter, Crowder, Dodson, Floyd, Gillespie, Jiggett, Revis, Talley, Taylor, Mecklenburg County, 1910 Supplementary Tobacco Schedules, Records of the USBC, entry 309, RG 29, NA; Manuscript Census, Virginia, Mecklenburg County, 1910, AGLL.

100. Manuscript Census, Virginia, Louisa County, 1910, AGLL.

101. Manuscript Census, Virginia, Mecklenburg County, 1910, AGLL.

102. Aubrey Mitchell, Melville Mitchell, Loga Mitchell, Charley Morris, Manuscript Census, Virginia, Louisa County, 1910, AGLL.

103. It should be added that the wives of household heads were usually listed without occupation, although Caroline Bennett's occupation was given as "housekeeper" and Frances Jiggett's and Laura Talley's were noted as "farm labor home farm." See Manuscript Census, Virginia, Mecklenburg County, 1910, AGLL.

104. Louisa County and Mecklenburg County, 1910 Supplementary Tobacco Schedules, Records of the USBC, entry 309, RG 29, NA; Manuscript Census, Virginia, Louisa County and Mecklenburg County, 1910, AGLL.

105. Jiggett, Mecklenburg County, 1910 Supplementary Tobacco Schedules, Records of the USBC, entry 309, RG 29, NA.

106. Manuscript Census, Virginia, Pittsylvania County, Dan River District, 1880, household 44–45, AGLL.

107. Pittsylvania County Land Tax Book, 1909, p. 99.

108. White, Pittsylvania County, 1909 Supplementary Tobacco Schedule, Records of the USBC, entry 309, RG 29, NA (letter attached [Appendix 3]).

109. A crude version of this social process already exists in the notion that black landholding was facilitated by black emigration because of a reduced populace in the countryside. But this explains nothing about why, under what conditions, and when freedpeople left. Nor does it tell us anything about how those who remained obtained land. Most importantly, it fails to address the seeming contradiction of simultaneous exodus and landholding. See Schweninger, "Vanishing Breed," 49–50; Ayers, *Promise*, 209.

110. USBC, *1890, Population*, 43; USBC, *1900, Abstract*, 34–35. The six states with lower population increases were Delaware (9.6 percent), New Hampshire (9.3 percent), Maine (5 percent), Vermont (3.4 percent), Kansas (3 percent), and Nebraska (0.3 percent).

111. Kelsey, *Negro Farmer*, 80–81.

112. USBC, *1900, Population*, 561–62.

113. Ibid.

114. Cohen, *Freedom's Edge*, 295–96; USBC, *1900, Population*, 43–44.

115. Kelsey, *Negro Farmer*, 80–81.

116. USBC, *1900, Population*, 561–62.

117. Bradshaw, *Prince Edward County*, 517.

118. Kelsey, *Negro Farmer*, 80–81; Dabney in Roberts, "Life and Labor of Rural Virginia Negroes," 57 n. 7.

119. Tilley, *Bright Tobacco*, 100.

120. Ibid.

121. Shifflett, *Patronage and Poverty*, 52, points out that black emigration was the most visible form of black resistance to patronage and poverty in postwar Louisa County, although this is not linked to the freedpeople's record landholdings.

122. For the river as a powerful metaphor for understanding black history, see Harding, *There Is a River*.

123. For a seminal articulation of the aspirations of freedom's first generation, see Engs, *Freedom's First Generation*. My emphasis differs somewhat; it focuses on the Virginia interior, it examines landholding and exodus as complimentary parts of social dissolution, and it differentiates between freedom's older and younger generations.

124. USBC, *1900, Abstract*, 148, 172–74; USBC, *1890, Population*, 483.

125. Virginia historian Allen Moger, in his useful article "Industrial and Urban Progress," writes of this period, "Old towns took on new life, increased their population, extended their borders, and became important centers of manufacturing and commerce. New towns appeared, and in a few cases sleepy country villages were transformed into flourishing cities of wealth and influence" (307). This Whiggish flourish repeats uncritically contemporary New South boosterism and fails to explain urbanization as a protracted process emanating from struggles between labor, land, agricultural transformations, and freedom's generations.

126. USBC, *1900, Abstract*, 357–58, 361–81; Moger, "Industrial and Urban Progress," 311.

127. Over the last two decades there has been much attention directed toward postwar urban Virginia, including black life in Hampton (Engs), Richmond (Rachleff), Petersburg (Hartzell), and Norfolk (Lewis); local politics in 1880s Lynchburg (Schewel) and Danville (Hamm); and white racial violence in 1890s Roanoke (Alexander). Much of this useful literature, however, is disparate and pays little attention to broad structural changes in late nineteenth-century Virginia, which, I argue, played such a crucial role in the making of these urban areas. What was the relationship between countryside and town, and how can this be broadly construed? For critiques of particularized black urban history that are suggestive for the South despite their northern focus, see Kusmer, "Black Urban Experience," in Hine, *Afro-American History*, and Trotter, "Afro-American Urban History," in *Black Milwaukee*.

128. Kelsey, *Negro Farmer*, 38.

129. Dawdy to Durand, Sept. 21, 1910, attached to Powhatan County, 1909 Supplementary Tobacco Schedule, Records of the USBC, entry 309, RG 29, NA.

130. Campbell County Land Tax Book, 1900. One can only wonder whether freedpeople who sold their land to the commonwealth for delinquent taxes also

moved to the town and city or elsewhere or stayed to work the land as rural proletarians.

131. Addie Luck Williams, "Interview." This interview provides an interesting insight into local black life. It is also very revealing about the politics of interviewing. The interviewer repeatedly asked why the Lucks moved to Danville, only to be met with the same response—that it was what Luvenia Luck wanted. This vague answer sat ill with the questioner, who seemed to be seeking a more dynamic explanation. See esp. pp. 236–37.

132. USBC, *1900, Population*, pt. 1, 704–5. It should also be noted that there were 44,564 white Virginia-born residents in West Virginia in 1900, many of whom worked in the coal mines.

133. Cohen, *Freedom's Edge*, 295; Ayers, *Promise*, 120–21; Trotter, *Coal, Class, and Color*, 9–38; Goggin, *Woodson*, 10–11.

134. USBC, *1900, Manufactures*, pt. 2, 60.

135. There were 3,088 women workers in the mills (25 percent of all women workers) and 5,129 women workers in the factories (42 percent). See USBC, *1900, Manufactures*, pt. 2, 499.

136. Ibid., pt. 3, 664–66.

137. Meade, *I Live in Virginia*, 298–99; Tilley, *Bright Tobacco*, 319.

138. Jacqueline Jones, *Labor of Love*, 152–95.

139. Addie Luck Williams, "Interview."

140. Davis, *Patience Gnomes*, 13–43.

141. Landhorne in Wynes, *Southern Sketches*, 68, 29.

142. Joe and Violet, the protagonists in Toni Morrison's novel *Jazz*, emigrated from imaginary Vesper County, Virginia, to New York City in 1906. For this Virginia-New York City connection later in the 1920s, see Eugene Kinckle Jones, "Negro Migration in New York State," *Opportunity Magazine*, Jan. 1926, reprinted in Adero, *Up South*, 85–96. Jones himself was born in Richmond. See also Osofsky, *Harlem*, 28–34, 129.

143. USBC, *1900, Population*, pt. 1, 688–89, 692–93, 704–5, 709–13.

144. Du Bois, *Philadelphia Negro*, 74–75.

145. Emmet J. Scott, *Negro Migration*; Kiser, *Sea Island to City*; Kennedy, *Negro Peasant*.

146. Henri, *Black Migration*; Hill, *Garvey Papers*.

147. For the ghetto approach, see Osofsky, *Harlem*; Kusmer, *Ghetto Takes Shape*. For the proletarian approach, see Trotter, *Black Milwaukee*; Gottlieb, *Making Their Own Way*; Grossman, *Land of Hope*.

148. Jacqueline Jones, *Labor of Love*; Gregg, *Sparks from the Anvil*; Adero, *Up South*; Griffin, "*Who Set You Flowin'?*"

149. Gregg, *Sparks from the Anvil*, is perhaps the exception to these generalizations.

150. Jacqueline Jones, *Labor of Love*, 153, lists "obvious" reasons for northward migration, including push factors such as oppressive sharecropping, disfranchisement, Jim Crow laws, and boll weevils, and pull factors such as high wages and a freer life. The pull factors are plausible for 1890s Virginia; the push factors are less relevant. As we have seen, sharecropping was mostly located in the tobacco southside, disfranchisement and Jim Crow laws came later, and the boll weevil was a cotton parasite.

151. Kelsey, *Negro Farmer*, 38.

152. Hewin, "Land and Business among Colored People," Hampton Annual Summer Conference, July 1904, 33–39.

153. Jacqueline Jones, *Labor of Love*, 159.

154. Gregg, *Sparks from the Anvil*, 151.

155. Toni Morrison's recent novel *Jazz* (1992), despite its eloquence and exquisite metaphor, strangely propagates an old migration historiography. On the main protagonists' emigration Morrison writes, "The wave of black people running from want and violence crested in the 1870s; the '80s; the '90s but was a steady stream in 1906 when Joe and Violet joined it. Like the others, they were country people, but how soon country people forget" (33). I would argue that this link was much stronger and more often reforged. August Wilson's plays are often full of references to country folk not forgetting their older ways in Pittsburgh. In his recent Broadway show *Seven Guitars*, for instance, one woman uses a rooster to awaken herself, much to the chagrin of her working-class neighbors.

156. Dabney, Manuscript Census, Virginia, Louisa County, 1910, AGLL; Alexander, Manuscript Census, Virginia, Mecklenburg County, 1910, AGLL.

157. This was probably limited since the sixteen black household names did not reappear in close proximity in the census as one might expect if an older son left the original household. See Manuscript Census, Virginia, Louisa County and Mecklenburg County, 1910, AGLL.

158. Kerr-Ritchie, " 'From Leaf to Cane.' "

159. For scattered comments on remittance, see Trotter, *Coal, Class, and Color*; Ayers, *Promise*, 121; Roberts, "Life and Labor of Rural Virginia Negroes," 100–101. Thanks to Harold Forsythe for pointing out the post office's role in this remitting process.

EPILOGUE

1. USBC, *1900, Abstract*, 274; USBC, *1860, Agriculture*, 154–62; Peterson, *Historical Study of Prices*, 101.

2. Daniel, *Breaking the Land*, 110–33; Garnet and Ellison, "Negro Life," 40–46; Gee and Corson, *Rural Depopulation*; Wingo, *Virginia's Soils*, 162; Schweninger, "Vanishing Breed," 60; Heinemann, *Depression and New Deal*, 105–28.

3. Daniel, *Breaking the Land*, 260, 268–70; Schweninger, "Vanishing Breed," 52; Fisher, "Negro Farm Ownership," 486; Brooks, "Decline of Black Landownership," 191–94.

4. My wife's stepfather lives in Philadelphia; his parents emigrated from Louisa County. A friend who works at the Public Theater in New York City has family from Mecklenburg County. Another friend who lives just outside New York City traces her family to southwest Virginia.

5. Edwards to author, July 24, 1994, Pittsylvania County.

BIBLIOGRAPHY

MANUSCRIPTS

American Genealogical Lending Library, Bountiful, Utah
    Louisa County Census, 1910 (microfilm)
    Mecklenburg County Census, 1910 (microfilm)
    Pittsylvania County Census, 1880, 1900 (microfilm)
    Prince Edward County Census, 1880, 1900 (microfilm)
Hampton Institute, Hampton, Va.
    Samuel Chapman Armstrong Collection
    Hampton Negro Conference Reports, 1897–1912
    Peabody Collection Newspaper Clippings
National Archives, Washington, D.C.
    Records of the Bureau of Refugees, Freedmen, and Abandoned Lands, 1865–69,
        Record Group 105
    Records of the Bureau of the Census, Supplementary Tobacco Schedules, 1910,
        Record Group 29
    Records of the Department of Treasury, Southern Claims Commission, 1871–80,
        Record Group 56
    Records of the National Recovery Administration, Records of the Tobacco Unit,
        Record Group 9
Southern Historical Collection, Chapel Hill, N.C.
    Fredericks Hall Plantation Books
    T. L. Jones Journal, 1862–69
    Edmund Ruffin Jr. Plantation Diary, 1851–73
University of Virginia, Charlottesville
    Baylor Family Papers
    Bremo Recess Papers
    Burwell Family Papers
    John H. Cocke Family Papers
    William G. Crenshaw Papers
    Gordon Family Papers
    Holland Family Papers
    Hubard Family Papers
    Irvine-Saunders Family Papers
    Minor Family Papers
    Joseph Palmore Papers
    Sarah P. Payne Family Papers
    Robert A. Schoolfield Papers

Shepherd Family Papers
Southside Virginia Family Papers
Tayloe Family Papers
Twyman Family Papers
Samuel Pannhill Wilson Papers
Virginia Historical Society, Richmond
    Allen Family Papers
    Ashlin Family Papers
    Baskerville Family Papers
    Dabney Family Papers
    Hannah Family Papers
    Harvie Family Papers
    Henry Family Papers
    George Hunt Diaries, 1873–81, 1883–92
    M. G. Rice Reminiscences
    Short Family Papers
    Skipworth Family Papers
    Winston Family Papers
Virginia Library, Richmond
    Amelia County Land Tax Book, 1900
    Amherst County Land Tax Book, 1900
    Appomattox County Land Tax Book, 1900
    Brunswick County Court Order Books, 1875–87
    Brunswick County Land Tax Books, 1890, 1900
    Buckingham County Land Tax Books, 1890, 1900
    Campbell County Land Tax Books, 1890, 1900
    Caroline County Land Tax Book, 1890
    Charlotte County Land Tax Books, 1890, 1900
    Cumberland County Land Tax Books, 1890, 1900
    Dinwiddie County Land Tax Books, 1890, 1900
    Fluvanna County Land Tax Books, 1890, 1901
    Franklin County Land Tax Books, 1890, 1900
    Gloucester County Land Tax Books, 1890, 1899, 1910
    Goochland County Circuit Court, Common Law Order Book, 1863–83
    Goochland County Land Tax Books, 1890, 1899
    Halifax County Court Order Books, 1875–78, 1879–81
    Halifax County Land Tax Books, 1870, 1880, 1890, 1900
    Henry County Land Tax Books, 1870, 1880, 1890, 1900
    Louisa County Land Tax Books, 1890, 1900
    Lunenburg County Court Judgments, 1885–89
    Lunenburg County Land Tax Books, 1890, 1900
    Mecklenburg County Land Tax Books, 1880, 1890, 1900
    Nelson County Land Tax Books, 1890, 1900
    Nottoway County Land Tax Books, 1890, 1900
    Pittsylvania County Land Tax Books, 1870, 1880, 1890, 1900, 1909
    Powhatan County Land Tax Books, 1890, 1900
    Prince Edward County Land Tax Books, 1880, 1900, 1901
    Works Projects Administration Virginia County Histories, 1943

Virginia State University, Petersburg
Luther Porter Jackson Papers
Harry W. Roberts Papers

GOVERNMENT PUBLICATIONS

Federal

Bowie, Walter W. W. "Culture and Management of Tobacco." In *Agricultural Report*, 179–84. U.S. Department of Agriculture, 1867.

Brewer, William H. "Report on the Cereal Production of the U.S." In *1880, Productions of Agriculture*, 1–173. U.S. Bureau of the Census, 1883.

Dodge, J. R. "Statistics of Manufacturers of Tobacco and of Its Commercial Distribution, Exportation, and Prices." In *1880, Productions of Agriculture*, 881–950. U.S. Bureau of the Census, 1883.

Du Bois, W. E. B. "The Negro Landholder of Georgia." *Bulletin of the Department of Labor*, no. 35 (July 1901): 647–777.

Floyd, Marcus. "Tobacco." In *1900, Agriculture*, pt. 2, section 6, pp. 499–511. U.S. Bureau of the Census, 1902.

Gage, Charles E. "American Tobacco Types, Uses, and Markets." In *Circular No. 249*, 1–129. U.S. Department of Agriculture, 1933.

Garber, John H. "Tobacco." In *1900, Manufactures*, pt. 3, pp. 639–72. U.S. Bureau of the Census, 1902.

Garner, W. W., E. G. Moss, H. S. Yohe, F. B. Wilkinson, and O. C. Stine. "History and Status of Tobacco Culture." In *Yearbook*, 395–465. U.S. Department of Agriculture, 1922.

Goodloe, Daniel R. "Resources and Industrial Condition of the Southern States." In *Agricultural Report*, 102–36. U.S. Department of Agriculture, 1865.

Holmes, George K. "Three Centuries of Tobacco." In *Yearbook*, 151–75. U.S. Department of Agriculture, 1919.

Janney, Samuel M. "Virginia: Her Past, Present, and Future." In *Agricultural Report*, 17–42. U.S. Department of Agriculture, 1864.

Killebrew, Joseph B. "Culture and Curing of Tobacco in Kentucky." In *1880, Productions of Agriculture*, 42–80. U.S. Bureau of the Census, 1883.

——. "Culture and Curing of Tobacco in Tennessee." In *1880, Productions of Agriculture*, 167–92. U.S. Bureau of the Census, 1883.

——. "Culture and Curing of Tobacco in the United States." In *1880, Productions of Agriculture*, 1–225. U.S. Bureau of the Census, 1883.

——. "Culture and Curing of Tobacco in Virginia." In *1880, Productions of Agriculture*, 192–225. U.S. Bureau of the Census, 1883.

——. "Tobacco Crop, 1911, by Types and Districts." In *Circular 27*, 3–8. U.S. Department of Agriculture, 1912.

——. "Tobacco Districts and Types." In *Circular 18*, 3–16. U.S. Department of Agriculture, 1909.

——. "Culture and Curing of Tobacco in North Carolina." In *1880, Productions of Agriculture*, 110–25. U.S. Bureau of the Census, 1883.

Secretary of Agriculture. "Status of Virginia Agriculture in 1870." In *Agricultural Report*, 267–91. U.S. Department of Agriculture, 1870.

——. "Tobacco." In *Agricultural Report*, 565–72. U.S. Department of Agriculture, 1878.

——. "Tobacco." In *Agricultural Report*, 257–59. U.S. Department of Agriculture, 1890.

——. "Wages of Farm Labor." In *Agricultural Report*, 312–16. U.S. Department of Agriculture, 1890.

Statistician. "The Tobacco Crop." In *Agricultural Report*, 42–59. U.S. Department of Agriculture, 1874.

——. "The Tobacco Crop." In *Agricultural Report*, 53–58. U.S. Department of Agriculture, 1875.

U.S. Bureau of the Census. *1860, Agriculture*. Washington, D.C., 1864.

——. *1860, Manufactures*. Washington, D.C., 1865.

——. *1860, Population*. Washington, D.C., 1864.

——. *1870, Compendium*. Washington, D.C., 1872.

——. *1870, Population*. Washington, D.C., 1872.

——. *1870, Wealth and Industry*. Washington, D.C., 1872.

——. *1880, Manufactures*. Washington, D.C., 1883.

——. *1880, Population*. Washington, D.C., 1883.

——. *1880, Productions of Agriculture*. Washington, D.C., 1883.

——. *1890, Agriculture*. Washington, D.C., 1895.

——. *1890, Manufacturing Industries*. Pts. 1 and 2. Washington, D.C., 1895.

——. *1890, Population*. Washington, D.C., 1895.

——. *1900, Abstract*. Washington, D.C., 1902.

——. *1900, Agriculture*. Pt. 2. Washington, D.C., 1902.

——. *1900, Manufactures*. Pt. 2. Washington, D.C., 1902.

——. *1900, Population*. Vol. 1, pts. 1 and 2. Washington, D.C., 1901.

——. *1900, Statistical Atlas*. Washington, D.C., 1903.

——. *1910, Agriculture*. Vol. 7. Washington, D.C., 1913.

——. *1920, Agriculture*. Vol. 6, pt. 2.

——. *Negro Population, 1790–1915*. Washington, D.C., 1918.

——. *Plantation Farming in the United States*. Washington, D.C., 1916.

U.S. Department of Agriculture. *Annual Reports of the Commissioner of Agriculture*. 1865–94.

——. *Office of Experiment Stations Farmer's Bulletins Nos. 1–120*. 1889–1900.

——. *Yearbooks*. 1895–1909.

Virginia

Flournoy, H. W., ed. *Calendar of Virginia State Papers and Other Major Manuscripts, January 1, 1836–April 15, 1869*. Vol. 11. Richmond, 1893.

Hansbrough, George W. *Reports of Cases Decided in the Supreme Court of Appeals in Virginia*. Vol. 81, *Parrish v. Commonwealth*, 1–17. Richmond, 1887.

Virginia Agricultural and Mechanical College Experimental Station. *Bulletins 1–327*. Blacksburg, Montgomery County, 1889–1940.

Virginia Census. Pittsylvania County. 1880, 1900.

——. Prince Edward County. 1880, 1900.

Virginia Department of Agriculture. *Annual Reports of the Commissioner of Agriculture*. Richmond, 1877–1906.

——. *Handbooks of Virginia*. Richmond, 1879–97.

BIBLIOGRAPHY

Virginia General Assembly. *Acts of the General Assembly.* 1860–1900.

——. *Code of Virginia.* 1860, 1887.

Virginia Supreme Court of Appeals. *Alexander H. Parrish v. Commonwealth.* 1884.

NEWSPAPERS AND PERIODICALS

Buckingham Informant, 1994–97

Danville Daily News, 1875

Danville Free Press, 1901

Danville Register, 1875, 1888, 1900

Hampton Southern Workman, 1872–1913

Harper's Weekly, 1870–80

Journal of the Royal Agricultural Society of England (London), 2nd ser., vols. 22–23, 1886–87; 3rd ser., vols. 1–9, 1890–98

Petersburg Index and Appeal, 1874–76

Richmond Southern Planter and Farmer, 1841, 1860–61, 1867–1900

Transactions of the Highland and Agricultural Society of Scotland (Edinburgh), 4th ser., vols. 12 and 15, 1880, 1883; 5th ser., vol. 6, 1894

PUBLISHED CONTEMPORARY SOURCES

Alvord, John W. "Semi-Annual Reports on Schools for Freedmen, nos. 1–10, Jan. 1866–July 1870." In *Freedmen's Schools and Textbooks,* edited by Robert C. Morris. New York: Ams, 1980.

Berlin, Ira, and Leslie S. Rowland, eds., *Families and Freedom: A Documentary History of African-American Kinship in the Civil War Era.* New York: New Press, 1997.

Berlin, Ira, Joseph P. Reidy, and Leslie S. Rowland, eds. *The Black Military Experience.* Ser. 2 of *Freedom: A Documentary History of Emancipation, 1861–1867.* Cambridge: Cambridge University Press, 1982.

Berlin, Ira, Barbara J. Fields, Thavolia Glymph, Joseph P. Reidy, and Leslie Rowland, eds. *The Destruction of Slavery.* Ser. 1, vol. 1, of *Freedom: A Documentary History of Emancipation, 1861–1867.* Cambridge: Cambridge University Press, 1985.

Berlin, Ira, Barbara J. Fields, Steven F. Miller, Joseph P. Reidy, and Leslie Rowland, eds. *Free at Last: A Documentary History of Slavery, Freedom, and the Civil War.* New York: New Press, 1992.

Bitting, Samuel T. *Rural Land Ownership among the Negroes of Virginia: With Special Reference to Albemarle County.* Charlottesville: University of Virginia Press, 1915.

Blanton, James M. *Confidential Address to the Patrons of Husbandry in Virginia.* Richmond: Clemmitt and Jones, 1876.

Boney, F. N., Richard L. Hume, and Rafia Zafar, eds. *God Made Man, Man Made the Slave: The Autobiography of George Teamah.* Macon, Ga.: Mercer University Press, 1990.

Bradley, A. G. *Other Days: Recollections of Rural England and Old Virginia, 1860–1880.* London: Constable, 1913.

Bruce, Philip A. *The Plantation Negro as a Freeman: Observations on His Character, Condition, and Prospects in Virginia.* New York: G. P. Putnam's Sons, 1889.

——. "A Tobacco Plantation." *Lippincott's Magazine*, Dec. 1885, 533–42.

Campbell, Sir George. *White and Black: The Outcome of a Visit to the U.S.* New York: R. Worthington, 1879.

Christian, Ashbury W. *Lynchburg and Its People.* Salem, Mass.: Higginson, 1900.

Dennett, John R. *The South As It Is, 1865–1866.* 1866. Reprint, Athens: University of Georgia Press, 1986.

Evans, Paul, and Thomas P. Govan, eds. "A Belgian Consul on Conditions in the South in 1860 and 1862." *Journal of Southern History* 3 (Feb.–Nov. 1937): 478–91.

Faust, Drew Gilpin, ed. *The Ideology of Slavery: Proslavery Thought in the Antebellum South, 1830–1860.* Baton Rouge: Louisiana State University Press, 1981.

Garvey, Marcus, and UNIA Papers. Vols. 1–7. Berkeley: University of California Press, 1983.

Glasgow, Ellen. *The Battle-Ground.* New York: Doubleday, Page, 1902.

——. *The Deliverance: A Romance of the Virginia Tobacco Fields.* New York: Doubleday, Page, 1904.

Greenberg, Kenneth S., ed. *The Confessions of Nat Turner and Related Documents.* Boston: Bedford Books, 1996.

Handy, M. P. "In a Tobacco Factory." *Harper's Weekly*, Oct. 1873, 713–19.

——. "On the Tobacco Plantation." *Scribner's Monthly*, Oct. 1872, 651–55.

Howard, Oliver Otis. *Autobiography of Oliver Otis Howard: Major General, United States Army.* New York: Baker and Taylor, 1908.

Jefferson, Thomas. *Notes on the State of Virginia.* 1787. Reprint, Chapel Hill: University of North Carolina Press, 1955.

Kelsey, Carl. *The Negro Farmer.* Chicago: Jennings and Pye, 1903.

Killebrew, J. B., and H. Myrick. *Tobacco Leaf: Its Culture and Cure, Marketing and Manufacture.* New York: Orange Judd, 1897.

King, Edward. *The Great South.* 1873–74. Reprint, Baton Rouge: Louisiana State University Press, 1972.

Lowe, Richard G., ed. "Virginia's Reconstruction Convention: General Schofield Rates the Delegates." *Virginia Magazine of History and Biography* 80, no. 3 (July 1972): 341–60.

Meade, Julian R. *I Live in Virginia.* New York: Longmans, 1935.

Miller, Kelly. *Radicals and Conservatives, and Other Essays on the Negro in America.* 1908. Reprint, New York: Schocken Books, 1968.

Minor, John B. *Institutes of Common and Statute Law.* 3rd ed. Vol 2. Richmond: for the author, 1882.

Mugleston, William F., ed. "The Freedman's Bureau and Reconstruction in Virginia: The Diary of Marcus Sterling Hopkins, a Union Officer." *Virginia Magazine of History and Biography* 86, no. 1 (Jan. 1978): 45–102.

Mumford, Beverley Bland. *Random Recollections.* New York: De Vinne, 1905.

Olmsted, Frederick L. *A Journey in the Seaboard Slave States, with Remarks on Their Economy.* New York: Mason Brothers, 1959.

Ott, John. *Danville as a Tobacco Centre.* Richmond: SFC, 1879.

——. *The Position Tobacco Has Ever Held as the Chief Source of Wealth to Virginia.* Richmond: SFC, 1876.

———. *Tobacco in Virginia and North Carolina.* Richmond: SFC, 1877.

———. *Tobacco: The Outlook in America for 1875; Production, Consumption and Movement in the United States, the German Empire, Hungary, Turkey, Cuba, Brazil, Japan, and the other Tobacco-growing Countries.* Richmond: SFC, 1875.

Pollock, Edward. *Illustrated Sketch Book of Danville, Virginia: Its Manufactures and Commerce.* Danville: E. R. Waddill, 1885.

Porter, Duval, ed. *Men, Places, and Things As Noted by Benjamin Simpson.* Danville: Dance Bros., 1891.

Purdue, Charles L., Thomas E. Barden, and Robert K. Phillips, eds. *Weevils in the Wheat: Interviews with Virginia Ex-Slaves.* Charlottesville: University Press of Virginia, 1976.

Reid, Whitelaw. *After the War: A Southern Tour.* New York: Moore, Wilstach and Baldwin, 1866.

Schofield, John M. *Forty-Six Years in the Army.* New York: Century, 1897.

Scott, John. "British Farming and Foreign Competition." *Transactions,* 5th ser., 5 (1893): 112–29.

"Some Recent Observations on Virginia." *Nation,* Sept. 1877, 163–65.

Somers, Robert. *The Southern States since the War, 1870–1871.* London: Macmillan, 1871.

State v. Elias Gay. South Carolina Law Reports 19 (1833–37): 364–65.

State v. John Jones. North Carolina Law Reports 19 (1834–39): 544–46.

Taylor, John N. *A Treatise on the American Law of Landlord and Tenant.* 7th ed. Boston: Little, Brown, 1879.

Thanet, Octave. "Plantation Life in Arkansas." *Atlantic Monthly,* July 1891, 32–49.

Trowbridge, John T. *The South: A Tour of Its Battle Fields and Ruined Cities, a Journey through the Desolated States, and Talks with the People.* Hartford, Conn.: L. Stebbins, 1866.

"The Virginia Judicial System." *Virginia Law Journal* 12 (Feb. 1888): 65–69.

Walker, T. C. "Development in the Tidewater Counties of Virginia." *Annals of American Academy of Political and Social Science* 49 (Sept. 1913): 28–31.

Warner, Charles D. "The Industrial South." *Harper's Weekly,* supplement, Jan. 29, 1887, 75.

Washington, Booker T. *Up from Slavery.* 1901. Reprint, New York: Avon, 1965.

Williams, Addie Luck. "Interview, Dec. 30, 1977." In *Black Women Oral History Project,* edited by Ruth E. Hill, 10:225–72. Westport, Conn.: Greenwood Press, 1990.

Wood, James P. *Industries of Richmond: Her Trade, Commerce, Manufactures, and Representative Establishments.* Richmond: Metropolitan, 1886.

Wynes, Charles E., ed. *Southern Sketches from Virginia, 1881–1901, by Orra Langhorne.* Charlottesville: University Press of Virginia, 1964.

Zola, Emile. *La Terre.* London: Penguin, 1980.

SECONDARY SOURCES

Adero, Malaika, ed. *Up South: Stories, Studies, and Letters of This Century's African-American Migrations.* New York: New Press, 1993.

Agee, Helene Barret. *Facets of Goochland County's History.* Richmond: Dietz, 1962.

Alexander, Ann Field. " 'Like an Evil Wind': The Roanoke Riot of 1893 and the Lynching of Thomas Smith." *Virginia Magazine of History and Biography* 100, no. 2 (Apr. 1992): 173–206.

Ambler, Charles Henry. *Sectionalism in Virginia from 1776 to 1861.* New York: Russell and Russell, 1964.

American Tobacco Company. *"Sold American!" The First Fifty Years.* New York: American Tobacco Co., 1954.

Anderson, James D. *The Education of Blacks in the South, 1860–1935.* Chapel Hill: University of North Carolina Press, 1988.

Aptheker, Herbert. *To Be Free: Pioneering Studies in Afro-American History.* New York: International Publishers, 1948.

Archer, John E. *By a Flash and a Scare: Incendiarism, Animal Maiming, and Poaching in East Anglia, 1815–1870.* Oxford: Clarendon Press, 1990.

Arnesen, Eric. *Waterfront Workers of New Orleans: Race, Class, and Politics, 1860–1920.* New York: Oxford University Press, 1991.

———. "Up from Exclusion: Black and White Workers, Race, and the State of Labor History." *Reviews in American History* 26 (1998): 146–74.

Arnold, Benjamin W. *History of the Tobacco Industry in Virginia from 1860 to 1894.* Baltimore: Johns Hopkins University Studies, 1897.

Ayers, Edward L. *The Promise of the New South: Life after Reconstruction.* New York: Oxford University Press, 1992.

Ayers, Edward L., and John C. Willis, eds. *The Edge of the South: Life in Nineteenth-Century Virginia.* Charlottesville: University Press of Virginia, 1991.

Barns, William D. *The West Virginia State Grange: The First Century, 1873–1973.* Morgantown: Morgantown Printing Co., 1973.

Beeman, Richard. *The Evolution of the Southern Backcountry: A Case Study of Lunenburg County, Virginia, 1746–1832.* Philadelphia: University of Pennsylvania Press, 1984.

Bentley, George R. *A History of the Freedmen's Bureau.* Philadelphia: University of Pennsylvania Press, 1955.

Berlin, Ira, and Philip D. Morgan, eds. *Cultivation and Culture: Labor and the Shaping of Slave Life in the Americas.* Charlottesville: University Press of Virginia, 1993.

Berlin, Ira, Barbara J. Fields, Steven F. Miller, Joseph P. Reidy, and Leslie S. Rowland, eds. *Slaves No More: Three Essays on Emancipation and the Civil War.* Cambridge: Cambridge University Press, 1992.

Billings, Dwight B., Jr. *Planters and the Making of a "New South": Class, Politics, and Development in North Carolina, 1865–1900.* Chapel Hill: University of North Carolina Press, 1979.

Blackburn, Robin. *The Making of New World Slavery: From the Baroque to the Modern, 1492–1800.* London: Verso, 1997.

Blake, Nelson M. *William Mahone of Virginia: Soldier and Political Insurgent.* Richmond: Garret and Massie, 1935.

Blassingame, John W. *The Slave Community: Plantation Life in the Antebellum South.* New York: Oxford University Press, 1972.

Bloch, Mark. *French Rural History: An Essay on Its Basic Characteristics.* Berkeley: University of California Press, 1966.

———. *The Historian's Craft.* New York: Vintage, 1953.

Bonekemper, Edward H., III. "Negro Ownership of Real Property in Hampton and Elizabeth City County, Virginia, 1860–1870." *Journal of Negro History* 55, no. 3 (July 1970): 165–81.

Bradford, Helen. "Highways, Byways, and Cul-de-Sacs: The Transition to Agrarian Capitalism in Revisionist South African History." *Radical History Review* 46 (1990): 59–88.

Bradshaw, Herbert C. *History of Prince Edward County, Virginia*. Richmond: Dietz, 1955.

Breen, T. H. *Tobacco Culture: The Mentality of the Great Tidewater Planters on the Eve of Revolution*. Princeton: Princeton University Press, 1985.

Brewer, James H. *The Confederate Negro: Virginia's Craftsmen and Military Laborers, 1861–1865*. Durham, N.C.: Duke University Press, 1969.

Brooks, Joseph. "The Decline of Black Landownership." *Freedomways* 24, no. 3 (1984): 191–94.

Brooks-Higginbotham, Evelyn. *Righteous Discontent: The Women's Movement in the Black Baptist Church, 1880–1920*. Cambridge: Harvard University Press, 1993.

Bruce, Kathleen. "Virginian Agricultural Decline to 1860: A Fallacy." *Agricultural History* 6, no. 1 (Jan. 1932): 3–13.

Buck, Solon J. *The Granger Movement: A Study of Agricultural Organization and Its Political, Economic, and Social Manifestations, 1870–1880*. Cambridge: Harvard University Press, 1933.

Burdick, John. "From Virtue to Fitness: The Accommodation of a Planter Family to Postbellum Virginia." *Virginia Magazine of History and Biography* 93, no. 1 (Jan. 1985): 14–35.

Byres, T. J., ed. "Sharecropping and Sharecroppers." *Journal of Peasant Studies* 10, nos. 2–3 (Jan–Apr. 1983): 3–283.

Campbell, Tracy. *The Politics of Despair: Power and Resistance in the Tobacco Wars*. Lexington: University Press of Kentucky, 1993.

Carrington, Wirt J. *A History of Halifax County, Virginia*. Baltimore: Regional Pub. Co., 1924.

Carter, Ian. *Farm Life in North East Scotland, 1840–1914*. Edinburgh: Donald, 1979.

Cecil-Fronsman, Bill. *Common Whites: Class and Culture in Antebellum North Carolina*. Lexington: University Press of Kentucky, 1992.

Cell, John W. *The Highest Stage of White Supremacy: The Origins of Segregation in South Africa and the American South*. Cambridge: Cambridge University Press, 1982.

Chakrabarty, Dipesh. *Rethinking Working-Class History: Bengal, 1890–1940*. Princeton: Princeton University Press, 1989.

Chandler, Alfred D. *The Visible Hand: The Managerial Revolution in American Business*. Cambridge: Belknap Press, 1977.

Chesson, Michael B. *Richmond after the War, 1865–1890*. Richmond: Virginia State Library, 1981.

Clark, Christopher. "The Household Economy, Market Exchange, and the Rise of Capitalism in the Connecticut Valley, 1800–1860." *Journal of Social History* 13 (Winter 1979): 169–89.

——. *The Roots of Rural Capitalism: Western Massachusetts, 1780–1869*. Ithaca: Cornell University Press, 1990.

Clark, Thomas D. *Pills, Petticoats, and Plows: The Southern Country Store.* New York: Bobbs-Merrill, 1944.

Clement, Maud C. *The History of Pittsylvania County, Virginia.* Baltimore: Regional Pub. Co., 1976.

Clifton, James M. "Twilight Comes to the Rice Kingdom: Postbellum Rice Culture on the South Atlantic Coast." *Georgia Historical Quarterly* 62 (Summer 1978): 146–54.

Cochran, Sherman. *Big Business in China: Sino-Foreign Rivalry in the Cigarette Industry, 1890–1930.* Cambridge: Harvard University Press, 1980.

Cohen, William. *At Freedom's Edge: Black Mobility and the Southern White Quest for Racial Control, 1861–1915.* Baton Rouge: Louisiana State University Press, 1991.

———. "Negro Involuntary Servitude in the South, 1865–1940: A Preliminary Analysis." *Journal of Southern History* 42, no. 1 (Feb. 1976): 31–60.

Cohen-Lack, Nancy. "A Struggle for Sovereignty: National Consolidation, Emancipation, and Free Labor in Texas, 1865." *Journal of Southern History* 58, no. 1 (Feb. 1992): 57–98.

Cooper, Frederick. *From Slaves to Squatters: Plantation Labor and Agriculture in Zanzibar and Coastal Kenya, 1890–1925.* New Haven: Yale University Press, 1980.

Craven, Avery O. *Soil Exhaustion as a Factor in the Agricultural History of Virginia and Maryland, 1606–1860.* Urbana: University of Illinois Press, 1925.

Crofts, Daniel W. *Reluctant Confederates: Upper South Unionists in the Secession Crisis.* Chapel Hill: University of North Carolina Press, 1988.

Croix, G. E. M. de Ste. *The Class Struggle in the Ancient Greek World from the Archaic Age to the Arab Conquest.* Ithaca: Cornell University Press, 1981.

Dabney, Virginius. *Virginia, the New Dominion: A History from 1607 to the Present.* Charlottesville: University Press of Virginia, 1971.

Daniel, Pete. *Breaking the Land: The Transformation of Cotton, Tobacco, and Rice Cultures since 1880.* Urbana: University of Illinois Press, 1985.

———. "The Metamorphosis of Slavery, 1865–1900." *Journal of American History* 66, no. 1 (June 1979): 88–99.

Davidson, Basil. *The Black Man's Burden: Africa and the Curse of the Nation-State.* New York: Random House, 1992.

Davis, Ronald L. *Good and Faithful Labor: From Slavery to Sharecropping in the Natchez District, 1860–1890.* Westport, Conn.: Greenwood Press, 1982.

Davis, Scott C. *The World of Patience Gnomes: Making and Unmaking a Black Community.* Lexington: University Press of Kentucky, 1988.

Dobb, Maurice. *Studies in the Development of Capitalism.* New York: International Publishers, 1949.

Du Bois, W. E. B. *Black Reconstruction: An Essay toward a History of the Part Which Black Folk Played in the Attempt to Reconstruct Democracy in America, 1860–1880.* New York: Russell and Russell, 1935.

———. *The Philadelphia Negro: A Social Study.* Philadelphia: University of Pennsylvania Press, 1996.

Dunn, Richard S. "A Tale of Two Plantations: Slave Life at Mesopotamia in Jamaica and Mount Airy in Virginia, 1799 to 1828." *William and Mary Quarterly*, 3rd ser., 34 (1977): 32–34.

Eaton, Clement. *A History of the Southern Confederacy.* New York: Collier, 1954.

Eckenrode, James H. *The Political History of Virginia during the Reconstruction.* Baltimore: Johns Hopkins University Press, 1904.

Engerman, S. L. "Economic Change amd Contract Labour in the British Caribbean: The End of Slavery and the Adjustment to Emancipation." In Richardson, *Abolition*, 225–44.

———. "Slavery and Emancipation in Comparative Perspective: A Look at Some Recent Debates." *Journal of Economic History* 46 (June 1986): 317–39.

Engs, Robert F. *Freedom's First Generation: Black Hampton, Virginia, 1861–1890.* Philadelphia: University of Pennsylvania Press, 1979.

Eustler, Roland B. "Agricultural Credit and the Negro Farmer." Pts. 1 and 2. *Journal of Social Forces* 8, nos. 3–4 (Mar.–June 1930): 416–25, 565–73.

Ferguson, Maxwell. *State Regulation of Railroads in the South.* New York: Columbia University Press, 1916.

Ferleger, Lou, ed. *Agriculture and National Development: Views on the Nineteenth Century.* Ames: Iowa State University Press, 1990.

Fields, Barbara J. "The Advent of Capitalist Agriculture: The New South in a Bourgeois World." In Glymph and Kushma, *Essays*, pp. 73–94.

———. "The Nineteenth Century American South: History and Theory." *Plantation Society in the Americas* 2 (Apr. 1983): 7–27.

———. *Slavery and Freedom on the Middle Ground: Maryland during the Nineteenth Century.* New Haven: Yale University Press, 1985.

———. "Slavery, Race, and Ideology in the USA." *New Left Review*, no. 181 (May–June 1990): 95–118.

Figes, Orlando. *Peasant Russia, Civil War: The Volga Countryside in Revolution, 1917–1921.* New York: Oxford University Press, 1989.

Fink, Leon. " 'Irrespective of Party, Color or Social Standing': The Knights of Labor and Opposition Politics in Richmond, Virginia." *Labor History* 19, no. 3 (Summer 1978): 325–49.

———. "The New Labor History and the Powers of Historical Pessimism: Consensus, Hegemony, and the Case of the Knights of Labor." *Journal of American History* 75, no. 1 (June 1988): 115–36.

Fisher, James S. "Negro Farm Ownership in the South." *Annals of the Association of American Geographers* 63 (1973): 478–89.

Fligstein, Neil. "The Underdevelopment of the South: State and Agriculture, 1865–1900." In *Studies in the Transformation of U.S. Agriculture*, edited by A. Eugene Havens, 60–103. Boulder, Colo.: Westview Press, 1986.

Fogel, Robert William, and Stanley L. Engerman. *Time on the Cross: The Economics of American Negro Slavery.* New York: Little, Brown, 1974.

Foner, Eric. *Freedom's Lawmakers: A Directory of Black Officeholders during Reconstruction.* New York: Oxford University Press, 1993.

———. *Free Soil, Free Labor, Free Men: The Ideology of the Republican Party before the Civil War.* New York: Oxford University Press, 1970.

———. "The Meaning of Freedom in the Age of Emancipation." *Journal of American History* 81 (Sept. 1994): 435–60.

———. *Nothing but Freedom: Emancipation and Its Legacy.* Baton Rouge: Louisiana State University Press, 1983.

———. *Reconstruction: America's Unfinished Revolution.* New York: Harper and Row, 1988.

———. "Reconstruction Revisited." *Reviews in American History* 10 (1982): 82–100.

Ford, Lacy. "Labor and Ideology in the South Carolina Up-Country: The Transition to Free-Labor Agriculture." In *The Southern Enigma: Essays on Race, Class, and Folk Culture*, edited by Walter J. Fraser and Winfred B. Moore, 25–41. Westport, Conn.: Greenwood Press, 1983.

Foster, R. F. *Modern Ireland, 1600–1972*. London: Penguin, 1988.

Foster-Carter, Adrian. "The Modes of Production Controversy." *New Left Review*, no. 107 (Jan.–Feb. 1978): 47–77.

Fox-Genovese, Elizabeth. *Within the Plantation Household: Black and White Women of the Old South*. Chapel Hill: University of North Carolina Press, 1988.

Fox-Genovese, Elizabeth, and Eugene D. Genovese. *Fruits of Merchant Capital: Slavery and Bourgeois Property in the Rise and Expansion of Capitalism*. New York: Oxford University Press, 1983.

Frader, Laura L. *Peasants and Protest: Agricultural Workers, Politics, and Unions in the Aude, 1850–1914*. Los Angeles: University of California Press, 1991.

Fraginals, M. M., F. M. Pons, and Stanley L. Engerman, eds. *Between Slavery and Free Labor: The Spanish-Speaking Caribbean in the Nineteenth Century*. Baltimore: Johns Hopkins University Press, 1985.

Fuke, Richard P. "Planters, Apprenticeship, and Forced Labor: The Black Family under Pressure in Post-Emancipation Maryland." *Agricultural History* 62, no. 4 (Fall 1988): 57–72.

Garnet, William E., and John Marcus Ellison. "Negro Life in Rural Virginia, 1865–1934." Virginia Agricultural Experiment Station. Bulletin 295. Blacksburg, Va., 1934.

Gaston, Paul M. *The New South Creed: A Study in Southern Mythmaking*. Baton Rouge: Louisiana State University Press, 1970.

Gates, Paul W. *The Farmer's Age: Agriculture, 1815–1860*. New York: Holt, Rinehart and Winston, 1960.

Gee, Wilson, and John J. Corson. *Rural Depopulation in Certain Tidewater and Piedmont Areas of Virginia*. Charlottesville: University Press of Virginia, 1929.

Genovese, Eugene D. *The Political Economy of Slavery: Studies in the Economy and Society of the Slave South*. New York: Pantheon, 1966.

———. *Roll, Jordan, Roll: The World the Slaves Made*. New York: Pantheon, 1972.

———. *The Slaveholders' Dilemma: Freedom and Progress in Southern Conservative Thought, 1820–1860*. Columbia: University of South Carolina Press, 1992.

———. *The Southern Front: History and Politics in the Cultural Wars*. Columbia: University of Missouri Press, 1995.

———. *The Southern Tradition: The Achievement and Limitations of an American Conservatism*. Cambridge: Harvard University Press, 1994.

———. *The World the Slaveholders Made: Two Essays in Interdependency*. New York: Vintage, 1971.

———. "Yeomen Farmers in a Slaveholders' Democracy." *Agricultural History* 49, no. 2 (Apr. 1973): 331–42.

Glymph, Thavolia, and John J. Kushma, eds. *Essays on the Postbellum Southern Economy*. College Station: Texas A&M University Press, 1985.

Goggin, Jacqueline. *Carter G. Woodson: A Life in History*. Baton Rouge: Louisiana State University Press, 1993.

Goodman, Jordan. *Tobacco in History: The Cultures of Dependence*. New York: Routledge, 1993.

Goodwyn, Lawrence. *The Populist Moment: A Short History of the Agrarian Revolt in America*. New York: Oxford University Press, 1978.

Gottlieb, Peter. *Making Their Own Way: Southern Blacks' Migration to Pittsburgh, 1916–30*. Urbana: University of Illinois Press, 1987.

Gray, Lewis C. *History of Agriculture in the Southern United States to 1860*. 2 vols. Washington, D.C.: Carnegie Institute, 1933.

Green, Gary P. "The Political Economy of Flue-cured Tobacco Production." *Rural Sociology* 52, no. 2 (1987): 221–41.

Green, Rodney D. "Black Tobacco Factory Workers and Social Conflict in Antebellum Richmond: Were Slavery and Urban Industry Really Compatible?" *Slavery and Abolition* 8, no. 2 (Sept. 1987): 183–203.

Gregg, Robert. *Sparks from the Anvil of Oppression: Philadelphia's African Methodists and Southern Migrants, 1890–1940*. Philadelphia: Temple University Press, 1993.

Griffin, Farah Jasmine. *"Who Set You Flowin'?" The African-American Migration Narrative*. New York: Oxford University Press, 1995.

Grossman, James R. *Land of Hope: Chicago, Black Southerners, and the Great Migration*. Chicago: University of Chicago Press, 1989.

Gutman, Herbert G. *The Black Family in Slavery and Freedom, 1750–1925*. New York: Vintage, 1976.

Hahn, Steven. "Class and State in Postemancipation Societies: Southern Planters in Comparative Perspective." *American Historical Review* 95 (Feb. 1990): 75–98.

———. "Hunting, Fishing, and Foraging: Common Rights and Class Relations in the Postbellum South." *Radical History Review* 26 (1982): 37–64.

———. "A Response: Common Cents or Historical Sense?" *Journal of Southern History* 59, no. 4 (May 1993): 243–58.

———. *The Roots of Southern Populism: Yeoman Farmers and the Transformation of the Georgia Upcountry, 1850–1890*. New York: Oxford University Press, 1983.

Hahn, Steven, and Jonathan Prude, eds. *The Countryside in the Age of Capitalist Transformation: Essays in the Social History of Rural America*. Chapel Hill: University of North Carolina Press, 1985.

Hall, Virginius Cornick, Jr. "Virginia Post Offices, 1798–1859." *Virginia Magazine of History and Biography* 81, no. 1 (Jan. 1973): 49–97.

Hamm, Richard F. "The Killing of John R. Moffett and the Trial of J. T. Clark: Race, Prohibition, and Politics in Danville, 1887–1893." *Virginia Magazine of History and Biography* 101, no. 3 (July 1993): 375–404.

Haraksingh, Kusha. "The Worker and the Wage in a Plantation Economy." In Mary Turner, *From Chattel Slaves to Wage Slaves*, 224–38.

Harding, Vincent. *There Is a River: The Black Struggle for Freedom in America*. New York: Vintage, 1983.

Harlan, Louis R. *Booker T. Washington: The Making of a Black Leader, 1856–1901*. New York: Oxford University Press, 1972.

Harris, William J. "Portrait of a Small Slaveholder: The Journal of Benton Miller." *Georgia Historical Quarterly* 74, no. 1 (Winter 1990): 1–19.

Harrison, John P. "The Evolution of the Colombian Tobacco Trade to 1875." *Hispanic American Historical Review* 32, no. 2 (May 1952): 163–74.

Hartzell, Lawrence L. "The Exploration of Freedom in Black Petersburg, Virginia, 1865–1902." In Ayers and Willis, *Edge of the South*, 134–56.

Hay, Douglas, et al., eds. *Albion's Fatal Tree: Crime and Society in Eighteenth-Century England*. Harmondsworth: Penguin, 1977.

Haywood, Harry. *Black Bolshevik: Autobiography of an Afro-American Communist*. Chicago: Liberator Press, 1978.

Heinemann, Ronald L. *Depression and New Deal in Virginia: The Enduring Dominion*. Charlottesville: University Press of Virginia, 1983.

Henderson, William D. *The Unredeemed City: Reconstruction in Petersburg, Virginia, 1865–1874*. Washington, D.C.: University Press of America, 1977.

Henri, Florette. *Black Migration: Movement North, 1900–1920*. New York: Anchor, 1975.

Higgs, Robert. *Competition and Coercion: Blacks in the American Economy, 1865–1914*. Cambridge: Cambridge University Press, 1977.

Hill, Christopher. *The English Bible and the Seventeenth-Century Revolution*. London: Penguin, 1993.

———. *Liberty against the Law: Some Seventeenth-Century Controversies*. London: Penguin, 1996.

Hill, J. P. A. *A History of Henry County, Virginia*. Baltimore: Regional Pub. Co., 1976.

Hilton, Rodney. *Class Conflict and the Crisis of Feudalism*. London: Verso, 1990.

———, ed. *The Transition from Feudalism to Capitalism*. London: New Left Books, 1976.

Hine, Darlene Clark, ed., *The State of Afro-American History: Past, Present, and Future*. Baton Rouge: Louisiana State University Press, 1986.

Hobsbawn, Eric J. *The Age of Capital, 1848–1875*. New York: Scribner's, 1875.

———. *The Age of Empire, 1875–1914*. New York: Vintage, 1987.

———. *Echoes of the Marseillaise: Two Centuries Look Back on the French Revolution*. New Brunswick: Rutgers University Press, 1990.

Hoggart, Richard. *The Uses of Literacy: Changing Patterns in English Mass Culture*. 1957. Reprint, London: Penguin, 1990.

Holmes, William F., ed. *American Populism*. Lexington, Miss.: D. C. Heath, 1994.

Holt, Sharon Ann. "Making Freedom Pay: Freedpeople Working for Themselves, North Carolina, 1865–1900." *Journal of Southern History* 60, no. 2 (May 1994): 229–62.

Holt, Thomas. *Black over White: Negro Political Leadership in South Carolina during Reconstruction*. Urbana: University of Illinois Press, 1977.

———. " 'An Empire over the Mind': Emancipation, Race, Ideology in the British West Indies and the American South." In Kousser and McPherson, *Region, Race, and Reconstruction*, 283–312.

———. *The Problem of Freedom: Race, Labor, and Politics in Jamaica, 1832–1938*. Baltimore: Johns Hopkins University Press, 1992.

Irwin, James R. "Farmers and Laborers: A Note on Black Occupations in the Postbellum South." *Agricultural History* 64, no. 1 (Winter 1990): 53–60.

Isaac, Rhys. *The Transformation of Virginia, 1740–1790*. Chapel Hill: University of North Carolina Press, 1982.

Jackson, Luther P. *Negro Office-Holders in Virginia, 1865–1895*. Norfolk: Guide Quality Press, 1945.

———. "The Virginia Free Negro Farmer and Property Owner, 1830–1860." *Journal of Negro History* 24 (1939): 390–439.

Janiewski, Dolores E. *Sisterhood Denied: Race, Gender, and Class in a New South Community*. Philadelphia: Temple University Press, 1985.

———. "Women and the Making of a Rural Proletariat in the Bright Tobacco Belt, 1880–1930." *Insurgent Sociologist* 10 (Summer 1980): 16–26.

Jaynes, Gerald D. *Branches without Roots: Genesis of the Black Working Class in the American South, 1862–1882*. New York: Oxford University Press, 1986.

Jenkins, John Wilber. *James B. Duke: Master Builder*. New York: George H. Doran, 1927.

Jones, Jacqueline. *Labor of Love, Labor of Sorrow: Black Women, Work, and the Family, from Slavery to the Present*. New York: Basic Books, 1985.

Jordan, Ervin L., Jr. *Black Confederates and Afro-Yankees in Civil War Virginia*. Charlottesville: University Press of Virginia, 1995.

Joyce, Patrick, ed. *Class*. New York: Oxford University Press, 1995.

Kantor, Shawn Everett, and J. Morgan Kousser. "Common Sense or Common-wealth? The Fence Law and Institutional Change in the Postbellum South." *Journal of Southern History* 59, no. 2 (May 1993): 201–42.

Kantrowitz, Steven. "The Crop, the Rent, and the Lien: Law and Society in the New South." *Reviews in American History* 24 (1996): 46–50.

Kautsky, Karl. *The Agrarian Question*. 2 vols. 1899. Reprint, London: Zwan, 1988.

Kennedy, Louise V. *The Negro Peasant Turns Cityward: Effects of Recent Migrations to Northern Centers*. New York: Columbia University Press, 1930.

Kenny, Kevin. *Making Sense of the Molly Maguires*. New York: Oxford University Press, 1998.

Kiernan, Victor G. *Tobacco: A History*. London: Hutchinson Radius, 1991.

Kiser, Clyde V. *Sea Island to City: A Study of St. Helena Islanders in Harlem and Other Urban Centers*. New York, 1932.

Kousser, J. Morgan. *The Shaping of Southern Politics: Suffrage Restriction and the Establishment of the One-Party South, 1880–1910*. New Haven: Yale University Press, 1974.

Kousser, J. Morgan, and James M. McPherson, eds. *Region, Race, and Reconstruction: Essays in Honor of C. Vann Woodward*. New York: Oxford University Press, 1982.

Kulikoff, Allan. *The Agrarian Origins of American Capitalism*. Charlottesville: University Press of Virginia, 1992.

———. *Tobacco and Slaves: The Development of Southern Cultures in the Chesapeake, 1680–1800*. Chapel Hill: University of North Carolina Press, 1986.

Kusmer, Kenneth L. *A Ghetto Takes Shape: Black Cleveland, 1870–1930*. Urbana: University of Illinois Press, 1976.

Lacerte, Robert K. "The Evolution of Land and Labor in the Haitian Revolution, 1791–1820." *Americas* 34, no. 4 (Apr. 1978): 449–59.

Lake, David A. "Export, Die, or Subsidize: The International Political Economy of American Agriculture, 1875–1940." *Comparative Studies in Society and History* 31, no. 1 (Jan. 1989): 81–105.

Lebsock, Suzanne. *The Free Women of Petersburg: Status and Culture in a Southern Town, 1784–1860*. New York: Norton, 1984.

Lenin, V. I. *The Development of Capitalism in Russia: The Process of the Formation of a Home Market for Large Scale Industry*. Moscow: Foreign Languages Publishing House, 1956.

Lewis, Earl. *In Their Own Interests: Race, Class, and Power in Twentieth-Century Norfolk, Virginia*. Los Angeles: University of California Press, 1991.

Lichtenstein, Alex. *Twice the Work of Free Labor: The Political Economy of Convict Labor in the New South*. London: Verso, 1996.

Link, William A. *A Hard Country and a Lonely Place: Schooling, Society, and Reform in Rural Virginia, 1870–1920*. Chapel Hill: University of North Carolina Press, 1986.

Litwack, Leon. *Been in the Storm So Long: The Aftermath of Slavery*. New York: Vintage, 1979.

Lowe, Richard. "Another Look at Reconstruction in Virginia." *Civil War History* 32, no. 1 (Mar. 1986): 56–76.

———. "Local Black Leaders during Reconstruction in Virginia." *Virginia Magazine of History and Biography* 103, no. 2 (Apr. 1995): 181–206.

———. *Republicans and Reconstruction in Virginia, 1856–1870*. Charlottesville: University Press of Virginia, 1991.

Lynchburg Sesqui-Centennial Association. *The Saga of a City: Lynchburg, Virginia*. Lynchburg: Lynchburg Sesqui-Centennial Association, 1936.

McConnell, John P. *Negroes and Their Treatment in Virginia from 1865 to 1867*. 1910. Reprint, New York: Negro Universities Press, 1969.

McFeeley, William S. *Yankee Stepfather: General O. O. Howard and the Freedmen*. New Haven: Yale University Press, 1968.

McKenzie, Robert Tracy. "Freedmen and the Soil in the Upper South: The Reorganization of Tennessee Agriculture, 1865–1880." *Journal of Southern History* 59, no. 1 (Feb. 1993): 63–84.

———. *One South or Many: Plantation Belt and Upcountry in Civil War–Era Tennessee*. Cambridge: Cambridge University Press, 1994.

McPherson, James M. *Battle Cry of Freedom: The Civil War Era*. New York: Oxford University Press, 1988.

Madden, Ida A. "The Housing Conditions of One Hundred and Fifty Negro Families in Campbell County, Virginia." *Virginia State College Gazette*, Nov. 1994, 41–43.

Maddex, Jack P. *The Virginia Conservatives, 1867–1879: A Study in Reconstruction Politics*. Chapel Hill: University of North Carolina Press, 1970.

———. "Virginia: The Persistence of Centrist Hegemony." In *Reconstruction and Redemption in the South*, edited by Otto H. Olsen, 113–55. Baton Rouge: Louisiana State University Press, 1980.

Mallon, Florencia E. *The Defense of Community in Peru's Central Highlands: Peasant Struggle and Capitalist Transition, 1860–1940*. Princeton: Princeton University Press, 1983.

Mandle, Jay R. *Nor Slave, Nor Free: The African American Economic Experience since the Civil War*. Durham, N.C.: Duke University Press, 1992.

———. *The Roots of Black Poverty: The Southern Plantation Economy after the Civil War*. Durham, N.C.: Duke University Press, 1978.

Mann, Susan Archer. *Agrarian Capitalism in Theory and Practice*. Chapel Hill: University of North Carolina Press, 1990.

Marcus, Alan I. *Agricultural Science and the Quest for Legitimacy: Farmers, Agricul-*

tural Colleges, and Experiment Stations, 1870–1890. Ames: Iowa State University Press, 1985.

Marti, Donald B. *Women of the Grange: Mutuality and Sisterhood in Rural America, 1866–1920.* New York: Greenwood Press, 1991.

Marx, Karl. *Capital: A Critical Analysis of Capitalist Production.* Vol. 1. New York: International Publishers, 1967.

———. *Capital: A Critique of Political Economy.* Vol. 3. London: Penguin, 1991.

———. *Capital: Theories of Surplus Value.* Vol. 4. Moscow: Progress Publishers, 1968.

———. *The Eighteenth Brumaire of Louis Bonaparte.* New York: International Publishers, 1963.

———. *Pre-Capitalist Economic Formations.* New York: International Publishers, 1964.

Matthew, William M. *Edmund Ruffin and the Crisis of Slavery in the Old South: The Failure of Agricultural Reform.* Athens: University of Georgia Press, 1988.

Meier, August, and Elliot Rudwick. *Black History and the Historical Profession, 1915–1980.* Urbana: University of Illinois Press, 1986.

Menard, Russel R. "The Tobacco Industry in the Chesapeake Colonies, 1617–1730: An Interpretation." *Research in Economic History* 5 (1980): 109–77.

Merrington, John. "Town and Country in the Transition to Capitalism." *New Left Review,* no. 93 (Sept.–Oct. 1975): 71–92.

Meyer, Jacobstein. *The Tobacco Industry in the U.S.* New York: Columbia University Press, 1968.

Mingay, G. E., ed. *The Agrarian History of England and Wales.* Vol. 6, *1750–1850.* Cambridge: Cambridge University Press, 1989.

Mintz, Sidney. *Caribbean Transformations.* Chicago: Aldine, 1974.

Moger, Allen W. "Industrial and Urban Progress in Virginia from 1880–1900." *Virginia Magazine of History and Biography* 66, no. 3 (July 1958): 307–36.

———. "Railroad Practices and Policies in Virginia after the Civil War." *Virginia Magazine of History and Biography* 59, no. 4 (Oct. 1951): 423–57.

———. *The Rebuilding of the Old Dominion, 1880–1902.* Ann Arbor: University of Michigan Press, 1940.

———. *Virginia: Bourbonism to Byrd, 1870–1925.* Charlottesville: University Press of Virginia, 1968.

Montgomery, David. *Beyond Equality: Labor and the Radical Republicans, 1862–1872.* Chicago: University of Illinois Press, 1981.

Mooney, P. H. "Desperately Seeking: One-Dimensional Mann and Dickinson." *Rural Sociology* 52, no. 2 (1987): 286–95.

———. "Labor Time, Production Time, and Capitalist Development in Agriculture: A Reconsideration of the Mann-Dickinson Thesis." *Sociologia Ruralis* 22 (1982): 279–92.

Moore, James T. "Black Militancy in Readjuster Virginia, 1879–1883." *Journal of Southern History* 41, no. 2 (May 1975): 167–86.

———. *Two Paths to the New South: The Virginia Debt Controversy, 1870–1883.* Lexington: University Press of Kentucky, 1974.

Morgan, Edmund S. *American Slavery, American Freedom: The Ordeal of Colonial Virginia.* New York: Norton, 1975.

Morgan, Lynda J. *Emancipation in Virginia's Tobacco Belt, 1850–1870*. Athens: University of Georgia Press, 1992.

Morgan, Philip D. "Slave Life in Piedmont Virginia, 1720–1800." In *Colonial Chesapeake Society*, edited by Lois Green Carr, Philip D. Morgan, and Jean B. Russo, 433–84. Chapel Hill: University of North Carolina Press, 1988.

Morgan, Philip D., and Michael L. Nicholls. "Slaves in Piedmont Virginia, 1720–1790." *William and Mary Quarterly* 46, no. 2 (Apr. 1989): 211–51.

Morris, Mike. "Social History and the Transition to Capitalism in the South African Countryside." *African Perspectives* 1, no. 5–6 (1987): 7–24.

Morrison, Toni. *Jazz*. New York: Plume, 1992.

Morton, Richard L. *Colonial Virginia: Westward Expansion and the Prelude to Revolution*. Chapel Hill: University of North Carolina Press, 1960.

———. *The Negro in Virginia Politics, 1865–1902*. Charlottesville: University Press of Virginia, 1919.

Moselle, Boaz. "Allotments, Enclosure, and Proletarianization in Early Nineteenth-Century Southern England." *Economic History Review* 48, no. 3 (1995): 482–500.

Mullin, Gerald W. *Africa in America: Slave Acculturation and Resistance in the American South and the British Caribbean, 1736–1831*. Urbana: University of Illinois Press, 1992.

———. *Flight and Rebellion: Slave Resistance in Eighteenth-Century Virginia*. New York: Oxford University Press, 1972.

Nanzig, Thomas P. *Third Virginia Cavalry*. Lynchburg, H. E. Howard, 1989.

Nelson, Margaret V. *A Study of Judicial Review in Virginia, 1789–1928*. New York: Columbia University Press, 1947.

Newby, I. A. *Plain Folk in the New South: Social Change and Cultural Persistence, 1880–1915*. Baton Rouge: Louisiana State University Press, 1989.

North, Douglas C. *The Economic Growth of the U.S., 1790–1860*. Englewood Cliffs, N.J.: Prentice Hall, 1961.

Northrup, Herbert R., and Richard L. Rowan. *Negro Employment in Basic Industry: A Study of Racial Policies in Six Industries*. Philadelphia: University of Pennsylvania Press, 1970.

Ortiz, Fernando. *Cuban Counterpoint: Tobacco and Sugar*. 1947. Reprint, Durham, N.C.: Duke University Press, 1995.

Osofsky, Gilbert. *Harlem, the Making of a Ghetto: Negro New York, 1890–1930*. New York: Harper, 1963.

Oubre, Claude F. *Forty Acres and a Mule: The Freedmen's Bureau and Black Land Ownership*. Baton Rouge: Louisiana State University Press, 1978.

Pearce, R. "Sharecropping: Towards a Marxist View." *Journal of Peasant Studies* 10, no. 2–3 (Jan.–Apr. 1983): 42–70.

Pearson, Charles C. *The Readjuster Movement in Virginia*. New Haven: Yale University Press, 1917.

Pedigo, Virginia G., and Lewis G. Pedigo. *History of Patrick and Henry Counties, Virginia*. Roanoke: Stone, 1933.

Peterson, Arthur G. *Historical Study of Prices Received by Producers of Farm Products in Virginia, 1801–1927*. Blacksburg: Virginia Agricultural Experiment Station, 1929.

Phillips, Ulrich B. *American Negro Slavery: A Survey of the Supply, Employment,* and *Control of Negro Labor as Determined by the Plantation Regime*. Baton Rouge: Louisiana State University Press, 1966.

———. *Life and Labor in the Old South*. Boston: Little, Brown, 1963.

Plumb, J. H. *England in the Eighteenth Century, 1714–1815*. London: Penguin, 1950.

Post, Charles. "The American Road to Capitalism." *New Left Review*, no. 133 (May–June 1982): 30–51.

Prakash, Gyan, ed. *The World of the Rural Labourer in Colonial India*. Delhi: Oxford University Press, 1994.

Pulley, Raymond H. *Old Virginia Restored: An Interpretation of the Progressive Impulse, 1870–1930*. Charlottesville: University Press of Virginia, 1968.

Rabinowitz, Howard N. "More Than the Woodward Thesis: Assessing the Strange Career of Jim Crow." *Journal of American History* 75, no. 3 (Dec. 1988): 842–56.

———. *Race, Ethnicity, and Urbanization: Selected Essays*. Columbia: University of Missouri Press, 1994.

———. *Race Relations in the Urban South, 1865–1890*. New York: Oxford University Press, 1978.

Rachleff, Peter J. *Black Labor in the South: Richmond, Virginia, 1865–1890*. Philadelphia: Temple University Press, 1984.

Ransom, Roger L. *Conflict and Compromise: The Political Economy of Slavery, Emancipation, and the American Civil War*. Cambridge: Cambridge University Press, 1989.

Ransom, Roger L., and Richard Sutch. *One Kind of Freedom: The Economic Consequences of Emancipation*. Cambridge: Cambridge University Press, 1977.

Rawick, George P., ed. *The American Slave: A Composite Autobiography*. Vol. 16, *Virginia Narratives*. Westport, Conn.: Greenwood Press, 1972.

———. *From Sunup to Sundown: The Making of the Black Community*. Westport, Conn.: Greenwood Press, 1972.

Reid, Joseph D. "Sharecropping as an Understandable Market Response: The Postbellum South." *Journal of Economic History* 33 (Mar. 1973): 106–30.

Reidy, Joseph P. *From Slavery to Agrarian Capitalism in the Cotton Plantation South: Central Georgia, 1800–1880*. Chapel Hill: University of North Carolina Press, 1992.

———. "Slavery, Emancipation, and the Capitalist Transformation of Southern Agriculture, 1850–1910." In Ferleger, *Agriculture and National Development*, 229–64.

Reiff, Janice L., and Michel R. Dahlin. "Rural Push and Urban Pull: Work and Family Experiences of Older Black Women in Southern Cities, 1880–1900." *Journal of Social History* 16, no. 4 (Dec. 1983): 39–48.

Renda, Lex. "The Advent of Agricultural Progressivism in Virginia." *Virginia Magazine of History and Biography* 96, no. 1 (Jan. 1988): 55–82.

Rezneck, Samuel. "Distress, Relief, and Discontent in the United States during the Depression of 1873–78." *Journal of Political Economy* 58 (Dec. 1950): 494–512.

Richardson, David, ed. *Abolition and Its Aftermath: The Historical Context, 1790–1916*. London: Frank Cass, 1985.

Riley, Sam G. *Magazines of the American South*. New York: Greenwood Press, 1986.

Robert, Joseph C. *The Story of Tobacco in America*. New York, 1949.

———. *The Tobacco Kingdom: Plantation, Market, and Factory in Virginia and North Carolina, 1800–1860*. Gloucester, Mass.: Peter Smith, 1965.

Roberts, Richard, and Suzanne Miers, eds. *The End of Slavery in Africa*. Madison: University of Wisconsin Press, 1988.

Roberts, W. C., and Richard F. Knapp. "Paving the Way for the Tobacco Trust: From Hand Rolling to Mechanized Cigarette Production by W. Duke, Sons and Company." *North Carolina Historical Review* 69, no. 3 (July 1992): 257–81.

Robinson, Armstead. "Beyond the Realm of Social Consensus: New Meanings of Reconstruction for American History." *Journal of American History* 68, no. 3 (June–Sept. 1981): 276–97.

Rodney, Walter. *History of the Guyanese Working People*. Baltimore: Johns Hopkins University Press, 1983.

———. *How Europe Underdeveloped Africa*. Washington, D.C.: Howard University Press, 1972.

Rose, Willie Lee. *Rehearsal for Reconstruction: The Port Royal Experiment*. Indianapolis: Bobbs-Merrill, 1964.

Rosengarten, Theodore. *All God's Dangers: The Life of Nate Shaw*. New York: Knopf, 1974.

Royce, Edward. *The Origins of Southern Sharecropping*. Philadelphia: Temple University Press, 1993.

Russel, Robert Royal. *Economic Aspects of Southern Sectionalism, 1840–1861*. New York: Russell and Russell, 1960.

Russell, James S. "Rural Economic Progress of the Negro in Virginia." *Journal of Negro History* 11, no. 4 (Oct. 1926): 556–62.

Russell, Lester F. *Black Baptist Secondary Schools in Virginia, 1887–1957: A Study in Black History*. Metuchen, N.J.: Scarecrow Press, 1981.

Saloutos, Theodore. *Farmer Movements in the South, 1865–1933*. Lincoln: University of Nebraska Press, 1960.

Saunders, Robert M. "Progressive Historians and the Late Nineteenth Century Agrarian Revolt: Virginia as Historiographical Test Case." *Virginia Magazine of History and Biography* 79, no. 4 (Oct. 1971): 484–92.

Saville, Julie. *The Work of Reconstruction: From Slave to Wage Laborer in South Carolina, 1860–1870*. Cambridge: Cambridge University Press, 1994.

Schewel, Michael J. "Local Politics in Lynchburg, Virginia, in the 1880's." *Virginia Magazine of History and Biography* 89, no. 2 (Apr. 1981): 170–80.

Schwartz, Michael. *Radical Protest and Social Structure: The Southern Farmers' Alliance and Cotton Tenancy, 1880–1890*. Chicago: University of Chicago Press, 1976.

Schwarz, Philip J. " 'A Sense of Their Own Power': Self Determination in Recent Writings on Black Virginians." *Virginia Magazine of History and Biography* 97, no. 3 (July 1989): 279–310.

Schweninger, Loren. "A Vanishing Breed: Black Farm Owners in the South, 1651–1982." *Agricultural History* 63, no. 3 (Summer 1989): 41–60.

Scott, Emmett J. *Negro Migration during the War*. New York: Oxford University Press, 1920.

Scott, James C. *The Moral Economy of the Peasant: Rebellion and Subsistence in Southeast Asia*. New Haven: Yale University Press, 1990.

Scott, Rebecca J. "Defining the Boundaries of Freedom in the World of Cane: Cuba, Brazil, and Louisiana after Emancipation." *American Historical Review* 99 (Feb. 1994): 70–102.

———. *Slave Emancipation in Cuba: The Transition to Free Labor, 1860–1899*. Princeton: Princeton University Press, 1985.

Scruggs, C. G., and Smith W. Moseley. "The Role of Agricultural Journalism in Building the Rural South." *Agricultural History* 53, no. 1 (Jan. 1979): 22–61.

Shammas, Carole. "Black Women's Work and the Evolution of Plantation Society in Virginia." *Labor History* 26, no. 1 (Winter 1985): 5–28.

———. *The Pre-Industrial Consumer in England and America*. Oxford: Clarendon Press, 1990.

Shanin, Theodore. *The Awkward Class*. Oxford: Oxford University Press, 1972.

Shanks, Henry T. *The Secession Movement in Virginia, 1847–1861*. Richmond: Garrett and Massie, 1934.

Shannon, Fred A. *The Farmer's Last Frontier: Agriculture, 1860–1897*. New York: Farrar and Rinehart, 1947.

Shaw, Barton C. *The Wool-Hat Boys: Georgia's Populist Party*. Baton Rouge: Louisiana State University Press, 1984.

Sheldon, William. *Populism in Virginia, 1885–1900*. Princeton: Princeton University Press, 1935.

Shepard, E. Lee. " 'This Being Court Day': Courthouses and Community Life in Rural Virginia." *Virginia Magazine of History and Biography* 103, no. 4 (Oct. 1995): 459–70.

Sheridan, Richard C. "Chemical Fertilizers in Southern Agriculture." *Agricultural History* 53, no. 1 (Jan. 1979): 308–18.

Shields, Emma L. "A Half-Century in the Tobacco Industry." *Southern Workman*, Sept. 1922, 419–25.

Shifflett, Crandall A. *Patronage and Poverty in the Tobacco South: Louisa County, Virginia, 1860–1900*. Knoxville: University of Tennessee Press, 1982.

Shlomowitz, Ralph. " 'Bound' or 'Free'? Black Labor in Cotton and Sugarcane Farming, 1865–1880." *Journal of Southern History* 50, no. 4 (Nov. 1984): 569–96.

———. "The Origins of Southern Sharecropping." *Agricultural History* 53, no. 1 (July 1979): 557–75.

Siegel, Frederick F. *The Roots of Southern Distinctiveness: Tobacco and Society in Danville, Virginia, 1780–1865*. Chapel Hill: University of North Carolina Press, 1987.

Sitterson, J. Carlyle. *Sugar Country: The Cane Sugar Industry in the South, 1753–1950*. Lexington: University Press of Kentucky, 1953.

Smith, R. E. *Wheat Fields and Markets of the World*. St. Louis: Modern Miller, 1908.

Smith, Robert S. *Mill on the Dan: A History of Dan River Mills, 1882–1950*. Durham, N.C.: Duke University Press, 1960.

Sobel, Mechal. *The World They Made Together: Black and White Values in Eighteenth Century Virginia*. Princeton: Princeton University Press, 1987.

Spriggs, William F. "The Virginia Colored Farmers' Alliance: A Case Study of Race and Class Identity." *Journal of Negro History* 64, no. 3 (Summer 1979): 191–204.

Stampp, Kenneth M. *The Peculiar Institution: Slavery in the Antebellum South*. New York: Knopf, 1986.

Starnes, George T., and John E. Hamm. *Some Phases of Labor Relations in Virginia*. Charlottesville: University Press of Virginia, 1934.

Stokes, Melvyn, and Stephen Conway, eds. *The Market Revolution in America: Social, Political, and Religious Expressions, 1800–1880*. Charlottesville: University Press of Virginia, 1996.

Stover, John F. *The Railroads of the South, 1865–1900: A Study in Finance and Control*. Chapel Hill: University of North Carolina Press, 1955.

Strickland, John Scott. " 'No More Mud Work': The Struggle for the Control of Labor and Production in Low Country South Carolina, 1863–1880." In *The Southern Enigma: Essays on Race, Class, and Folk Culture*, edited by Walter J. Fraser and Winfred B. Moore, 43–62. Westport, Conn.: Greenwood Press, 1983.

Stubbs, Jean. *Tobacco on the Periphery: A Case Study in Cuban Labor History, 1860–1958*. Cambridge: Cambridge University Press, 1985.

Tadman, Michael. *Speculators and Slaves: Masters, Traders, and Slaves in the Old South*. Madison: University of Wisconsin Press, 1989.

Taylor, Alrutheus A. *The Negro in the Reconstruction of Virginia*. Washington, D.C.: Associated Publishers, 1926.

Thompson, Edward P. *Customs in Common*. New York: New Press, 1993.

———. "Eighteenth-Century English Society: Class Struggle without Class?" *Social History* 3, no. 2 (May 1978): 133–65.

———. *The Making of the English Working Class*. New York: Vintage, 1966.

———. *Whigs and Hunters: The Origins of the Black Act*. New York: Pantheon, 1975.

Tilley, Nannie M. *The Bright Tobacco Industry, 1860–1929*. Chapel Hill: University of North Carolina Press, 1948.

Tise, Larry E. *Proslavery: A History of the Defense of Slavery in America, 1701–1840*. Athens: University of Georgia Press, 1987.

Today and Yesterday in the Heart of Virginia. Farmville, Va.: *Farmville Herald*, 1935.

Townes, Jane A. "The Effect of Emancipation on Large Landholdings, Nelson and Goochland Counties, Virginia." *Journal of Southern History* 45, no. 3 (Aug. 1979): 403–12.

Treadway, Sandra Gioia. "New Directions in Virginia Women's History." *Virginia Magazine of History and Biography* 100, no. 1 (Jan. 1992): 5–28.

Trotter, Joe William. *Black Milwaukee: The Making of an Industrial Proletariat, 1915–45*. Urbana: University of Illinois Press, 1985.

———. *Coal, Class, and Color: Blacks in Southern West Virginia, 1915–32*. Urbana: University of Illinois Press, 1990.

Tucker, Robert C., ed. *The Marx-Engels Reader*. New York: Norton, 1978.

Turner, Charles W. "Virginia Agricultural Reform, 1815–1860." *Agricultural History* 26, no. 3 (July 1952): 80–89.

Turner, Mary, ed. *From Chattel Slaves to Wage Slaves: The Dynamics of Labour Bargaining in the Americas*. Bloomington: Indiana University Press, 1995.

Vaughan, Alden T. "The Origins Debate: Slavery and Racism in Seventeenth Century Virginia." *Virginia Magazine of History and Biography* 97, no. 3 (July 1989): 311–54.

Walvin, James. *Fruits of Empire: Exotic Produce and British Taste, 1660–1800*. London: Macmillan, 1997.

Watkinson, James D. "William Washington Browne and the True Reformers of Richmond, Virginia." *Virginia Magazine of History and Biography* 97, no. 3 (July 1989): 375–98.

Wawrzyczek, Irmina. *Unfree Labour in Early Modern English Culture: England and Colonial Virginia*. Lublin, Poland: Uniwersytetu Marii Curie-Skłodowskiej, 1990.

Wayne, Michael. *The Reshaping of Plantation Society: The Natchez District, 1860–1880*. Baton Rouge: Louisiana State University Press, 1983.

Weber, Max. "Capitalism and Rural Society in Germany." In *From Max Weber: Essays in Sociology*, edited by H. H. Gerth and C. W. Mills, 363–85. New York, 1946.

Wharton, Vernon Lane. *The Negro in Mississippi, 1865–1890*. New York: Harper, 1947.

White, Charles W. *The Hidden and Forgotten: Buckingham County*. Marceline, Mo.: Walsworth Press, 1990.

White, Deborah Gray. *Ar'n't I a Woman: Female Slaves in the Plantation South*. New York: Oxford University Press, 1985.

Wiener, Jonathan M. "Class Structure and Economic Development in the American South, 1865–1955." *American Historical Review* 84 (Oct.–Dec. 1979): 970–92.

———. *Social Origins of the New South: Alabama, 1860–1880*. Baton Rouge: Louisiana State University Press, 1978.

Wiley, Bell I. "Salient Changes in Southern Agriculture since the Civil War." *Agricultural History* 13, no. 1 (Jan. 1939): 65–76.

———. *Southern Negroes*. New Haven: Yale University Press, 1938.

Williams, Raymond. *The Country and the City*. New York: Oxford University Press, 1973.

———. "Culture Is Ordinary." In *Resources of Hope: Culture, Democracy, Socialism*. London: Verso, 1989.

Williams, William Appleman. *The Tragedy of American Diplomacy*. New York: Delta, 1962.

Wingfield, Marshall. *A History of Caroline County, Virginia*. Baltimore: Regional Pub. Co., 1969.

Wingo, Alfred L. *Virginia's Soils and Land Use*. Richmond: Baughman, 1949.

Woodman, Harold D. "Class, Race, Politics, and the Modernization of the Postbellum South." *Journal of Southern History* 68, no. 1 (Feb. 1997): 3–22.

———. "How New Was the New South?" *Agricultural History* 58, no. 4 (Oct. 1984): 529–45.

———. *King Cotton and His Retainers: Financing and Marketing the Cotton Crop of the South, 1800–1925*. Lexington: University Press of Kentucky, 1968.

———. *New South—New Law: The Legal Foundations of Credit and Labor Relations in the Postbellum Agricultural South*. Baton Rouge: Louisiana State University Press, 1995.

———. "Post–Civil War Southern Agriculture and the Law." *Agricultural History* 53, no. 1 (Jan. 1979): 319–37.

———. "Sequel to Slavery: The New History Views the Postbellum South." *Journal of Southern History* 43, no. 4 (Nov. 1977): 523–54.

Woods, Thomas A. *Knights of the Plow: Oliver H. Kelley and the Origins of the Grange in Republican Ideology*. Ames: Iowa State University Press, 1991.

Woodson, Carter G. *The Rural Negro*. Washington, D.C.: Association for Study of Negro Life and History, 1930.

Woodward, Comer V. "Emancipations and Reconstructions: A Comparative Study." *International Congress of Historical Sciences* (Moscow) (1970): 155–78.

———. *Origins of the New South, 1877–1913*. Baton Rouge: Louisiana State University Press, 1951.

———. "Strange Career Critics: Long May They Persevere." *Journal of American History* 75, no. 3 (Dec. 1988): 857–68.

———. *The Strange Career of Jim Crow*. New York: Oxford University Press, 1955.

———. *Tom Watson: Agrarian Rebel*. New York: Oxford University Press, 1938.

Woofter, T. J., Jr. *The Plight of Cigarette Tobacco*. Chapel Hill: University of North Carolina Press, 1931.

Wright, Gavin. *Old South, New South: Revolutions in the Southern Economy since the Civil War*. New York: Basic Books, 1986.

———. "The Strange Career of the New Southern Economic History." *Reviews in American History* 10 (1982): 164–80.

Wyatt, Edward A. "Rise of Industry in Antebellum Petersburg." *William and Mary Quarterly*, 1st ser., 7, no. 1 (Jan. 1937): 1–36.

Wynes, Charles. *Race Relations in Virginia, 1870–1902*. Charlottesville: University Press of Virginia, 1961.

Yoshiaki, Nishida. "Growth of the Meiji Landlord System and Tenancy Disputes after World War I: A Critique of Richard Smethurst, *Agricultural Development and Tenancy Disputes in Japan, 1870–1940*." *Journal of Japanese Studies* 15, no. 2 (1989): 389–437.

UNPUBLISHED SOURCES

Alderson, William T. "The Freedmen's Bureau in Virginia." M.A. thesis, Vanderbilt University, 1949.

Brown, Elsa Barkley. "Uncle Ned's Children: Negotiating Community and Freedom in Postemancipation Richmond, Virginia." Ph.D. diss., Kent State University, 1994.

Ellison, John Marcus. "Negro Ownership and Leadership in Relation to Rural Life in Virginia." Ph.D. diss., Drew University, 1933.

Fields, Emmett B. "The Agricultural Population of Virginia, 1850–1860." Ph.D. diss., Vanderbilt University, 1953.

Forsythe, Harold. " 'But My Friends Are Poor': Ross Hamilton and Freedpeople's Politics in Mecklenburg County, Virginia, 1869–1892." Manuscript, 1992.

Hall, Arthur R. "Soil Erosion and Agriculture in the Southern Piedmont: A History." Ph.D. diss., Duke University, 1948.

Hough, Leslie S. "Discontent in a Southern Tobacco Town: Lynchburg, Virginia, Workers in the 1880's." M.A. thesis, University of Virginia, 1973.

Irwin, James R. "Slave Agriculture and Staple Crops in the Virginia Piedmont." Ph.D. diss., University of Rochester, 1986.

Jones, Susannah H. "Labor and Landownership in Halifax County, Virginia, 1865–1880." M.A. thesis, University of Virginia, 1980.

Kerr-Ritchie, Jeffrey R. "Francis-Forty-Acres-and-a-Mule Moss." Manuscript.

———. "Freedpeople and Schooling in the Virginia Interior during the 1870's." Paper for National Association of African American Studies, Petersburg, Feb. 1994.

———. "Free Labor in the Virginia Tobacco Piedmont, 1865–1900." Ph.D. diss., University of Pennsylvania, 1993.

——. " 'From Leaf to Cane': Freedpeople, Temporary Migration, and Cash/Credit Networks in the Postbellum South." Paper for Association for the Study of Afro-American Life and Culture, Atlanta, Oct. 1994.

——. "Life in the Postwar Virginia Interior: The Diary of George Hunt, 1873–1891." Manuscript.

Link, William A. "Cavaliers and Mudsills: The Farmers' Alliance and the Emergence of Virginia Populism." M.A. thesis, University of Virginia, 1979.

McDonald, Roderick A. "The Transition from Slavery to Freedom in the British West Indies: The Journal of John Anderson, St. Vincent Special Magistrate, 1836–1839." Manuscript, 1990.

McGuire, M. Jennie. "The Worlds the Land Made: Postbellum Land Ownership and Social Change in Beaufort, South Carolina." Manuscript, 1988.

Medford, Edna G. "The Transition from Slavery to Freedom in a Diversified Economy: Virginia's Lower Peninsula, 1860–1900." Ph.D. diss., University of Maryland, 1987.

Nicholls, Michael L. "Origins of the Virginia Southside, 1703–1753." Ph.D. diss., College of William and Mary, 1972.

Perry, Kathleen S. "The History of Farm Tenancy in the Tobacco Region of Virginia, 1865–1950." Ph.D. diss., Radcliffe College, Harvard University, 1956.

Roberts, Harry W. "The Life and Labor of Rural Virginia Negroes." Ph.D. diss., Yale University, 1942.

Schlotterbeck, John. "Plantation and Farm: Social and Economic Change in Orange and Greene Counties, Virginia, 1716–1860." Ph.D. diss., Johns Hopkins University, 1980.

Schwalm, Leslie A. "The Meaning of Freedom: African-American Women and Their Transition from Slavery to Freedom in Lowcountry South Carolina." Ph.D. diss., University of Wisconsin, Madison, 1991.

Spriggs, William Edward. "Afro-American Wealth Accumulation, Virginia, 1900–1914." Ph.D. diss., University of Wisconsin, Madison, 1984.

Thomas, Percival. "Plantations in Transition: A Study of Four Virginia Plantations, 1860–1870." Ph.D. diss., University of Virginia, 1979.

Wheaton, Kathleen A. "Virginia's Failure to Attract Immigration, 1865–1880." M.A. thesis, University of Virginia, 1973.

REFERENCE SOURCES

Bottomore, Tom, ed. *A Dictionary of Marxist Thought.* Oxford: Blackwell, 1991.

Clark, Thomas D., ed. *Travels in the New South: A Bibliography.* Vol. 1, *The Postwar South, 1865–1900: An Era of Reconstruction and Readjustment.* Norman: University of Oklahoma Press, 1962.

Encyclopaedia Britannica. 11th ed. 1910–11.

Jahn, Raymond, ed. *Tobacco Dictionary.* New York: Philosophical Library, 1954.

Kolbe, J. Christian, and Lyndon H. Hart III. *Auditor of Public Accounts: Inventory.* Richmond: Virginia State Library and Archives, n.d.

Lankford, Nelson D., ed. *Guide to the Manuscript Collections of the Virginia Historical Society.* Richmond: VHS Publications, 1985.

Malval, Fritz J. *A Guide to the Archives of Hampton Institute.* Westport, Conn.: Greenwood Press, 1985.

National Archives and Records Administration. *Guide to the National Archives of the U.S.* Washington, D.C., 1987.

Plunkett, Michael. *Afro-American Sources in Virginia: A Guide to Manuscripts.* Charlottesville: University Press of Virginia, 1990.

Ray, Suzanne Smith, Lyndon H. Hart III, and J. Christian Kolbe. *A Preliminary Guide to Pre-1904 County Records in the Archives Branch of Virginia State Library and Archives.* Richmond: Virginia State Archives and Library, 1988.

Salmon, Emily J., and Edward D. C. Campbell Jr., eds. *The Hornbook of Virginia History: A Ready-Reference Guide to the Old Dominion's People, Places, and Past.* Richmond: Library of Virginia, 1994.

Suggs, Henry Lewis, ed. *The Black Press in the South, 1865–1979.* Westport, Conn.: Greenwood Press, 1983.

in, 197; CFA in, 205; freedpeople's
landholding in, 211, 219, 229
Buck, Delphy, 226
Buckingham County, 28, 40; freedpeople and labor contracting in, 47–48,
51–52, 63, 86; freedpeople's political
activity in, 77, 78, 80; Grange in, 144,
145; Farmers' Alliance in, 197; freedpeople's landholding in, 220, 222,
228, 296 (n. 62)
Buffum, George, 61, 68, 69, 83, 268
(n. 108)
Bull Durham Company, 185, 189
Bureau of Refugees, Freedmen, and
Abandoned Lands (BRFAL): and
postwar social relations, 5, 30; ideology of, 7, 53–54, 58, 65–66, 83, 117,
123, 266 (n. 70); reports by, 10, 35,
89; and free labor contract system,
33, 34, 47–48, 71, 82, 84, 88, 159;
transitional role of, 34–35; operation
of, 35, 37, 54, 60–61; and welfare
support, 39, 40–41; and refugees, 40;
landholding of, 40, 94, 262 (n. 18);
function of, 40–42, 46, 48–49, 168,
263 (n. 25); and vagrancy act, 49;
power of, 52, 54; and freedpeople's
education, 59, 89, 90, 97; and emigration, 63–64, 267 (n. 100); and
rental agreements, 68, 86; and contract laws, 72; and Black Republicanism, 74, 76, 82, 83–84, 87; and
whites' assaults on freedpeople, 88;
withdrawal of, 89–91, 117
Burns, Susie, 229
Bush and Biery Agricultural Club, 140

Cabell, Walker, 51
Callis, Ruffin, 229
Campbell, Charles, 172
Campbell County, 29, 96; emigration
of freedpeople from, 63, 239; freed-
people's political activity in, 77;
freedpeople's landholding in, 217,
218, 220, 224, 226, 227, 230
Canada, David, 77
Capitalism: industrial, 4, 126; agrarian,

4, 171, 176, 210; monopoly, 6, 181–82,
184–85, 189, 203, 207; and free labor,
39
Caribbean region, 32, 262 (n. 16)
Caroline County, freedpeople's political
activity in, 74
Carr, Julian, 185
Carse, G. B., 80, 87
Carter, James B., 77
Carter, Thad, 231
Cash crop production, 14, 15, 55, 68,
98, 113–14, 133–38, 184
Cayton, Thomas, 122
Cereal production, 2, 14, 17, 95, 109,
110, 114, 127, 129, 223
Chambers, Archer, 51
Chambers, Willis, 51
Charlotte County, 28, 29, 276 (n. 48);
freedpeople and labor contracting in,
52, 56–57, 63, 66; postwar planters
in, 54–56, 57, 58–59; freedwomen's
labor in, 57–58, 60; freedpeople and
tenancy in, 67, 105; freedpeople's
political activity in, 76, 80, 86;
tobacco production in, 95; freedpeo-
ple and cash labor system in, 105;
freedpeople's landholding in, 224,
297 (n. 85)
Charlottesville, Va., 35
Cheatham, W. J., 49
Cheatwood, J. J., 166
Chesapeake region, 4, 129, 132–33
Chesterfield County, freedpeople's
political activity in, 77
Chilton, Sam, 172
Christopher, E. A., 161
Christopher, Ella, 221
Christopher, William, 221
Cigarette industry: and tobacco econ-
omy, 6, 17, 135; and tobacco manu-
facturers, 181; and W. Duke, Sons &
Co., 185–86; expansion of, 187–88,
192, 207; and freedpeople's landhold-
ing, 213; and freedwomen, 240
Civil Rights Act (1866), 73
Civil War: effects on Virginia, 1, 71, 94,
96; African Virginians' role in, 3; and

and land transfers, 225; and freed-
people's emigration, 234
Davenport, Peter, 173
Dawdy, J. S., 238–39
Debt peonage, 66, 83, 159, 268 (n. 108)
De Give, Laurent Marcellin Joseph, 17
Democratic Party, 88, 206–7
Dennis, Dr. (planter), 55, 57, 58–59, 65
Dew, Thomas Roderick, 21, 112
Dibrell, William E., 100, 197
Dillard, Thomas, 87
Dinwiddie County, 31, 262 (n. 18);
freedpeople and tenancy in, 68;
freedpeople's political activity in, 81;
tobacco production in, 183; CFA in,
205; freedpeople's landholding in,
220, 222–23, 228
Disfranchisement, 271 (nn. 36, 42);
Confederate, 73, 78, 80, 88
Dodd, Samuel H., 200
Dodd, T. W., 202
Dodge, Sanford M., 77
Dodson, Alexander, 88
Dodson, George, 231
Dodson, Richard, 231
Duke, Benjamin, 191
Duke, James, 187, 292 (n. 68)
Duke, Washington, 185–86, 189. *See
also* W. Duke, Sons & Co.
Dunn, George, 197
Durand, E. Dana, 238, 255
Durham, N.C., 182, 185
Durham Fertilizer Company (DFC),
201, 202, 292 (n. 68)

Eaton, Clement, 29
Education: of freedmen, 38, 40, 59–60;
and BRFAL, 59, 89, 90, 97; and
Bland, 78; and Moss, 79; and effects
of climatic conditions, 97–98; and
Morrill Act, 118; of freedchildren,
122; and household economy, 278
(n. 96). *See also* Hampton Agricultural and Normal Institute
Edwards, Roger, 248
Egbert, A. R., 85
Emancipation: effects of, 2, 91, 93,
95–96, 98–99, 274 (n. 23); and postwar social relations, 4–5, 93; and
exploitation, 7; and self-emancipation, 25, 28, 29, 65, 179, 236; in
Jamaica, 32; as dialectical process,
56; politicization of, 73–74; and
freedwomen's political activities, 75;
and land values, 94, 95; and tobacco
economy, 99, 150, 154; and land-
labor ratios, 106
Emancipatory aspirations of freedpeople: and mobility, 53, 204; and free
labor, 56, 66; and withdrawal from
agricultural labor, 57; and landholding, 71, 209, 211, 223, 224, 247; and
class consciousness, 73, 80; and
Underwood Convention, 77, 78; and
rural protest, 196, 207; and familial
cooperation, 210, 231; and younger
generations, 236, 244, 247; and emigration, 247
Emigration: effects of, 2, 6; and postwar
social relations, 6, 244; and freedpeople's local attachments, 56; and
BRFAL, 63–64, 267 (n. 100); and
contract disputes, 63–65, 83; and
financial crisis, 127; of whites westward, 133–34; statistics on, 175, 233–
34, 267 (n. 104); and freedpeople's
landholding, 209, 243, 298 (n. 109);
of whites to cities, 224; and labor
scarcity, 235, 238–39; and self-emancipation, 236; and Great Migration,
236, 241–42; and families, 240–44;
and younger generations, 242–44;
and resistance, 299 (n. 121)
Employee-employer relations: equaliza-
tion of, 39; and BRFAL enforcement,
46, 89–90; and contract laws, 72; and
Black Republicanism, 80–83, 86, 87;
and contract disputes, 84, 88; and
Bankruptcy Act, 84–85; and *Parrish
v. The Commonwealth*, 170; and crop
lien laws, 178
Europe, 13, 126, 129–30, 131, 132
Exploitation, 10, 22, 170, 171, 240, 258
(n. 15), 272 (n. 54); definition of, 7–8

and Grange organizations, 144, 281 (n. 56), 282–83 (n. 81); and Hunt, 145, 282 (n. 61); and crop lien system, 159, 163; leadership among, 219–20; and land trustees, 222; farming knowledge of, 231, 232–33, 261 (n. 31); family relations of, 231, 243; population of, 233; and Lyon's survey, 265 (n. 59); and urban-rural relations, 267 (n. 99); and peanut production, 277 (n. 73). *See also* Black Republicanism; Emancipatory aspirations of freedpeople; Emigration; Free labor contract system

Freedwomen: and gender, 8–9; withdrawal from agricultural production, 57–58, 60, 106, 266 (n. 70); and domestic work, 66; and Black Republicanism, 75; whites' assaults on, 87; wages of, 172; and CFA, 206; as landholders, 217, 218, 220, 221, 224, 226–30; as proletariat, 240

Free labor: and urbanization, 1; definitions of, 4; and postwar social relations, 5, 247, 285 (n. 30); in trans-Allegheny region, 19; and proslavery ideology, 22; BRFAL constitution for, 39; and self-support, 40; time, 47–48; and free market, 53; and emancipatory aspirations of freedpeople, 56, 66; mobility of, 68, 104, 106, 110, 159, 287 (n. 70); and Hampton Institute, 93; and climatic conditions, 98; and VAS, 101–2; and local attachments, 102, 104, 152, 178, 275 (n. 38); and labor-saving machinery, 109; and soil conditions, 109–13; and promotion of bright tobacco cultivation, 116–17; and Orlando Brown, 120, 251–52; and tobacco economy, 138, 143

—contract system: and BRFAL, 33, 34, 41–42, 46–49, 60–63, 71, 82, 84, 88, 89–90, 159, 263 (n. 25), 264 (n. 36); disputes over, 33, 45–48, 50, 57, 60–62, 64–65, 67, 71, 80–85, 87–90, 263–64 (n. 33); and ideology, 37–38,

45, 71, 272 (n. 54); conditions of, 42–44, 48, 49–52, 56–57, 61–62, 66–67, 69, 71, 85–86, 268 (n. 108); enticements to break contracts, 53, 265 (n. 58); and Black Republicanism, 81–83, 86, 87

—ideology: and BRFAL reports, 35, 37; of Republican Party, 35, 37, 39, 48, 52, 71; and independence, 60; and freedmen's political activities, 74, 84; clashes in, 84; and industriousness, 120; and exploitation, 272 (n. 54)

—management: debates over, 101, 275 (n. 33); and VAS, 101–2; and *Southern Planter and Farmer*, 103–6, 114; and labor scarcity, 108; and former masters, 123; and Ott, 151–52; and paternalism, 152, 178; and crop lien system, 160, 162

—relations: and property rights, 5, 170; and BRFAL, 37, 41, 67, 91; and political activities, 82, 271 (n. 42); and crop lien system, 158, 160, 161, 162, 284 (n. 15); and *Parrish v. The Commonwealth*, 158, 165; and agricultural proletariat, 171, 175, 179, 189, 289 (n. 22); and sharecropping, 174–75; and tenant farming, 176–77; and Readjusters, 179, 271 (n. 42); and bright tobacco production, 184; and freedpeople's landholdings, 219

Freeman, Martin, 228

Freeman, Robert, 228

Free market: and household economy, 8; slaves' familiarity with, 18; and wage labor, 32; and free labor, 53, 64, 106; and tobacco economy, 82, 138, 143; and employee dismissals, 82–83; freedpeople's conversion to, 91; and labor-saving machinery, 108; and fertilizer sales, 111; and tobacco production, 137; and Grange organizations, 147; and crop lien system, 159; and cigarette industry, 186

Friend, William G., 227

F. S. Kinney Company, 186, 189

Fuller, G., 219

Fuller, J. W., 219
Fuller, W. T., 206
Funders, 157, 158

Gaines, R. V., 145
Garber, John H., 181, 192
Gardiner, Wyatt, 66
Georgia, 127, 275 (n. 31)
Gillespie, Scott, 231
Gilliam, John G., 47
Gilliam, Willis, 173
Gilmer, G. C., 109–10, 112
Given, John V., 75
Gloucester County, freedpeople's land-
holding in, 218, 227–28, 294 (nn. 24,
33), 295 (n. 52), 297–98 (n. 95)
Gnomes, Frank, 240–41
Gnomes, Patience, 240–41
Gooch, William, 139
Goochland County, 28, 96; freedpeople
and tenancy in, 67, 165–68, 176–77;
freedpeople's political activity in, 77,
81; freedpeople's landholding in, 213,
218; freedpeople-employer disputes
in, 267 (n. 94)
Goode, Edward B., 41, 42, 66, 69, 86
Goode, J. Thomas, 206–7
Good Samaritans, 222
Goodwin, Charles C., 43
Goodwin & Company, 186, 189
Goodwyn, Martha, 228
Goodwyn, Susun, 228
Goodwyn Agricultural Club, 105
Grange organizations, 143–48, 150, 281
(n. 49), 282 (nn. 63, 81)
Grant, Ulysses S., 34
Graves, Stonewall J., 224, 230
Great Britain, 13, 127, 135, 138, 186,
194
Great Depression, 126, 248
Green, Cornelius, 66
Green, Harry C., 205
Green, J. W., 161
Green, William, 179
Greene, J. N., 211
Greene, J. W., 211
Gregory, J. W., 235

Gregory, James, 66
Gregory, Nathaniel A., 105

Hackney, James, 229
Hairston, Peter, 145
Hairston, Tom Ely, 172
Haiti, 275 (n. 31)
Halifax County, 94, 262 (n. 18); tobacco
production in, 60, 68, 95, 114, 175,
182–83; freedpeople and labor con-
tracting in, 61, 69; freedpeople's
political activity in, 74, 76, 77, 83, 86;
freedpeople-employer disputes in,
90; Grange in, 144; freedpeople and
tenancy in, 175–76; Farmers' Alliance
in, 197; freedpeople's landholding in,
218
Hambleton, Robert, 172
Hammond, James Henry, 21–22
Hampton Agricultural and Normal
Institute, 93, 117, 118, 206, 211, 222,
267 (n. 100), 278 (n. 88). See also
Southern Workman
Hancock, H. R., 221
Hancock, J., 219
Handy, M. P., 99
Hankins, J. D., 197
Hannah, George C., 66, 69
Hanover County, freedpeople's school
activity in, 122
Hardaway, Dick, 42
Hardcastle, Philip, 179
Harrah, Tom, 66
Harris, H. J., 197
Harris, Nelson, 229
Harrison, G. F., 174
Harrison, George, 211
Harrison, O. A., 160
Harvie, Edwin James, 52
Harvie, Lewis E., 42, 43, 48, 49, 52,
145, 282 (n. 81)
Haskins, Eliza B., 52
Haskins, W. W., 197
Havana Commercial Company, 193
Hazelwood, N. W., 143, 145
Hellagner, William, 161
Henry County: tobacco production in,

King, Edward, 99
Knight, William F. D., 61, 80

Labor-saving machinery, 108–9, 276 (n. 54)
Labor theory of value, 79
Lacey, Robert S., 34–35
Lacy, Horace, 66
Land: redistribution of, 78, 79; taxes on, 78, 79, 213, 223, 228–29, 294 (n. 18); value of, 94, 95, 99, 102, 158; sales of, 223, 224
Landholding: postemancipation transformation of, 6, 40, 42; and postwar social relations, 6, 244; and ideology, 8; and subsistence farming, 32; and success for freedpeople, 32–33; of BRFAL, 40, 94, 262 (n. 18); freedpeople's access to, 71; and Underwood Convention, 77; and former masters' retention of land, 94; of CFA members, 205; and emancipatory aspirations of freedpeople, 209, 211, 218–19, 222; of freedpeople in piedmont region, 209–10; records of freedpeople's land acquisition, 211–13, 214, 215, 218, 219; and agricultural depression, 212; and freedpeople's acreage, 213, 215–16, 219, 220–21, 294 (n. 24), 295 (n. 52); and freedpeople's family cooperation, 213, 244; and freedpeople's land value, 216–17, 219; and freedpeople's buildings, 217–18; and freedpeople's leadership, 219–20; and agricultural proletariat, 221; and freedpeople as trustees, 222; communal, 222–23, 296 (n. 62); and land sales, 224; and land transfers, 224, 225–28, 230; and freedpeople's persistence, 229–30, 298 (n. 97); and freedpeople's tobacco production, 230–31; and freedpeople's emigration, 243, 298 (n. 109)
Land-labor ratios, 106, 276 (n. 44)
Landlords: and exploitation, 7; and labor scarcity, 33–34, 222; and free labor relations, 158; and crop lien

laws, 161, 162, 164; and wage labor, 172; and sharecropping, 174; and freedpeople's landholding, 222
Langan, William E., 42
Langhorne, Orra, 241
Leahey, Thomas, 86
Leahy, William, 87–88
Leake, A. K., 168
Lee, Robert E., 34
Lee, William T., 23
Lewis, Jessie, 51
Lin, Jennie, 226
Lindsay, Lewis, 78, 273 (n. 76)
Liny, John L., 46
Livestock, 96
Long Depression, 126, 248
Louisa County, 28, 96; freedpeople and labor contracting in, 42, 43, 61, 62, 263 (nn. 25, 33); freedpeople's political activity in, 74; Grange in, 144, 147, 283 (n. 81); Farmers' Alliance in, 197; freedpeople's landholding in, 213, 215, 218, 219, 226–27, 228–29, 230, 231–32, 297 (n. 78); tobacco production in, 230, 231
Louisiana, 275 (n. 31)
Lowe, Richard, 71
Lowry, C. B., 52
Luck, Jerry, 239
Luck, Luvenia Smith, 239
Lundy, J. B., 17
Lunenburg County: freedpeople and labor contracting in, 61, 62–63, 85; emigration of freedpeople from, 64; freedpeople and tenancy in, 67–68, 85; freedpeople's political activity in, 74, 80; freedpeople-employer disputes in, 84, 85; tobacco production in, 95, 154, 183; rural protest in, 178–79; freedpeople's landholding in, 217, 220, 222
Lynchburg, Va., 14, 19, 35, 63, 136, 197–98, 217, 218, 237, 239
Lynn, William G., 87
Lyon, Edwin, 54, 59–60, 67, 105, 265 (n. 59)

freedpeople and labor contracting in, 53, 63; emigration of freedpeople from, 63, 235, 238, 243; freedpeople's political activity in, 74, 77, 78, 80, 119; freedpeople and tenancy in, 85, 176; tobacco marketing in, 140; Grange in, 144, 145, 146, 147, 282–83 (n. 81); freedpeople and cash labor system in, 173; rural protest in, 178; Farmers' Alliance in, 198; freedpeople's landholding in, 217, 218, 220, 224–25, 228

Progressive Farmer, 143, 196

Property rights, 5, 170, 171, 179

Proslavery ideology: of former masters, 8, 40; and paternalism, 21–22; and free labor contract system, 44, 52; and family discipline, 59; and postwar social relations, 91; vindications of, 101; and slave management, 106; and Readjusterism, 179; and freedpeople's landholding, 222; and freedpeople's competence, 261 (n. 31); and attitudes toward Black Republicanism, 271 (n. 36)

Protest. *See* Rural protest

Puryear, Henry, 86

Puryear, James, 86

Race relations: in Virginia, 3; and class, 8; postemancipation readjustments in, 32; and BRFAL, 35; and freedwomen's political activities, 75; and Black Republicanism, 86–87; and Danville race riot, 157, 289 (n. 26)

Ragland, Robert L., 142, 151, 182–83

Railroads, 188, 205–6, 228, 241, 297 (n. 85)

Readjusters, 157–58, 179, 204, 207, 271 (n. 42)

Reconstruction, 72–73, 74, 89, 90

Reconstruction Acts of 1867, 73

Reece, Ann, 172

Reece, Marinda, 172

Religion: and proslavery views, 21; and free labor, 39; and landholding, 74, . 295 (n. 43)

Republican Party: as dominant party, 2; free labor ideology of, 35, 37, 39, 48, 52–53, 71; and Reconstruction Acts, 73; and voter registration, 74; and tobacco tax, 148; coalition with Readjusters, 158; and monopoly capitalism, 181; and Schofield, 270 (n. 24)

Rice, Va., 198

Richardson, William H., 107

Richmond, Va.: as tobacco market, 14, 140, 142, 147; slavery in, 19; as Confederate capital, 72; and Kentucky tobacco production, 136; and Grange organizations, 144; and cigarette industry, 185; and CFA, 204, 205; and emigration, 236; and proletarianization, 237

Richmond Tobacco Exchange, 140, 142, 147

Roanoke, Va., 236, 237–38, 239

Roberts, Harry, 230

Robinson, A. L., 224

Robinson, John, 45, 76, 77

Rogers, Joseph J., 204, 205

Rover, B. C., 200

Rover, Emma, 200

Ruffin, Frank G., 106, 145

Rural protest: and theft, 178–79; and ATC, 182, 197–98; characteristics of, 195, 198–99; and PCATU, 199–204; and CFA, 204–6

Sargent, John S., 44

Saunders, R. S., 166

Schofield, John M., 72, 73, 74, 76, 77, 79, 86, 270 (n. 24)

Scott, Archie, 228

Scott, Charles, 67

Scott, Cornelius, 42

Scott, John A., 140

Scott, Peter, 228

Scott, William L., 55, 56, 57, 58, 59

Sears, Albert, 222

Secessionism, 3, 25, 72

Sharecropping: and free labor contract system, 50–51, 85; and Moss, 79; and freedpeople, 100, 178; and *Southern Planter and Farmer*, 103; compared to wage labor, 103, 105; and free labor management, 104–5; and Ott, 153; and *Parrish v. The Commonwealth*, 158; and agricultural proletariat, 171; compared to tenant farming, 174–75, 177–78; prevalence of, 175–76; and landholding, 212, 213

Sharp, George, 51

Sharp, J. W., 31–34, 40, 41, 45, 46, 47, 68, 69, 253–54, 266 (n. 76)

Shaun, B. F., 61, 81, 82

Shelton, David R., 43–44

Shelton, Samuel C., 115–16

Sherman Antitrust Act, 194–95

Shields, Camelia, 200

Shields, Taylor L., 200

Shifflett, Crandall, 225

Skipworth, Grey, 31, 52

Slade, Abisha, 182

Slavery: dissolution of, 1; in Virginian society, 3, 13, 17–18; and postwar social relations, 4; social organization of, 5, 19, 25; and market relations, 8; and European colonization, 13; Aristotle on, 21; and geographical expansionism, 21; Civil War's effects on, 25; and transition to freedom, 35, 39, 56, 211, 264 (nn. 34, 84), 293–94 (n. 16); and training for children, 59; and emancipatory aspirations of freedpeople, 211

Slaves: population of, 18, 20; as hirees, 19, 25, 260 (n. 16); trade in, 21, 260 (n. 17); management of, 22–23, 28–29, 52, 57, 71, 103, 106, 123, 260 (n. 26); farming knowledge of, 23–25, 30, 261 (n. 31); self-emancipation of, 25, 28, 29, 267 (n. 98); capital invested in, 94–95

Small, John, 135

Smith, H. M., 109

Smith, Jim, 42

Smith, John, 45

Smith, Louisa, 220

Smith, M., 51

Smith, N., 51

Smith, William A., 55, 56–57, 58

Social relations, postwar: and tobacco economy, 4, 154–55; emancipation's effect on, 4–5, 93, 209; and BRFAL, 5, 30; and *Southern Workman*, 5, 120–21; and former masters, 6–7, 10–11; and culture, 7–8; and proslavery ideology, 91; and tobacco production, 117; and landholding, 244; and free labor relations, 247, 285 (n. 30)

South Carolina, 21, 76, 170, 183, 187, 275 (n. 31)

Southern Fertilizing Company (SFC), 111, 150, 151, 154, 188

Southern Planter, 103, 260 (n. 26)

Southern Planter and Farmer: and postwar social relations, 5; and land values, 94; and climatic conditions, 97, 98; and J. F. Jackson, 100; and effects of emancipation, 102–3, 154; and free labor management, 103–6, 178; and white labor, 106–7; and labor-saving machinery, 108–9; and soil conditions, 110–13; and bright tobacco cultivation, 115–16, 183; and tobacco inspection system, 142–43; and Grange organizations, 145, 147; and taxation, 148–49; and Ott, 151; and crop lien system, 159–60, 162–63; and rural mercantilism, 161; and rural protest, 195, 197

Southern Tobacco Journal, 192

Southern Tobacconist and Manufacturers Record, 100

Southern Workman: and postwar social relations, 5, 120–21; motto of, 93, 119; and Hampton Agricultural and Normal Institute, 117, 119; and families, 121–22; and CFA, 204, 206; and landholding reports, 211–12

Spanish-American War, 193

Spaulding, William, 55, 56, 57, 58

Spencer, John A., 55, 57, 65

Spencer, Moses A., 47

Spiece, John B., 25

Spraggins, I. D., 52, 55, 58
Staple crop production, 129, 212
State v. Elias Gay, 170
Stearns, Franklin, 145
Stevenson, Louis W., 63, 64, 68, 80, 82
Stowell, W. H. H., 84, 86, 90
Subsistence farming, 8, 31–32, 68, 96
Suffrage: and freedmen's registration, 73–74; and freedmen circuit riders, 75–76; and freedmen voting, 76, 86, 205; and employee opposition, 80–83, 86; and BRFAL opposition, 83
Sugar production, 21, 101, 275 (n. 31)
Sutherlin, C. T., 145
Sutherlin, William T., 102, 104, 108, 145, 148

Taxation. *See* Land: taxes on; Tobacco economy: and taxation
Taylor, H. W., 161–62
Taylor, J. E., 202
Taylor, James T. S., 77, 78
Taylor, John N., 170
Taylor, Miles, 87
Taylor, T., 211
Taylor, William, 145
Tedway, J. L., 202
Tenant farming: postemancipation transformation of, 6; and free labor contract system, 67–68, 85, 86, 263–64 (n. 33); and free labor management, 104–5; and tobacco economy, 154; and crop lien laws, 158, 161, 162; and *Parrish v. The Commonwealth*, 169–70; compared to sharecropping, 174–75, 177–78; and agricultural proletariat, 175; regional nature of, 179–80; and rural protest, 196, 205; and PCATU, 200; and landholding, 212, 213; and wage labor, 287 (n. 53)
Tennessee, 64, 95, 133, 137–38, 153, 280 (nn. 25, 33)
Terry, Alfred H., 49, 72
Thomas, Emily R., 219
Thomas, James A., 194

Thompson, A. W., 31, 45, 47
Thompson, C. L., 77
Thompson, John, 42
Thornhill, John, 224
Thorton, G. W., 217
Thrower, Lewis, 161
Tidball, William L., 61–62
Tidewater region: interaction with piedmont region, 18; mixed economy of, 19; abandoned lands in, 40; land values in, 94; and Civil War, 96; and tobacco inspection system, 139; and freedpeople's landholdings, 210, 212, 295 (n. 52); slave trade in, 260 (n. 17)
Tinsely, J. W., 88
Tobacco Association, 147–48
Tobacco capitalists, 185–87, 189, 191–95
Tobacco economy: transformation of, 2, 6, 211; and postwar social relations, 4; agricultural depression's effects on, 5, 129; and competition, 5, 136, 153; and cigarette industry, 6, 17, 184, 187; and exports, 14, 130–41 passim, 151; Civil War's effects on, 17, 135, 137; and free market, 82, 138; effects of emancipation on, 99, 150; and financial crisis of 1873, 126–27; and global production, 130, 131, 132–33, 151, 153, 279 (n. 17), 283 (n. 84); growth of, 133, 134; and inspection system, 19, 63–64, 138–42, 147, 150; and auctions, 141; and Grange organizations, 147; and taxation, 148–50, 153, 195; and prices, 154; and credit crisis, 159; and bright tobacco production, 183; and ATC, 185; specialization in, 191–92; and landholding, 223; and emigration, 235; and agribusiness, 248
Tobacco factories, 19, 63–64, 188, 191–93, 240
Tobacco farmers, 127, 141–50, 154, 173, 196, 198, 200–204, 230–33, 248
Tobacco manufacturers: and preferences for bright tobacco, 15, 133; and